Shaw's Dramatic Criticism
(1895-98)

Shaw's Dramatic Criticism (1895-98)

A *Selection by* John F. Matthews

GREENWOOD PRESS, PUBLISHERS
WESTPORT, CONNECTICUT

The present selection of Bernard Shaw's dramatic criticism has been made from contributions to *The Saturday Review* from January 1895 to May 1898. They have appeared in *Our Theatres in the Nineties,* published by Constable & Co., Ltd., London, 1932. Other of Shaw's dramatic criticisms also were collected in *Dramatic Opinions and Essays* (and containing as well a word on the dramatic opinions and essays of Bernard Shaw by James Huneker), published by Brentano's, New York, 1906; and in *Plays and Players,* Oxford University Press, New York, 1954.

Originally published in 1959
by Hill and Wang, New York

Reprinted with the permission
of The Society of Authors, London

First Greenwood Reprinting 1971

Library of Congress Catalogue Card Number 77-136084

SBN 8371-5234-8

Printed in the United States of America

Foreword

There seems no need, nowadays, to pronounce a panegyric on Shaw as a drama critic. Like Lewes and Hazlitt, whom he considered in some ways his critical progenitors, and like Beerbohm, whom he chose as his successor on *The Saturday Review,* his position in the field of English criticism is secure.

Indeed, leaving aside those elements of bias and affection which were, after all, merely the mark of his humanity, the only defect in his criticism was the fact that he wrote too well. Not that he was always equally interesting; as a journalist he had his bad days, just as, as a dramatist, he had his bad plays. But on the whole, his work was so intensely readable that, like Mozart, he could almost be said to have written nothing really bad—only a few things a little less good. This literary Midas touch was a great advantage to Shaw personally—but it makes the task of his editors almost insuperable.

Shaw wrote 151 weekly theatre pieces during his stint on *The Saturday Review* (January, 1895 through May, 1898). Approximately one third of these make up this selection. As St. John Ervine has remarked, "publishers are not philanthropists, even though they sometimes behave as if they were." Short of philanthropy, it is impossible in a volume of this nature to include all of Shaw's reviews.

In a somewhat comparable situation, Mr. James Huneker, in 1905, picked what he seemed to enjoy reading himself. This is a perfectly respectable procedure especially when one has two 400-page volumes to fill—but for present purposes it was not entirely adequate. Granted that the essays included here represent to some extent the preferences of the editor—still an attempt has been made to justify each inclusion somewhat systematically.

Three aspects of Shaw's criticism seem of greatest interest to the modern reader, and have therefore formed the basis of these selections. First, there is the playwright-critic commenting on his predecessors—Shakespeare, Marlowe, Robertson, and in a special sense, Ibsen. The present

v

volume includes nearly everything of this sort, except a few essays which seem to add nothing new to the reader's understanding of Shaw's views. Secondly, there is Shaw's reactions to the work of his contemporary rivals—dramatists whose fame his own was so soon to eclipse. The selections here offer most of what he had to say about the major figures, including Sardou, Pinero, Wilde, and Jones, along with a sampling of reviews showing his response to ordinary farce, ordinary melodrama, and even that peculiarly English institution, the Christmas pantomime.

Finally, and perhaps most important, an attempt has been made to emphasize Shaw's role as a critic of the executive branch of the theatre—giving the fullest possible expression to his views on directing (which he usually calls "stage-management"), producing, scenic design, and especially acting. (With this in mind, nearly all the selections deal with plays Shaw saw in actual performance.)

In an age when acting has declined in America almost to the level of mere behavior, it seems particularly useful to reprint Shaw's vivid reports and analyses of what acting could and should be at its best, and his equally vivid denunciations of what he thought was wrong with it at its worst. Thus, all the principal essays about such artists as Henry Irving, Duse, Sarah Bernhardt, Ellen Terry, and Forbes-Robertson are included, along with many other pieces chosen mainly to display Shaw's detailed, sympathetic and expert interest in acting of all sorts, even amateur.

Of the fifty-four essays in this volume, thirty-two are reprinted in their entirety. In the remaining twenty-two, cuts have been made—in most cases by deleting one or more reviews from essays in which Shaw reviewed two or more plays. These deletions are indicated with ellipses under the title of the article. The few places where minor cuts have been made within a review are also indicated with ellipses.

This volume, then, attempts simply to provide a characteristic self-portrait of Shaw as a dramatic critic, using as his subject the London Theatre of the Nineties. As for the columns he wrote on many other topics—ranging from religion to bicycle accidents—we are sorry, they had to go.

JOHN F. MATTHEWS

Westport, Connecticut

Contents

Shaw's Dramatic Criticism
(1895-98)

Two New Plays

GUY DOMVILLE. A play in three acts. By Henry James. St. James's Theatre, 5 January 1895.

AN IDEAL HUSBAND. A new and original play of modern life. By Oscar Wilde. Haymarket Theatre, 3 January 1895.

[12 *January* 1895]

The truth about Mr James's play is no worse than that it is out of fashion. Any dramatically disposed young gentleman who, cultivating sentiment on a little alcohol, and gaining an insight to the mysteries of the eternal feminine by a couple of squalid intrigues, meanwhile keeps well aloof from art and philosophy, and thus preserves his innocence of the higher life of the senses and of the intellect, can patch up a play tomorrow which will pass as real drama with the gentlemen who deny that distinction to the works of Mr Henry James. No doubt, if the literary world were as completely dominated by the admirers of Mr Rider Haggard as the dramatic world is by their first cousins, we should be told that Mr James cannot write a novel. That is not criticism: it is a mere begging of the question. There is no reason why life as we find it in Mr James's novels—life, that is, in which passion is subordinate to intellect and to fastidious artistic taste—should not be represented on the stage. If it is real to Mr James, it must be real to others; and why should not these others have their drama instead of being banished from the theatre (to the theatre's great loss) by the monotony and vulgarity of drama in which passion is everything, intellect nothing, and art only brought in by the incidental outrages upon it. As it happens, I am not myself in Mr James's camp: in all the life that has energy enough to be interesting to me, subjective volition, passion, will, make intellect the merest tool. But there is in the centre of that cyclone a certain calm spot where cultivated ladies and gentlemen live on independent incomes or by pleasant artistic occupations. It is there that Mr James's art touches life, selecting whatever is graceful, exquisite, or dignified in its serenity. It is not life as imagined by the pit or gallery, or even by the stalls: it is, let us say, the ideal of the balcony; but that is no reason why the pit and gallery should excommunicate it on the ground that it has no blood and entrails in it, and have its sentence formulated for it by the fiercely ambitious

1

and wilful professional man in the stalls. The whole case against its adequacy really rests on its violation of the cardinal stage convention that love is the most irresistible of all the passions. Since most people go to the theatre to escape from reality, this convention is naturally dear to a world in which love, all powerful in the secret, unreal, day-dreaming life of the imagination, is in the real active life the abject slave of every trifling habit, prejudice, and cowardice, easily stifled by shyness, class feeling, and pecuniary prudence, or diverted from what is theatrically assumed to be its hurricane course by such obstacles as a thick ankle, a cockney accent, or an unfashionable hat. In the face of this, is it good sense to accuse Mr Henry James of a want of grip of the realities of life because he gives us a hero who sacrifices his love to a strong and noble vocation for the Church? And yet when some unmannerly playgoer, untouched by either love or religion, chooses to send a derisive howl from the gallery at such a situation, we are to sorrowfully admit, if you please, that Mr James is no dramatist, on the general ground that "the drama's laws the drama's patrons give." Pray, which of its patrons? —the cultivated majority who, like myself and all the ablest of my colleagues, applauded Mr James on Saturday, or the handful of rowdies who brawled at him? It is the business of the dramatic critic to educate these dunces, not to echo them.

Admitting, then, that Mr James's dramatic authorship is valid, and that his plays are *du théâtre* when the right people are in the theatre, what are the qualities and faults of Guy Domville? First among the qualities, a rare charm of speech. Line after line comes with such a delicate turn and fall that I unhesitatingly challenge any of our popular dramatists to write a scene in verse with half the beauty of Mr James's prose. I am not now speaking of the verbal fitness, which is a matter of careful workmanship merely. I am speaking of the delicate inflexions of feeling conveyed by the cadences of the line, inflexions and cadences which, after so long a course of the ordinary theatrical splashes and daubs of passion and emphasis, are as grateful to my ear as the music of Mozart's Entführung aus dem Serail would be after a year of Ernani and Il Trovatore. Second, Guy Domville is a story, and not a mere situation hung out on a gallows of plot. And it is a story of fine sentiment and delicate manners, with an entirely worthy and touching ending. Third, it relies on the performers, not for the brute force of their personalities and popularities, but for their finest accomplishments in grace of manner, delicacy of diction, and dignity of style. It is pleasant to be able to add that this reliance, rash as it undeniably is in these days, was not disappointed. Mr Alexander, having been treated little better than a tailor's dummy by Mr Wilde, Mr Pinero, and Mr Henry Arthur Jones successively, found himself treated as an artist by Mr James, and repaid the compliment, not only, as his manager, by charming eighteenth-century stage setting of the piece, but, as actor, by his fine execution of the principal part, which he touched with great skill and judgment. Miss Marion Terry, as Mrs Peveril, was altogether charming, every movement, every tone, harmonized perfectly with the dainty grace and feeling of her lines. In fact, had the second act been equal to the first and third, and the acting as fine throughout as in the scenes between Mr Alexander and Miss Terry (in which, by the way, they were well supported by Mr Waring), the result would have been less doubtful. It will be a deplorable misfortune if Guy Domville does not hold the stage long enough to justify Mr Alexander's enterprise in producing it.

Unfortunately, the second act dissolved the charm rather badly; and what was more, the actors felt it. The Falstaffian make-up of Mrs Saker, and the senseless drunken scene, which Mr Alexander played with the sobriety of desperation, made fuss instead of drama; and the dialogue, except for a brief and very pretty episode in which Miss Millard and Mr Esmond took part, fell off into mere rococo. Little of this act can be remembered with pleasure except Miss Millard's "Forgive me a little," and a few cognate scraps of dialogue. It had better have been left out, and the wanderings of the prodigal taken for granted. And, to weight it still further, it contained a great deal of the gentleman who played Lord Devenish, and played him just as he might have played an elderly marquis in a comic opera, grimacing over a snuff-box, and withering all sense and music out of Mr James's lines with a diction which I forbear to describe. He was very largely responsible for the irritation which subsequently vented itself on the author; and I am far from sure that I ought not to borrow a weapon from the Speaker of the House of Commons, and go to the extreme length of naming him.

Guy Domville is preceded by a farce (called in the bill a comedy) by Julian Field, entitled Too Happy by Half. It is deftly turned out from old and seasoned materials, and is capital fun for the audience and for Mr Esmond and Miss Millard. Miss Millard is not yet quite experienced enough to do very easy work quite well: she is the least bit crude occasionally.

Mr Oscar Wilde's new play at the Haymarket is a dangerous subject, because he has the property of making his critics dull. They laugh angrily at his epigrams, like a child who is coaxed into being amused in the very act of setting up a yell of rage and agony. They protest that the trick is obvious, and that such epigrams can be turned out by the score by any one lightminded enough to condescend to such frivolity. As far as I can ascertain, I am the only person in London who cannot sit down and write an Oscar Wilde play at will. The fact that his plays, though apparently lucrative, remain unique under these circumstances, says much for the self-denial of our scribes. In a certain sense Mr Wilde is to me our only thorough playwright. He plays with everything: with wit, with philosophy, with drama, with actors and audience, with the whole theatre. Such a feat scandalizes the Englishman, who can no more play with wit and philosophy than he can with a football or a cricket bat. He works at both, and has the consolation, if he cannot make people laugh, of being the best cricketer and footballer in the world. Now it is the mark of the artist that he will not work. Just as people with social ambitions will practise the meanest economies in order to live expensively; so the artist will starve his way through incredible toil and discouragement sooner than go and earn a week's honest wages. Mr Wilde, an arch-artist, is so colossally lazy that he trifles even with the work by which an artist escapes work. He distils the very quintessence, and gets as product plays which are so unapproachably playful that they are the delight of every playgoer with twopenn'orth of brains. The English critic, always protesting that the drama should not be didactic, and yet always complaining if the dramatist does not find sermons in stones and good in everything, will be conscious of a subtle and pervading levity in An Ideal Husband. All the literary dignity of the play, all the imperturbable good sense and good manners with which Mr Wilde makes his wit pleasant to his comparatively stupid audience, cannot quite overcome the fact that Ireland is of all countries the most foreign to England, and that to the Irishman (and Mr Wilde is almost as acutely Irish an Irishman as the Iron Duke of Wellington) there is nothing in the world quite so exquisitely comic as an Englishman's seriousness. It becomes tragic, perhaps, when the Englishman acts on it; but that occurs too seldom to be taken into account, a fact which intensifies the humor of the situation, the total result being the Englishman utterly unconscious of his real self, Mr Wilde keenly observant of it and playing on the self-unconsciousness with irresistible humor, and finally, of course, the Englishman annoyed with himself for being amused at his own expense, and for being unable to convict Mr Wilde of what seems an obvious misunderstanding of human nature. He is shocked, too, at the danger to the foundations of society when seriousness is publicly laughed at. And to complete the oddity of the situation, Mr Wilde, touching what he himself reverences, is absolutely the most sentimental dramatist of the day.

It is useless to describe a play which has no thesis: which is, in the purest integrity, a play and nothing less. The six worst epigrams are mere alms handed with a kind smile to the average suburban playgoer; the three best remain secrets between Mr Wilde and a few choice spirits. The modern note is struck in Sir Robert Chiltern's assertion of the individuality and courage of his wrongdoing as against the mechanical idealism of his stupidly good wife, and in his bitter criticism of a love that is only the reward of merit. It is from the philosophy on which this scene is based that the most pregnant epigrams in the play have been condensed. Indeed, this is the only philosophy that ever has produced epigrams. In contriving the stage expedients by which the action of the piece is kept going, Mr Wilde has been once or twice a little too careless of stage illusion: for example, why on earth should Mrs Cheveley, hiding in Lord Goring's room, knock down a chair? That is my sole criticism.

The performance is very amusing. The audience laughs conscientiously: each person comes to the theatre prepared, like a special artist, with the background of a laugh ready sketched in on his or her features. Some of the performers labor intensely at being epigrammatic. I am sure Miss Vane Featherstone and Miss Forsyth could play Lady Macbeth and Medea with less effort than Lady Basildon and Mrs Marchmont, who have nothing to do but sit on a sofa and be politely silly for ten minutes. There is no doubt that these glimpses of expensive receptions in Park Lane, with the servants announcing titles *ad libitum,* are enormously attractive to social outsiders (say ninety-nine hundredths of us); but the stage reproduction is not convincing: everybody has an outrageous air of being at a party; of not being used to it; and, worst of all, of enjoying themselves immensely. Mr Charles Hawtrey has the best of the fun among the principals. As everyone's guide, philosopher, and friend, he has moments in which he is, I think, intended to be deep, strong, and tender. These moments, to say the least, do not quite come off; but his lighter serious episodes are excellent, and his drollery conquers without effort. When Miss Neilson sits still and lets her gifts of beauty and grace be eloquent for her, she is highly satisfying; but I cannot say the same for the passages in which she has to take the stage herself and try to act. She becomes merely artificial and superficially imitative. Miss Fanny Brough makes Lady Markby, an eminently possible person, quite impossible; and Miss Maude Millet, playing very well indeed as Mabel Chiltern, nevertheless occasionally spoils a word by certain vowel sounds which are only permissible to actresses of the second rank. As an adventuress who, like the real and unlike the stage adventuress, is not in love with any one, and is simply selfish, dishonest, and third rate, Miss Florence West is kinetoscopically realistic. The portrait is true to nature; but it has no artistic character: Miss West has not the art of being agreeably disagreeable. Mr Brookfield, a great artist in small things, makes the valet in the third act one of the heroes of the performance. And Mr Waller is handsome and dignified as the ideal husband, a part easily within his means. His management could not have been more auspiciously inaugurated.

King Arthur

KING ARTHUR. A drama in a prologue and four acts. By J. Comyns Carr. Lyceum Theatre, 12 January 1895.

[19 *January* 1895]

Mr Irving is to be congratulated on the impulse which has led him to exclaim, on this occasion, "Let us get rid

of that insufferably ignorant specialist, the dramatist, and
try whether something fresh cannot be done by a man
equipped with all the culture of the age." It was an inevitable step in the movement which is bringing the stage more
and more into contact with life. When I was young, the
banquets on the stage were made by the property man: his
goblets and pasties, and epergnes laden with grapes, regaled guests who walked off and on through illusory wain-
scoting simulated by the precarious perspective of the
wings. The scene-painter built the rooms; the costumier
made the dresses; the armor was made apparently by dip-
ping the legs of the knights in a solution of salt of spangles
and precipitating the metal on their calves by some electro-
process; the leader of the band made the music; and the
author wrote the verse and invented the law, the morals,
the religion, the art, the jurisprudence, and whatever else
might be needed in the abstract department of the play.
Since then we have seen great changes. Real walls, ceilings,
and doors are made by real carpenters; real tailors and
dressmakers clothe the performers; real armorers harness
them; and real musicians write the music and have it performed with full orchestral honors at the Crystal Palace
and the Philharmonic. All that remains is to get a real poet
to write the verse, a real philosopher to do the morals, a
real divine to put in the religion, a real lawyer to adjust
the law, and a real painter to design the pictorial effects.
This is too much to achieve at one blow; but Mr Irving
made a brave step towards it when he resolved to get rid
of the author and put in his place his dear old friend
Comyns Carr as an encyclopædic gentleman well up to
date in most of these matters. And Mr Comyns Carr, of
course, was at once able to tell him that there was an
immense mass of artistic and poetic tradition, accumulated
by generations of poets and painters, lying at hand all
ready for exploitation by any experienced dealer with
ingenuity and literary faculty enough to focus it in a stage
entertainment. Such a man would have to know, for instance, that educated people have ceased to believe that
architecture means "ruins by moonlight" (style, ecclesiastical Gothic); that the once fashionable admiration of the
Renascence and "the old masters" of the sixteenth and
seventeenth centuries has been swept away by the growth
of a genuine sense of the naïve dignity and charm of
thirteenth-century work, and a passionate affection for the

exquisite beauty of fifteenth-century work, so that nowadays ten acres of Carracci, Giulio Romano, Guido,
Domenichino, and Pietro di Cortona will not buy an inch
of Botticelli, or Lippi, or John Bellini—no, not even with
a few yards of Raphael thrown in; and that the whole
rhetorical school in English literature, from Shakespear to
Byron, appears to us in our present mood only another
side of the terrible *degringolade* from Michael Angelo to
Canova and Thorwaldsen, all of whose works would not
now tempt us to part with a single fragment by Donatello,
or even a pretty foundling baby by Della Robbia. And yet
this, which is the real art culture of England today, is only
dimly known to our dramatic authors as a momentary
bygone craze out of which a couple of successful pieces,
Patience, and The Colonel, made some money in their day.
Mr Comyns Carr knows better. He knows that Burne-Jones
has made himself the greatest among English decorative
painters by picking up the tradition of his art where Lippi
left it, and utterly ignoring "their Raphaels, Correggios,
and stuff." He knows that William Morris has made himself the greatest living master of the English language,
both in prose and verse, by picking up the tradition of
the literary art where Chaucer left it, and that Morris and
Burne-Jones, close friends and co-operators in many a
masterpiece, form the highest aristocracy of English art
today. And he knows exactly how far their culture has
spread and penetrated, and how much simply noble beauty
of Romanesque architecture, what touching loveliness and
delicate splendor of fifteenth-century Italian dresses and
armor, what blue from the hills round Florence and what
sunset gloom deepening into splendid black shadow from
the horizons of Giorgione will be recognized with delight
on the stage if they be well counterfeited there; also what
stories we long to have as the subject of these deeply desired pictures. Foremost among such stories stands that of
King Arthur, Lancelot, and Guinevere; and what Mr
Comyns Carr has done is to contrive a play in which we
have our heart's wish, and see these figures come to life,
and move through halls and colonnades that might have
been raised by the master-builders of San Zeno or San
Ambrogio, out into the eternal beauty of the woodland
spring acting their legend just as we know it, in just such
vestures and against just such backgrounds of blue hill and
fiery sunset. No mere dramatic author could have wrought

this miracle. Mr Comyns Carr has done it with ease, by
simply knowing whom to send for. His long business experience as a man of art and letters, and the contact with
artists and poets which it has involved, have equipped him
completely for the work. In Mr Irving's theatre, with
Burne-Jones to design for him, Harker and Hawes Craven
to paint for him, and Malory and Tennyson and many
another on his bookshelves, he has put out his hand cleverly on a ready-made success, and tasted the joy of victory
without the terror of battle.

But how am I to praise this deed when my own art, the
art of literature, is left shabby and ashamed amid the triumph of the arts of the painter and the actor? I sometimes
wonder where Mr Irving will go to when he dies—whether
he will dare to claim, as a master artist, to walk where he
may any day meet Shakespear whom he has mutilated,
Goethe whom he has travestied, and the nameless creator
of the hero-king out of whose mouth he has uttered jobbing
verses. For in poetry Mr Comyns Carr is frankly a jobber
and nothing else. There is one scene in the play in which
Mr Irving rises to the height of his art, and impersonates,
with the noblest feeling, and the most sensitive refinement
of execution, the King Arthur of all our imaginations in
the moment when he learns that his wife loves his friend
instead of himself. And all the time, whilst the voice, the
gesture, the emotion expressed are those of the hero-king,
the talk is the talk of an angry and jealous costermonger,
exalted by the abject submission of the other parties to a
transport of magnanimity in refraining from reviling his
wife and punching her lover's head. I do not suppose that
Mr Irving said to Mr Comyns Carr in so many words,
"Write what trash you like: I'll play the real King Arthur
over the head of your stuff"; but that was what it came to.
And the end of it was that Mr Comyns Carr was too much
for Mr Irving. When King Arthur, having broken down in
an attempt to hit Lancelot with his sword, left Guinevere
grovelling on the floor with her head within an inch of his
toes, and stood plainly conveying to the numerous by-
standers that this was the proper position for a female
who had forgotten herself so far as to prefer another man
to him, one's gorge rose at the Tappertitian vulgarity and
ínfamy of the thing; and it was a relief when the scene
ended with a fine old Richard the Third effect of Arthur
leading his mail-clad knights off to battle. That vision of

a fine figure of a woman, torn with sobs and remorse,
stretched at the feet of a nobly superior and deeply
wronged lord of creation, is no doubt still as popular with
the men whose sentimental vanity it flatters as it was in the
days of the Idylls of the King. But since then we have been
learning that a woman is something more than a piece of
sweetstuff to fatten a man's emotions; and our amateur
King Arthurs are beginning to realize, with shocked surprise, that the more generous the race grows, the stronger
becomes its disposition to bring them to their senses with
a stinging dose of wholesome ridicule. Mr Comyns Carr
miscalculated the spirit of the age on this point; and the
result was that he dragged Mr Irving down from the height
of the loftiest passage in his acting to the abyss of the
lowest depth of the dialogue.

Whilst not sparing my protest against this unpardonable
scene, I can hardly blame Mr Comyns Carr for the touch
of human frailty which made him reserve to himself the
honor of providing the "book of the words" for Burne-
Jones's picture-opera. No doubt, since Mr Carr is no more
a poet than I am, the consistent course would have been to
call in Mr William Morris to provide the verse. Perhaps, if
Mr Irving, in his black harness, with his visor down and
Excalibur ready to hand and well in view, were to present
himself at the Kelmscott Press fortified with a propitiatory
appeal from the great painter, the poet might, without absolutely swearing, listen to a proposal that he should condescend to touch up those little rhymed acrostics in which
Merlin utters his prophecies, leaving the blank verse pad-
ding to Mr Comyns Carr. For the blank verse is at all
events accurately metrical, a fact which distinguishes the
author sharply from most modern dramatists. The ideas
are second-hand, and are dovetailed into a coherent struc-
ture instead of developing into one another by any life of
their own; but they are sometimes very well chosen; and
Mr Carr is often guided to his choice of them by the
strength and sincerity of their effect on his own feelings.
At such moments, if he does not create, he reflects so well,
and sometimes reflects such fine rays too, that one gladly
admits that there are men whose originality might have
been worse than his receptivity. There are excellent moments in the love scenes: indeed, Lancelot's confession of
his love to Guinevere all but earns for the author the poet's
privilege of having his chain tested by its strongest link.

The only great bit of acting in the piece is that passage of Mr Irving's to which I have already alluded—a masterly fulfilment of the promise of one or two quiet but eloquent touches in his scene with Guinevere in the second act. Popularly speaking, Mr Forbes Robertson as Lancelot is the hero of the piece. He has a beautiful costume, mostly of plate-armor of Burne-Jonesian design; and he wears it beautifully, like a fifteenth-century St George, the spiritual, interesting face completing a rarely attractive living picture. He was more than applauded on his entrance: he was positively adored. His voice is an organ with only one stop on it: to the musician it suggests a clarionet in A, played only in the chalumeau register; but then the chalumeau, sympathetically sounded, has a richly melancholy and noble effect. The one tune he had to play throughout suited it perfectly: its subdued passion, both in love and devotion, affected the house deeply; and the crowning moment of the drama for most of those present was his clasping of Guinevere's waist as he knelt at her feet when she intoxicated him by answering his confession with her own. As to Miss Ellen Terry, it was the old story, a born actress of real women's parts condemned to figure as a mere artist's model in costume plays which, from the woman's point of view, are foolish flatteries written by gentlemen for gentlemen. It is pathetic to see Miss Terry snatching at some fleeting touch of nature in her part, and playing it not only to perfection, but often with a parting caress that brings it beyond that for an instant as she relinquishes it, very loth, and passes on to the next length of arid sham-feminine twaddle in blank verse, which she pumps out in little rhythmic strokes in a desperate and all too obvious effort to make music of it. I should prove myself void of the true critic's passion if I could pass with polite commonplaces over what seems to me a heartless waste of an exquisite talent. What a theatre for a woman of genius to be attached to! Obsolete tomfooleries like Robert Macaire, schoolgirl charades like Nance Oldfield, blank verse by Wills, Comyns Carr, and Calmour, with intervals of hashed Shakespear; and all the time a stream of splendid women's parts pouring from the Ibsen volcano and minor craters, and being snapped up by the rising generation. Strange, under these circumstances, that it is Mr Irving and not Miss Terry who feels the want of a municipal theatre. He has certainly done his best to make everyone else feel it.

The rest of the acting is the merest stock company routine, there being only three real parts in the play. Sir Arthur Sullivan (who, in the playbill, drops his knighthood whilst Burne-Jones parades his baronetcy) sweetens the sentiment of the scenes here and there by penn'orths of orchestral sugarstick, for which the dramatic critics, in their soft-eared innocence, praise him above Wagner. The overture and the vocal pieces are pretty specimens of his best late work. Some awkwardness in the construction of the play towards the end has led the stage manager into a couple of absurdities. For instance, when the body of Elaine is done with, it should be taken off the stage and not put in the corner like a portmanteau at a railway station. I do not know what is supposed to happen in the last act—whether Guinevere is alive or a ghost when she comes in at Arthur's death (I understood she was being burnt behind the scenes), or what becomes of Lancelot and Mordred, or who on earth the two gentlemen are who come in successively to interview the dying Arthur, or why the funeral barge should leave Mr Irving lying on the stage and bear off to bliss an impostor with a strikingly different nose. In fact I understand nothing that happened after the sudden blossoming out of Arthur into Lohengrin, Guinevere into Elsa, Mordred into Telramund, and Morgan le Fay into Ortruda in the combat scene, in which, by the way, Mr Comyns Carr kills the wrong man, probably from having read Wagner carelessly. But I certainly think something might be done to relieve the shock of the whole court suddenly bolting and leaving the mortally wounded king floundering on the floor without a soul to look after him. These trifles are mere specks of dust on a splendid picture; but they could easily be brushed off.

Poor Shakespear!

ALL'S WELL THAT ENDS WELL. Performance by the Irving Dramatic Club at St George's Hall, 22 and 24 January 1895.

[2 *February* 1895]

What a pity it is that the people who love the sound of Shakespear so seldom go on the stage! The ear is the sure clue to him: only a musician can understand the play of feeling which is the real rarity in his early plays. In a deaf nation these plays would have died long ago. The moral

attitude in them is conventional and secondhand: the borrowed ideas, however finely expressed, have not the overpowering human interest of those original criticisms of life
which supply the rhetorical element in his later works.
Even the individualization which produces that old-estab-
lished British speciality, the Shakespearean "delineation of
character," owes all its magic to the turn of the line, which
lets you into the secret of its utterer's mood and temperament, not by its commonplace meaning, but by some subtle exaltation, or stultification, or slyness, or delicacy, or
hesitancy, or what not in the sound of it. In short, it is the
score and not the libretto that keeps the work alive and
fresh; and this is why only musical critics should be allowed to meddle with Shakespear—especially early Shakespear. Unhappily, though the nation still retains its ears,
the players and playgoers of this generation are for the
most part deaf as adders. Their appreciation of Shakespear
is sheer hypocrisy, the proof being that where an early
play of his is revived, they take the utmost pains to suppress as much of it as possible, and disguise the rest past
recognition, relying for success on extraordinary scenic
attractions; on very popular performers, including, if possible, a famously beautiful actress in the leading part; and,
above all, on Shakespear's reputation and the consequent
submission of the British public to be mercilessly bored by
each of his plays once in their lives, for the sake of being
able to say they have seen it. And not a soul has the hardihood to yawn in the face of the imposture. The manager
is praised; the bard is praised; the beautiful actress is
praised; and the free list comes early and comes often,
not without a distinct sense of conferring a handsome
compliment on the acting manager. And it certainly is hard
to face such a disappointment without being paid for it.
For the more enchanting the play is at home by the fireside
in winter, or out on the heather of a summer evening—the
more the manager, in his efforts to realize this enchantment by reckless expenditure on incidental music, colored
lights, dances, dresses, and elaborate rearrangements and
dislocations of the play—the more, in fact, he departs from
the old platform with its curtains and its placards inscribed
"A street in Mantua," and so forth, the more hopelessly
and vulgarly does he miss his mark. Such crown jewels of
dramatic poetry as Twelfth Night and A Midsummer
Night's Dream, fade into shabby colored glass in his purse;

and sincere people who do not know what the matter is, begin to babble insufferably about plays that are meant for the study and not for the stage.

Yet once in a blue moon or so there wanders on to the stage some happy fair whose eyes are lodestars and whose tongue's sweet air's more tunable than lark to shepherd's ear. And the moment she strikes up the true Shakespearean music, and feels her way to her part altogether by her sense of that music, the play returns to life and all the magic is there. She may make nonsense of the verses by wrong conjunctions and misplaced commas, which shew that she has never worked out the logical construction of a single sentence in her part; but if her heart is in the song, the protesting commentator-critic may save his breath to cool his porridge: the soul of the play is there, no matter where the sense of it may be. We have all heard Miss Rehan perform this miracle with Twelfth Night, and turn it, in spite of the impossible Mr Daly, from a hopelessly ineffective actress show into something like the exquisite poem its author left it. All I can remember of the last performance I witnessed of A Midsummer Night's Dream is that Miss Kate Rorke got on the stage somehow and began to make some music with Helena's lines, with the result that Shakespear, who had up to that moment lain without sense or motion, immediately began to stir uneasily and shew signs of quickening, which lasted until the others took up the word and struck him dead.

Powerful among the enemies of Shakespear are the commentator and the elocutionist: the commentator because, not knowing Shakespear's language, he sharpens his reasoning faculty to examine propositions advanced by an eminent lecturer from the Midlands, instead of sensitizing his artistic faculty to receive the impression of moods and inflexions of feeling conveyed by word-music; the elocutionist because he is a born fool, in which capacity, observing with pain that poets have a weakness for imparting to their dramatic dialogue a quality which he describes and deplores as "sing-song," he devotes his life to the art of breaking up verse in such a way as to make it sound like insanely pompous prose. The effect of this on Shakespear's earlier verse, which is full of the naïve delight of pure oscillation, to be enjoyed as an Italian enjoys a barcarolle, or a child a swing, or a baby a rocking-cradle, is destructively stupid. In the later plays, where the barcarolle measure has evolved into much more varied and complex rhythms, it does not matter so much, since the work is no longer simple enough for a fool to pick to pieces. But in every play from Love's Labour Lost to Henry V, the elocutionist meddles simply as a murderer, and ought to be dealt with as such without benefit of clergy. To our young people studying for the stage I say, with all solemnity, learn how to pronounce the English alphabet clearly and beautifully from some person who is at once an artist and a phonetic expert. And then leave blank verse patiently alone until you have experienced emotion deep enough to crave for poetic expression, at which point verse will seem an absolutely natural and real form of speech to you. Meanwhile, if any pedant, with an uncultivated heart and a theoretic ear, proposes to teach you to recite, send instantly for the police.

Among Shakespear's earlier plays, All's Well that Ends Well stands out artistically by the sovereign charm of the young Helena and the old Countess of Rousillon, and intellectually by the experiment, repeated nearly three hundred years later in A Doll's House, of making the hero a perfectly ordinary young man, whose unimaginative prejudices and selfish conventionality make him cut a very fine mean figure in the atmosphere created by the nobler nature of his wife. That is what gives a certain plausibility to the otherwise doubtful tradition that Shakespear did not succeed in getting his play produced (founded on the absence of any record of a performance of it during his lifetime). It certainly explains why Phelps, the only modern actor-manager tempted by it, was attracted by the part of Parolles, a capital study of the adventurous yarn-spinning society-struck coward, who also crops up again in modern fiction as the hero of Charles Lever's underrated novel, A Day's Ride: a Life's Romance. When I saw All's Well announced for performance by the Irving Dramatic Club, I was highly interested, especially as the performers were free, for once, to play Shakespear for Shakespear's sake. Alas! at this amateur performance, at which there need have been none of the miserable commercialization compulsory at the regular theatres, I suffered all the vulgarity and absurdity of that commercialism without its efficiency. We all know the stock objection of the Brixton Family Shakespear to All's Well—that the heroine is a lady doctor, and that no lady of any delicacy could possibly adopt

a profession which involves the possibility of her having
to attend cases such as that of the king in this play, who
suffers from a fistula. How any sensible and humane person can have ever read this sort of thing without a deep
sense of its insult to every charitable woman's humanity
and every sick man's suffering is, fortunately, getting
harder to understand nowadays than it once was. Nevertheless All's Well was minced with strict deference to it
for the members of the Irving Dramatic Club. The rule
for expurgation was to omit everything that the most
pestiferously prurient person could find improper. For
example, when the non-commissioned officer, with quite
becoming earnestness and force, says to the disgraced
Parolles: "If you could find out a country where but
women were that had received so much shame, you might
begin an impudent nation," the speech was suppressed as
if it were on all fours with the obsolete Elizabethan badi-
nage which is and should be cut out as a matter of course.
And to save Helena from anything so shocking as a reference to her virginity, she was robbed of that rapturous outburst beginning

> There shall your master have a thousand loves—
> A mother and a mistress and a friend, etc.

But perhaps this was sacrificed in deference to the opinion
of the editor of those pretty and handy little books called
the Temple Shakespear, who compares the passage to "the
nonsense of some foolish conceited player"—a criticism
which only a commentator could hope to live down.

The play was, of course, pulled to pieces in order that
some bad scenery, totally unconnected with Florence or
Rousillon, might destroy all the illusion which the simple
stage directions in the book create, and which they would
equally have created had they been printed on a placard
and hung up on a curtain. The passage of the Florentine
army beneath the walls of the city was managed in the
manner of the end of the first act of Robertson's Ours,
the widow and the girls looking out of their sitting-room
window, whilst a few of the band gave a precarious selection from the orchestral parts of Berlioz's version of the
Rackoczy March. The dresses were the usual fancy ball
odds and ends, Helena especially distinguishing herself by
playing the first scene partly in the costume of Hamlet and
partly in that of a waitress in an Aerated Bread shop, set

off by a monstrous auburn wig which could by no stretch
of imagination be taken for her own hair. Briefly, the
whole play was vivisected, and the fragments mutilated,
for the sake of accessories which were in every particular
silly and ridiculous. If they were meant to heighten the
illusion, they were worse than failures, since they rendered
illusion almost impossible. If they were intended as illustrations of place and period, they were ignorant impos-
tures. I have seen poetic plays performed without costumes before a pair of curtains by ladies and gentlemen
in evening dress wtih twenty times the effect: nay, I will
pledge my reputation that if the members of the Irving
Dramatic Club will take their books in their hands, sit in
a Christy Minstrel semicircle, and read the play decently
as it was written, the result will be a vast improvement on
this St George's Hall travesty.

Perhaps it would not be altogether kind to leave these
misguided but no doubt well-intentioned ladies and gentlemen without a word of appreciation from their own point
of view. Only, there is not much to be said for them even
from that point of view. Few living actresses could throw
themselves into the sustained transport of exquisite tenderness and impulsive courage which makes poetry the natural speech of Helena. The cool young woman, with a
superior understanding, excellent manners, and a habit of
reciting Shakespear, presented before us by Miss Olive
Kennett, could not conceivably have been even Helena's
thirty-second cousin. Miss Lena Heinekey, with the most
beautiful old woman's part ever written in her hands, discovered none of its wonderfully pleasant good sense, humanity, and originality: she grieved stagily all through in
the manner of the Duchess of York in Cibber's Richard
III. Mr Lewin-Mannering did not for any instant make it
possible to believe that Parolles was a real person to him.
They all insisted on calling him *parole,* instead of Parolles,
in three syllables, with the *s* sounded at the end, as Shakespear intended: consequently, when he came to the couplet
which cannot be negotiated on any other terms:

> Rust, sword; cool, blushes; and, Parolles, thrive;
> Theres place and means for every man alive,

he made a desperate effort to get even with it by saying:

> Rust, rapier; cool, blushes; and, *parole,* thrive,

and seemed quite disconcerted when he found that it would
not do. Lafeu is hardly a part that can be acted: it comes
right if the right man is available: if not, no acting can
conceal the makeshift. Mr Herbert Everitt was not the right
man; but he made the best of it. The clown was evidently
willing to relish his own humor if only he could have seen
it; but there are few actors who would not have gone that
far. Bertram (Mr Patrick Munro), if not the most intelligent of Bertrams, played the love scene with Diana with
some passion. The rest of the parts, not being character
studies, are tolerably straightforward and easy of execution; and they were creditably played, the king (Mr Ernest
Meads) carrying off the honors, and Diana (Mrs Herbert
Morris) acquitting herself with comparative distinction.
But I should not like to see another such performance of
All's Well or any other play that is equally rooted in my
deeper affections.

An Old New Play and a New Old One

THE IMPORTANCE OF BEING EARNEST. A trivial comedy for
serious people. By Oscar Wilde. St James's Theatre, 14
February 1895.

? A play in ? acts. By ?. Opera Comique, 16 February 1895.

THE SECOND MRS TANQUERAY. A play in four acts. By Arthur
W. Pinero. London: W. Heinemann. 1895.

[23 *February* 1895]

It is somewhat surprising to find Mr Oscar Wilde, who
does not usually model himself on Mr Henry Arthur Jones,
giving his latest play a five-chambered title like The Case
of Rebellious Susan. So I suggest with some confidence
that The Importance of Being Earnest dates from a period
long anterior to Susan. However it may have been re-
touched immediately before its production, it must certainly have been written before Lady Windermere's Fan.
I do not suppose it to be Mr Wilde's first play: he is too
susceptible to fine art to have begun otherwise than with
a strenuous imitation of a great dramatic poem, Greek or
Shakespearean; but it was perhaps the first which he designed for practical commercial use at the West End
theatres. The evidence of this is abundant. The play has a
plot—a gross anachronism; there is a scene between the
two girls in the second act quite in the literary style of

Mr Gilbert, and almost inhuman enough to have been conceived by him; the humor is adulterated by stock mechanical fun to an extent that absolutely scandalizes one in a play with such an author's name to it; and the punning title and several of the more farcical passages recall the epoch of the late H. J. Byron. The whole has been varnished, and here and there veneered, by the author of A Woman of no Importance; but the general effect is that of a farcical comedy dating from the seventies, unplayed during that period because it was too clever and too decent, and brought up to date as far as possible by Mr Wilde in his now completely formed style. Such is the impression left by the play on me. But I find other critics, equally entitled to respect, declaring that The Importance of Being Earnest is a strained effort of Mr Wilde's at ultra-modernity, and that it could never have been written but for the opening up of entirely new paths in drama last year by Arms and the Man. At which I confess to a chuckle.

I cannot say that I greatly cared for The Importance of Being Earnest. It amused me, of course; but unless comedy touches me as well as amuses me, it leaves me with a sense of having wasted my evening. I go to the theatre to be moved to laughter, not to be tickled or bustled into it; and that is why, though I laugh as much as anybody at a farcical comedy, I am out of spirits before the end of the second act, and out of temper before the end of the third, my miserable mechanical laughter intensifying these symptoms at every outburst. If the public ever becomes intelligent enough to know when it is really enjoying itself and when it is not, there will be an end of farcical comedy. Now in The Importance of Being Earnest there is plenty of this rib-tickling: for instance, the lies, the deceptions, the cross purposes, the sham mourning, the christening of the two grown-up men, the muffin eating, and so forth. These could only have been raised from the farcical plane by making them occur to characters who had, like Don Quixote, convinced us of their reality and obtained some hold on our sympathy. But that unfortunate moment of Gilbertism breaks our belief in the humanity of the play. Thus we are thrown back on the force and daintiness of its wit, brought home by an exquisitely grave, natural, and unconscious execution on the part of the actors. Alas! the latter is not forthcoming. Mr Kinsey Peile as a man-servant, and Miss Irene Vanbrugh as Gwendolen Fairfax, alone escaped from a devastating consciousness of Mr Wilde's reputation, which more or less preoccupied all the rest, except perhaps Miss Millard, with whom all comedy is a preoccupation, since she is essentially a sentimental actress. In such passages as the Gilbertian quarrel with Gwendolen, her charm rebuked the scene instead of enhancing it. The older ladies were, if they will excuse my saying so, quite maddening. The violence of their affectation, the insufferable low comedy soars and swoops of the voice, the rigid shivers of elbow, shoulder, and neck, which are supposed on the stage to characterize the behavior of ladies after the age of forty, played havoc with the piece. In Miss Rose Leclerq a good deal of this sort of thing is only the mannerism of a genuine if somewhat impossible style; but Miss Leclerq was absent through indisposition on the night of my visit; so that I had not her style to console me. Mr Aynesworth's easy-going Our Boys style of play suited his part rather happily; and Mr Alexander's graver and more refined manner made the right contrast with it. But Mr Alexander, after playing with very nearly if not quite perfect conviction in the first two acts, suddenly lost confidence in the third, and began to spur up for a rattling finish. From the moment that began, the play was done with. The speech in which Worthing forgives his supposed mother, and the business of searching the army lists, which should have been conducted with subdued earnestness, was bustled through to the destruction of all verisimilitude and consequently all interest. That is the worst of having anyone who is not an inveterate and hardened comedian in a leading comedy part. His faith, patience, and relish begin to give out after a time; and he finally commits the unpardonable sin against the author of giving the signal that the play is over ten minutes before the fall of the curtain, instead of speaking the last line as if the whole evening were still before the audience. Mr Alexander does not throw himself genuinely into comedy: he condescends to amuse himself with it; and in the end he finds that he cannot condescend enough. On the whole I must decline to accept The Importance of Being Earnest as a day less than ten years old; and I am altogether unable to perceive any uncommon excellence in its presentation.

I am in a somewhat foolish position concerning a play at the Opera Comique, whither I was bidden this day week. For some reason I was not supplied with a program; so that I never learnt the name of the play. I believe I recognized some of the members of the company—generally a very difficult thing to do in a country where, with a few talented exceptions, every actor is just like every other actor—but they have now faded from my memory. At the end of the second act the play had advanced about as far as an ordinary dramatist would have brought it five minutes after the first rising of the curtain; or, say, as far as Ibsen would have brought it ten years before that event. Taking advantage of the second interval to stroll out into the Strand for a little exercise, I unfortunately forgot all about my business, and actually reached home before it occurred to me that I had not seen the end of the play. Under these circumstances it would ill become me to dogmatize on the merits of the work or its performance. I can only offer the management my apologies.

I am indebted to Mr Heinemann for a copy of The Second Mrs Tanqueray, which he has just published in a five-shilling volume, with an excellent photographic portrait of the author by Mr Hollyer. Those who did not see the play at the St James's Theatre can now examine the literary basis of the work that so immoderately fascinated playgoing London in 1893. But they must not expect the play to be as imposing in the library as it was on the stage. Its merit there was relative to the culture of the playgoing public. Paula Tanqueray is an astonishingly well-drawn figure as stage figures go nowadays, even allowing for the fact that there is no cheaper subject for the character draughtsman than the ill-tempered sensual woman seen from the point of view of the conventional man. But off the stage her distinction vanishes. The novels of Anthony Trollope, Charles Lever, Bulwer Lytton, Charles Reade, and many other novelists, whom nobody praised thirty years ago in the terms in which Mr Pinero is praised now, are full of feats of character-drawing in no way inferior— to say the least—to Mr Pinero's. The theatre was not ready for that class of work then: it is now; and accordingly Mr Pinero, who in literature is a humble and somewhat belated follower of the novelists of the middle of the nineteenth century, and who has never written a line from which it could be guessed that he is a contemporary of Ibsen, Tolstoi, Meredith, or Sarah Grand, finds himself at the dawn of the twentieth hailed as a man of new ideas, of daring originality, of supreme literary distinction, and even—which is perhaps oddest—of consummate stage craft. Stage craft, after all, is very narrowly limited by the physical conditions of stage representation; but when one turns over the pages of The Second Mrs Tanqueray, and notes the naïve machinery of the exposition in the first act, in which two whole actors are wasted on sham parts, and the hero, at his own dinner party, is compelled to get up and go ignominiously into the next room "to write some letters" when something has to be said behind his back; when one follows Cayley Drummle, the confidant to whom both Paula and her husband explain themselves for the benefit of the audience; when one counts the number of doors which Mr Pinero needs to get his characters on and off the stage, and how they have finally to be supplemented by the inevitable "French windows" (two of them); and when the activity of the postman is taken into consideration, it is impossible to avoid the conclusion that what most of our critics mean by mastery of stage craft is reckless-ness in the substitution of dead machinery and lay figures for vital action and real characters. I do not deny that an author may be driven by his own limitations to ingenuities which Shakespear had no occasion to cultivate, just as a painter without hands or feet learns to surpass Michael Angelo in the art of drawing with the brush held in the mouth; but I regard such ingenuity as an extremity to be deplored, not as an art to be admired. In the Second Mrs Tanqueray I find little except a scaffold for the situation of a step-daughter and step-mother finding themselves in the positions respectively of affianced wife and discarded mis-tress to the same man. Obviously, the only necessary con-ditions of this situation are that the persons concerned shall be respectable enough to be shocked by it, and that the step-mother shall be an improper person. Mr Pinero has not got above this minimum. He is, of course, sufficiently skilled in fiction to give Ellean, Mrs Cortelyon, Ardale, Tanqueray, and Cayley Drummle a passable air of being human beings. He has even touched up Cayley into a Thackerayan *flâneur* in order to secure toleration of his intrusiveness. But who will pretend that any of these figures are more than the barest accessories to the main situation? To compare them with the characters in Robert-son's Caste would be almost as ridiculous as to compare Caste with A Doll's House. The two vulgar characters produce the requisite jar—a pitilessly disagreeable jar—and that is all. Still, all the seven seem good as far as they go; and that very little way may suggest that Mr Pinero might have done good creative work if he had carried them further. Unfortunately for this surmise, he has carried Paula further; and with what result? The moment the point is reached at which the comparatively common gift of "an eye for character" has to be supplemented by the higher dramatic gift of sympathy with character—of the power of seeing the world from the point of view of others instead of merely describing or judging them from one's own point of view in terms of the conventional systems of morals, Mr Pinero breaks down. I remember that when I saw the play acted I sat up very attentively when Tanqueray said to Paula, "I know what you were at Ellean's age. You hadnt a thought that wasnt a wholesome one; you hadnt an impulse that didnt tend towards good; you never harbored a notion you couldnt have gossiped about to a parcel of children. And this was a very few years back, etc. etc." On the reply to that fatuous but not unnatural speech depended the whole question of Mr Pinero's rank as a dramatist. One can imagine how, in a play by a master-hand, Paula's reply would have opened Tanqueray's foolish eyes to the fact that a woman of that sort is already the same at three as she is at thirty-three, and that however she may have found by experience that her nature is in conflict with the ideals of differently constituted people, she remains perfectly valid to herself, and despises herself, if she sincerely does so at all, for the hypocrisy that the world forces on her instead of for being what she is. What reply does Mr Pinero put into her mouth? Here it is, with the stage directions: "A few—years ago! (*She walks slowly towards the door, then suddenly drops upon the ottoman in a paroxysm of weeping.*) O God! A few years ago!" That is to say, she makes her reply from the Tanqueray-Ellean-Pinero point of view, and thus betrays the fact that she is a work of prejudiced observation instead of comprehension, and that the other characters only owe their faint humanity to the fact that they are projections of Mr Pinero's own personal amiabilities and beliefs and conventions. Mr Pinero, then, is no interpreter of character, but simply an adroit describer of people as the ordinary man sees and judges them. Add to this a clear head, a love of the stage, and a fair talent for fiction, all

highly cultivated by hard and honorable work as a writer
of effective stage plays for the modern commercial theatre;
and you have him on his real level. On that level he is
entitled to all the praise The Second Mrs Tanqueray has
won him; and I very heartily regret that the glamor which
Mrs Patrick Campbell cast round the play has forced me
to examine pretensions which Mr Pinero himself never put
forward rather than to acknowledge the merits with which
his work is so concisely packed.

Mr Pinero's New Play

THE NOTORIOUS MRS EBBSMITH. An original play in four
acts. By A. W. Pinero. Garrick Theatre, 13 March 1895.

[16 *March* 1895]

Mr Pinero's new play is an attempt to reproduce that
peculiar stage effect of intellectual drama, of social problem, of subtle psychological study of character, in short, of
a great play, with which he was so successful in The
Profligate and The Second Mrs Tanqueray. In the two
earlier plays, it will be remembered, he was careful to
support this stage effect with a substantial basis of ordinary dramatic material, consisting of a well worked-up
and well worn situation which would have secured the
success of a conventional Adelphi piece. In this way he
conquered the public by the exquisite flattery of giving
them plays that they really liked, whilst persuading them
that such appreciation was only possible from persons of
great culture and intellectual acuteness. The vogue of The
Second Mrs Tanqueray was due to the fact that the commonplace playgoer, as he admired Mrs Patrick Campbell,
and was moved for the twentieth time by the conventional
wicked woman with a past, consumed with remorse at
the recollection of her innocent girlhood, and unable to
look her pure step-daughter (from a convent) in the face,
believed that he was one of the select few for whom "the
literary drama" exists, and thus combined the delights of
an evening at a play which would not have puzzled Madame Celeste with a sense of being immensely in the modern movement. Mr Pinero, in effect, invented a new sort
of play by taking the ordinary article and giving it an air
of novel, profound, and original thought. This he was able

to do because he was an inveterate "character actor" (a technical term denoting a clever stage performer who cannot act, and therefore makes an elaborate study of the disguises and stage tricks by which acting can be grotesquely simulated) as well as a competent dramatist on customary lines. His performance as a thinker and social philosopher is simply character acting in the domain of authorship, and can impose only on those who are taken in by character acting on the stage. It is only the make-up of an actor who does not understand his part, but who knows—because he shares—the popular notion of its externals. As such, it can never be the governing factor in his success, which must always depend on the commonplace but real substratum of ordinary drama in his works. Thus his power to provide Mrs Tanqueray with equally popular successors depends on his freedom from the illusion he has himself created as to his real strength lying in his acuteness as a critic of life. Given a good play, the stage effect of philosophy will pass with those who are no better philosophers than he; but when the play is bad, the air of philosophy can only add to its insufferableness. In the case of The Notorious Mrs Ebbsmith, the play is bad. But one of its defects: to wit, the unreality of the chief female character, who is fully as artificial as Mrs Tanqueray herself, has the lucky effect of setting Mrs Patrick Campbell free to do as she pleases in it, the result being an irresistible projection of that lady's personal genius, a projection which sweeps the play aside and imperiously becomes the play itself. Mrs Patrick Campbell, in fact, pulls her author through by playing him clean off the stage. She creates all sorts of illusions, and gives one all sorts of searching sensations. It is impossible not to feel that those haunting eyes are brooding on a momentous past, and the parted lips anticipating a thrilling imminent future, whilst some enigmatic present must no less surely be working underneath all that subtle play of limb and stealthy intensity of tone. Clearly there must be a great tragedy somewhere in the immediate neighborhood; and most of my colleagues will no doubt tell us that this imaginary masterpiece is Mr Pinero's Notorious Mrs Ebbsmith. But Mr Pinero has hardly anything to do with it. When the curtain comes down, you are compelled to admit that, after all, nothing has come of it except your conviction that Mrs Patrick Campbell is a wonderful woman. Let us put her out of the question for a moment and take a look at Mrs Ebbsmith.

To begin with, she is what has been called "a platform woman." She is the daughter of a secularist agitator—say a minor Bradlaugh. After eight years of married life, during which she was for one year her husband's sultana, and for the other seven his housekeeper, she has emerged into widowhood and an active career as an agitator, speaking from the platforms formerly occupied by her father. Although educated, well conducted, beautiful, and a sufficiently powerful speaker to produce a great effect in Trafalgar Square, she loses her voice from starvation, and has to fall back on nursing—a piece of fiction which shews that Mr Pinero has not the faintest idea of what such a woman's career is in reality. He may take my word for it that a lady with such qualifications would be very much better off than a nurse; and that the plinth of the Nelson column, the "pitch" in the park, and the little meeting halls in poor parishes, all of which he speaks of with such an exquisitely suburban sense of their being the dark places of the earth, enter nowadays very largely into the political education of almost all publicly active men and women; so that the Duke of St Olpherts, when he went to that iron building in St Luke's, and saw "Mad Agnes" on the platform, might much more probably have found there a future Cabinet Minister, a lady of his own ducal family, or even a dramatic critic. However, the mistakes into which Mr Pinero has been led by his want of practical acquaintance with the business of political agitation are of no great dramatic moment. We may forgive a modern British dramatist for supposing that Mrs Besant, for example, was an outcast on the brink of starvation in the days when she graduated on the platform, although we should certainly not tolerate such nonsense from any intellectually responsible person. But Mr Pinero has made a deeper mistake. He has fallen into the common error of supposing that the woman who speaks in public and takes an interest in wider concerns than those of her own household is a special variety of the human species; that she "Trafalgar Squares" aristocratic visitors in her drawing room; and that there is something dramatic in her discovery that she has the common passions of humanity.

Mrs Ebbsmith, in the course of her nursing, finds a pa-

tient who falls in love with her. He is married to a shrew;
and he proposes to spend the rest of his life with his nurse,
preaching the horrors of marriage. Off the stage it is not
customary for a man and woman to assume that they cannot co-operate in bringing about social reform without
living together as man and wife: on the stage, this is considered inevitable. Mrs Ebbsmith rebels against the stage
so far as to propose that they shall prove their disinter-
estedness by making the partnership a friendly business
one only. She then finds out that he does not really care a
rap about her ideas, and that his attachment to her is
simply sexual. Here we start with a dramatic theme capable
of interesting development. Mr Pinero, unable to develop
it, lets it slip through his fingers after one feeble clutch at
it, and proceeds to degrade his drama below the ordinary
level by making the woman declare that her discovery of
the nature of the man's feelings puts within her reach "the
only one hour in a woman's life," in pursuance of which
detestable view she puts on an indecent dress and utterly
abandons herself to him. A clergyman appears at this crisis,
and offers her a Bible. She promptly pitches it into the
stove; and a thrill of horror runs through the audience as
they see, in imagination, the whole Christian Church totter-
ing before their eyes. Suddenly, with a wild scream, she
plunges her hand into the glowing stove and pulls out the
Bible again. The Church is saved; and the curtain descends
amid thunders of applause. In that applause I hope I need
not say I did not join. A less sensible and less courageous
stage effect I have never witnessed. If Mr Pinero had
created for us a woman whose childhood had been made
miserable by the gloomy terrorism which vulgar, fanatical
parents extract from the Bible, then he might fitly have
given some of the public a very wholesome lesson by making the woman thrust the Bible into the stove and leave it
there. Many of the most devoted clergymen of the Church
of England would, I can assure him, have publicly thanked
him for such a lesson. But to introduce a woman as to
whom we are carefully assured that she was educated as a
secularist, and whose one misfortune—her unhappy marriage—can hardly by any stretch of casuistry be laid to
the charge of St Paul's teaching; to make this woman
senselessly say that all her misfortunes are due to the Bible; to make her throw it into the stove, and then injure
herself horribly in pulling it out again: this, I submit, is a

piece of claptrap so gross that it absolves me from all
obligation to treat Mr Pinero's art as anything higher than
the barest art of theatrical sensation. As in The Profligate,
as in The Second Mrs Tanqueray, he has had no idea beyond that of doing something daring and bringing down
the house by running away from the consequences.

I must confess that I have no criticism for all this stuff.
Mr Pinero is quite right to try his hand at the higher
drama; only he will never succeed on his present method
of trusting to his imagination, which seems to me to have
been fed originally on the novels and American humor of
forty years ago, and of late to have been entirely starved. I
strongly recommend him to air his ideas a little in Hyde
Park or "the Iron Hall, St Luke's," before he writes his
next play. I shall be happy to take the chair for him.

I should, by the way, like to know the truth about the
great stage effect at the end of the second act, where Mrs
Patrick Campbell enters with her plain and very becoming
dress changed for a horrifying confection apparently made
of Japanese bronze wall-paper with a bold pattern of
stamped gold. Lest the maker should take an action against
me and obtain ruinous damages, I hasten to say that the
garment was well made, the skirt and train perfectly hung,
and the bodice, or rather waistband, fitting flawlessly. But,
as I know nothing of the fashion in evening dresses, it was
cut rather lower in the pectoral region than I expected;
and it was, to my taste, appallingly ugly. So I fully believed
that the effect intended was a terrible rebuke to the man's
complaint that Mrs Ebbsmith's previous dress was only fit
for "a dowdy demagogue." Conceive my feelings when
everyone on the stage went into ecstasies of admiration.
Can Mr Pinero have shared that admiration? As the hero of
a recent play observes, "That is the question that torments
me."

A great deal of the performance is extremely tedious.
The first twenty minutes, with its intolerable, unnecessary,
and unintelligible explanations about the relationships of
the characters, should be ruthlessly cut out. Half the stage
business is only Mr Pinero's old "character actor" nonsense; and much of the other half might be executed during the dialogue, and not between the sentences. The company need to be reminded that the Garrick is a theatre in
which very distinct utterance is desirable. The worrying
from time to time about the stove should be dropped, as

it does not in the least fulfil its purpose of making the Bible incident—which is badly stage managed—seem more natural when it comes.

Mr Hare, in the stalest of parts, gives us a perfect piece of acting, not only executed with extraordinary fineness, but conceived so as to produce a strong illusion that there is a real character there, whereas there is really nothing but that hackneyed simulacrum of a cynical and epigrammatic old libertine who has helped to carry on so many plots. Mr Forbes Robertson lent himself to the hero, and so enabled him to become interesting on credit. Miss Jeffreys, miraculously ill fitted with her part, was pleasant for the first five minutes, during which she was suggesting a perfectly different sort of person to that which she afterwards vainly pretended to become. The other characters were the merest stock figures, convincing us that Mr Pinero either never meets anybody now, or else that he has lost the power of observation. Many passages in the play, of course, have all the qualities which have gained Mr Pinero his position as a dramatist; but I shall not dwell on them, as, to tell the truth, I disliked the play so much that nothing would induce me to say anything good of it. And here let me warn the reader to carefully discount my opinion in view of the fact that I write plays myself, and that my school is in violent reaction against that of Mr Pinero. But my criticism has not, I hope, any other fault than the inevitable one of extreme unfairness.

I must change the subject here to say that Mr Clement Scott has been kind enough to let me know that he did not write the obituary notice which I ascribed to him throughout my recent utterance on the subject of the Censorship in these columns. Not that Mr Scott has at all changed his views on that subject. The continuity of his policy was strictly maintained by the actual writer of the article; so that the argument between us on that point remains, I am sorry to say, where it was. But as I have incidentally made it appear that Mr Scott wrote an anonymous obituary notice of his late friend, and made it the occasion for a defence of him against certain strictures of mine, I am bound not only to comply with Mr Scott's request to make it known that he did not write the article, but to express my sense of the very considerate terms in which he has pointed out my mistake, and to beg him to excuse it.

The Independent Theatre Repents

A MAN'S LOVE, a Play in three acts, from the Dutch of J. C.
de Vos; and SALVÊ, a Dramatic Fragment in one act, by
Mrs Oscar Beringer. The Independent Theatre (Opéra
Comique), 15 March 1895.

[23 *March* 1895]

The Independent Theatre is becoming wretchedly respectable. Nobody now clamors for the prosecution of Mr
Grein under Lord Campbell's Act, or denounces myself
and the other frequenters of the performances as neurotic,
cretinous degenerates. This is not as it should be. In my
barbarous youth, when one of the pleasures of theatre-
going was the fierce struggle at the pit-door, I learnt a
lesson which I have never forgotten: namely, that the secret
of getting in was to wedge myself into the worst of the
crush. When ribs and breastbone were on the verge of collapse, and the stout lady in front, after passionately calling
on her escort to take her out of it if he considered himself
a man, had resigned herself to death, my hopes of a place
in the front row ran high. If the pressure slackened I knew
I was being extruded into the side eddies where the feeble
and half-hearted were throwing away their chance of a
good seat for such paltry indulgences as freedom to breathe
and a fully expanded skeleton. The progressive man goes
through life on the same principle, instinctively making for
the focus of struggle and resisting the tendency to edge
him out into the place of ease. When the Independent
Theatre was started, its supporters all made for it, I presume—certainly I did—because it was being heavily
squeezed. There was one crowded moment when, after the
first performance of Ghosts, the atmosphere of London
was black with vituperation, with threats, with clamor for
suppression and extinction, with everything that makes life
worth living in modern society. I have myself stood before
the Independent footlights in obedience to my vocation
(literally) as dramatic author, drinking in the rapture of
such a hooting from the outraged conventional first-nighter
as even Mr Henry James might have envied. But now that
glory has departed to the regular theatres. My poor little
audacity of a heroine who lost her temper and shook her
housemaid has been eclipsed by heroines who throw the
Bible into the fire. Mr Grein, no longer a revolutionist, is

modestly bidding for the position left vacant by the death of German Reed, and will shortly be consecrated by public opinion as the manager of the one theatre in London that is not a real wicked Pinerotic theatre, and is, consequently, the only theatre in London that it is not wrong for good people to go to. His latest playbill is conclusive on this point. It begins with A Man's Love, from the Dutch of J. C. de Vos, and ends with Salvê, by Mrs Oscar Beringer. The first would be contemptuously rejected by Mr Hare as a snivelling, pietistic insult to the spirit of the age; and the second might without the least incongruity be played as a curtain-raiser before Green Bushes or The Wreck Ashore.

The defence to this grave disparagement will probably be that, in A Man's Love, the hero makes advances to his undeceased wife's sister, and that Salvê ends unhappily. I cannot allow the excuse. Any man, on the stage or off it, may make love to his sister-in-law without rousing the faintest sense of unexpectedness in the spectator. And when, as in Mr de Vos's play, the young lady tells him he ought to be ashamed of himself, and leaves the house without making her sister miserable by telling her why, the situation becomes positively triter than if he had not made love to her at all. There is only one Independent Theatre drama to be got out of such a theme; and that is the drama of the discovery by the man that he has married the wrong sister, and that the most earnest desire on the part of all concerned to do their duty does not avail against that solid fact. Such a drama occurred in the life of one of the greatest English writers of the nineteenth century, one who was never accused by his worst enemies of being a loose liver. But Mr de Vos has not written that drama, or even pretended to write it. As to the unhappy ending of Salvê, unhappy endings are not a new development in the theatre, but a reversion to an older stage phase. I take it that the recently defunct happy ending, which is merely a means of sending the audience away in good humor, was brought in by the disappearance of the farce. Formerly you had The Gamester to begin with; and then, when Beverley had expired yelling from the effects of swallowing some powerful mineral irritant, there was a screaming farce to finish with. When it suddenly occurred to the managers that for twenty-five years or so no experienced playgoer had ever been known to wait for the farce, it was dropped; and nothing was left in the bill except the play of the evening and a

curtain-raiser to keep the gallery amused whilst waiting for
the plutocracy to finish their dinners and get down to their
reserved seats. Still the idea of sending away the audience
in a cheerful temper survived, and led to the incorporation
of that function of the farce into the end of the play.
Hence the happy ending. But in course of time this produced the same effect as the farce. The people got up and
made for the doors the moment they saw it coming; and
managers were reduced to the abject expedient of publish-
ing in the program a request to the audience not to rise
until the fall of the curtain. When even this appeal *ad
misericordiam* failed, there was nothing for it but to abolish
the happy ending, and venture on the wild innovation of
ringing down the curtain the moment the play was really
over. This brought back the old tragic ending of the farce
days, which was of course immediately hailed, as the custom is whenever some particularly ghastly antiquity is
trotted out, as the newest feature of the new drama.

So much then for the novelty of Mrs Beringer's idea of
ending her little play by making the mother slay her long-
lost cheeyild, and go mad then and there like Lucia di
Lammermoor. Indeed, if Mrs Theodore Wright had struck
up Spargi d' amaro pianto, with flute obbligato and variations, my old Italian operatic training would have saved
me from the least feeling of surprise, though the younger
generation would certainly have thought us both mad. The
variations would have been quite in keeping with the bags
of gold poured out on the table, and with the spectacle of
a mother taking up the breadknife and transfixing her
healthy young son full in the public view. Is it possible that
Mrs Beringer has not yet realized that these mock butcher-
ies belong to the babyhood of the drama? She may depend
on it there is a solid reason for Hedda Gabler shooting
herself behind the scenes instead of stabbing herself before
them. In that, Ibsen shakes hands with the Greek dramatic
poets just as clearly as Mrs Beringer, with her gory breadknife, shakes hands with the most infantile melodramatists
of the Donizettian epoch. Salvê is not at all a bad piece of
work of its naïve kind: indeed, except for a few unactable
little bits here and there, it would merit high praise at the
Pavilion or Marylebone theatres; but what, in the name of
all thats Independent, has it to do with the aims of Mr
Grein's society?

To find any sort of justification for the performance I

must turn to the acting—for let me say that I should consider Mr Grein quite in order in giving a performance of
Robertson's Caste, followed by Box and Cox, if he could
handle them so as to suggest fresh developments in stage
art. Unfortunately, the management made an incompre-
hensible mistake in casting A Man's Love. It had at its
disposal Miss Winifred Fraser and Miss Mary Keegan; and
the two women's parts in the play were well suited to their
strongly contrasted personalities. Accordingly, it put Miss
Keegan into the part which suited Miss Fraser, and Miss
Fraser into the part which suited Miss Keegan. The two
ladies did what they could under the circumstances; but
their predicament was hopeless from the outset. The resultant awkwardness made the worst of the very clumsy
devices by which the action of the play is maintained—
impossible soliloquies, incidents off the stage described by
people on it as they stare at them through the wings, and
the like: all, by the way, reasons why the Independent
Theatre should not have produced the work unless these
crudities were atoned for by boldness or novelty in some
other direction.

The two ladies being practically out of the question, the
burden of the play fell upon Mr Herbert Flemming, whose
work presented a striking contrast to the sort of thing we
are accustomed to from our popular "leading men." We all
know the faultlessly dressed, funereally wooden, carefully
phrased walking negation who is so careful not to do anything that could help or hinder our imaginations in mend-
ing him into a hero. His great secret is to keep quiet, look
serious, and, above all, not act. To this day you see Mr
Lewis Waller and Mr George Alexander struggling, even
in the freedom of management, with the habits of the days
when they were expected to supply this particular style of
article, and to live under the unwritten law: "Be a nonentity, or you will get cast for villains," a fate which has
actually overtaken Mr Waring because his efforts to suppress himself stopped short of absolute inanity. Only for
certain attractive individual peculiarities which have enabled Mr Forbes-Robertson to place himself above this
law occasionally as a personal privilege, our stage heroes
would be as little distinguishable from one another as bricks
in a wall. Under these circumstances, I was quite staggered
to find Mr Flemming, though neither a comic actor nor
a "character actor," acting—positively acting—in a senti-

mental leading part. He was all initiative, life, expression, with the unhesitating certainty of execution which stamps an actor as perfectly safe for every effect within his range. This amounted to a combination of the proficiency and positive power (as distinguished from negative discretion) of the old stock actor, with the spontaneity, sensitiveness, and touch with the cultivated non-professional world which the latest developments of the drama demand. Mr Flemming first made his mark here by his performances in certain Ibsen parts, and by his playing of the hero in Voss's Alexandra, Stuttgart's pet tragedy. Yet when he appeared recently in such an absurd melodrama as Robbery Under Arms, he was as equal to the occasion as the veteran Mr Clarence Holt; and his return without effort to the new style in A Man's Love is interesting as a sign that the new drama is at last beginning to bring in its harvest of technically efficient actors, instead of being, as it was at first, thrown into hands which were, with one or two brilliant exceptions, comparatively unskilled. The occasion was not a favorable one for Mr Flemming—quite the contrary. He was not on his mettle; he was in the unmistakeable attitude of an experienced actor towards a play which he knows to be beyond saving; the extent to which he fell back on his mere stage habits shewed that he had refused to waste much time in useless study of a dramatically worthless character, and was simply using his professional skill to get through his part without damage to his reputation; and he was sometimes taken out of the character by his very free recourse to that frankly feminine style of play which is up to a certain point the secret, and beyond it the mere stage trick, of modern acting, and which is enormously effective in a man who, like Mr Flemming, is virile enough to be feminine without risk of effeminacy. None the less this half-studied performance in a third-rate play at a depressing matinée (I was not present at the first performance) was striking enough to demand, at the present moment, all the attention I have given to it.

Mrs Theodore Wright, as the mother in Salvê, had no difficulty in touching and harrowing the audience to the necessary degree. Her acting, also, has the imaginative quality which the reviving drama requires. She made a mistake or two over Mrs Beringer's unactable bits, trying to worry some acting into them instead of letting them quietly slip by; but that was a fault on the right side; and one felt sorry for her sake when the breadknife reduced the little play to absurdity, and half spoiled the admirable effect of her playing in the scenes just before and after her journey of intercession. Happily, the audience did not mind the breadknife at all, and made her an ovation.

.   .   .   .

L'Œuvre

THÉÂTRE DE L'ŒUVRE DE PARIS. Performances at the Opéra Comique, London, of Ibsen's Rosmersholm and Master Builder, and of Maeterlinck's L'Intruse and Pelléas et Mélisande, 25-30 March 1895.

[30 *March* 1895]

M. Lugné-Poë and his dramatic company called L'Œuvre came to us with the reputation of having made Ibsen cry by their performance of one of his works. There was not much in that: I have seen performances by English players which would have driven him to suicide. But the first act of Rosmersholm had hardly begun on Monday night, when I recognized, with something like excitement, the true atmosphere of this most enthralling of all Ibsen's works rising like an enchanted mist for the first time on an English stage. There were drawbacks, of course. The shabbiness of the scenery did not trouble me; but the library of Pastor Rosmer got on my nerves a little. What on earth did he want, for instance, with Sell's World's Press? That he should have provided himself with a volume of my own dramatic works I thought right and natural enough, though when he took that particular volume down and opened it, I began to speculate rather uneasily on the chances of his presently becoming so absorbed as to forget all about his part. I was surprised, too, when it appeared that the Conservative paper which attacked the Pastor for his conversion to Radicalism was none other than our own Globe; and the thrill which passed through the house when Rebecca West contemptuously tore it across and flung it down, far exceeded that which Mrs Ebbsmith sends nightly through the Garrick audiences. Then I was heavily taken aback by Mortensgard. He, in his determination to be modern and original, had entrusted the making-up of his face to an ultra-Impressionist painter who had recklessly abused his opportunity. Kroll, too, had a frankly incredible

wig, and a costume of which every detail was a mistake.
We know Kroll perfectly well in this country: he is one out
of many instances of that essential and consequently universal knowledge of mankind which enables Ibsen to make
his pictures of social and political life in outlandish little
Norwegian parishes instantly recognizable in London and
Chicago (where Mr Beerbohm Tree, by the way, has just
made a remarkable sensation with An Enemy of the People). For saying this I may be asked whether I am aware
that many of our critical authorities have pointed out how
absurdly irrelevant the petty parochial squabblings which
stand for public life in Ibsen's prose comedies are to the
complex greatness of public affairs in our huge cities. I
reply that I am. And if I am further pressed to declare
straightforwardly whether I mean to disparage these authorities, I reply, pointedly, that I do. I affirm that such
criticisms are written by men who know as much of political life as I know of navigation. Any person who has helped
to "nurse" an English constituency, local or parliamentary,
and organized the election from the inside, or served for a
year on a vestry, or attempted to set on foot a movement
for broadening the religious and social views of an English
village, will not only vouch for it that The League of
Youth, An Enemy of the People, and Rosmersholm, are as
true to English as they can possibly be to Norwegian society, but will probably offer to supply from his own
acquaintances originals for all the public characters in these
plays.

I took exception, then, to Kroll, because I know Kroll by
sight perfectly well (was he not for a long time chairman
of the London School Board?); and I am certain he would
die sooner than pay a visit to the rector in a coat and
trousers which would make a superannuated coffee-stall
keeper feel apologetic, and with his haircutting and sham-
pooing considerably more than three months overdue.

I take a further exception which goes a good deal deeper
than this. Mdlle Marthe Mellot, the clever actress who
appeared as Rebecca West, Pelléas, and Kaia, played
Rebecca in the manner of Sarah Bernhardt, the least appropriate of all manners for the part. Rebecca's passion is
not the cold passion of the North—that essentially human
passion which embodies itself in objective purposes and
interests, and in attachments which again embody themselves in objective purposes and interests on behalf of

others—that fruitful, contained, governed, instinctively
utilized passion which makes nations and individuals great,
as distinguished from the explosive, hysterical, wasteful
passion which makes nothing but a scene. Now in the third
and fourth acts of Rosmersholm, Mdlle Mellot, who had
played excellently in the first and second, suddenly let the
part slip through her fingers by turning to the wrong sort of
passion. Take, for example, the situation in the third act.
Rosmer, who has hitherto believed that his wife was mad
when she committed suicide, is now convinced (by Mortensgard) that she did it because he transferred his affection
to Rebecca West. Rebecca, seeing that Rosmer will be
utterly broken by his own conscience if he is left to believe
that he is almost a murderer, confesses that it was she who
drove the unfortunate wife to suicide by telling her certain
lies. The deliberate character of this self-sacrifice is carefully
marked by Ibsen both in Rebecca's cold rebuke to Kroll's
attempt to improve the occasion by a gaol chaplain's
homily, and in the scene with Madame Helseth in which she
calmly arranges for her departure after the men have left
her in horror. It was here that Mdlle Mellot yielded to the
temptation to have a tearing finish in the Bernhardt style.
The confession became the mere hysterical incontinence of
a guilty and worthless woman; the scene with Madame
Helseth had to be spiced with gasps and sobs and clutches;
and the curtain fell on applause that belonged not to Rosmersholm, but to Frou-frou. Rebecca West, therefore, still
remains to be created in England. Her vicissitudes have
already been curious enough to the student of acting. Miss
Farr, the first to attempt the part here, played it as the New
Woman, fascinated by Rebecca's unscrupulousness, asking
amazed interviewers why such a useless Old Woman as
Mrs Rosmer should not have been cleared out of Rosmer's
way into the millrace, and generally combining an admirable clearness as to the logic of the situation with an exasperating insensibility to the gravity, or even the reality,
of the issues. The result was that the point which Mdlle
Mellot has just missed was hit by Miss Farr, who, in spite
of failures in whole sections of the play through want of
faith in Rebecca's final phase of development, and in various details through the awkwardness of a somewhat amateurish attempt to find a new stage method for a new style
of play, yet succeeded on the whole in leaving an impression of at least one side of Rebecca—and that the side

which was then strangest—which has not been obliterated
by any subsequent performance. A second attempt was
made by Miss Elizabeth Robins; and from this a great deal
was expected, Miss Robins having been remarkably successful in The Master Builder as Hilda Wangel, who is
clearly the earlier Rebecca West of the "free fearless will."
But that devastating stage pathos which is Miss Robins's
most formidable professional specialty, and which made her
so heartrending in Alan's Wife, and so touching as Agnes
in Brand, suddenly rose in Rosmersholm and submerged
Rebecca in an ocean of grief. So that opportunity, too, was
lost; and we still wait the perfect Rebecca, leaving Miss
Farr with the honors of having at least done most to make
us curious about her.

The performance of Maeterlinck's Pelléas and Mélisande, in which Mdlle Mellot, who was altogether charming as Pelléas, brought down the house in the Rapunzel
scene, settled the artistic superiority of M. Lugné-Poë's
company to the Comédie Française. When I recall the last
evening I spent at that institution, looking at its laboriously
drilled upper-housemaid queens and flunkey heroes, and
listening to the insensate, inhuman delivery by which every
half Alexandrine is made to sound exactly like a street cry
—when I compare this depressing experience with last
Tuesday evening at the Théâtre de l'Œuvre, I can hardly
believe that the same city has produced the two. In the
Comédie Française there is nothing but costly and highly
organized routine, deliberately used, like the ceremonial
of a court, to make second-rate human material presentable. In the Théâtre de l'Œuvre there is not merely the
ordinary theatrical intention, but a vigilant artistic conscience in the diction, the stage action, and the stage picture, producing a true poetic atmosphere, and triumphing
easily over shabby appointments and ridiculous incidents.
Of course, this is so much the worse for the Théâtre de
l'Œuvre from the point of view of the critics who represent
the Philistinism against which all genuinely artistic enterprises are crusades. It is a stinging criticism on our theatre
that ten years of constant playgoing in London seem to
reduce all but the strongest men to a condition in which
any attempt to secure in stage-work the higher qualities of
artistic execution—qualities which have been familiar for
thousands of years to all art students—appears an aberra-
tion absurd enough to justify reputable newspapers in pub-

lishing as criticism stuff which is mere street-boy guying. I am not here quarrelling with dispraise of the Théâtre de l'Œuvre and M. Maeterlinck. I set the highest value on a strong Opposition both in art and politics; and if Herr Max Nordau were made critic of the Standard (for instance) I should rejoice exceedingly. But when I find players speaking with such skill and delicacy that they can deliver M. Maeterlinck's fragile word-music throughout five acts without one harsh or strained note, and with remarkable subtlety and conviction of expression; and when I see these artists, simply because their wigs are not up to Mr Clarkson's English standard, and the curtain accidentally goes up at the wrong time, denounced as "amateurs" by gentlemen who go into obedient raptures when M. Mounet Sully plasters his cheeks with white and his lips with vermilion, and positively howls his lines at them for a whole evening with a meaningless and discordant violence which would secure his dismissal from M. Lugné-Poë's company at the end of the first act, then—Well, what then? Shall I violate the sacredness of professional etiquette, and confess to a foreigner that the distinction some of our critics make between the amateur and the expert is really a distinction between a rich enterprise and a poor one, and has nothing in the world to do with the distinction made by the trained senses of the critic who recognizes art directly through his eyes and ears, and not by its business associations? Never! Besides, it would not be fair; no man, be he ever so accomplished a critic, can effectively look at or listen to plays that he really does not want to see or hear.

The interest taken in the performances culminated at that of The Master Builder on Wednesday. At first it seemed as if M. Lugné-Poë's elaborate and completely realized study of a self-made man breaking up, was going to carry all before it, a hope raised to the highest by the delightful boldness and youthfulness of Mdlle Suzanne Despres in the earlier scenes of Hilda. Unfortunately, Madam Gay as Mrs Solness was quite impossible; Miss Florence St John as Lady Macbeth would have been better suited. And in the second act, where Solness, the dominator and mesmerizer of Kaia, becomes himself dominated and mesmerized by the impulsive, irresponsible, abounding youth and force of Hilda, Mdlle Despres lost ground, and actually began to play Kaia—Kaia prettily mutinous, perhaps, but still Kaia. The last act, with a subjugated Hilda, and a Mrs

Solness, who was visibly struggling with a natural propensity to cheerful common sense, all but failed; and it was
perhaps just as well that an offensive Frenchman in the pit
circle, by attempting to guy Mdlle Despres, provoked a
sympathetic demonstration from the decent members of the
audience at the fall of the curtain. Probably he had been
reading the English papers.

Comparing the performance with those which we have
achieved in England, it must be admitted that neither Mr
Waring nor Mr Waller were in a position to play Solness
as M. Lugné-Poë played him. They would never have got
another engagement in genteel comedy if they had worn
those vulgar trousers, painted that red eruption on their
faces, and given life to that portrait which, in every stroke,
from its domineering energy, talent, and covetousness, to
its half witted egotism and crazy philandering sentiment,
is so amazingly true to life. Mr Waring and Mr Waller
failed because they were under the spell of Ibsen's fame
as a dramatic magician, and grasped at his poetic treatment
of the man instead of at the man himself. M. Lugné-Poë
succeeded because he recognized Solness as a person he had
met a dozen times in ordinary life, and just reddened his
nose and played him without preoccupation.

With Hilda it was a different matter. Except for the first
five minutes, in which she was so bright and girlish, Mdlle
Despres could not touch Miss Robins as Hilda Wangel.
Whether Miss Robins would know Hilda if she met her in
the street, any more than Mr Waring would know Solness,
I doubt; but Miss Robins *was* Hilda; and it is an essential
part of Hilda that she does not realize her own humanity,
much less that of the poor wretch whom she destroys, or
the woman whom she widows both before and after his
actual bodily death. This merciless insensibility, which gives
such appalling force to youth, and which, when combined
with vivid imagination, high brain power, and personal
fascination, makes the young person in search of the
"frightfully thrilling" more dangerous than a lion in the
path, was presented by Miss Robins with such reality that
she made The Master Builder seem almost a one-part play.
It was a great achievement, the danger of which was realized here for the first time perhaps, on Wednesday last,
when Mdlle Despres failed to hold the house at the critical
moment. Had there been the most trifling bereavement in
the part to call forth the tear-deluge which swamped

Rebecca and Mrs Lessingham, Heaven only knows what
would have happened to Miss Robins's Hilda. Happily the
part is grief proof; and a Hilda who can even approach
Miss Robins has not yet been seen in London.

Many thanks to the Independent Theatre for its share in
bringing about the visit of the Théâtre de l'Œuvre to this
country. Mr Grein could have rendered no better service
to English art.

The Living Pictures

[6 *April* 1895]

I have been to see the Living Pictures at the Palace
Theatre. The moment Lady Henry Somerset called public
attention to the fact that they were obnoxious to the National Vigilance Association, I resolved to try whether they
would offend me. But this, like many other good resolutions
of mine, remained unfulfilled until I was reminded of it by
the address recently delivered by Mr William Alexander
Coote, the secretary of the Association, to the Church and
Stage Guild, as reported verbatim in that excellent little
paper the Church Reformer. In this address, Mr Coote said
that he considered the Living Pictures "the ideal form of
indecency." I at first supposed this to mean an ideally
desirable form of indecency; but later on I found Mr Coote
denouncing the pictures as "shameful productions, deserv-
ing the condemnation of all right-thinking people." That
cured my procrastination, and incidentally brought five
shillings into the till of the Palace Theatre. For I hurried off
to see the Living Pictures at once, not because I wanted to
wallow in indecency—no man in his senses would go to a
public theatre with that object even in the most abandoned
condition of public taste, privacy being a necessary condition of thorough-going indecency—but because, as a critic,
I at once perceived that Mr Coote had placed before the
public an issue of considerable moment: namely, whether
Mr Coote's opinion is worth anything or not. For Mr Coote
is a person of real importance, active, useful, convinced,
thoroughly respectable, able to point to achievements which
we must all admit honorable to him, and backed by an
Association strong enough to enable him to bring his convictions to bear effectively on our licensing authorities. But
all this is quite compatible with Mr Coote being in artistic

matters a most intensely stupid man, and on sexual questions something of a monomaniac.

I sat out the entire list of sixteen Living Pictures. Half
a dozen represented naiads, mountain sprites, peris, and
Lady Godiva, all practically undraped, and all, except perhaps Lady Godiva, who was posed after a well-known picture by Van Lerius (who should have read Landor's imaginary conversation between Lady Godiva and her husband),
very pretty. I need hardly say that the ladies who impersonated the figures in these pictures were not actually braving
our climate without any protection. It was only too obvious
to a practised art critic's eye that what was presented as
flesh was really spun silk. But the illusion produced on the
ordinary music-hall frequenter was that of the undraped
human figure, exquisitely clean, graceful, and, in striking
contrast to many of the completely draped and elaborately
dressed ladies who were looking at them, perfectly modest.
Many of the younger and poorer girls in the audience must
have gone away with a greater respect for their own persons, a greater regard for the virtues of the bath, and a
quickened sense of the repulsiveness of that personal slovenliness and gluttony which are the real indecencies of popular life, in addition to the valuable recreation of an escape
for a moment into the enchanted land to which naiads
and peris belong. In short, the living pictures are not only
works of art: they are excellent practical sermons; and I
urge every father of a family who cannot afford to send
his daughters the round of the picture galleries in the Haymarket and Bond Street, to take them all (with their brothers) to the Palace Theatre.

This is how they struck me. Now let Mr Coote explain
how they struck him.

"What cant to talk about 'Art' in connection with these
living picture exhibitions! They are so obviously 'living.'
Human nature is so very much in evidence. The nude as
represented by the true artist on canvas never has the slightest tendency to demoralize. The artist's soul so consciously
pervades the work that the beauty of form and pose hides
that which would mar or vulgarize the picture. The subject
is spiritualized, and becomes an inspiration for good and
lovely thoughts. It is very different with the 'living picture.'
There is no art in it. Paradoxical as it may seem, there is
no life in the living picture: it is even posed as a lifeless
mass. There is a marked difference between the canvas or

marble and the living picture, much to the disadvantage of the latter."

In discussing the above utterance, I do not want to take an unfair advantage of the fact that in writing about art I am a trained expert, and Mr Coote a novice. Mr Coote's object in undertaking a task so far beyond my powers as an explanation of the operation of the artist's soul is clearly to persuade us that he sees a distinction between an art that is false and an art that is true, and that it is his passionate devotion to the former that makes him so wroth with the latter. Let us see.

First, Mr Coote tells us that there is no art in the Palace pictures. Well, I can quite believe that Mr Coote conceives that the posing and lighting of the figures so as to throw the figure into the required light and shadow is pure accident. Let me therefore make a suggestion. Let Mr Morton, the manager of the Palace, request Mr Dando, the arranger of the pictures, to stand aside and entrust his functions for one night (on which a stall may be reserved for me at any price the management chooses to exact) to Mr William Alexander Coote. Let the entire resources of the establishment be placed absolutely under his direction; and let us then see whether he can take advantage of there being "no art in it" to produce a single tableau that will not be ludicrously and outrageously deficient in the artistic qualities without which Mr Dando's compositions would be hooted off the stage.

Now as to Mr Coote's assertion that the artist's soul spiritualizes his subject, and finds in it an inspiration for good and lovely thoughts. I can assure Mr Coote that he never made a greater mistake in his life. There are artists, and very able artists too, whose souls exactly resemble those of some members of the National Vigilance Association in debauching every subject, and finding in it an inspiration for obscene and unlovely thoughts. If Mr Coote, in the course of his next holiday, will travel from Padua to Mantua, and compare Giotto's pictorial decoration of the arena chapel with Giulio Romano's decoration of the Palazzo Té, he will learn that the artist's soul can commune with the satyrs as well as with the saints. He need go no further than our own National Gallery to see the work of great artists who, like Paul Veronese, or Rubens, materialize all their subjects and appeal to our love of physical splendor and vitality, exhibited under the same roof with those of the pre-Raphaelites (the real ones), whose works of art were also works of devotion. What is more, he will find the same artist expressing his devotional mood in one picture and his voluptuous mood in another; and if he will go as far as Venice—and the journey will be well worth his while—he can see there, in Titian's Virgin of the Assumption, a union of the flesh and the spirit so triumphantly beautiful, that he will return abashed to the Church and Stage Guild, and apologize to them very humbly for having mixed up his account of his Vigilance stewardship with a sham lecture on a subject of which he does not know enough to be even conscious of his own ignorance.

Let me now help Mr Coote out of his difficulty. He admits by implication that works of art are above the law, and should be tolerated at all hazards. He then attempts to shew that the works he objects to are not "true art," and that therefore his hostility to them does not imply any hostility to Phidias and Raphael and the Royal Academy and so on. No person who really understands Art would make any such admission. A work of art is no more above the law than anything else. An old bridge may be a beautiful work of mediaeval art; but if it obstructs navigation, causes the river to silt up, or becomes insufficient for the traffic, it must come down. A palace may be a gem of the builder's art; but if its site is imperatively required for a better lighted and drained modern building, however ugly, or for a new thoroughfare, down it must come too. And if the living pictures, or M. Jules Garnier's illustrations to Rabelais, can be proved to be doing more harm than good, then Mr Coote is quite right to demand their suppression, works of art or no works of art. Mr Coote is quite entitled to carry out all his aims, to forbid the circulation of cheap unexpurgated Shakespears; to make it a punishable offence for an artist to paint from a nude model; and to send the manager of the Palace Theatre to prison, if he can convince us that it is for the public interest that these things should be done. No plea as to the sacredness of art could in that case be admitted for a moment. If Mr Coote feels modest about claiming so much, let him consult the gentleman whom he describes as "that strange, peculiar, yet splendid man, Mr Stead." Mr Stead will, I think, as a matter of common sense, at once assure him that I am right.

Having now got rid of the Art question, and pulled Mr

Coote out of that morass on to solid ground, I am almost tempted to begin by exhorting him to go to his Bible, and ponder the saying, "He which is filthy, let him be filthy still." But no public man in these islands ever believes that the Bible means what it says: he is always convinced that it says what he means; and I have no reason to hope that Mr Coote may be an exception to the rule. What, then, does Mr Coote found himself on? Apparently on this position, which I state in his own words: "Nothing in the management of our public entertainments can justify the exhibition of nude and semi-nude women as a means of amusement for a mixed audience." But why not, if the audience thinks the woman prettier and no less decent in that state than when fully draped, and she agrees with them; or if nudity or semi-nudity is appropriate to the character she is impersonating; or if she is performing athletic feats which skirts would hinder? Here is an instance which fulfils all three conditions. When Sir Augustus Harris first introduced at Covent Garden the Walpurgis ballet, which is one of the features of Gounod's Faust as performed at the Paris Grand Opéra, the dancer who impersonated Phryne dispensed with skirts altogether, and danced to the one exquisite tune that the ballet contains, in a costume which produced the illusion of nudity (I presume Mr Coote knows that it is only an illusion). She wore certain decorative ribbons, but no dress. She looked very graceful and quite modest; nobody in that huge theatre, which was crowded from floor to ceiling, objected in the least; it did not occur to us for a moment to complain of the absence of the ballet skirts and petticoats which make a woman look like an ostrich or a teetotum.

I will not pretend to misunderstand Mr Coote's objection to this. There are in the world a certain number of persons who, owing to morbid irritability in certain directions, are greatly incommoded by circumstances which are indifferent, or even agreeable, to the normal man. For instance, London is rather an ill-smelling place; and people with exceptionally acute noses suffer agonies on stagnant days when ordinary people notice nothing. Carlyle, even in the comparative quietude of Chelsea, had to take special measures to keep the noises of the streets from his irritable ears; people with tender eyes have to resort to blue spectacles; humane people are made miserable by the treatment of our beasts of burden; and we find people oppressed by a special susceptibility to the dread inspired by hydrophobia, cholera, the Jesuits, the possibility of being damned, and many other contingencies which only occur to normal persons when they are out of health. On the other hand, we find people who are deficient in certain faculties—blind people, deaf people, color-blind people, people with no musical faculty, callous people, unsocial people, and so on. And we also find people in whom a deficiency in one respect is associated with an excess of sensitiveness in others. Now, it is quite impossible to legislate and administer with a view to the comfort of these abnormal people, even though there may, in so large a population as ours, be enough of any one variety of them to form an association and make a vigorous agitation. For instance, the Church will not modify the rite of communion because certain deplorable cases are on record in which the taste of the sacramental wine has brought on a ruinous attack of drink craze in the communicant. We do not suppress public meetings and abolish the right of free speech because people who are peculiarly susceptible to political excitement and the stimulus of platform oratory are led to behave foolishly and misuse their votes on such occasions. We do not prohibit "revivalist" prayer meetings because of the mischievously hysterical condition into which weak people are thrown by them, a condition which the ignorant preacher glories in producing. We shall not stop the performances of The Notorious Mrs Ebbsmith because it has produced a case of suicide. In short, we shall not lead the life of invalids for the sake of a handful of unfortunate people to whom such a life is the only safe one.

The application of all this to Mr Coote's position is obvious. We have among us a certain number of people who are morbidly sensitive to sexual impressions, and quite insensible to artistic ones. We have certain sects in which such a condition is artificially induced as a matter of religious duty. Children have their affections repressed, and their susceptibility to emotional excitement nursed on sin, wrath, terror, and vengeance, whilst they are forbidden to go to the theatre or to amuse themselves with stories or "profane" pictures. Naturally, when such people grow up, life becomes to them a prolonged temptation of St Anthony. You try to please them by a picture which appeals to their delight in graceful form and bright warm color, to their share in the romance which peoples the woods and streams

with sylphs and water maidens, to the innocent and highly
recreative love of personal beauty, which is one of the
great advantages of having a sex at all. To your horror and
discomposure, you are met by a shriek of "Nude woman:
nude woman: police!" The one thing that the normal spectator overlooks in the picture is the one thing that St
Anthony sees in it. Let me again put his protest in Mr
Coote's own words: "Nothing can justify the exhibition of
nude and semi-nude women as a means of amusement for
a mixed audience. They are shameful productions, and
deserve the condemnation of all right-thinking people. The
manager deserves, and should have, the immediate attention of the County Council." You remonstrate, perhaps,
from the point of view of the artist. Mr Coote at once
pleads: "They are so very obviously *living*. Human nature
is so very much in evidence." And there you have the whole
of Mr Coote's pessimistic, misanthropic philosophy in two
sentences. Human nature and the human body are to him
nasty things. Sex is a scourge. Woman is a walking temptation which should be covered up as much as possible. Well,
let us be charitable to Mr Coote's infirmity, and ask him,
as kindly as may be, what good covering women up will do.
Carmencita is covered up; our skirt dancers are all petticoats; each of our serpentine dancers carries drapery
enough to make skirts for a whole dozen schoolgirls. And
yet they appeal far more to the sex instinct and far less to
the artistic instinct than the Naiads and Phryne. There is
only one solution of the difficulty; and that is for Mr Coote
and those that sympathize with him to keep away from the
Palace Theatre. Of course that will not protect them altogether. Every low-necked dress, every gust of wind that
catches a skirt and reveals an ankle, perhaps every child in
whom "human nature is in evidence" to the extent of a pair
of sturdy little legs, may be a torment to the victims of this
most pitiable of all obsessions. A quarrel with human nature admits of no fundamental remedy except the knife;
and I should be sorry to see the members of the Vigilance
Association cutting their own throats; they are useful and
even necessary in keeping order among the people who
suffer from morbid attractions instead of morbid repulsions.
For it must not be forgotten that Mr Coote's error does not
lie in his claim that the community shall suppress indecent
exhibitions, but in his attempt to make nudity or semi-
nudity the criterion of indecency. Perhaps I should qualify

this statement of his position by limiting nudity to the
female sex; for I notice that the semi-nudity which is quite
a common spectacle in the case of male athletes is not
complained of, though, if there were anything in the Vigilance Association's view of such exhibitions as demoralizing, our women ought by this time to be much more demoralized than our men.

Two Bad Plays

THE GIRL I LEFT BEHIND ME. A Drama in four acts. By
Franklin Fyles and David Belasco. Adelphi Theatre, 13 April
1895.

DELIA HARDING. By Victorien Sardou. Adapted by J. Comyns
Carr. Comedy Theatre, 17 April 1895.

[20 *April* 1895]

Last Saturday was made memorable to me by my first
visit to the Adelphi Theatre. My frequent allusions to
Adelphi melodrama were all founded on a knowledge so
perfect that there was no need to verify it experimentally;
and now that the experiment has been imposed on me in
the course of my professional duty, it has confirmed my
deductions to the minutest particular.

Should anyone rush to the conclusion hereupon that my
attitude towards the Adelphi Theatre is that of a superior
person, he will be quite right. It is precisely because I am
able to visit all theatres as a superior person that I am
entrusted with my present critical function. As a superior
person, then, I hold Adelphi melodrama in high consideration. A really good Adelphi melodrama is of first-rate
literary importance, because it only needs elaboration to
become a masterpiece. Molière's Festin de Pierre and
Mozart's Don Juan are elaborations of Punch and Judy,
just as Hamlet, Faust, and Peer Gynt are elaborations of
popular stories. Unfortunately, a really good Adelphi melodrama is very hard to get. It should be a simple and sincere
drama of action and feeling, kept well within that vast tract
of passion and motive which is common to the philosopher
and the laborer, relieved by plenty of fun, and depending
for variety of human character, not on the high comedy
idiosyncrasies which individualize people in spite of the
closest similarity of age, sex, and circumstances, but on
broad contrasts between types of youth and age, sympathy

and selfishness, the masculine and the feminine, the serious
and the frivolous, the sublime and the ridiculous, and so
on. The whole character of the piece must be allegorical,
idealistic, full of generalizations and moral lessons; and it
must represent conduct as producing swiftly and certainly
on the individual the results which in actual life it only
produces on the race in the course of many centuries. All
of which, obviously, requires for its accomplishment rather
greater heads and surer hands than we commonly find in
the service of the playhouse.

The latest Adelphi melodrama, The Girl I Left Behind
Me, is a very bad one. The only stroke in it that comes
home is at the close of the second act, where the heroine
sends her soldier lover, who has been accused of cowardice,
off on a dangerous duty, and tells him that she loves him.
The authors, I need hardly say, did not invent this situation,
nor did they freshen it or add anything to it; but they at
least brought it off without bungling it, and so saved the
piece from the hostility of that sceptical spirit which is now
growing among first-night audiences in a very marked degree. This is an inevitable reaction against the artificialities,
insincerities, and impossibilities which form about three-
fourths of the stock-in-trade of those playwrights who seek
safety and success in the assumption that it is impossible
to underrate the taste and intelligence of the British public.
But there is a profound error in this policy. It is true that
the public consists largely of people who are incapable of
fully appreciating the best sort of artistic work. It is even
true that in every audience, especially on first nights, there
is an appreciable number of persons whose condition is
such that—to turn Tennyson's shallow claptrap into a terrible truth—they needs must hate the highest when they see
it. But why should we credit these unhappy persons with
that attribute of the highest character, the power of liking
what pleases them, of believing in it, of standing by those
who give it to them? For the most part they never enjoy
anything; they are always craving for stimulants, whereas
the essence of art is recreation; let their flatterer slip, as he
always does sooner or later, and they are at his throat
mercilessly before he can recover himself. But if you speak
in their hearing as the great men speak (which is easy
enough if you happen to be a great man), then you will find
that their speciality is self-torture, and that they are always
hankering, in spite of themselves, after their own boredom

and bewilderment, driven, probably, by some sort of uneasy hope that Ibsen or Wagner or some other gigantic bore may exorcise the devils which rend them. The fact is, there is nothing the public despises so much as an attempt to please it. Torment is its natural element: it is only the saint who has any capacity for happiness. There is no greater mistake in theology than to suppose that it is necessary to lock people into hell or out of heaven. You might as well suppose that it is necessary to lock a professional tramp into a public-house or out of a Monday popular concert, on the ground that the concert is the better and cheaper place of the two. The artist's rule must be Cromwell's: "Not what they want, but what is good for them." That rule, carried out in a kindly and sociable way, is the secret to success in the long run at the theatre as elsewhere.

My strong propensity for preaching is, I fear, leading me to deal with The Girl I Left Behind Me in rather too abstract a fashion. But it is only in its abstract bearings that the play provides interesting material to the critic. Instead of being natural and sincere, it is artificial and sanctimonious. The language, which should be vividly vernacular, is ineptly literary. Its fun runs too much on the underclothing of the ladies, which they tear up to make bandages for wounds, or offer, without detachment, to be used by gentlemen at a loss for towels after washing. The characters, instead of being consistent and typical, are patched and rickety, the author's grip constantly slipping from them. The villain and coward of the piece punches the hero's head with pluck and promptitude in the first act, lapses into abject poltroonery in the second, and in the third faces without concern a military emergency which drives all the rest into hysterical desperation. The hero, assaulted as aforesaid, ingloriously brings down the curtain with a stage villain's retort, "You shall rrepent—thiss—bblow," and subsequently becomes the sport of circumstances, which turn out happily for him without much aid from himself. As to Kennion, the sympathetic general, I cannot believe that even in the army so incapable a man could rise to high command. It is, of course, usual on the stage for all army commanders to be superseded at critical moments by their daughters; but still there is no good reason why they should not have moments of efficiency when nothing but routine business is in hand. Private Jones, who is cordially received by his officer when he describes, with an air of conscious

merit, how he has just run away on being actually fired at
by the enemy, and who calmly quits his post as sentry (at
a stockade which may be surprised at any moment) to sit
down beside his sleeping lady love, and is supported in that
proceeding by the general against a not unnatural remonstrance from his lieutenant—Private Jones is certainly consistent; but what he is consistent with is not himself—for
as an individual human being he has no credible existence
—but the trained incapacity of the Adelphi audience to
understand true military valor. Instead of being, as he
should be in a popular melodrama, a typically good soldier,
he is a mere folly of the ignorant civil imagination. There
is also a medical man, an army surgeon, who makes love to
a girl of sixteen by way of comic relief. He relaxed the
tension of the third act very happily by a slight but astonishingly effective alteration of a single syllable in the author's text. In the agony of the siege, when all hope was
gone, he sat down with heroic calmness to write two
documents: one a prescription which there was no apparent
means of getting compounded, and the other a farewell—
I did not quite catch to whom—probably to his mother.
The last touching words of this communication were pref-
aced by the author with the sentence, "I will add a post-
script." The doctor, however, adroitly substituted, "I will
add a postcard," and sent the audience, just at the moment
when their feelings could bear no further harrowing, into
shrieks of refreshing laughter.

The third act, by the way, is an adaptation of the Relief
of Lucknow, which, as a dramatic situation, is so strong
and familiar that it is hardly possible to spoil it, though the
authors have done their best. The main difficulty is the fore-
knowledge of the hopelessly sophisticated audience that Mr
Terriss will rush in at the last moment, sword in hand, and
rescue everybody. The authors' business was to carry us on
from incident to incident so convincingly and interestingly
as to preoccupy us with the illusion of the situation sufficiently to put Mr Terriss out of our heads. Messrs Fyles
and Belasco have not been equal to this. They have lamely
staved off Mr Terriss for the necessary time by a flabbily
commonplace treatment of the question of killing the
women to save them from the Indians, and by bringing in
the Indian chief's daughter to die in the stockade at the
instant when the sound of her voice would have won quarter for the garrison. This is ill contrived, and only passes

because the explanation is deferred until the last act, which is so transcendently imbecile that an absurdity more or less does not matter. As to the heroine, who had to kneel in the middle of the stage and rave her way through the burial service whilst her father, the general, hopped about, pulling horrible faces, and trying to make up his mind to shoot her, she was so completely out of the question from any rational human point of view, that I think the effort to impersonate her temporarily unhinged Miss Millward's reason; for when the rescue came, and she had to wave the American flag instead of expressing her feelings naturally, she all but impaled the general on it in a frightful manner. Miss Millward and Mr Terriss and the rest of the company must bear with my irreverent way of describing the performance. I quite appreciate their skill, which is perhaps more indispensable for nonsense of this kind than for plays good enough to be comparatively "actor-proof"; but the better the skill, the more annoying it is to see it nine-tenths wasted.

All the same, the evening was not a dull one. The play is not good drama, nor good melodrama; but it is tolerable pastime. I have spun out my criticism of it in order to leave as little room as possible for another play which was not tolerable even as pastime. When Mr Comyns Carr came before the curtain at the end of Sardou's Delia Harding at the Comedy Theatre on Wednesday, I found myself instinctively repeating the words of Sam Weller, "You rayther want somebody to look arter you, sir, ven your judgment goes out a wisitin'." Delia Harding is the worst play I ever saw. Taking it as a work bearing the same relation to the tastes of the upper middle class as the Adelphi drama to those of the lower middle class, I declare enthusiastically in favor of the Adelphi. Sardou's plan of playwriting is first to invent the action of his piece, and then to carefully keep it off the stage and have it announced merely by letters and telegrams. The people open the letters and read them, whether they are addressed to them or not; and then they talk either about what the letters announce as having occurred already or about what they intend to do tomorrow in consequence of receiving them. When the news is not brought by post, the characters are pressed into the service. Delia Harding, for instance, consists largely of the fashionable intelligence in Bellagio. As thus: "Stanley French arrived in Bellagio this morning," "Mr Harding will

arrive in Bellagio tomorrow afternoon," "Miss Harding
lives in that villa on the lake," "Sir Christopher Carstairs
will remain here for another month at least," "This is my
brother, Sir Arthur Studley," "Janet: we shall pack up and
leave tomorrow morning," etc. etc., the person addressed
invariably echoing with subdued horror, "This morning!"
"Tomorrow afternoon!" "In *that* villa!" and so on. The
whole business was so stale, so obviously factitious, so
barrenly inept, that at last the gallery broke out into open
derision, almost as if they were listening to a particularly
touching and delicate passage in a really good play. As for
me, I felt ashamed and remorseful. The time has now come
for pity rather than vengeance on the poor old "well made
play." Fifteen years ago I was almost alone in my contempt
for these clumsy booby traps. Nowadays an actor cannot
open a letter or toss off somebody else's glass of poison
without having to face a brutal outburst of jeering. At the
Comedy on Thursday, some low fellow shouted out "Rats!"
in the middle of the second act. Why was he not removed
by the police? Such a step would be highly popular in the
gallery: ninety-nine out of every hundred people in it are
incommoded by rowdyism, and are only too glad to be pro-
tected from neighbors who cannot express their disapproval
or approval decently. At political meetings the public is
not only allowed but expected to exercise a freedom of
comment and interruption which no sane person would
propose to tolerate in a theatre; but of late first nights have
been disturbed by interruptions which would expose the
interrupter to serious risk of a remarkably summary expul-
sion from a political meeting. Besides, public speakers are
helped by interruptions: they deliberately provoke them
for the sake of an effective retort. But the actor is helpless:
he must not say a word that is not set down for him; and
the nature of his work makes it terribly easy for any half
drunk fool to cruelly disconcert and annoy him. Even the
applause on first nights, the receptions and exit demonstrations, are silly enough: the rule ought to be silence whilst
the curtain is up and as much noise as you please when it
is down. But that is a matter of taste and custom rather
than of police. Where the police ought to come in without
mercy is in the case of offensive and disorderly remarks or
exclamations shouted at the stage during the performance.
One or two well chosen examples pursued to the police
court would settle the matter for the next ten years.

The acting of Delia Harding calls for no special notice. Mr Mackintosh, who appeared as Stanley French, was warmly received. His acting was not lacking in force; but his gesture and facial expression were grotesque and caricatured, though there was nothing in the part to give occasion for such extravagant handling.

Vanity Fair

VANITY FAIR. A Caricature. By G. W. Godfrey. Court Theatre, 27 April 1895. [*From* "At the Theatres."]

.   .   .   .   .

[4 *May* 1895]

On the whole, I am inclined to congratulate Mr Godfrey on Mrs John Wood, rather than Mrs John Wood on Mr Godfrey, in the matter of Vanity Fair. Mrs John Wood is herself a character; and by providing her with some new dialogue Mr Godfrey has given himself an air of creation; but I doubt if the other parts can be said to bear him out on this point. When I saw the piece, on the third night, Mr Arthur Cecil was still so unequal to the mere taskwork of remembering long strings of sentences which were about as characteristic and human as the instructions on the back of a telegram form, that he had to be spoon-fed by the prompter all the evening. Mr Anson as Bill Feltoe, the blackmailer, had a part which was certainly memorable in the sense that he could preserve the continuity of his ideas; but it did not go beyond that. The play, as a drama, is nothing. As an entertainment "written round" Mrs John Wood, it is a success. But it also pretends to be Vanity Fair, a picture of society. Mr Godfrey guards himself by calling it a caricature; but he none the less presents it as a morality, a satire, a sermon. And here he appeals to the love of the public for edification. Dickens's group of cronies at the Maypole inn, with their cry of "Go on improvin' of us, Johnny," exactly typifies the playgoing public in England. When an English playgoer is not by temperament, if not by actual practice, nine-tenths a chapel-goer, he is generally ten-tenths a blackguard; and so, if you cannot produce a genuine drama, and conquer him legitimately in that way, you must either be licentious at the cost of your respectability, or else moral and idealistic. Mr Godfrey, running short for the moment of character and drama, of course

chose the respectable alternative, and resorted to idealism.
He moralizes on fine lady spectators at murder trials, on
matrimonial scandals in high life, on Christianity conquer-
ing Africa with the Maxim gun, and on the prevarications
of the Treasury Bench. As further evidence of the corrup-
tion of society, he instances the interest taken by it in eminent explorers, in Buffalo Bill, and in foreign violinists, the
inference being, as I understand it, that to invite Mr Stanley
to dine, or Herr Joachim to play a partita by Bach, is a
proceeding as fraught with degenerate heartlessness as to
shew your "horror" of a crime by rushing down to the court
to gloat over the trial, or to give a gentleman who pays your
wife's bills the right to call you to account for being seen in
her company. Mr Godfrey's explanation of all this depravity is simple. It is the work of the New Woman and of the
Problem Play.

You are now in a position to appreciate the scene at the
beginning of the third act, where Mr Arthur Cecil, as the
gently cynical Thackerayan observer of Vanity Fair, receives, with the assistance of the prompter, the wondering
questions of Miss Nancy Noel as to whether the relations
between young men and young women ever really were as
they are represented in the novels of Sir Walter Scott. To
which I regret to say Mr Cecil does not hesitate to reply in
the affirmative, without mentioning that no change that has
taken place in this century has been more obviously a
change for the better than the change in the relations between men and women. "Goodnight, little girl," he adds
with unction, after a brief reference to his guide, philosopher, and friend in the prompter's box. "Trust to the teach-
ings of your own pure heart. God bless you!"

Mr Godfrey must excuse me; but that sort of social philosophy is not good enough for me. It does not matter,
perhaps, because I am far from attributing to the claptrap
play the devastating social influence he apparently attaches
to the problem play (which I am getting rather anxious to
see, by the way). But I must at least declare my belief that
Mr Godfrey will never succeed as a critic of society by
merely jumbling together all the splenetic commonplaces
that sound effective to him, and tacking on an Adelphi
moral. In order to make a stage drawing room a microcosm
of Vanity Fair, you may, I grant, mix your sets to any
extent you please; but you need not therefore produce an
impression that the sort of man who never reads a serious

book or ventures above burlesque and farcical comedy at the theatre, has been led into his habit of not paying his bills, and of winking at his wife's relations with useful acquaintances, by The Heavenly Twins and Ibsen's plays. I do not say that Mr Godfrey has produced such impressions intentionally: my quarrel with him is that he has begun to criticize life without first arranging his ideas. The result is, that it is impossible for the most credulous person to believe in Mrs Brabazon-Tegg's Grosvenor Square reception even to the extent of recognizing it as a caricature. It is not that the real thing is more respectable, or that the most extravagant bits (the scene with the sham millionaire, for instance) are the least lifelike: quite the contrary. But a drawing room is not like Margate sands for all that: however loose the selection of guests, there is enough logic in it to keep the music, bad though it may be, in one predominant key. It requires a very nice knowledge of what is reasonable to be safely outrageous in society of any grade; and this knowledge is as essential to the dramatist depicting society on the stage as to the diner-out who wishes to be allowed the privilege of unconventionality. In putting the drawing room on the stage, Mr Godfrey's master is obviously Mr Oscar Wilde. Now Mr Wilde has written scenes in which there is hardly a speech which could conceivably be uttered by one real person at a real at-home; but the deflection from common-sense is so subtle that it is evidently produced as a tuner tunes a piano: that is, he first tunes a fifth perfectly, and then flattens it a shade. If he could not tune the perfect fifth he could not produce the practicable one. This condition is imposed on the sociological humorist also. For instance, Don Quixote's irresistibly laughable address to the galley slaves, like the rest of his nonsense, is so close to the verge of good sense that thickwitted people, and even some clever ones, take the Don for a man of exceptionally sound understanding. None the less he is a hopeless lunatic, the sound understanding which he skirts so funnily being that of Cervantes. Mr Godfrey fails to produce the same effect because he tries to say the absurd thing without precisely knowing the sensible thing, with the result that, though he makes epigrams most industriously, he never tickles the audience except by strokes of pure fun, such as Mrs Brabazon-Tegg's "Dont disturb my maid: she's upstairs doing my hair." There are passages which are effective because they give voice to grievances or allude to abuses

upon which the audience feels, or feels obliged to pretend
to feel, highly indignant; but this is not art or drama: the
effect would be the same if the point were made on a political platform: indeed, it would be better there. For example,
in Mrs Brabazon-Tegg's dream of her trial for bigamy, she
is made to complain of the practice of eminent counsel
accepting retainers in more cases than they can possibly
attend to. The complaint would be more effective at an
ordinary public meeting, because the trial represented on
the stage is precisely the sort of one from which no counsel
would dream of absenting himself. Such effect, then, as
Mrs Brabazon-Tegg's speech from the dock actually does
produce is due, not to the author's knowledge of his subject, but to the extraordinary spontaneity and conviction
with which Mrs John Wood delivers herself.

There is one point on which I am unable to say whether
Mr Godfrey was satirical or sincere. When Mrs Brabazon-
Tegg's conscience is awakened, she does what most rich
people do under similar circumstances: that is to say, the
most mischievous thing possible. She begins to scatter
hundred pound cheques in conscience-money to various
charities. Whether Mr Godfrey approves of this proceeding I do not know; but he at any rate conquered my respect
by remorselessly making his woman of fashion presently
reduce all the cheques to five pounds and replunge into
fashionable life not a whit the better for her hard experience. This seems to indicate that Mr Godfrey has that
courage of his profession in which most of our dramatists
are shamelessly wanting. For its sake he may very well be
forgiven his random satire, and even—on condition that
he undertakes not to do it again—the insufferable conversations of Mr Arthur Cecil and Miss Granville.

Mr Irving Takes Paregoric

BYGONES. By A. W. Pinero. A STORY OF WATERLOO. By A.
Conan Doyle. A CHAPTER FROM DON QUIXOTE. By the late
W. G. Wills. Lyceum Theatre, 4 May 1895.

[11 *May* 1895]

It was Mr Grant Allen, I think, who familiarized us
with the fact that all attempts to sustain our conduct at a
higher level than is natural to us produce violent reactions.
Was there not a certain Africa divine, the Reverend Mr

Creedy, who tamed the barbarian within him and lived the
higher life of the Caledonian Road for a while, only to end
by "going Fantee" with a vengeance? This liability to reaction is a serious matter for the actor—not, perhaps, for the
actor of villains, who becomes by reaction the most amiable
of men in private life, but certainly for the actor of heroes,
who is occasionally to be found off the stage in a state of
very violent reaction indeed. But there are some actors—
not many, but some—who have solid private characters
which stand like rocks in the midst of the ebb and tide of
their stage emotions; and in their case the reaction must
take place in their art itself. Such men, when they have to
be unnaturally dignified on the stage, cannot relieve themselves by being ridiculous in private life, since the good
sense of their private characters makes that impossible to
them. When they can bear it no longer, they must make
themselves ridiculous on the stage or burst. No actor suffers
from the tyranny of this grotesque necessity more than Mr
Irving. His career, ever since he became a heroic actor, has
been studded by relapses into the most impish buffoonery.
I remember years ago going into the Lyceum Theatre under the impression that I was about to witness a performance of Richard III. After one act of that tragedy, however, Mr Irving relapsed into an impersonation of Alfred
Jingle. He concealed piles of sandwiches in his hat; so
that when he afterwards raised it to introduce himself as
"Alfred Jingle, Esq., of No Hall, Nowhere," a rain of ham
and bread descended on him. He knelt on the stage on one
knee and seated Miss Pauncefort (the spinster aunt) on
the other, and then upset himself and her, head over heels.
He beat a refractory horse with a bandbox; inked the
glimpses of shirt that appeared through the holes in his
coat; and insulted all the other characters by turning their
coats back with the idiotic remark, "From the country,
sir?" He was not acting: nothing less like the scenes
created by Dickens could possibly have been put on the
stage. He was simply taking his revenge on Shakespear and
himself for months of sustained dignity. Later on we had
the same phenomenon repeated in his Robert Macaire.
There was, and, I suppose, still is in the market a version
of that little melodrama by Mr Henley and the late Louis
Stevenson which was full of literary distinction; but Mr
Irving stuck to the old third-class version, which gave him
unlimited scope for absurdity. He made one or two mem-

orable effects in it: a more horribly evil-looking beast of
prey than his Macaire never crossed the stage; and I can
recall a point or two where the feeling produced was terrible. But what Mr Irving enjoyed, and obviously what
attracted him in the business, was rushing Mr Weedon
Grossmith upstairs by the back of the neck, breaking plates
on his stomach, standing on a barrel boyishly pretending
to play the fiddle, singing a chanson to an accompaniment
improvised by himself on an old harpsichord, and, above
all—for here his glee attained its climax—inadvertently
pulling a large assortment of stolen handkerchiefs out of his
pocket whilst explaining matters to the police officer, and
clinching his account by throwing one into his hat, which,
having no crown, allowed it to fall through to the floor.
This alternation of the grotesque, the impish, the farcical,
with the serious and exalted, is characteristic of the nineteenth century. Goethe anticipated it in his Faust and
Mephistopheles, obviously two sides of the same character; and it was in the foolish travesty of Faust perpetrated
by Wills that Mr Irving found a part in which he could
be melodramatic actor, mocker, and buffoon all in one
evening. Since then he has had a trying time of it. Becket
on top of Wolsey was enough to provoke a graver man to
go Fantee; and Lear followed Becket. But when King
Arthur capped Lear, all of us who knew Mr Irving's constitution felt that a terrific reaction must be imminent. It
has come in the shape of Don Quixote, in which he makes
his own dignity ridiculous to his heart's content. He rides
a slim white horse, made up as Rozinante with painted
hollows just as a face is made up; he has a set of imitation
geese waggling on springs to mistake for swans; he tumbles
about the stage with his legs in the air; and he has a single
combat, on refreshingly indecorous provocation, with a
pump. And he is perfectly happy. I am the last person in
the world to object; for I, too, have something of that
aboriginal need for an occasional carnival in me. When he
came before the curtain at the end, he informed us, with
transparent good faith, that the little play practically covered the whole of Cervantes' novel, a statement which we
listened to with respectful stupefaction. I get into trouble
often enough by my ignorance of authors whom every
literate person is expected to have at his fingers' ends; but
I believe Mr Irving can beat me holllow in that respect. If
I have not read Don Quixote all through, I have at least

looked at the pictures; and I am prepared to swear that Mr
Irving never got beyond the second chapter.

Anyone who consults recent visitors to the Lyceum, or
who seeks for information in the Press as to the merits of
Mr Conan Doyle's Story of Waterloo, will in nineteen
cases out of twenty learn that the piece is a trifle raised
into importance by the marvellous acting of Mr Irving as
Corporal Gregory Brewster. As a matter of fact, the entire effect is contrived by the author, and is due to him
alone. There is absolutely no acting in it—none whatever.
There is a make-up in it, and a little cheap and simple
mimicry which Mr Irving does indifferently because he is
neither apt nor observant as a mimic of doddering old
men, and because his finely cultivated voice and diction
again and again rebel against the indignity of the Corporal's
squeakings and mumblings and vulgarities of pronunciation. But all the rest is an illusion produced by the machinery of "a good acting play," by which is always meant
a play that requires from the performers no qualifications
beyond a plausible appearance and a little experience and
address in stage business. I had better make this clear by
explaining the process of doing without acting as exemplified by A Story of Waterloo, in which Mr Conan Doyle has
carried the art of constructing an "acting" play to such an
extreme that I almost suspect him of satirically revenging
himself, as a literary man, on a profession which has such
a dread of "literary plays." (A "literary play," I should
explain, is a play that the actors have to act, in opposition
to the "acting play," which acts them.)

Before the curtain rises, you read the playbill; and the
process commences at once with the suggestive effect on
your imagination of "Corporal Gregory Brewster, age
eighty-six, a Waterloo veteran," of "Nora Brewster, the
corporal's grandniece," and of "Scene—Brewster's lodgings." By the time you have read that, your own imagination, with the author pulling the strings, has done half
the work you afterwards give Mr Irving credit for. Up goes
the curtain; and the lodgings are before you, with the
humble breakfast table, the cheery fire, the old man's spectacles and Bible, and a medal hung up in a frame over the
chimney-piece. Lest you should be unobservant enough to
miss the significance of all this, Miss Annie Hughes comes
in with a basket of butter and bacon, ostensibly to impersonate the grandniece, really to carefully point out all these

things to you, and to lead up to the entry of the hero by
preparing breakfast for him. When the background is sufficiently laid in by this artifice, the drawing of the figure
commences. Mr Fuller Mellish enters in the uniform of a
modern artillery sergeant, with a breech-loading carbine.
You are touched: here is the young soldier come to see the
old—two figures from the Seven Ages of Man. Miss Hughes
tells Mr Mellish all about Corporal Gregory. She takes
down the medal, and makes him read aloud to her the
press-cutting pasted beside it which describes the feat for
which the medal was given. In short, the pair work at the
picture of the old warrior until the very dullest dog in the
audience knows what he is to see, or to imagine he sees,
when the great moment comes. Thus is Brewster already
created, though Mr Irving has not yet left his dressing
room. At last, everything being ready, Mr Fuller Mellish
is packed off so as not to divide the interest. A squeak is
heard behind the scenes: it is the childish treble that once
rang like a trumpet on the powder-waggon at Waterloo.
Enter Mr Irving, in a dirty white wig, toothless, blear-eyed,
palsied, shaky at the knees, stooping at the shoulders, in-
credibly aged and very poor, but respectable. He makes his
way to his chair, and can only sit down, so stiff are his aged
limbs, very slowly and creakily. This sitting down business
is not acting: the callboy could do it; but we are so thoroughly primed by the playbill, the scene-painter, the stage-
manager, Miss Hughes and Mr Mellish, that we go off in
enthusiastic whispers, "What superb acting! How wonderfully he does it!" The corporal cannot recognize his grandniece at first. When he does, he asks her questions about
children—children who have long gone to their graves at
ripe ages. She prepares his tea: he sups it noisily and
ineptly, like an infant. More whispers: "How masterly a
touch of second childhood!" He gets a bronchial attack
and gasps for paregoric, which Miss Hughes administers
with a spoon, whilst our faces glisten with tearful smiles.
"Is there another living actor who could take paregoric
like that?" The sun shines through the window: the old
man would fain sit there and peacefully enjoy the fragrant
air and life-giving warmth of the world's summer, contrast-
ing so pathetically with his own winter. He rises, more
creakily than before, but with his faithful grandniece's
arm fondly supporting him. He dodders across the stage,
expressing a hope that the flies will not be too "owdacious,"

and sits down on another chair with his joints crying more
loudly than ever for some of the oil of youth. We feel that
we could watch him sitting down for ever. Hark! a band
in the street without. Soldiers pass: the old war-horse snorts
feebly, but complains that bands dont play so loud as they
used to. The band being duly exploited for all it is worth,
the Bible comes into play. What he likes in it are the cam-
paigns of Joshua and the battle of Armageddon, which the
poor dear old thing can hardly pronounce, though he had
it from "our clergyman." How sweet of the clergyman to
humor him! Blessings on his kindly face and on his silver
hair! Mr Fuller Mellish comes back with the breechloading
carbine. The old man handles it; calls it a firelock; and
goes crazily through his manual with it. Finally, he unlocks
the breech, and as the barrel drops, believes that he has
broken the weapon in two. Matters being explained, he expresses his unalterable conviction that England will have
to fall back on Brown Bess when the moment for action
arrives again. He takes out his pipe. It falls and is broken.
He whimpers, and is petted and consoled by a present of
the sergeant's beautiful pipe with "a hamber mouthpiece."
Mr Fuller Mellish, becoming again superfluous, is again
got rid of. Enter a haughty gentleman. It is the Colonel of
the Royal Scots Guards, the corporal's old regiment. According to the well-known custom of colonels, he has called
on the old pensioner to give him a five-pound note. The
old man, as if electrically shocked, staggers up and desperately tries to stand for a moment at "attention" and
salute his officer. He collapses, almost slain by the effort,
into his chair, mumbling pathetically that he "were a'most
gone that time, Colonel." "A masterstroke! who but a
great actor could have executed this heart-searching movement?" The veteran returns to the fireside: once more he
depicts with convincing art the state of an old man's joints.
The Colonel goes; Mr Fuller Mellish comes; the old man
dozes. Suddenly he springs up. "The Guards want powder;
and, by God, the Guards shall have it." With these words
he falls back in his chair. Mr Fuller Mellish, lest there
should be any mistake about it (it is never safe to trust the
intelligence of the British public), delicately informs Miss
Hughes that her granduncle is dead. The curtain falls amid
thunders of applause.

Every old actor into whose hands this article falls will
understand perfectly from my description how the whole

thing is done, and will wish that he could get such Press
notices for a little hobbling and piping, and a few bits of
mechanical business with a pipe, a carbine, and two chairs.
The whole performance does not involve one gesture, one
line, one thought outside the commonest routine of automatic stage illusion. What, I wonder, must Mr Irving, who
of course knows this better than anyone else, feel when he
finds this pitiful little handful of hackneyed stage tricks
received exactly as if it were a crowning instance of his
most difficult and finest art? No doubt he expected and
intended that the public, on being touched and pleased
by machinery, should imagine that they were being touched
and pleased by acting. But the critics! What can he think
of the analytic powers of those of us who, when an organized and successful attack is made on our emotions, are
unable to discriminate between the execution done by the
actor's art and that done by Mr Conan Doyle's ingenious
exploitation of the ready-made pathos of old age, the
ignorant and maudlin sentiment attaching to the army and
"the Dook," and the vulgar conception of the battle of
Waterloo as a stand-up street fight between an Englishman
and a Frenchman, a conception infinitely less respectable
than that which led Byron to exclaim, when he heard of
Napoleon's defeat, "I'm damned sorry"?

The first item in the Lyceum triple bill is Mr Pinero's
Bygones, in which Mr Sydney Valentine, as Professor
Mazzoni, acts with notable skill and judgment. Mr Pinero
used to play the part himself; but he was bitten then, like
everyone else at that time, with the notion that "character
acting," especially in parts that admitted of a foreign accent, was the perfection of stage art; and his Mazzoni was
accordingly worse than anyone could believe without having seen it. Matters were made worse by the detestable
and irredeemable scene in which the old man proposes
marriage to the girl. Mazzoni might excusably offer her, as
a means of escape from her humiliating predicament, the
position of his wife, and his friendly affection and fatherly
care until he left her a widow; and he might make this
offer being secretly in love with her, and so preserve the
pathos of his subsequent disappointment. But to propose a
serious love match to her as he does seems to me abominable: the scene makes my flesh creep: it always did. Mr
Valentine could not reconcile me to it; nor should I have
thanked him if he had; but he softened it as far as it could

be softened; and his final leavetaking, with its effect of
sparing us the exhibition of a grief which he nevertheless
made us feel keenly behind that last sincere and kindly
smile, was a fine stroke of art. He here, as elsewhere in the
play, shewed himself able to do with a few light and sure
touches what most of our actors vainly struggle with by
publicly wallowing in self-pity for minutes at a stretch.

I hope I have not conveyed an impression that the triple
bill makes a bad evening's entertainment. Though it is my
steady purpose to do what I can to drive such sketches as
A Story of Waterloo, with their ready-made feeling and
prearranged effects, away to the music-hall, which is their
proper place now that we no longer have a "Gallery of
Illustration," I enjoy them, and am entirely in favor of
their multiplication so long as it is understood that they are
not the business of fine actors and first-class theatres. And,
abortive as Don Quixote is, there are moments in it when
Wills vanishes, and we have Cervantes as the author and
Mr Irving as the actor—no cheap combination. Apart from
the merits of the three plays, I suggest that it is a mistake
—easily avoidable by a manager with Mr Irving's resources
at his disposal—to cast Miss Annie Hughes and Mr
Webster for parts in two different pieces. I half expected
to see Miss Hughes again in the third play; but Mr Irving
drew the line there, and entrusted the leading young lady's
part in Don Quixote to Miss de Silva. In Bygones, Miss
Ailsa Craig succeeds in giving a touch of interest to the
part of the ill-conditioned servant who works the plot.
Miss Hughes grows younger and prettier, and acts better,
continually; only her voice still slyly contradicts her efforts
to be pathetic, which are in all other respects credible and
graceful enough.

A New Lady Macbeth and
a New Mrs Ebbsmith

[25 *May* 1895]

Last Saturday evening found me lurking, an uninvited
guest, in an obscure corner of the Garrick Theatre, giving
Mrs Ebbsmith another trial in the person of Miss Olga
Nethersole. This time I carefully regulated the dose, coming late for the preliminary explanations, and hurrying
home at the end of the second act, when Mrs Ehbsmith had

put her fine dress on, and was beginning to work up towards the stove. I cannot say I enjoyed myself very much; for the play bored me more than ever; but I perceived better than I did before that the fault was not altogether Mr Pinero's. The interest of the first act depends on Mrs Thorpe really affecting and interesting her audience in her scene with Agnes. Miss Ellice Jeffries fails to do this. I do not blame her, just as I should not blame Mr Charles Hawtrey if he were cast for the ghost in Hamlet and played it somewhat disappointingly. On the contrary, I congratulate her on her hopeless incapacity to persuade us that she is the victim of an unhappy marriage, or that she lives in a dreary country rectory where she walks like a ghost about her dead child's room in the intervals of housekeeping for her parson brother. She has obviously not a scrap of anything of the kind in her whole disposition; and that Mr Pinero should have cast her for such business in a part on which his whole first act and a good deal of the rest of the play depends, suggests that his experience of the impossibility of getting all his characters fitted in a metropolis which has more theatres than companies is making him reckless. The impression left is that the scene between Agnes and Mrs Thorpe is tedious and colorless, and that between Agnes and the Duke biting and full of character. But really one scene is as good as the other; only Mr Hare's Duke of St Olpherts is a consummate piece of acting, whilst Miss Jeffries' Mrs Thorpe is at best a graceful evasion of an impossible task. This was less noticeable before, because Mrs Patrick Campbell counted for so much in both scenes that the second factor in them mattered less. With Miss Nethersole, who failed to touch the character of Agnes at any point as far as I witnessed her performance, it mattered a great deal. I have no doubt that Miss Nethersole pulled the bible out of the stove, and played all the "emotional" scenes as well as Mrs Campbell or any one else could play them; but certainly in the first two acts, where Mrs Ebbsmith, not yet reduced to a mere phase of hysteria, is a self-possessed individual character, Miss Nethersole gave us nothing but the stage fashion of the day in a very accentuated and conscious manner. Mrs Campbell's extraordinary power of doing anything surely and swiftly with her hands whilst she is acting, preoccupation seeming an embarrassment unknown to her, is a personal peculiarity which cannot reasonably be demanded from her competi-

tors. But Miss Nethersole seems to set a positive value on
such preoccupation. When she pretends to darn a stocking
she brings it down to the footlights, and poses in profile
with the stockinged hand raised above the level of her head.
She touches nothing without first poising her hand above
it like a bird about to alight, or a pianist's fingers descending on a chord. She cannot even take up the box containing
the rich dress to bundle it off into the next room, without
disposing her hands round it with an unmistakeable reference to the conventional laws of grace. The effect in these
first two acts, throughout which Mrs Ebbsmith is supposed
to be setting Lucas Cleeve's teeth on edge at every turn by
her businesslike ways, plain dress, and impatience of the
effects that charm the voluptuary, may be imagined. The
change of dress, with which Mrs Campbell achieved such
a very startling effect, produced hardly any with Miss
Nethersole, and would have produced none but for the
dialogue; for Mrs Ebbsmith had been so obviously concerned all through with the effect of her attitudes, that one
quite expected that she would not neglect herself when it
came to dressing for dinner. The "Trafalgar Squaring" of
the Duke, a complete success on Mr Hare's part, was a
complete failure on Miss Nethersole's. Mrs Campbell
caught the right platform tone of political invective and
contemptuous social criticism to perfection: Miss Nethersole made the speech an emotional outburst, flying out at
the Duke exactly as, in a melodrama, she would have
flown out at the villain who had betrayed her. My inference
is that Miss Nethersole has force and emotion without
sense of character. With force and emotion, and an interesting and plastic person, one can play "the heroine" under
a hundred different names with entire success. But the
individualized heroine is another matter; and that is where
Mrs Patrick Campbell comes in.

It is usual to describe Mr Hare as an actor who does not
do himself justice on first nights because he is nervous. His
Duke of St Olpherts is certainly not an instance of this. It
is still capital; but compared to his superb performance on
the first night, it is minced in diction and almost off-hand
in deportment. I have come to the conclusion that Mr
Forbes-Robertson is only less out of place as Lucas Cleeve
than Miss Jeffries as Mrs Thorpe. In contrast to the cool
intensity of Mrs Campbell, his strong, resolute manner,
slackened as much as he could slacken it, barely passed

muster on the first night as the manner of the weak neurotic
creature described by the Duke. But with Miss Nethersole,
whose Mrs Ebbsmith is really not Mrs Ebbsmith at all, but
a female Lucas Cleeve, even that faint scrap of illusion
vanishes, and is replaced by a contrast of personal style in
flat contradiction to the character relationship which is the
subject of the drama. I still do not think The Notorious
Mrs Ebbsmith could be made a good play by anything short
of treating Agnes's sudden resolution to make Lucas fall in
love with her as a comedy motive (as it essentially is), and
getting rid of the claptrap about the bible, finishing the
play with Lucas's discovery that his wife is quite as good
a woman as he could stand life with, and possibly—though
on this I do not insist—with Agnes's return to the political
platform as the Radical Duchess of St Olpherts. But I am
at least quite convinced now that the play as it stands
would be much more interesting if the other characters
were only half as appropriately impersonated as the Duke
of St Olpherts is by Mr Hare, or as Mrs Ebbsmith was by
Mrs Campbell.

By the way, I have received a sixpenny pamphlet, by Mr
H. Schütz Wilson, entitled The Notorious Mrs Ebbsmith,
published by Messrs Bickers. My opinion being thus challenged, I cheerfully acknowledge the pre-eminence of the
pamphlet, from my point of view, as the worst pamphlet I
ever read on any subject whatsoever. That, however, is
only a way of saying that I cannot agree with Mr Schütz
Wilson. The difference may be my fault as well as my misfortune. He accepts the play as a great "spiritual tragedy,"
and considers that the casting of it at the Garrick Theatre
was perfect in every part. And so, as he says, "Farewell,
Agnes! and may all good go with you in the future. After
all, you did not burn THE BOOK."

Readers who have noticed the heading of this article may
possibly want to know what Lady Macbeth has to do with
it. Well, I have discovered a new Lady Macbeth. It is one
of my eccentricities to be old-fashioned in my artistic tastes.
For instance, I am fond—unaffectedly fond—of Shakespear's plays. I do not mean actor-managers' editions and
revivals; I mean the plays as Shakespear wrote them, played
straight through line by line and scene by scene as nearly
as possible under the conditions of representation for
which they were designed. I have seen the suburban amateurs of the Shakespear Reading Society, seated like Christy

minstrels on the platform of the lecture hall at the London
Institution, produce, at a moderate computation, about
sixty-six times as much effect by reading straight through
Much Ado About Nothing as Mr Irving with his expensively mounted and superlatively dull Lyceum version.
When these same amateurs invited me to a regular stage
performance of Macbeth in aid of the Siddons Memorial
Fund, I went, not for the sake of Sarah the Respectable,
whose great memory can take care of itself (how much
fresher it is, by the way, than those of many writers and
painters of her day, though no actor ever makes a speech
without complaining that he is cheated out of the immortal-
ity every other sort of artist enjoys!), but simply because
I wanted to see Macbeth. Mind, I am no admirer of the
Elizabethan school. When Mr Henry Arthur Jones, whose
collected essays on the English drama I am now engaged
in reading, says: "Surely the crowning glory of our nation
is our Shakespear; and remember he was one of a great
school," I almost burst with the intensity of my repudiation
of the second clause in that utterance. What Shakespear
got from his "school" was the insane and hideous rhetoric
which is all that he has in common with Jonson, Webster,
and the whole crew of insufferable bunglers and dullards
whose work stands out as vile even at the beginning of
the seventeenth century, when every art was corrupted
to the marrow by the orgie called the Renaissance, which
was nothing but the vulgar exploitation in the artistic professions of the territory won by the Protestant movement.
The leaders of that great self-assertion of the growing spirit
of man were dead long before the Elizabethan literary
rabble became conscious that "ideas" were in fashion, and
that any author who could gather a cheap stock of them
from murder, lust, and obscenity, and formulate them in
rhetorical blank verse, might make the stage pestiferous
with plays that have no ray of noble feeling, no touch of
faith, beauty, or even common kindness in them from beginning to end. I really cannot keep my temper over the
Elizabethan dramatists and the Renaissance; nor would I
if I could. The generation which admired them equally
admired the pictures of Guido, Giulio Romano, Domenichino, and the Carracci; and I trust it is not nowadays
necessary to offer any further samples of its folly. A masterpiece by Carracci—say the smirking Susanna in the National Gallery—would not fetch seven pounds ten at

Christie's today; but our literary men, always fifty years behind their time because they never look at anything nor listen to anything, but go on working up what they learnt in their boyhood when they read books instead of writing them, still serve up Charles Lamb's hobby, and please themselves by observing that Cyril Tourneur could turn out pretty pairs of lines and string them monotonously together, or that Greene had a genuine groatsworth of popular wit, or that Marlowe, who was perhaps good enough to make it possible to believe that if he had been born thirty years ago he might now have been a tolerable imitator of Mr Rudyard Kipling, dealt in a single special quality of "mighty line." On the strength of these discoveries, they keep up the tradition that these men were slightly inferior Shakespears. Beaumont and Fletcher are, indeed, sometimes cited as hardly inferior; but I will not go into that. I could not do justice to it in moderate language.

As to this performance of Macbeth at St George's Hall, of course it was, from the ordinary professional standpoint, a very bad one. I say this because I well know what happens to a critic when he incautiously praises an amateur. He gets by the next post a letter in the following terms: "Dear Sir,—I am perhaps transgressing the bounds of etiquette in writing privately to you; but I thought you might like to know that your kind notice of my performance as Guildenstern has encouraged me to take a step which I have long been meditating. I have resigned my position as Governor of the Bank of England with a view to adopting the stage as a profession, and trust that the result may justify your too favorable opinion of my humble powers." Therefore I desire it to be distinctly understood that I do not recommend any members of the Macbeth cast to go on the stage. The three witches, Miss Florence Bourne, Miss Longvil, and Miss Munro, were as good as any three witches I ever saw; but the impersonation of witches, as a profession, is almost as precarious as the provision of smoked glasses for looking at eclipses through. Macduff was bad: I am not sure that with his natural advantages he could very easily have been worse; but still, if he feels himself driven to some artistic career by a radical aversion to earning an honest livelihood, and is prepared for a hard apprenticeship of twenty years in mastering the art of the stage—for that period still holds as good as when Talma prescribed it—he can become an actor if he likes. As to Lady Macbeth, she, too, was bad; but it is clear to me that unless she at once resolutely marries some rich gentleman who disapproves of the theatre on principle, she will not be able to keep herself off the stage. She is as handsome as Miss Neilson; and she can hold an audience whilst she is doing everything wrongly. The murder scene was not very good, because Macbeth belonged to the school of the Irish fiddler who, when Ole Bull asked him whether he played by ear or from notes, replied that he played "by main strength"; and you cannot get the brooding horror of the dagger scene by that method. Besides, Miss Lillah McCarthy—that is the lady's name as given in my program—is happily too young to conceive ambition and murder, or the temptation of a husband with a sickly conscience, as realities: they are to her delicious excitements of the imagination, with a beautiful, splendid terror about them, to be conveyed by strenuous pose, and flashing eye, and indomitable bearing. She went at them bravely in this spirit; and they came off more or less happily as her instinct and courage helped her, or her skill failed her. The banquet scene and the sleep-walking scene, which are the easiest passages in the part technically to a lady with the requisite pluck and personal fascination, were quite successful; and if the earlier scenes were immature, unskilful, and entirely artificial and rhetorical in their conception, still, they were very nearly thrilling. In short, I should like to see Miss Lillah McCarthy play again. I venture on the responsibility of saying that her Lady Macbeth was a highly promising performance, and that some years of hard work would make her a valuable recruit to the London stage. And with that very rash remark I will leave Macbeth, with a fervent wish that Mr Pinero, Mr Grundy, and Monsieur Sardou could be persuaded to learn from it how to write a play without wasting the first hour of the performance in tediously explaining its "construction." They really are mistaken in supposing that Scribe was cleverer than Shakespear.

Sardoodledom

FEDORA (Herman Merivale's English version). By Victorien Sardou. Haymarket Theatre, 25 May 1895.

GISMONDA. By Victorien Sardou. Daly's Theatre, 27 May 1895.

. . . . .

[1 *June* 1895]

Up to this day week I had preserved my innocence as a playgoer sufficiently never to have seen Fedora. Of course I was not altogether new to it, since I had seen Diplomacy Dora, and Theodora, and La Toscadora, and other machine dolls from the same firm. And yet the thing took me aback. To see that curtain go up again and again only to disclose a bewildering profusion of everything that has no business in a play, was an experience for which nothing could quite prepare me. The postal arrangements, the telegraphic arrangements, the police arrangements, the names and addresses, the hours and seasons, the tables of consanguinity, the railway and shipping time-tables, the arrivals and departures, the whole welter of Bradshaw and Baedeker, Court Guide and Post Office Directory, whirling round one incredible little stage murder and finally vanishing in a gulp of impossible stage poison, made up an entertainment too Bedlamite for any man with settled wits to preconceive. Even the murder was arranged, in pure wantonness, flatly contrary to common sense. The hero is suspected by the heroine of having been a Nihilist at a period when matters were so bad in Russia that refugees who made no secret of their sympathy with the Terrorists were sympathetically welcomed by the strictest Constitutionalists in every other country in Europe. He completely regains her sympathy by proving to her that he is no Nihilist at all, but a common assassin who has deliberately murdered a man out of jealousy. Surely, if dramatists are bent on the fundamentally impossible task of inventing pardonable assassinations, they should recognize that the man who, for no reward or satisfaction to his direct personal instincts, but at the risk of his own life, kills for the sake of an idea, believing that he is striking in the cause of the general weal, is at any rate more respectable than the dehumanized creature who stabs or shoots to slake a passion which he has in common with

a stag. I strongly object to heroic criminals, whether political or personal; but if the stage cannot yet get on without its illustrated police news, let us at least shun the most
repulsive motives for the stage crimes we are expected to
condone. This Loris Ipanoff is a vulgar scoundrel as far
as he is credibly human at all; and Fedora, who has at first
the excuse of being the avenger of blood, sinks to his level
when, on learning that her husband preferred another
woman to her, she gloats over his murder, and is disappointed because Loris did not kill his wife on the spot too.
Why need plays be so brutally, callously, barbarously im-
moral as this? I wish Sir Henry Irving would give us at least
a matinée of The Lady from the Sea to shew the playgoing
public how a humane gentleman acts when he finds he has
had the misfortune to lose the affection of his wife. Miss
Terry as Ellida would be quite as worthy of the Lyceum
Theatre as Nance Oldfield as Miss Terry.

It is greatly to Mrs Patrick Campbell's credit that, bad
as the play was, her acting was worse. It was a masterpiece
of failure. Not, pray observe, that Mrs Campbell herself
did not succeed. The moment she was seen, our reason
collapsed and our judgment fled. Every time the curtain
fell there was a delirious roar. If the play was not tragic,
our infatuation was. I solemnly warn all and sundry that no
common man's opinion of the artistic merits of that performance was worth a farthing after the first flash of the
heroine's eyes. It was not Fedora; but it was Circe; and I,
as sworn critic, must make the best attempt I can to be
Ulysses.

It cannot, I think, be disputed now that Mrs Campbell's
force, which is intense enough, has only one mode, and
that one the vituperative. This was proved at one stroke
in the first act, when Fedora goes to her husband's bedside
and discovers him dead. Mrs Campbell uttered a shriek,
as any actress would; but it was a shriek that suggested
nothing of grief, or mortally wounded tenderness, or even
horror. What it did suggest very strongly was that Fedora
had surprised the secret which Loris reveals to her in the
third act. In short, it was a scream of rage. Again in the
second act, when Loris admitted the killing of Vladimir,
her cry of "Murderer, assassin," might have been any
abusive term hurled at a man, appropriately or not, under
an impulse of violent anger. Last week I politely attributed
to Mrs Campbell's sense of character her catching, as Mrs

Ebbsmith, what Miss Nethersole misses: namely, the tone
of invective in "Trafalgar Squaring" the Duke of St Olpherts. But it now appears that, her emotion declines to
take any other form than that of invective. When she is
not abusing somebody, she sits visibly concentrating her
forces to restrain the vituperative pressure which is struggling to expand in reckless aggression, the general effect
being that of a magnificent woman with a magnificent temper, which she holds in or lets loose with exciting uncer-
tainty. This of course means that Mrs Campbell is not yet
mistress of her art, though she has a rare equipment for
it. Even her diction is technically defective. In order to
secure refinement of tone, she articulates with the tip of her
tongue against her front teeth as much as possible. This
enters for what it is worth and no more into the method
of every fine speaker; but it should not suggest the snobbish
Irishman who uses it as a cheap recipe for speaking genteel
English; and once or twice Mrs Campbell came dangerously
near to producing this mincing effect. For instance, "One
absorbing thought which meeks a sleeve of me," is clearly
not the excess of a genuine refinement of diction, like Sir
Henry Irving's pure vowel method, which would lead him
to say "One ap-sorbing thot which mĕks a slèv of me" (the
p in absorbing being a German b, and the italic letters
pronounced as in the French *fidèle*). I am only moderately
pedantic in this matter, and do not object at all to Mrs
Campbell's saying "Forgimme" for "Forgive me," or the
traditional and ugly "Be't so" for the correct and pretty
"Be it so"; but I protest against "hatrid" and "disseived,"
which are pure inaccuracies produced by that Irish recipe.
I make no apology for going into these details; for stage
usage is one of our few standards of diction; and it is rather
alarming to hear the extent to which our younger actresses
are left to pick up the stage trick of speech without in the
least understanding the phonetic part of it.

The death scene begins like a feeble drawing room pla-
giarism of the murder of Nancy by Bill Sykes, and ends
with the Gilbertian absurdity of the woman, as she realizes
with disgust that her husband actually proposes to commit
the vulgarity of strangling her, rising with a dignity which
paralyzes him, and saying, "Oh, if you are determined to
behave in that way, I will poison myself like a lady; and
you, I hope, will look on quietly like a gentleman," or
words to that effect. Here Mrs Campbell did for a moment

produce the effect which Sardou has so tediously and laboriously lath-and-plastered up, and produce it in a way which shewed unmistakeably that she is quite capable of the modern equivalents of the whole Bernhardtian range of sensational effects—effects so enormously popular and lucrative that, though their production is hardly more of a fine art than lion-taming, few women who are able for them can resist the temptation to devote their lives to them. At every other point, Mrs Campbell threw Sardou out of the window and substituted her own personal magnetism for the stale mechanical tragedy of Fedora. It was irrelevant; but it was effective.

Sardou's latest edition of the Kiralfian entertainment which Madame Bernhardt has for years past dragged from sea to sea in her Armada of transports, is called Gismonda, and is surpassingly dreary, although it is happily relieved four times by very long waits between the acts. The scene being laid in the Middle Ages, there are no newspapers, letters, or telegrams; but this is far from being an advantage, as the characters tell each other the news all through except when a child is dropped into a tiger's cage as a cue for Madame Bernhardt's popular scream; or when the inevitable stale, puerile love scene is turned on to shew off that "voix céleste" stop which Madame Bernhardt, like a sentimental New England villager with an American organ, keeps always pulled out; or when, in a paroxysm of the basest sensationalism, we are treated to the spectacle of Gismonda chopping a man to death with a hatchet as a preliminary to appearing as a mediæval saint with a palm in her hand at the head of a religious procession. What does it matter whether such an entertainment is called Gismonda, or Theodora, or Venice, or Constantinople, or The Orient, or Captain Boyton's water show? Personally, I prefer the water show, because the sixty-foot header interested me, which Madame Bernhardt has long ceased to do; and the sensation of shooting the chute thrilled me, which Gismonda does not. As a pageant the affair may pass very well with people who, never having been touched by the peculiar spiritual beauty of the art of the Middle Ages, compare the scene-painter's titivated imitations with the Lord Mayor's Show and the architecture of Regent Street instead of with the originals; but it is no more to be compared to the pageantry of King Arthur at the Lyceum than the clever but throughly shoppy stage business of Madame

Bernhardt is to be compared to the acting of Miss Ellen
Terry. I confess I regard with a certain jealousy the extent
to which this ex-artist, having deliberately exercised her
unquestioned right to step down from the national theatre
in which she became famous to posture in a travelling
show, is still permitted the privileges and courtesies proper
to her former rank. It is open to all actresses to say either,
"Give me a dignified living wage and let me work at my
art," or, "Give me as much money and applause as can
possibly be got out of me, and let my art go hang." Only,
when the choice is made, it is the business of the critic to
see that the chooser of the lower level does not take prece-
dence of the devoted artist who takes the higher one.
Madame Bernhardt has elected to go round the world
pretending to kill people with hatchets and hairpins, and
making, I presume, heaps of money. I wish her every success; but I shall certainly not treat her as a dramatic artist
of the first rank unless she pays me well for it. As a self-
respecting critic I decline to be bought for nothing.

It seems a strange thing to me that we should still be so
little awake to the fact that in these plays which depend
wholly on poignant intensity of expression for the simple
emotions the sceptre has passed to the operatic artist.
What surprises me is not that this exhibition of Madame
Bernhardt's should be flagrantly vulgar and commercial,
or that it should be hackneyed and old-fashioned, but
that we should dream of going to see it now that we have
seen Calvé as Carmen and La Navarraise. In the front
ranks of art there is a place for the methods of Duse, and
for the drama in which emotion exists only to make
thought live and move us, but none for Sarah Bernhardt
and the claptraps which Sardou contrives for her. To me,
at least, the whole affair seems antiquated and ridiculous,
except when I regard it as a high modern development of
the circus and the waxworks. I have seen it, just as I have
seen, in my time, Madame Celeste in Green Bushes and
The Red Woman. Though I always preferred Buckstone
to Sardou as a tragic dramatist, and still do, I used to think
Madame Bernhardt a greater actress than Celeste. But I
almost believe now that this must have been a delusion of
the departed days when Madame Bernhardt was so slim
that when she went for a trip in a captive balloon, it was
said that her stepping into the car had the same effect as
throwing out ballast. At all events, I am quite sure that if

I had to choose between seeing Miami and Gismonda again, I should vote eagerly for Miami, who was at least amusing.

To revert for a moment to Fedora, I hope Mrs Campbell will note that Sarah Bernhardt's career cannot be repeated now—that her art is out of date and her dramas dead. The proof is that Mrs Campbell cannot act Fedora, although to any actress over forty-five Fedora is more natural than Mrs Tanqueray. By the way, I have forgotten to say that Mrs Bancroft is in the cast, and is as amusing and skilful as ever. Mr Tree, confonted with the impossible Loris Ipanoff, was forced to take the part seriously, and, with the help of a Polish make-up, try to pull it through by a creditably awkward attempt at conventional melodramatic acting. Besides, Mrs Campbell ruined his clothes. Wherever her beautiful white arms touched him they left their mark. She knelt at his feet and made a perfect zebra of his left leg with bars across it. Then she flung her arms convulsively right round him; and the next time he turned his back to the footlights there was little to choose between his coatback and his shirtfront. Before the act was over a gallon of benzine would hardly have set him right again. Mr Tree had his revenge at the end of the play, when, in falling on Fedora's body, he managed to transfer a large black patch to her cheek, which was strikingly in evidence when she bowed her acknowledgment of the frantic applause with which the evening ended; but he was still so unhinged by the futility of Loris and the ill-treatment of his garments, that when the audience called for Mr Bancroft he informed them that Mr Bancroft was prevented from coming forward by modesty, but that Mrs Bancroft —and here Mrs Bancroft came forward smiling; and the audience naturally chuckled hugely.

May I suggest that soap and water is an excellent cosmetic for the arms, and that it does not mark coats? Also that this white-washing malpractice has become an intolerable absurdity, and that there is at least one critic who means to try whether ridicule can kill it.

•   •   •   •   •   •   •

La Femme de Claude

LA FEMME DE CLAUDE. By Alexandre Dumas *fils*. Drury
Lane Theatre, 5 June 1895. [*From* "Two Plays."]

.   .   .   .   .

[8 *June* 1895]

The appearance of Duse at Drury Lane on Wednesday
in La Femme de Claude, is too recent for my judgment to
have recovered from the emotional disturbance produced
by such an appeal as she made to my passion for very
fine acting. The furthest extremes of Duse's range as an
artist must always, even in this greatest art centre in the
world, remain a secret between herself and a few fine
observers. I should say without qualification that it is the
best modern acting I have ever seen, were it not that the
phrase suggests a larger experience of first-rate acting in
this department than I possess. I have only seen Salvini
and Ristori in their historic-heroic parts, or in Shakespear;
and my experience of Coquelin is limited to Molière and
such plays of our own day as Les Surprises de Divorce.
The work of these three great artists seemed to me (humanly speaking) quite thorough and perfect in its application to their conception of the parts they played; and their
conception was, for the most part, adequate, and more
than adequate, to the culture of their generation. But their
incubatory period was the period before the theatre had
advanced to the point at which Wagner and Ibsen became
its master spirits. Duse is the first actress whom we have
seen applying the method of the great school to characteristically modern parts or to characteristically modern
conceptions of old parts. Her style is not, to the attentive
observer of the stage, entirely new: nothing arrives at such
perfection without many tentative approaches to it. I remember years ago, when The Lady of Lyons was first produced at the Lyceum, being struck with two things about
it: first, the fact that Henry Irving, after much striving
and, if I may be allowed the expression, not a little
floundering, had at last discovered the method of heroic
acting; and, second, that in the scene where Claude brings
Pauline home after their wedding, Miss Ellen Terry, by a
number of delicate touches, slipped into the scene a play
of subtle emotion quite foreign to its traditions, with such

effect that I can conjure up those moments perfectly to
this day, though my utmost effort of memory cannot bring
back the very faintest adumbration of any other scene in
Pauline's part, which was as useless as material for Miss
Terry's peculiar genius as most of those twenty-three
Lyceum heroines—Catherine Duval in A Dead Heart, and
so forth—of which Mr Clement Scott has made a list for
my benefit, evidently to make me cry afresh over the
wicked waste of so rare a talent. Of course the twenty-
three parts are not all bad parts as parts are reckoned con-
ventionally; and equally of course Miss Terry has not
exactly played any of them badly. But neither is Shakespear's Cleopatra a bad part; and neither did Duse exactly
play it badly. Yet who on earth would know that Duse
was a great actress if he had never seen her play anything
but Cleopatra? And who on earth will ever know what
Miss Terry can do if we are never to see her except in
plays that date, in feeling if not in actual composition,
from the dark ages before the Married Women's Property
Act? I can only guess at her powers myself from my
recollections of the old Court Theatre, and the little inter-
polations in the Lyceum parts by which her genius so often
instinctively thrusts through the old play to the new style,
only, of course, to be beaten back by the giving out of the
material. Still, just in these thrustings you could see Duse's
style coming. Long after the Lady of Lyons came Miss
Janet Achurch, whose playing as Alexandra, in Voss's
play, came nearer to Duse's work in subtlety, continuity
and variety of detail, and in beauty of execution, than anything I have seen on the English stage. But Duse has been
helped to her supremacy by the fortunate sternness of
Nature in giving her nothing but her genius. Miss Ellen
Terry is a woman of quite peculiar and irresistible personal
charm. Miss Achurch has been kept in constant danger of
missing the highest distinction in her art by having, as an
extra and cheaper string to her bow, an endowment of
conventional good looks, and a large share of that power
of expressing all the common emotions with extraordinary
intensity which makes the vulgar great actress of the Bernhardt school. Consequently you have two Miss Achurches:
the Miss Achurch of Nora and Alexandra, and the Miss
Achurch of Adrienne and Forget-me-not; and there are
moments when the two get mixed. But in Duse you necessarily get the great school in its perfect integrity, because

Duse without her genius would be a plain little woman of
no use to any manager, whereas Miss Terry or Miss
Achurch, if they had no more skill than can be acquired
by any person of ordinary capacity in the course of a few
years' experience, would always find a certain degree of
favor as pretty leading ladies. Duse, *with* her genius, is so
fascinating that it is positively difficult to attend to the
play instead of attending wholly to her. The extraordinary
richness of her art can only be understood by those who
have studied the process by which an actress is built up.
You offer a part to a young lady who is an enthusiastic
beginner. She reads it devoutly, and forms, say, half a
dozen great ideas as to points which she will make. The
difficulty then is to induce her to do nothing between these
points; so that the play may be allowed at such moments
to play itself. Probably when it comes to the point, these
intervals will prove the only effective periods during her
performance, the points being ill chosen or awkwardly
executed. The majority of actresses never get beyond
learning not to invent new points for themselves, but rather
to pick out in their parts the passages which admit of certain well worn and tried old points being reapplied. When
they have learnt to make these points smoothly and to
keep quiet between whiles with a graceful air of having
good reasons for doing nothing, they are finished actresses.
The great actress has a harder struggle. She goes on inventing her points and her business determinedly, constantly increasing the original half-dozen, and constantly
executing them with greater force and smoothness. A time
comes when she is always making points, and making them
well; and this is the finishing point with some actresses.
But with the greatest artists there soon commences an
integration of the points into a continuous whole, at which
stage the actress appears to make no points at all, and to
proceed in the most unstudied and "natural" way. This
rare consummation Duse has reached. An attentive study
of her Marguerite Gauthier, for instance, by a highly
trained observer of such things, will bring to light how
its apparently simple strokes are combinations of a whole
series of strokes, separately conceived originally, and
added one by one to the part, until finally, after many
years of evolution, they have integrated into one single
highly complex stroke. Take, as a very simple illustration,
the business of Camille's tying up the flowers in the third

act. It seems the most natural thing in the world; but it is
really the final development of a highly evolved dance
with the arms—even, when you watch it consciously, a
rather prolonged and elaborate one. The strokes of character have grown up in just the same way. And this is
the secret of the extraordinary interest of such acting.
There are years of work, bodily and mental, behind every
instant of it—work, mind, not mere practice and habit,
which is quite a different thing. It is the rarity of the gigantic energy needed to sustain this work which makes
Duse so exceptional; for the work is in her case highly
intellectual work, and so requires energy of a quality
altogether superior to the mere head of steam needed to
produce Bernhardtian explosions with the requisite regu-
larity. With such high energy, mere personal fascination
becomes a thing which the actress can put off and on like
a garment. Sarah Bernhardt has nothing but her own
charm, for the exhibition of which Sardou contrives love
scenes—save the mark. Duse's own private charm has not
yet been given to the public. She gives you Césarine's
charm, Marguerite Gauthier's charm, the charm of La
Locandiera, the charm, in short, belonging to the character she impersonates; and you are enthralled by its reality
and delighted by the magical skill of the artist without for
a moment feeling any complicity either on your own part
or hers in the passion represented. And with that clue to
the consistency of supreme admiration for the artist with
perfect respect for the woman—a combination so rare that
some people doubt its possibility—I must leave discussion
of the plays she has appeared in this week to my next
article.

Duse and Bernhardt

[15 *June* 1895]

Mr William Archer's defence of the dramatic critics
against Mr Street's indictment of them for their indifference to acting appears to be falling through. Mr Archer
pleads that whereas Hazlitt and Leigh Hunt had frequent
opportunities of comparing ambitious actors in famous
parts, the modern dramatic critic spends his life in contemplating "good acting plays" without any real people
in them, and performers who do not create or interpret

characters, but simply lend their pretty or popular persons, for a consideration, to fill up the parts. Mr Archer might have added another reason which applies to nearly all modern works: to wit, the operation of our copyright laws, whereby actors and actresses acquire the right not only to perform new plays but to prevent anyone else from performing them. Nevertheless we critics can now at last outdo Hazlitt and Leigh Hunt if we have a mind to; for we have just had two Mrs Ebbsmiths to compare, besides a fourth Fedora, and Duse and Sarah Bernhardt playing La Dame aux Camélias and Sudermann's Heimat against one another at Daly's Theatre and at Drury Lane. Clearly now or never is the time for a triumphant refutation of the grievance of the English actor against the English Press: namely, that hardly any critic knows enough about acting to be able to distinguish between an effective part and a well played one, or between the bag of tricks which every old hand carries and the stock of ideas and sense of character which distinguish the master-actor from the mere handy man.

This week began with the relapse of Sarah Bernhardt into her old profession of serious actress. She played Magda in Sudermann's Heimat, and was promptly challenged by Duse in the same part at Drury Lane on Wednesday. The contrast between the two Magdas is as extreme as any contrast could possibly be between artists who have finished their twenty years apprenticeship to the same profession under closely similar conditions. Madame Bernhardt has the charm of a jolly maturity, rather spoilt and petulant, perhaps, but always ready with a sunshine-through-the-clouds smile if only she is made much of. Her dresses and diamonds, if not exactly splendid, are at least splendacious; her figure, far too scantily upholstered in the old days, is at its best; and her complexion shews that she has not studied modern art in vain. Those charming roseate effects which French painters produce by giving flesh the pretty color of strawberries and cream, and painting the shadows pink and crimson, are cunningly reproduced by Madame Bernhardt in the living picture. She paints her ears crimson and allows them to peep enchantingly through a few loose braids of her auburn hair. Every dimple has its dab of pink; and her finger-tips are so delicately incarnadined that you fancy they are transparent like her ears, and that the light is shining through their delicate blood-vessels. Her lips are like a newly painted pillar box; her cheeks, right up to the languid lashes, have the bloom and surface of a peach; she is beautiful with the beauty of her school, and entirely inhuman and incredible. But the incredibility is pardonable, because, though it is all the greatest nonsense, nobody believing in it, the actress herself least of all, it is so artful, so clever, so well recognized a part of the business, and carried off with such a genial air, that it is impossible not to accept it with good-humor. One feels, when the heroine bursts on the scene, a dazzling vision of beauty, that instead of imposing on you, she adds to her own piquancy by looking you straight in the face, and saying, in effect: "Now who would ever suppose that I am a grandmother?" That, of course, is irresistible; and one is not sorry to have been coaxed to relax one's notions of the dignity of art when she gets to serious business and shews how ably she does her work. The coaxing suits well with the childishly egotistical character of her acting, which is not the art of making you think more highly or feel more deeply, but the art of making you admire her, pity her, champion her, weep with her, laugh at her jokes, follow her fortunes breathlessly, and applaud her wildly when the curtain falls. It is the art of finding out all your weaknesses and practising on them— cajoling you, harrowing you, exciting you—on the whole, fooling you. And it is always Sarah Bernhardt in her own capacity who does this to you. The dress, the title of the play, the order of the words may vary; but the woman is always the same. She does not enter into the leading character: she substitutes herself for it.

All this is precisely what does not happen in the case of Duse, whose every part is a separate creation. When she comes on the stage, you are quite welcome to take your opera-glass and count whatever lines time and care have so far traced on her. They are the credentials of her humanity; and she knows better than to obliterate that significant handwriting beneath a layer of peach-bloom from the chemist's. The shadows on her face are grey, not crimson; her lips are sometimes nearly grey also; there are neither dabs nor dimples; her charm could never be imitated by a barmaid with unlimited pin money and a row of footlights before her instead of the handles of a beer-engine. The result is not so discouraging as the patrons of the bar might suppose. Wilkes, who squinted atrociously, boasted that he was only quarter of an hour behind the handsomest man in Europe: Duse is not in action five minutes before she is quarter of a century ahead of the handsomest woman in the world. I grant that Sarah's elaborate Mona Lisa smile, with the conscious droop of the eyelashes and the long carmined lips coyly disclosing the brilliant row of teeth, is effective of its kind—that it not only appeals to your susceptibilities, but positively jogs them. And it lasts quite a minute, sometimes longer. But Duse, with a tremor of the lip which you feel rather than see, and which lasts half an instant, touches you straight on the very heart; and there is not a line in the face, or a cold tone in the grey shadow that does not give poignancy to that tremor. As to youth and age, who can associate purity and delicacy of emotion, and simplicity of expression, with the sordid craft that repels us in age; or voluptuous appeal and egotistical self-insistence with the candor and generosity that attract us in youth? Who ever thinks of Potiphar's wife as a young woman, or St Elizabeth of Hungary as an old one? These associations are horribly unjust to age, and undeserved by youth: they belong of right to differences of character, not of years; but they rule our imaginations; and the great artist profits by them to appear eternally young. However, it would be a critical blunder as well as a personal folly on my part to suggest that Duse, any more than Sarah Bernhardt, neglects any art that could heighten the effect of her acting when she is impersonating young and pretty women. The truth is that in the art of being beautiful, Madame Bernhardt is a child beside her. The French artist's stock of attitudes and facial effects could be catalogued as easily as her stock of dramatic ideas: the counting would hardly go beyond the fingers of both hands. Duse produces the illusion of being infinite in variety of beautiful pose and motion. Every idea, every shade of thought and mood, expresses itself delicately but vividly to the eye; and yet, in an apparent million of changes and inflexions, it is impossible to catch any line at an awkward angle, or any strain interfering with the perfect abandonment of all the limbs to what appears to be their natural gravitation towards the finest grace. She is ambidextrous and supple, like a gymnast or a panther; only the multitude of ideas which find physical expression in her movements are all of that high quality which marks off humanity from the animals, and, I fear I must add, from a good many gymnasts. When it is remembered that the majority of tragic actors excel only in explosions of those passions which are common to man and brute, there will be no difficulty in understanding the indescribable distinction which Duse's acting acquires from the fact that behind every stroke of it is a distinctively human idea. In nothing is this more apparent than in the vigilance in her of that high human instinct which seeks to awaken the deepest responsive feeling without giving pain. In La Dame aux Camélias, for instance, it is easy for an intense actress to harrow us with her sorrows and paroxysms of phthisis, leaving us with a liberal pennyworth of sensation, not fundamentally distinguishable from that offered by a public execution, or any other evil in which we still take a hideous delight. As different from this as light from darkness is the method of the actress who shews us how human sorrow can express itself only in its appeal for the sympathy it needs, whilst striving by strong endurance to shield others from the infection of its torment. That is the charm of Duse's interpretation of the stage poem of Marguerite Gauthier. It is unspeakably touching because it is exquisitely considerate: that is, exquisitely sympathetic. No physical charm is noble as well as beautiful unless it is the expression of a moral charm; and it is because Duse's range includes these moral high notes, if I may so express myself, that her compass, extending from the depths of a mere predatory creature like Claude's wife up to Marguerite Gauthier at her kindest or Magda at her bravest, so immeasurably dwarfs the poor little octave and a half on which Sarah Bernhardt plays such pretty canzonets and stirring marches.

Obvious as the disparity of the two famous artists has been to many of us since we first saw Duse, I doubt whether any of us realized, after Madame Bernhardt's very clever performance as Magda on Monday night, that there was room in the nature of things for its annihilation within forty-eight hours by so comparatively quiet a talent as Duse's. And yet annihilation is the only word for it. Sarah was very charming, very jolly when the sun shone, very petulant when the clouds covered it, and positively angry when they wanted to take her child away from her. And she did not trouble us with any fuss about the main theme of Sudermann's play, the revolt of the modern woman against that ideal of home which exacts the sacrifice of her

whole life to its care, not by her grace, and as its own sole
help and refuge, but as a right which it has to the services
of all females as abject slaves. In fact, there is not the
slightest reason to suspect Madame Bernhardt of having
discovered any such theme in the play; though Duse, with
one look at Schwartze, the father, nailed it to the stage as
the subject of the impending dramatic struggle before she
had been five minutes on the scene. Before long, there
came a stroke of acting which will probably never be forgotten by those who saw it, and which explained at once
why those artifices of the dressing-table which help Madame Bernhardt would hinder Duse almost as much as a
screen placed in front of her. I should explain, first, that
the real name of the play is not Magda but Home. Magda
is a daughter who has been turned out of doors for defy-
ing her father, one of those outrageous persons who mistake their desire to have everything their own way in the
house for a sacred principle of home life. She has a hard
time of it, but at last makes a success as an opera singer,
though not until her lonely struggles have thrown her for
sympathy on a fellow student, who in due time goes his
way, and leaves her to face motherhood as best she can.
In the fullness of her fame she returns to her native town,
and in an attack of homesickness makes advances to her
father, who consents to receive her again. No sooner is
she installed in the house than she finds that one of the
most intimate friends of the family is the father of her
child. In the third act of the play she is on the stage when
he is announced as a visitor. It must be admitted that Sarah
Bernhardt played this scene very lightly and pleasantly:
there was genuine good fellowship in the way in which she
reassured the embarrassed gallant and made him understand that she was not going to play off the sorrows of
Gretchen on him after all those years, and that she felt
that she owed him the priceless experience of maternity,
even if she did not particularly respect him for it. Her
self-possession at this point was immense: the peach-bloom
never altered by a shade. Not so with Duse. The moment
she read the card handed her by the servant, you realized
what it was to have to face a meeting with the man. It was
interesting to watch how she got through it when he came
in, and how, on the whole, she got through it pretty well.
He paid his compliments and offered his flowers; they sat
down; and she evidently felt that she had got it safely over

and might allow herself to think at her ease, and to look at him to see how much he had altered. Then a terrible thing happened to her. She began to blush; and in another moment she was conscious of it, and the blush was slowly spreading and deepening until, after a few vain efforts to avert her face or to obstruct his view of it without seeming to do so, she gave up and hid the blush in her hands. After that feat of acting I did not need to be told why Duse does not paint an inch thick. I could detect no trick in it: it seemed to me a perfectly genuine effect of the dramatic imagination. In the third act of La Dame aux Camélias, where she produces a touching effect by throwing herself down, and presently rises with her face changed and flushed with weeping, the flush is secured by the preliminary plunge to a stooping attitude, imagination or no imagination; but Magda's blush did not admit of that explanation; and I must confess to an intense professional curiosity as to whether it always comes spontaneously.

I shall make no attempt to describe the rest of that unforgettable act. To say that it left the house not only frantically applauding, but actually roaring, is to say nothing; for had we not applauded Sarah as Gismonda and roared at Mrs Patrick Campbell as Fedora? But there really was something to roar at this time. There was a real play, and an actress who understood the author and was a greater artist than he. And for me, at least, there was a confirmation of my sometimes flagging faith that a dramatic critic is really the servant of a high art, and not a mere advertiser of entertainments of questionable respectability of motive.

La Princesse Lointaine

LA PRINCESSE LOINTAINE. By Edmond Rostand. Daly's Theatre, 17 June 1895.

[22 *June* 1895]

The romance of chivalry has its good points; but it always dies of the Unwomanly Woman. And M. Rostand's Princess Far Away will die of Melissinde. A first act in which the men do nothing but describe their hysterical visions of a wonderful goddess-princess whom they have never seen is bad enough; but it is pardonable, because men do make fools of themselves about women, sometimes in an interesting and poetic fashion. But when the woman appears and plays up to the height of their folly, intoning her speeches to an accompaniment of harps and horns, distributing lilies and languors to pilgrims, and roses and raptures to troubadours, always in the character which their ravings have ascribed to her, what can one feel except that an excellent opportunity for a good comedy is being thrown away? If Melissinde would only eat something, or speak in prose, or only swear in it, or do anything human —were it even smoking a cigaret—to bring these silly Argonauts to their senses for a moment, one could forgive her. But she remains an unredeemed humbug from one end of the play to the other; and when, at the climax of one of her most deliberately piled-up theatrical entrances, a poor green mariner exclaims, with open-mouthed awe, "The Blessed Virgin!" it sends a twinge of frightful blasphemous irony down one's spine. Having felt that, I now understand better than before why the Dulcinea episodes in Don Quixote are so coarse in comparison to the rest of the book. Cervantes had been driven into reactionary savagery by too much Melissinde.

It is a pity that the part of M. Rostand's play which deals with the shipful of enthusiasts did not get over the footlights better; for it is touched here and there with a certain modern freedom of spirit, and has some grace, youth, and imagination in it. But it lacks the force which comes from wisdom and originality. The prettiest descriptions of Melissinde are spoiled by the reflection—inevitable in an audience saturated with the Bernhardt tradition—that they are only leading up to the entrance of the star. Besides, they are in the verse of a rhythmless language. I know that many English people declare that they appreciate this verse; and I know also that they sometimes follow up their declaration by asking you whether you pronounce Fédora as Fay'dera or Fido'ra, a question which no Frenchman could even understand. But to me French verse is simply not verse at all. I know it as a blind man knows color: that is, by the current explanations of it. When I read alexandrines, I cook them, in spite of myself, so as to make them scan like the last line of a stanza in Childe Harold: for instance, if I may illustrate by combining Rostand and Byron:

Te voyant accoutré d'une manière telle,
He rushed into the field, and, foremost fighting, fell,

Pour porter monseigneur vers sa Dame Lointaine
And fertilize the field that each pretends to gain.

This, I know, is deplorable; but it would be useless for me
to attempt to conceal my hopeless deficiencies as a linguist.
I am very sorry; but I cannot learn languages. I have tried
hard, only to find that men of ordinary capacity can learn
Sanscrit in less time than it takes me to buy a German
dictionary. The worst of it is that this disability of mine
seems to be most humiliatingly exceptional. My colleagues
sit at French plays, German plays, and Italian plays, laughing at all the jokes, thrilling with all the fine sentiments,
and obviously seizing the finest shades of the language;
whilst I, unless I have read the play beforehand, or asked
someone during the interval what it is about, must either
struggle with a sixpenny "synopsis" which invariably
misses the real point of the drama, or else sit with a guilty
conscience and a blank countenance, drawing the most
extravagantly wrong inferences from the dumb show of the
piece. The torture of this can only be adequately appre-
hended when it is considered that in ordinary novels, or
plays, or conversations, the majority of sentences have no
definite meaning at all; and that an energetic intellectual
effort to grapple with them, such as one makes in trying
to understand a foreign language, would at once discover
their inconclusiveness, inaccuracy, and emptiness. When
I listen to an English play I am not troubled by not understanding when there is nothing to understand, because I
understand at once that there is nothing to understand. But
at a foreign play I do not understand this; and every sentence that means nothing in particular—say five out of six
in the slacker moments of the action—seems to me to be
a sentence of which I have missed the meaning through my
unhappy and disgraceful ignorance of the language. Hence
torments of shame and inefficiency, the betrayal of which
would destroy my reputation as a critic at one blow. Of
course I have a phrase or two ready at the end of my
tongue to conceal my ignorance. My command of operatic
Italian is almost copious, as might be expected from my
experience as a musical critic. I can make love in Italian;
I could challenge a foe to a duel in Italian if I were not
afraid of him; and if I swallowed some agonizing mineral
poison, I could describe my sensations very eloquently.
And I could manage a prayer pretty well. But these accomplishments are too special for modern comedy and ordi-

nary conversation. As to French, I can neither speak it nor understand it when spoken without an impracticably long interval for reflection; and I am, besides, subject to a curious propensity, when addressed by Italian or French people, to reply in fluent German, though on all other occasions that language utterly baffles me. On the whole, I come off best at the theatre in such a case as that of Magda, where I began by reading the synopsis, then picked up a little of the play in French at Daly's Theatre, then a little more in Italian at Drury Lane, then a little more in German from the book, and finally looked at Duse and was illuminated beyond all the powers of all the books and languages on earth.

I may now return to M. Rostand's play with an easy conscience, since I have made it plain that my sense that its versification is a drawback to it may be the effect of pure ignorance on my part. Certainly it made it verbose, and destroyed the illusion of the seafaring scenes by setting all the sailors monotonously bawling their phrases like street cries, in the manner of M. Mounet Sully and the Comédie Française, though of course they stopped short of the worst declamatory horrors of that institution. And in some subtle way, it led on the two troubadours, Joffroy Rudel and Bertrand d'Allamanon, to make themselves ridiculous. About Joffroy (M. de Max) there was no mistake from the very beginning. As he lay moribund on his litter, his large dark eyes were fixed in profound pity for himself; and his lips were wreathed in a smile of ineffable complacency at the thought of how well his eyes looked. He smiled all poor M. Rostand's poetry overboard within a minute of his entrance; and it then became a question whether Bertrand (M. Guitry) could raise it from the depths in the second and third acts, in which Joffroy does not appear. But though M. Guitry did not smile at all, being, in fact, as serious a man as any poet could desire, the audience laughed outright at Bertrand. In vain did Madame Bernhardt work up his entrance by tearing off her white sleeves and throwing them out of the window to him, enjoining him to redden them in the gore of the gigantic green knight. In vain did he dash in spinning with the impetus of his charge, whirling his falchion in the air, and bearing on his brow a gash which suggested that the green knight, before succumbing, had sliced the top off his head like the lid of a saucepan. The audience only laughed.

They laughed again when he fainted; they shrieked when
Sorismonde (the inevitable confidante) said "He is better"; and they might have ended by laughing the piece off
the stage had he not reminded Melissinde that she had no
sleeves on, whereupon she became conscious of herself,
and a blushing silence fell on the house. It was really not
M. Guitry's fault: for the life of me I cannot see what he
could have done other than what he did; but I cannot pretend that I take a very severe view of the bad manners
of the audience in laughing. However, his entrance, like
several of the exciting events on the ship in the first act,
might have been better stage-managed. The great modern
master of such effects is Richard Wagner, with regard to
whom the French nation is still in a comparatively benighted condition. The stage manager who wishes to work
up the arrival of a champion or the sighting of land from
a ship had better go to Bayreuth and watch the first acts of
Lohengrin and Tristan, unless he is content to run the risk
of making modern audiences laugh. But I do not think
very much could be done with M. Rostand's scene leading
up to Bertrand's arrival in any case. Melissinde and Sorismonde describing the attack from the window—"Oh, quel
superbe élan!" and so on—is not to be compared either to
Rebecca describing the onslaught of the black knight to
Ivanhoe, or Klingsor's running commentary to Kundry on
the havoc made by Parsifal among the knights of the
flower maidens.

As to Madame Bernhardt's own performance, it is not
humanly possible for an actress to do very much with a
play in which, when the other characters are not describing
what a peerlessly beautiful and wonderful creature she is,
she is herself on the stage accepting that ridiculous position. But the moment Madame Bernhardt entered one very
welcome reform was evident. The elaborate make-up
which I took the liberty of describing in some detail in my
last article, and which made Gismonda and Magda so im-
possibly like goddesses in a Tiepolesque ceiling, had all
but disappeared. Melissinde had a face, not a stucco mask:
she was a real woman, not a hairdresser's shop-window
image. And what an improvement it was! How Madame
Bernhardt can ever have supposed that her face is less
interesting or attractive than the complexion which she
carries in her dressing-bag, or that she has anything to
gain by trying to make herself look like the silliest sort of

lady of fashion, would be a mystery to me if it were not only too evident that she no longer brings to her art the immense pressure of thought and labor which earns for the greatest artists that rarest of all faiths, faith in their real selves. She looked much better; but there was very little thought, very little work, and consequently very little interest in her performance. Fortunately for her, she still has exceptional nervous power; and she has not altogether forgotten those situations in her old parts which repeat themselves with more or less inessential modification in her new ones. This, to so clever a woman, with such a reputation, is enough to enable her to play the great actress still. But it should not satisfy London criticism. Take, for example, the end of the third act of this Princesse Lointaine, which she selects as her opportunity for one of those displays of vehemence which are expected from her as part of the conventional Bernhardt exhibition. It is pure rant and nothing else. When once she begins to tear through her lines at the utmost pitch and power of her voice, she shews no further sense of what she is saying, and is unable to recover herself when, in the final speech, the feeling changes. As her physical endurance threatens to fail she tears along the faster, and finally rushes off the stage in a forced frenzy. I do not deny that there is something very exciting in a blind whirlwind of roaring energy. I have seen a working-class audience spring to their feet and cheer madly for three minutes at it. But then the artist was Mr John Burns, who can give Madame Bernhardt a start of several miles at that particular sort of effect, and beat her easily. And I am bound to say, in justice to Mr Burns, that I have never seen him bring down the curtain in this fashion until the play was really over, or substitute the peroration for the business part of the speech, whereas Madame Bernhardt does deliberately substitute rant for the business of the play. Again, Mr Burns does it to amuse an election meeting of working men who are tired of sitting still: he does not offer it as serious political oratory in the House of Commons. I need hardly say that it is not the sort of effect that improves as the artist grows older, since it can only be produced by sustained physical violence. It is quite different from those effects which great players produce at a dramatic climax by working up the scene, through sheer force of acting, to the pitch at which, when the crucial moment comes, the effect makes itself,

the artist's work being then over, though the audience is
persuaded that some stupendous magnetic explosion has
taken place. No doubt some of my readers have witnessed
that scene in which Queen Elizabeth and her court seemed
to vanish miraculously from the stage, apparently swept
into nothingness when Ristori let loose her wrath as Marie
Stuart; or they may have seen the same effect produced by
Salvini when the king flies in disorder from the play scene
in Hamlet. But it is only the critic, watching and listening
with the same intensity with which the performer acts,
who, when asked what extraordinary thing Ristori or Salvini did at that supreme moment to work such a miracle,
is able to reply that they did nothing. Elizabeth and Claudius ran off the stage with their courts after them: that
was all. Ristori and Salvini simply looked on, having already wrought the scene to the point at which the flight
of the rest produced the necessary effect on the imagination of the audience. I need hardly refer again to the effect
made last week by the third act of Sudermann's Home, as
Duse played it. I only ask anyone who saw that performance to try to imagine—if he has the heart to do it—such
an artistic scandal as that great actress suddenly throwing
her part to the winds and substituting for it a good two
minutes rant, like the finish to the third act of La Princesse Lointaine. The public should learn to distinguish in
these matters consciously as well as unconsciously. Ranting is not, as it is generally assumed to be, bad acting. It
is not acting at all, but the introduction of an exhibition of
force for the sake of force. And let us not affect to deny
that when the performer has strength enough to raise the
pressure to hurricane pitch, a successful rant is attractive
and exciting, provided only the performer is clearly doing
it on purpose, and is not an epileptic or a lunatic. But it
takes not only purpose but reason to humanize force and
raise it to the rank of a factor in fine art. It is the strength
that is completely controlled and utilized that takes the
crown: it is your Ristori, your Salvini, your Duse, with
their unfailing hold and yet exquisitely delicate touch upon
their parts, their sleeplessly vigilant sense of beauty of
thought, feeling, and action, and their prodigious industry,
that are recognized as the real athletes of the stage, compared with whom the ranters are weaklings and sluggards.
That, at least, must be the judgment of London. Artists of
international fame do not come to this capital of the world

for money, but for reputation; and the London critic should be jealous above all things of letting that reputation go cheaply. When Duse gives us her best work, we cannot be too emphatic in declaring that it is best of the best and magnificent; so that our hall-mark may be carried through the nations on a piece of sterling gold. But when Madame Bernhardt gives us pinchbeck plays and acting that is poor in thought and eked out with odds and ends stripped from her old parts; when she rants at us and brings down the house in a London theatre just as she brings it down in a provincial American one, we must tell her that she can do better than that, and that we will have nothing less than her best. When she offers us her reputation instead of first-rate acting, we must reply that we give reputations instead of taking them, and that we accept nothing in exchange except first-rate acting down on the counter, without a moment's credit. Already there are signs that she is waking up to the situation. The failure of Gismonda to elicit any expression of the deep respect which really fine work imposes, even on those who prefer something cheaper; the sudden and complete obliteration of her Magda by Duse's first five minutes in the part; the fatal compliments by which her most enthusiastic champions have exposed the commonness and obviousness of the intellectual material of her acting: something of all this may have penetrated to her through the barrier of language and the incense-clouds of flattery; for it looked as if on Monday the disappearance of the Gismonda make-up were only a symptom of a more serious attitude towards London. I suggest, now, that the rant should be discarded as well, and replaced by a genuine study and interpretation of the passages which are sacrificed to it. I further suggest, as a musical critic, that the shallow trick of intoning which sets so many of my musically neglected colleagues babbling about the "golden voice" should be discarded too. Miss Rehan, who is coming next week, will expose the musical emptiness of Madame Bernhardt's habit of monotonously chanting sentences on one note, as effectually as Duse has exposed the intellectual emptiness of her Magda. Of course, intoning is easy—as easy as holding down one key of an accordion and keeping up a mellifluous smile all the time; but it dehumanizes speech, and after some minutes becomes maddening, so that a flash of fun or a burst of rage is doubly welcome because it for a moment alters that

eternal pitch and timbre. Some critics speak of "the
melody" of it, as to which I can only say that the man
who finds melody in one sustained note would find exquisite curves in a packing case. I therefore respectfully urge
Madame Bernhardt to add a complete set of strings to her
lyre before Miss Rehan comes. Otherwise there will be
fresh comparisons of the most disparaging kind.

. . . .

Toujours Daly

A MIDSUMMER NIGHT'S DREAM. Daly's Theatre, 9 July 1895.

. . . . . .

[13 *July* 1895]

The Two Gentlemen of Verona has been succeeded at
Daly's Theatre by A Midsummer Night's Dream. Mr Daly
is in great form. In my last article I was rash enough to
hint that he had not quite realized what could be done with
electric lighting on the stage. He triumphantly answers me
by fitting up all his fairies with portable batteries and in-
candescent lights, which they switch on and off from time
to time, like children with a new toy. He has trained Miss
Lillian Swain in the part of Puck until it is safe to say that
she does not take one step, strike one attitude, or modify
her voice by a single inflexion that is not violently, wan-
tonly, and ridiculously wrong and absurd. Instead of being
mercurial, she poses academically, like a cheap Italian
statuette; instead of being impish and childish, she is elegant and affected; she laughs a solemn, measured laugh,
like a heavy German Zamiel; she announces her ability to
girdle the earth in forty minutes in the attitude of a professional skater, and then begins the journey awkwardly
in a swing, which takes her in the opposite direction to
that in which she indicated her intention of going: in short,
she illustrates every folly and superstition that still clings
round what Mr Daly no doubt calls "the legitimate." Another stroke of his is to make Oberon a woman. It must
not be supposed that he does this solely because it is
wrong, though there is no other reason apparent. He does
it partly because he was brought up to do such things, and
partly because they seem to him to be a tribute to Shakespear's greatness, which, being uncommon, ought not to be
interpreted according to the dictates of common sense. A

female Oberon and a Puck who behaves like a page-boy
earnestly training himself for the post of footman recommend themselves to him because they totally destroy the
naturalness of the representation, and so accord with his
conception of the Shakespearean drama as the most artificial of all forms of stage entertainment. That is how you
find out the man who is not an artist. Verse, music, the
beauties of dress, gesture, and movement are to him interesting aberrations instead of being the natural expression
which human feeling seeks at a certain degree of delicacy
and intensity. He regards art as a quaint and costly ring
in the nose of Nature. I am loth to say that Mr Daly is
such a man; but after studying all his Shakespearean revivals with the thirstiest desire to find as much art as possible in them, I must mournfully confess that the only idea
I can see in them is the idea of titivation. As to his
slaughterings of the text, how can one help feeling them
acutely in a play like A Midsummer Night's Dream, in
which Shakespear, having to bring Nature in its most enchanting aspect before an audience without the help of
theatrical scenery, used all his power of description and
expression in verse with such effect that the utmost any
scene-painter can hope for is to produce a picture that
shall not bitterly disappoint the spectator who has read the
play beforehand? Mr Daly is, I should say, one of those
people who are unable to conceive that there could have
been any illusion at all about the play before scenery was
introduced. He certainly has no suspicion of the fact that
every accessory he employs is brought in at the deadliest
risk of destroying the magic spell woven by the poet. He
swings Puck away on a clumsy trapeze with a ridiculous
clash of the cymbals in the orchestra, in the fullest belief
that he is thereby completing instead of destroying the
effect of Puck's lines. His "panoramic illusion of the passage of Theseus's barge to Athens" is more absurd than
anything that occurs in the tragedy of Pyramus and Thisbe
in the last act. The stage management blunders again and
again through feeble imaginative realization of the circumstances of the drama. In the first act it should be clear to
any stage manager that Lysander's speech, beginning, "I
am, my lord, as well derived as he," should be spoken
privately and not publicly to Theseus. In the rehearsal
scene in the wood, Titania should not be conspicuously
exhibited under a limelight in the very centre of the stage,

where the clowns have, in defiance of all common sanity, to pretend not to see her. We are expected, no doubt, to assume that she is invisible because she is a fairy, though Bottom's conversation with her when she wakes and addresses him flatly contradicts that hypothesis. In the fourth act, Theseus has to enter from his barge down a bank, picking his way through the sleeping Lysander and Hermia, Demetrius and Helena. The four lions in Trafalgar Square are not more conspicuous and unoverlookable than these four figures are. Yet Theseus has to make all his hunting speeches in an impossible unconsciousness of them, and then to look at them amazedly and exclaim, "But soft, what nymphs are these?" as if he could in any extremity of absence of mind have missed seeing them all along. Most of these absurdities are part of a systematic policy of sacrificing the credibility of the play to the chance of exhibiting an effective "living picture."

I very soon gave up the attempt to keep a record of the outrages practiced by Mr Daly on the text. Everyone knows the lines:

> I swear to thee by Cupid's strongest bow,
> By his best arrow with the golden head,
> By the simplicity of Venus' doves,
> By that which knitteth souls and prospers loves, etc.

Mr Daly's powerful mind perceived at a glance that the second and third lines are superfluous, as their omission does not destroy the sense of the passage. He accordingly omitted them. In the same scene, Shakespear makes the two star-crossed lovers speak in alternate lines with an effect which sets the whole scene throbbing with their absorption in one another:

> LYSANDER. The course of true love never did run smooth.
>   But either it was different in blood—
> HERMIA. O cross! too high to be enthralled to low!
> LYSANDER. Or else misgraffed in respect of years,
> HERMIA. O spite! too old to be engaged to young!
> LYSANDER. Or else it stood upon the choice of friends,
> HERMIA. O hell! to choose love by another's eye!
> LYSANDER. Or if there were a sympathy in choice,
>   War, death, or sickness did lay siege to it, etc.

With a Hermia who knew how to breathe out these parentheses, the duet would be an exquisite one; but Mr Daly, shocked, as an American and an Irishman, at a young lady using such an expression as "Oh hell!" cuts out the whole antiphony, and leaves Lysander to deliver a long lecture without interruption from the lady. At such moments, the episode of the ass's head rises to the dignity of allegory. From any other manager I should accept the excuse that the effects of verse for which I am pleading require a virtuosity of delivery on the part of the actor which is practically not to be had at present. But Mr Daly has Miss Rehan, who is specially famous for just this virtuosity of speech; and yet her lines are treated just as the others are. The fact is, beautiful elocution is rare because the managers have no ears.

The play, though of course very poorly spoken in comparison with how it ought to be spoken, is tolerably acted. Mr George Clarke, clad in the armor of Alcibiades and the red silk gown of Charley's Aunt, articulates most industriously, and waves his arms and flexes his wrists in strict accordance, not for a moment with the poetry, but with those laws of dramatic elocution and gesture which veteran actors are always willing to impart to novices at a reasonable price per dozen lessons. Mr Lewis as Bottom is not as funny as his part, whereas in modern plays he is always funnier than his part. He seemed to me to miss the stolid, obstinate, self-sufficient temperament of Bottom altogether. There is a definite conception of some particular sort of man at the back of all Shakespear's characters. The quantity of fun to be got out of Bottom and Autolycus, for instance, is about the same; but underneath the fun there are two widely different persons, of types still extant and familiar. Mr Lewis would be as funny in Autolycus as he is in Bottom; but he would be exactly the same man in both parts.

As to Miss Rehan, her scenes in the wood with Demetrius were very fine, although, in the passage where Hermia frightens her, she condescends to arrant clowning. Her treatment of Shakespearean verse is delightful after the mechanical intoning of Sarah Bernhardt. She gives us beauty of tone, grace of measure, delicacy of articulation: in short, all the technical qualities of verse music, along with the rich feeling and fine intelligence without which those technical qualities would soon become monotonous. When she is at her best, the music melts in the caress of the emotion it expresses, and thus completes the conditions necessary for obtaining Shakespear's effects in Shakespear's

way. When she is on the stage, the play asserts its full
charm; and when she is gone, and the stage carpenters and
the orchestra are doing their best to pull the entertainment
through in Mr Daly's way, down drops the whole affair
into mild tedium. But it is impossible to watch the most
recent developments of Miss Rehan's style without some
uneasiness. I wonder whether she is old enough to remember the late Barry Sullivan when he was still in his physical
prime. Those who do will recall, not an obsolete provincial
tragedian, trading on the wreck of an unaccountable reputation, but an actor who possessed in an extraordinary
degree just the imposing grace, the sensitive personal dignity of style, the force and self-reliance into which Miss
Rehan's style is settling. Miss Rehan's exit in the second
act of A Midsummer Night's Dream, with the couplet,

> I'll follow thee, and make a heaven of hell
> To die upon the hand I love so well,

is an exact reproduction of the Barry Sullivan exit. Again,
in the first act, when Miss Rehan, prone on a couch, raises
herself on her left hand, and, with her right raised "to
heaven," solemnly declaims the lines:

> For ere Demetrius look'd on Hermia's eyne
> He hailed down oaths, that he was only mine;
> And when this hail some heat from Hermia felt,
> So he dissolved, and showers of oaths did melt,

you are, once more, not forward with Duse, but back with
Barry Sullivan, who would in just the same way, when led
into it by a touch of stateliness and sonority in the lines,
abandon his part, and become for the moment a sort of
majestic incarnation of abstract solemnity and magnifi-
cence. His skill and intense belief in himself gave him the
dangerous power of doing so without making himself
ridiculous; and it was by this power, and by the fascination, the grace, and the force which are implied by it, that
he gave life to old-fashioned and mutilated representations
of Shakespear's plays, poorly acted and ignorantly
mounted. This was all very well whilst the fascination
lasted; but when his voice lost its tone, his figure its resili-
ence and grace, and his force its spontaneity and natural
dignity, there was nothing left but a mannered, elderly,
truculent, and, except to his old admirers, rather absurd
tragedian of the palmy school. As I was a small boy when

I first saw Barry Sullivan, and as I lost sight of him before his waning charm had quite vanished, I remember him, not as he is remembered by those who saw him only in the last ten years of his life, but as an actor who was in his day much further superior in pictorial, vocal, and rhetorical qualities to his next best rival than any actor or actress can easily be nowadays. And it strikes me forcibly that unless Miss Rehan takes to playing Imogen instead of such comparatively childish stuff as Julia or even Helena, and unless she throws herself into sympathy with the contemporary movement by identifying herself with characteristically modern parts of the Magda or Nora type, she may find herself left behind in the race by competitors of much less physical genius, just as Barry Sullivan did. Miss Rehan is clearly absolute mistress of the situation at Daly's Theatre: nobody can persuade me that if she says Cymbeline, Mr Daly can say The Two Gentlemen of Verona, or that if she says Sudermann or Ibsen, Mr Daly can insist on the author of Dollars and Cents. But the self-culture which has produced her superb graces of manner and diction seems to have isolated her instead of quickening her sympathy and drawing closer her contact with the world. Every woman who sees Duse play Magda feels that Duse is acting and speaking for her and for all women as they are hardly ever able to speak and act for themselves. The same may be said of Miss Achurch as Nora. But no woman has ever had the very faintest sensation of that kind about any part that Miss Rehan has yet played. We admire, not what she is doing, but the charm with which she does it. That sort of admiration will not last. Miss Rehan's voice is not henceforth going to grow fresher, nor her dignity less conscious, nor her grace of gesture less studied and mannered, nor her movements swifter and more spontaneous. Already I find that young people who see her for the first time cannot quite agree that our raptures about her Katharine and her Rosalind are borne out by her Julia and Helena. Five years hence she will be still more rhetorical and less real: further ahead I dare not look with Barry Sullivan in my mind. There is only one way to defy Time; and that is to have young ideas, which may always be trusted to find youthful and vivid expression. I am afraid this means avoiding the company of Mr Daly; but it is useless to blink the fact that unless a modern actress can and will force her manager, in

spite of his manly prejudices, to produce plays with real
women's parts in them, she had better, at all hazards, make
shift to manage for herself. With Grandfather Daly to
choose her plays for her, there is no future for Ada Rehan.

The Chili Widow

THE CHILI WIDOW. Adapted by Arthur Bourchier and Alfred
Sutro from Monsieur le Directeur, by MM. Bisson and
Carré. Royalty Theatre.

[12 *October* 1895]

On paying a somewhat belated visit to The Chili Widow
the other evening, I was astonished to find that Mr Bourchier has not only taken the Royalty Theatre—many have
done that before him, and some have repented it—but has
actually founded there, with apparent success, a new
school of stage art. At least it is new to the regular professional stage, though not to the country house or the
university dramatic club. It is the school of the romping,
gleeful amateur, not he with the contracted brow, the
Elizabethan imagination, and the patent method of voice
production, but the facetious undergraduate who dresses
up for a lark, the awfully jolly girl who can act like anything, and the funny man with accomplishments, including
the banjo. I am not intolerant of such sportiveness: the
majesty of criticism can unbend on occasion and enjoy a
bit of fun, served up with ridiculous home-made art, as
much as the humblest member of the domestic staff admitted to the drawing room to see the daughters of the
house in their stage glory. Even at the Royalty Theatre I
do not object to it: only, it is my duty to be perfectly
explicit with the public as to the nature of the entertainment. Let me therefore explain.

The accomplishments which distinguish the trained actor
from the amateur are not the same as the qualities which
distinguish great actors from ordinary ones. Take, first,
the difference between the trained actor and the man in the
street—the layman. When the layman walks, his only object is to get to Charing Cross; when he makes a gesture,
it is to attract the attention of a cab-driver or bus-conduc-
tor; when he speaks, it is to convey or demand information, or tell a lie, or otherwise further his prosaic ends;
when he moves his hands, it is to put up his umbrella or

take out his handkerchief. On the stage these merely utilitarian purposes are only simulated: the real purpose is to
produce an effect on the senses and imagination of the
spectator. The actor's walk is addressed to the spectator's
sense of grace, dignity, or strength of movement, and his
voice to the listener's sense of expressive or beautiful tone.
Impersonations even of ugly or deformed creatures with
harsh voices have the same artistic character, and are
agreeably disagreeable, just as the most extreme discords
in a symphony or opera are distinctly musical, and perfectly different to the random cacophonies which arise
from the tuning of the orchestra. Now, the power of complying with artistic conditions without being so preoccupied by them as to be incapable of thinking of anything
else is hard to acquire, and can be perfected only by long
practice. Talma estimated the apprenticeship at twenty
years. The habit can never become as instinctive as keeping one's balance, for instance, because failure in that for
even an instant means a fall, so that the practice in it is
lifelong and constant; whereas the artistic habit lapses
more or less in the absence of an audience, and even on
the stage can be forgotten for long periods without any
worse consequences than a loss of charm which nothing
may bring to the actor's attention. The real safeguard
against such lapses is a sense of beauty—the artistic sense
—cultivated to such a degree of sensitiveness that a coarse
or prosaic tone, or an awkward gesture, jars instantly on
the artist as a note out of tune jars on the musician. The
defect of the old-fashioned systems of training for the stage
was that they attempted to prescribe the conclusions of
this constantly evolving artistic sense instead of cultivating
it and leaving the artist to its guidance. Thus they taught
you an old-fashioned stage-walk, an old-fashioned stage-
voice, an old-fashioned stage way of kneeling, of sitting
down, of shaking hands, of picking up a handkerchief, and
so on, each of them supposed to be the final and perfect
way of doing it. The end of that was, of course, to dis-
credit training altogether. But neglect of training very
quickly discredits itself; and it will now perhaps be admitted that the awakening and culture of the artistic conscience is a real service which a teacher can render to an
actor. When that conscience is thoroughly awakened and
cultivated, when a person can maintain vigilant artistic
sensitiveness throughout a performance whilst making all

the movements required by the action of a drama, and
speaking all its dialogue graphically without preoccupation
or embarrassment, then that person is a technically competent artistic actor, able to play a part of which he hardly
comprehends one line, in a play of which he knows nothing except his own words and speeches and the cues
thereto, much more intelligibly and effectively, as well as
agreeably, than a statesman with ten times his general
ability could. He can only be beaten, in fact, by the professional rival who has equal skill in execution, but has
more numerous and valuable ideas to execute. The finest
actors—Jefferson, Coquelin, Salvini, Duse—carry this
technical skill to such a point that though they act so
beautifully that you cannot take your eyes off them even
when you do not understand what they are saying, yet the
beauty seems so spontaneous and inevitable that it is generally quite impossible to persuade their admirers that
there is any art or study in their acting at all.

The effect on an ordinary man of making him suddenly
conscious of the artistic aspect of his movements and
speech is to plunge him into a condition of terror and
bewilderment in which he forgets how to do anything. It
gives him stage fright, in short. Take a humble tradesman
who has demolished his boiled mutton and turnips for half
a century without misgiving. Invite him to meet a peer or
two at dinner in Grosvenor Square, and he will refuse
dish after dish because he no longer feels sure of how he
ought to eat it. Take a lady who habitually talks the heads
off all her acquaintances, and put her on a platform to
make the simplest statement to an audience, and she will
be struck dumb. The nervous agonies of the young have
caused more discomfort in the world than the torments of
the Inquisition. If this happens on the large stage of the
world to people who have all had at least some social
training, what must be the anguish of the wretch who, with
his face absurdly painted, and dressed in an outlandish
costume that does not fit him, is thrust on a stage for the
first time in his life to speak Elizabethan stage English
as Rosencrantz or Guildenstern, or even to stand as a
mute courtier and look on at some fellow creature making
the like horrible exhibition of himself!

All this, however, presupposes that the victim has an
artistic conscience, only just born and still blind. There
are plenty of people who have either no artistic conscience

at all or else one which is very easily satisfied. Just as you
have soldiers who are not frightened under fire because
they have not imagination enough to conceive their danger, whilst your imaginative Napoleon or Nelson turns
pale, and your serene Goethe sees yellow, so there are
debutters, both on the social and theatrical stage, who get
through their ordeal easily because they are only imper-
fectly conscious of it. And there are happy people whose
artistic conscience has always been awake, and to whom
sufficient conscious grace and beauty to begin with are
second nature. There is also the person with high animal
spirits, a strong sense of fun, and a turn for mimicry. He,
with an utterly unawakened artistic conscience, will flourish greatly at private theatricals, and sometimes also at
public ones. With a good ear for musical pitch and tune
and measure, and some physical agility, he will do excellently at the music-halls; but he very often has no ear to
speak of; and then, incapable of singing, dancing, fine
diction or graceful movement, he delights himself with
tomfoolery, and is hugely pleased with himself when the
people laugh. And since the people do laugh, there is a
constant tendency to substitute tomfoolery for artistic
comedy on the stage, since artistic comedians are in the
nature of things much scarcer than buffoons. Then it is
that the skilled critic must act as the watchdog of art, and
begin to bark vigorously. Unfortunately, he can only bark:
it is the manager who must bite. The artistic manager, as
distinguished from the man who merely takes a theatre
and puts up a play, is also a critic, and, knowing the difference between finished stage execution and mere larking,
picks and drills his company accordingly. That is how
theatres come to have styles as well as individuals.

The nature of my criticism of the Royalty performance
will now be intelligible. I do not deny that it is amusing
—sometimes; but I do most emphatically deny that the
performance, as a whole, has any artistic character. I go
further: I sorrowfully profess my conviction, based on an
attentive examination of the stage business, that the performers have been not only encouraged, but positively ordered, to clown as much as possible so as to keep the fun
going and make the play lively. The back drawing room
has never produced a company of comedians so intensely
and ostentatiously conscious of their own funniness.
Squawking voices, grinning faces, foolish antics, pervade

the play to such an extent that though, as I have admitted (very magnanimously, believe me), the second act amused me, yet I could not face the third, having lost my old robust schoolboy appetite for large doses of that sort of merriment. The jar on my nerves began in Harmony, a little play by Mr Henry Arthur Jones, one of his early pieces, in which you can plainly see the feeling, imagination, and humor of the future author of The Crusaders and Rebellious Susan, along with the stage asides and soliloquies of a cruder period. The gentleman who played the youthful lover in this nearly drove me out of my senses with his determination to be breezy and not to let the play down. His voice rattled and his figure bounded, until I gave up trying to imagine that I was looking at a scene in a primitive country parish, and fell to wondering what quality over and above a cheerful effrontery can be needed to make any able-bodied young gentleman into an actor in three weeks nowadays. Mr Kinghorne hardly improved matters by doing his business as the blind organist in the safest of old stage styles, piling it on and working it up tremendously, and never touching nature at any point. And Miss Ettie Williams, pretty, self-possessed, and resolutely metropolitan, gave the final blow to the illusion. But it was not until The Chili Widow came on that I began to suspect that breeziness, and rattle, and intense comic consciousness were parts of the managerial policy. Mr Bourchier seemed determined that there should be no mistake about our being there to make a regular evening of it; and it is possible that the profound depression into which this attitude naturally threw me—as I think it would any reasonable person—may have made me somewhat captious. At all events, I soon felt that I could willingly mow down the whole of that stage Home Office staff with a Maxim gun. It was not mere extravagance of caricature that annoyed me; for Mr Blakeley and Miss Larkin, who are hardened veterans in broad caricature, managed their business smoothly and easily, and at least did not play the part of the audience as well by laughing at their own performances; whilst Miss Phillips clowned only when a silly part absolutely forced her to, and made the most of the rest. What was wrong with the performance was its persistent Philistinism. It is fortunate for Mr Bourchier and for Miss Violet and Miss Irene Vanbrugh that they are such very pleasant people and that the play is such an amusing play. Mr Bourchier is a born comedian: he has ease, humor, geniality, and plenty of natural grace of speech and manner. Happy in these endowments, he insists on sharing the fun himself, and is evidently quite persuaded that if all the others will only rattle along in the same careless way, the result will be as pleasant in their case as in his. He enjoys himself so robustly that the audience cannot help feeling good-humored. The very thoughtlessness of his performance is an element in its popularity: one feels that a thoroughly healthy person never thinks. Miss Violet Vanbrugh is very attractive; but she is much more conscious of Miss Violet Vanbrugh than of her part: in other words, she lacks conviction. The fact is, she is not a comedian: all this man-killing archness does not belong to her: one sees that it is only her fun, not her nature; and the result is, not an artist at work, but a pretty lady at play, a spectacle always agreeable, but not to the purpose of the connoisseur in dramatic art. Miss Irene Vanbrugh has more genuine comic force, and is better fitted in her part; but as far as I saw the play she only appeared in the first act, which might with great advantage be cut out. Mr Kinghorne plays the office-keeper much more naturally than the organist in the first piece, and much more entertainingly. The others funnify their parts more or less blatantly, the whole ill-concerted attempt to produce a facetious atmosphere without any reference to the finer artistic conditions being, as I have said, discordant and amateurish. Even the audience struck me as a somewhat unsophisticated, not to say chuckleheaded one; but I am glad to be able to add that it was numerous and well pleased. It had the air of having at last discovered a play which was better fun than a smoking concert.

On a point of pronunciation may I be allowed to say that Ballymacklerush, with a strong stress on the rush, is a credible Irish name, but that Bally McKillrush, with the stress on the kill, is impossible. The only safe rule about the pronunciation of an Irish name is that whatever way comes naturally to an Englishman is quite certain to be the wrong way.

. . . .

Pinero as He Is Acted

THE BENEFIT OF THE DOUBT. A new and original comedy, in three acts. By Arthur W. Pinero. Comedy Theatre, 16 October 1895.

POOR MR POTTON. A new and original farce, in three acts. By Clarence Hamlyn and H. M. Paull. Vaudeville Theatre, 10 October 1895.

[19 *October* 1895]

This time Mr Pinero has succeeded. The Benefit of the Doubt is worth The Profligate, Mrs Tanqueray, and Mrs Ebbsmith rolled into one and multiplied by ten. It is melancholy to have to add that it has broken the back of our London stage, and may even fail through the sniffing monotony and dreary ugliness of the acting; but about the merit of the play there can be no question. Mr Pinero, concentrating himself on a phase of life and sentiment which he thoroughly understands, has extracted abundant drama from it, and maintained it at an astonishingly high and even pressure for two hours, without for a moment being driven back on the woman with a past, the cynical libertine peer, the angel of purity, the Cayley Drummle confidant, or any other of the conventional figures which inevitably appear in his plays whenever he conceives himself to be dealing as a sociologist with public questions of which he has no solid knowledge, but only a purely conventional and theatrical conceit. In The Benefit of the Doubt he keeps within the territory he has actually explored; and the result is at once apparent in the higher dramatic pressure, the closer-knit action, the substitution of a homogeneous slice of life for the old theatrical sandwich of sentiment and comic relief, and the comparative originality, naturalness, and free development of the characters. Even in the machinery by which the persons of the play are got on and off the stage there is a marked improvement. It is artificial enough—Mr Pinero has not exactly been born again—but at least there are no intercepted letters, or sendings of one set of people to France and another to India in order to enable a lady to arrive unexpectedly or a gentleman to walk in by night at the drawing room window. There certainly is one nocturnal visit through a window; but it is pardonable; and for the rest, the people come and go in

a normal and respectable manner. The play is of a frivolous widow with three fast, slangy, pretty daughters, two
of them married. An amiable young gentleman named
John Allingham, tormented by a frightfully jealous wife,
confides his miseries to one of the married daughters, a
Mrs Fraser (Fraser being much away from home). The
jealous Mrs Allingham sues for a judicial separation, and
the play opens at the point where her petition is refused.
Mrs Fraser, however, only escapes very narrowly, as the
Judge comments strongly on her indiscretion, and suggests
nothing more complimentary for her than "the benefit of
the doubt." When Mr Fraser comes home, he acts on this
suggestion so very grudgingly that Mrs Fraser rushes off to
throw herself upon the more sympathetic Allingham. But
that ill-starred example of the perils of excessive goodnature has meanwhile succumbed to his wife's appeal for
a reconciliation, she being nearly as violent in her remorse
as in her jealousy, and much less reasonable. There you
have your drama: first, in the suspense of awaiting the
verdict, ended by the return of Mrs Fraser from the
divorce court to face out her disgrace before her family
and be driven to desperation by the rebuff from her husband; and second, her arrival at Allingham's house just
as the demon of jealousy has been reinstalled there on the
domestic throne. In handling all this Mr Pinero is never
at a loss. He knows what pretty daughters and frivolous
mothers are like in those circles which used to be called
demi-mondaine before that distinction was audaciously
annexed by people who are not *mondaine* at all; he knows
what the divorce court and the newspapers mean to them;
he knows what a jealous woman is like; and he has dramatized them all with an intensity never attained by him
before. Consciously or unconsciously, he has this time
seen his world as it really is: that is, a world which never
dreams of bothering its little head with large questions or
general ideas. He no longer attempts to dress up Mrs
Ponsonby de Tomkins like Mrs Besant, and to present the
ridiculous result as a portrait of a typical modern "advanced" woman: he sticks to the Bayswater-Kensington
genre, of which he is a master. He does not even adul-
terate it with conventional stage sentiment: for instance,
none of Mrs Emptage's fast and rather raffish daughters
burst into tears at the thought of the holy purity of their
sixteenth year, when they could look angels in the face

unashamed, as Paula Tanqueray did. His early weaknesses
have disappeared along with his late affectations; and the
happy issue is the best serious play he has yet produced.

The subject of the acting is almost too painful to face.
The second act, which lasts for more than an hour, is pervaded by the violently jealous wife. She only leaves the
stage to give place to her wearied and desperate rival,
who ends by drinking champagne cup to save herself from
fainting, and, having fed on nothing all day but excitement, naturally gets tipsy and hysterical. Such scenes,
however moving and interesting they may be, and however skilfully written, can only be made tolerable by sheer
beauty of execution. Tact and experience—the best substitutes our unfortunate stage can offer—may do something to steer the performance clear of positive offensiveness; but tact and experience are not enough: unless the
lines are spoken by voices of which the ear never tires,
with gestures and action which never lose their fascination, the result can be no better than a disagreeable experience, drawing a crowd and holding it only as a street
accident does. The reason why the second act made the
audience uneasy was that long before the end of it we
had had enough, and more than enough, not of the play,
but of the performers. We all know the melodramatic
style which grew up in the days when actors who played
"emotional" parts habitually got themselves into the requisite maudlin condition by making themselves half drunk.
This was the true origin of the detestable veiled voice
and muzzy utterance which no longer produce any illusion
except that of the odor of spirits. The actor of the past did
not walk across the stage to open the door: he plunged
headlong at the handle, and, when he had safely grasped
it, rolled his eye round to give some pretence of dramatic
significance to an action which really expressed nothing
but his doubts as to his ability to walk straight. He hung
over the furniture, leant against the staircase, wallowed,
collapsed tragically when he sat down, did everything, in
short, to conceal his condition and cover up the absence
of that clear, sober, elegant speech and movement which
mark the self-possessed and accomplished artist. The old
drunken habits have nearly passed away—at least, I hope
future generations of critics will not often have to write
sympathetic obituary notices deploring the "breakdown in
health" of actors and actresses who notoriously drank

themselves first off the stage and then out of the world—
but the style of acting that arose in the days when everybody drank remains with us as a senseless superstition,
and is still laboriously acquired and cultivated by perfectly
sober actors. Unhappily for Mr Pinero's play, Mr Leonard
Boyne, who probably has no suspicion of the real origin
of the traditional style of which he has made himself, next
to Mr Charles Warner, the most popular exponent, played
John Allingham as he would have played an Adelphi or
Drury Lane hero. Miss Lily Hanbury, as the jealous Mrs
Allingham, soon proved the weakness of our system of
promoting young ladies to leading parts on the strength
of good looks and general intelligence and address. Miss
Hanbury acted as acting is understood on the London
stage. That is, she expressed emotion by catching the left
side of her under lip between her front teeth, and twisting
the right corner as much out of its natural place as possible. She cried, and declared that she was "bad," meaning
that she was mad. Her voice, which careful cultivation
might by this time have made a very agreeable one, still
has all its girlish, nasal character. Five minutes of Mr
Boyne and Miss Hanbury, doing some light and pleasant
work in an ordinary play, would leave the impression that
they were charming and clever people, and encourage our
fatuous satisfaction with the most incompetent profession
in the world; but half an hour of them—such a half-hour
as Mr Pinero has set them—may I never spend such another! They did their best; but they were hopelessly over-
parted. As to Miss Winifred Emery, she received boundless
applause, but as it burst out in all its enthusiasm in the
first act, before she had uttered a word or made a gesture,
it may safely be discounted. All the same, Miss Emery
played astonishingly well, considering that she is virtually
a beginner at work so difficult as that cut out for her by
Mr Pinero. She was, of course, powerfully aided by her
natural charm, and by the confidence in it which experience
has given her. The champagne scene and the passages of
querulous lassitude were frankly realistic; and I rather
doubt whether a less pretty and popular lady dare have
treated them so without greater art to help her. Even as it
was, Miss Emery sometimes lost her style and allowed
her intonation to become decidedly disagreeable. But for
the most part, and especially in the first act, she got far
beyond any point I have seen her reach before, and, in-

deed, beyond any point that is commonly reached by our
London "leading ladies." She evidently only wants plenty
of that sort of work to make her, within the limits of her
temperament, a highly accomplished actress.

Miss Rose Leclerq, not this time condemned to play
the usual caricature of herself, had a real part, and played
it with real distinction. The other parts are of the usual
type; that is to say, they require a certain professional
habit for their effective presentation, but involve little
knowledge of the art of acting. The best of them are in the
hands of Miss Esme Beringer, Mr Cyril Maude, and Mr
Aubrey Fitzgerald. Mr Pinero, always a bad hand at casting a play, has not fitted Miss Beringer very happily—
more's the pity, as she is one of the few young actresses
now on the stage who have studied their profession, or
even realized that there is anything to study in it.

Poor Mr Potton, at the Vaudeville, is called a farce,
even a new and original farce; but it is hardly more than
a romp. However, it is tolerably good fun of its kind,
childish fun mostly as regards the action, clever fun occasionally as regards the lines. The scenes, especially the
last act, are not at all ill-planned: there is a certain incongruity between the jejune flimsiness of the general
notion of the play and the comparative solidity and intelligence with which it is put together. Probably this is a
natural consequence of the collaboration between Mr
Clarence Hamlyn and Mr Paull. From the critical point of
view the play is chiefly interesting as an example of the
extent to which brutality and silliness are still in demand
in our theatres, just as the performance is an example of
the impudent artlessness with which long scenes can be
gabbled through on the London stage without provoking
as much criticism as a company of children performing
in a nursery would receive from their parents. The brutality is, of course, unconscious, though that is an excellent
reason for a critical attempt to induce some consciousness
of it. The fun of the play lies in the engagement of Mr
Potton (Mr Weedon Grossmith) to an elderly and several
times widowed heroine (Miss Gladys Homfrey). Miss
Gladys Homfrey is a lady of very ample proportions. I
shall not attempt to estimate the excess of her weight over
that of Mr Weedon Grossmith with precision; let me put
it roughly and safely at not less than fifty pounds. Need
I add that the main joke in Poor Mr Potton is the spectacle

of Miss Homfrey throwing herself ponderously on Mr
Grossmith's neck, and being petted and kissed and courted
by him. I am obliged to make the strange confession that
I do not enjoy this sort of stage effect; though I admit
that the guffaws which it invariably elicits shew that London audiences do not agree with me. Mr Gilbert quite
understood his public when he furnished his operas so
carefully with stout and mature ladies for the express
purpose of making fun of their age and figure. Such fun
has always revolted me; and I am waiting for the time
when it will revolt the public too. I have by me a book
called The Elizabethan Hamlet, by Mr John Corbin, published by Mr Elkin Mathews, in which the author succeeds
in fully driving home the fact, not of course hitherto unknown, but certainly hitherto underestimated, that Hamlet
first became popular on the stage as a madman: that is, as
a comic person according to the ideas of that time. I say
of that time as a matter of politeness to my contemporaries, though anyone who has ever seen a village idiot at
large must have seen also a crowd of villagers teasing him,
encouraging him to make uncouth sounds and cut deplorable capers, and laughing at him with gross enjoyment as
at one of Nature's primest jokes. It has always been so, I
am afraid. The old-fashioned king's jester was not a clever,
satirical, able person like Dumas's Chicot: he was a zany,
a poor idiot, a butt, not a wit. Fortunately we have at last
reached a point at which the old Hamlet play is out of the
question, whilst the masterpiece which Shakespear built
on it is the most popular play we have. But is there any
distinction, except in degree of atrocity, between the old
brutal laughter at "Hamblet's" madness and murderous
cunning, and our laughter today at the Lady Janes of Mr
Gilbert, and at certain comedians and music-hall artists
who are commercially fortunate enough to be abnormally
small or grotesque in appearance? And if Shakespear, in a
much coarser age, could take subjects which were reeking
with the vilest stage traditions, and lift them at one stroke
to the highest tragic dignity, is it too much to ask that our
modern dramatists should habitually assume that "the
British public" consists of humane persons with developed
sympathies, and not of rowdy undergraduates and street
arabs? I presume that Miss Gladys Homfrey has an honorable ambition to distinguish herself in the art of acting,
as Mrs Stirling and Mrs Gilbert have distinguished them-

selves. Why then should she be condemned to merely
exhibit herself as a fat lady? I am not pretending to ignore
the fact that personality is an element in the qualification
of an actor or actress as well as skill, and that our stage
affords so little training that practical dramatic authorship
has become the art of exploiting the personalities of popular favorites instead of setting tasks to the executive skill
of accomplished artists. If a young author were to come
to me and announce his intention of striving to win fame
by creating an imaginary heroine who should survive mil-
lions of real women as Imogen and Gretchen have, I
should, in the paternal character of a man of the world,
immediately reply, "Bless your innocence, you mustnt do
that. You must vamp up a serious part that will fit Mrs
Patrick Campbell, and a serio-comic part that will fit Miss
Fanny Brough, bearing carefully in mind that neither of
these ladies ever acts anybody but herself, nor indeed dare
do it, since the public goes to the theatre to see them playing themselves and not to enjoy dramatic poetry or fine
acting." Still, there are limits even to the compulsory
cynicism of dramatic authorship. The author may be
forced to exploit a lady's temperament and appearance because she cannot act; but he need not condescend to exploit her circumference. Characters like Falstaff are not
added to dramatic literature by any process so cheap as
making game of the stoutest member of the profession.

Two parts in Poor Mr Potton are well played. Mr
Weedon Grossmith succeeds in making Potton perfectly
real, and quite a different person from the other characters of his creation. His perplexed conviction, the apparent
unconsciousness with which he allows his funniest points
to make themselves, the art with which he takes care that
they shall make themselves, and the adroitness of his
execution, leave nothing for the critic to say except that
the part is as well done as it can be done. Miss Haydon,
as Mrs Potton, makes a charming old lady, preserving her
own dignity and that of her art, as well as the verisimilitude of the play, without losing a scrap of comic effect. I
will not say that none of the rest were amusing; but they
certainly were often quite as annoying as amusing, gab-
bling and guying as if the play were being performed for
their entertainment much more than for that of the audience. Accustomed as I am becoming to see important
parts given to clowning novices and to young women

whose flippant personal vanity, bad manners, vulgarly titivated costumes, and slipshod carelessness of speech and action would not be tolerated from a parlormaid by the people who are expected to pay half a guinea for a seat at the theatre, it hardly now seems worth while to complain of an outrage more or less in this direction. The Vaudeville company, apart from Mr Grossmith and Miss Haydon, is neither better nor worse than I expected to find it. The exceptions were Miss Beet, who gave a capital sketch of an irritable general servant, and Mr Tom Terriss, whose father has endowed him handsomely with an admirable voice and an attractive figure and face, disinheriting him only in the matter of his chin, which is a comparatively unfamiliar feature. If Mr Terriss's part was not a very exacting one, he at least got a thorough grip of it, and would have pleased the audience even if his name had been an unknown one.

The Case for the Critic-Dramatist

· · · · ·

[16 *November* 1895]

A discussion has arisen recently as to whether a dramatic critic can also be a dramatic author without injury to his integrity and impartiality. The feebleness with which the point has been debated may be guessed from the fact that the favorite opinion seems to be that a critic is either an honest man or he is not. If honest, then dramatic authorship can make no difference to him. If not, he will be dishonest whether he writes plays or not. This childish evasion cannot, for the honor of the craft, be allowed to stand. If I wanted to ascertain the melting-point of a certain metal, and how far it would be altered by an alloy of some other metal, and an expert were to tell me that a metal is either fusible or it is not—that if not, no temperature will melt it; and if so, it will melt anyhow—I am afraid I should ask that expert whether he was a fool himself or took me for one. Absolute honesty is as absurd an abstraction as absolute temperature or absolute value. A dramatic critic who would die rather than read an American pirated edition of a copyrighted English book might be considered an absolutely honest man for all practical purposes on that particular subject—I say on that one, because very few men have more than one point of honor; but as far as I am aware, no such dramatic critic exists. If he did, I should regard him as a highly dangerous monomaniac. That honesty varies inversely with temptation is proved by the fact that every additional penny on the income-tax yields a less return than the penny before it, shewing that men state their incomes less honestly for the purposes of taxation at sevenpence in the pound than sixpence. The matter may be tested by a simple experiment. Go to one of the gentlemen whose theory is that a man is either honest or he is not, and obtain from him the loan of half a crown on some plausible pretext of a lost purse or some such petty emergency. He will not ask you for a written acknowledgment of the debt. Return next day and ask for a loan of £500 without a promissory note, on the ground that you are either honest or not honest, and that a man who will pay back half a crown without compulsion will also pay back £500. You will find that the theory of absolute honesty will collapse at once.

Are we then to believe that the critic-dramatist who stands to make anything from five hundred to ten thousand pounds by persuading a manager to produce his plays, will be prevented by his honesty from writing about that manager otherwise than he would if he had never written a play and were quite certain that he never should write one? I can only say that people who believe such a thing would believe anything. I am myself a particularly flagrant example of the critic-dramatist. It is not with me a mere case of an adaptation or two raked up against me as incidents in my past. I have written half a dozen "original" plays, four of which have never been performed; and I shall presently write half a dozen more. The production of one of them, even if it attained the merest success of esteem, would be more remunerative to me than a couple of years of criticism. Clearly, since I am no honester than other people, I should be the most corrupt flatterer in London if there were nothing but honesty to restrain me. How is it, then, that the most severe criticisms of managers come from me and from my fellow critic-dramatists, and that the most servile puffery comes from writers whose every sentence proves that they have nothing to hope or fear from any manager? There are a good many answers to this question, one of the most obvious being that as the respect inspired by a good criticism is permanent, whilst the irritation it causes is temporary, and as, on the other hand, the pleasure given by a venal criticism is temporary and the contempt it inspires permanent, no man really secures his advancement as a dramatist by making himself despised as a critic. The thing has been tried extensively during the last twenty years; and it has failed. For example, the late Frank Marshall, a dramatist and an extravagantly enthusiastic admirer of Sir Henry Irving's genius, followed a fashion which at one time made the Lyceum Theatre a sort of court formed by a retinue of literary gentlemen. I need not question either their sincerity or the superiority of Canute to their idolatry; for Canute never produced their plays: Robert Emmett and the rest of their masterpieces remain unacted to this day. It may be said that this brings us back to honesty as the best policy; but honesty has nothing to do with it: plenty of the men who know that they can get along faster fighting than crawling, are no more honest than the first Napoleon was. No virtue, least of all courage, implies any other virtue. The cardinal guarantee for a critic's integrity is simply the force of the critical instinct itself. To try to prevent me from criticizing by pointing out to me the superior pecuniary advantages of puffing is like trying to keep a young Irving from going on the stage by pointing out the superior pecuniary advantages of stockbroking. If my own father were an actor-manager, and his life depended on his getting favorable notices of his performance, I should orphan myself without an instant's hesitation if he acted badly. I am by no means the willing victim of this instinct. I am keenly susceptible to contrary influences—to flattery, which I swallow greedily if the quality is sufficiently good; to the need of money, to private friendship or even acquaintanceship, to the pleasure of giving pleasure and the pain of giving pain, to consideration for people's circumstances and prospects, to personal likes and dislikes, to sentimentality, pity, chivalry, pugnacity and mischief, laziness and cowardice, and a dozen other human conditions which make the critic vulnerable; but the critical instinct gets the better of them all. I spare no effort to mitigate its inhumanity, trying to detect and strike out of my articles anything that would give pain without doing any good. Those who think the things I say severe, or even malicious, should just see the things I do *not* say.

I do my best to be partial, to hit out at remediable abuses
rather than at accidental shortcomings, and at strong and
responsible people rather than weak and helpless ones.
And yet all my efforts do not alter the result very much.
So stubborn is the critic within me, that with every disposition to be as goodnatured and as popular an authority as
the worst enemy of art could desire, I am to all intents and
purposes incorruptible. And that is how the dramatist-
critic, if only he is critic enough, "slates" the actor-manager in defiance of the interest he has in conciliating him.
He cannot help himself, any more than the ancient mariner could help telling his story. And the actor-manager
can no more help listening than the wedding guest could.
In short, the better formula would have been, that a man
is either a critic or not a critic; that to the extent to which
he is one he will criticize the managers in spite of heaven
or earth; and that to the extent to which he is not, he will
flatter them anyhow, to save himself trouble.

The advantage of having a play criticized by a critic
who is also a playwright is as obvious as the advantage of
having a ship criticized by a critic who is also a master
shipwright. Pray observe that I do not speak of the criticism of dramas and ships by dramatists and shipwrights
who are not also critics; for that would be no more convincing than the criticism of acting by actors. Dramatic
authorship no more constitutes a man a critic than actor-
ship constitutes him a dramatic author; but a dramatic critic
learns as much from having been a dramatic author as
Shakespear or Mr Pinero from having been actors. The
average London critic, for want of practical experience,
has no real confidence in himself: he is always searching
for an imaginary "right" opinion, with which he never
dares to identify his own. Consequently every public
man finds that as far as the press is concerned his career
divides itself into two parts: the first, during which the
critics are afraid to praise him; and the second, during
which they are afraid to do anything else. In the first, the
critic is uncomfortably trying to find faults enough to
make out a case for his timid coldness: in the second, he
is eagerly picking out excellences to justify his eulogies.
And of course he blunders equally in both phases. The
faults he finds are either inessential or are positive re-
forms, or he blames the wrong people for them: the
triumphs of acting which he announces are stage tricks

that any old hand could play. In criticizing actresses he is an open and shameless voluptuary. If a woman is pretty, well dressed, and self-satisfied enough to be at her ease on the stage, he is delighted; and if she is a walking monument of handsome incompetence, so much the better, as your voluptuary rarely likes a woman to be cleverer than himself, or to force him to feel deeply and think energetically when he only wants to wallow in her good looks. Confront him with an actress who will not condescend to attack him on this side—who takes her work with thorough seriousness and self-respect—and his resentment, his humiliation, his sense of being snubbed, break out ludicrously in his writing, even when he dare not write otherwise than favorably. A great deal of this nonsense would be taken out of him if he could only write a play and have it produced. No dramatist begins by writing plays merely as excuses for the exhibition of pretty women on the stage. He comes to that ultimately perhaps; but at first he does his best to create real characters and make them pass through three acts of real experiences. Bring a critic who has done this face to face with the practical question of selecting an actress for his heroine, and he suddenly realizes for the first time that there is not such a galaxy of talent on the London stage as he thought, and that the handsome walking ladies whom he always thought good enough for other people's plays are not good enough for his own. That is already an immense step in his education. There are other steps, too, which he will have taken before the curtain falls on the first public representation of his play; but they may be summed up in the fact that the author of a play is the only person who really wants to have it well done in every respect, and who therefore has every drawback brought fully home to him. The man who has had that awakening about one play will thenceforth have his eyes open at all other plays; and there you have at once the first moral with the first technical qualification of the critic—the determination to have every play as well done as possible, and the knowledge of what is standing in the way of that consummation. Those of our critics who, either as original dramatists or adapters and translators, have superintended the production of plays with paternal anxiety, are never guilty of the wittily disguised indifference of clever critics who have never seen a drama through from its first beginnings behind the scenes. Compare the

genuine excitement of Mr Clement Scott, or the almost
Calvinistic seriousness of Mr William Archer, with the
gaily easy what-does-it-matterness of Mr Walkley, and
you see at once how the two critic-dramatists influence the
drama, whilst the critic-playgoer only makes it a pretext
for entertaining his readers. On the whole there is only as
much validity in the theory that a critic should not be a
dramatist, as in the theory that a judge should not be a
lawyer nor a general a soldier. You cannot have qualifications without experience; and you cannot have experience
without personal interest and bias. That may not be an
ideal arrangement; but it is the way the world is built;
and we must make the best of it.

. . . .

Manxsome and Traditional

THE MANXMAN. In four acts. Adapted from Hall Caine's
celebrated novel. Shaftesbury Theatre, 18 November 1895.

. . . . . .

[23 *November* 1895]
In the bill The Manxman is described as "adapted from
HALL CAINE'S celebrated novel." Who is Hall Caine?
How did he become celebrated? At what period did he
flourish? Are there any other Manx authors of his calibre?
If there are, the matter will soon become serious; for if
that gift of intolerably copious and intolerably common
imagination is a national characteristic in the Isle of Man,
it will swamp the stage with Manx melodramas the moment the islanders pick up the trick of writing for the
stage.

Whether the speeches in The Manxman are interpolated
Wilson Barrett or aboriginal Hall Caine I cannot say, as I
have not read the celebrated novel, and am prepared to
go to the stake rather than face the least chapter of it. But
if they correctly represent the colloquial habits of the
island, the Manx race are without a vernacular, and only
communicate with one another by extracts from Cassell's
National Library, the Chandos Classics, and the like. In
the Isle of Man you do not use the word "always": you
say "Come weal come woe, come life come death." The
most useful phrases for the tourist are "Dust and ashes,
dust and ashes," "Dead sea fruit," "The lone watches of

the night," "What a hell is conscience!" "The storm clouds
are descending and the tempest is at hand," and so on.
The Manx do not speak of a little baby, but of a baby
"fresh from God." Their philosophy is that "love is best
—is everything—is the cream of life—better than worldly
success"; and they conceive woman—or, as they probably
call her, "the fair sex"—as a creature "giving herself body
and soul, and never thinking what she gets by it. Thats
the glory of Woman!" And the Manx woman rather deserves this. Her idea of pleasantry is to sit on a plank
over a stream dangling her legs; to call her young swain's
attention to her reflection in the water; and then, lest he
should miss the coquetry of the exhibition, to cut off the
reflected view of her knees by wrapping her skirt round
her ankles in a paroxysm of affected bashfulness. And
when she sprains her ankle, and the gentleman tenders
some surgical aid, she requests him to turn his head the
other way. In short, the keynote of your perfect Manxman is tawdry vulgarity aping the heroic, the hearty, the
primevally passionate, and sometimes, though here the
show of vigor in the affectation tumbles into lame ineptitude, the gallant and humorous.

Even when I put my personal distaste for The Manxman
as far as possible on one side, I cannot persuade myself
that it is likely to live very long, although no device is
spared to move the audience, from a cascade of real water
to a poor little baby, which is exploited as shamelessly
as if it had been let out on hire to an organ-grinder or a
beggar. Thirty years hence, no doubt, we shall have some
newly risen star telling the interviewers of a first appearance as the baby in The Manxman; but that interesting
possibility cannot reconcile me to the meanness of such
ways of fishing for sympathy. In the great Doll's House
itself, where children are introduced with so serious a
purpose that no one can have any sense of their being
unworthily used, I always feel that I should prefer the
baby to be an amateur. At the Shaftesbury melodrama,
where there was no serious purpose, but only an ostenta-
tious cradling and cuddling and dandling and bless-its-
little-hearting in order to work up the greatest possible
quantity of sentiment on the cheapest possible terms, I felt
thoroughly ashamed of the business. What with the real
water, the infant, and the well-worn incident of the fond
and simple-hearted husband returning home to find his

wife gone, the drama passes the time tolerably up to the
end of the second act. The rest of it is as null and dull as
the most cautious manager could desire. The third act is
nothing but a "front scene" bulked out to fill up the
evening; and the fourth act, with its offensively noisy
street music, does not produce a moment's illusion. The
play, originally designed for an actor-manager who played
Quilliam, has evidently been a good deal botched in alter-
ing it to fit another actor-manager who plays Christian;
but it never can have been a good play, because it is not
really a drama at all, but an acted narrative. Any competent playwright could make the third act effectively dramatic if only he were released from all obligation to
consult "the celebrated novel." As it is, it is a chapter in
a story, not an act in a drama.

As to the acting, most of the sixteen parts are so in-
definite in spite of their portentous names—Black Tom,
Ross Christian, Jemmy y Lord, and so on—that there is
nothing to act in them. Mr Cockburn is just the man for
Pete Quilliam, a rather fortunate circumstance for him,
as there is little art and no husbandry in his acting, though
his natural equipment is first-rate of its kind. Miss Kate
Phillips, with much greater skill, divided the honors with
him. There were no other personal successes. Mr Fernandez, in one of those characters which the celebrated
Hall Caine apparently copies very vilely from Sir Walter
Scott, mouthed texts of Scripture in a manner which
exposed him to the most serious risk of being described
as "a sound actor." Professional methods were also illustrated by Mr Hamilton Knight as the Manxsome governor.
He, having to leave the stage with the innocent words,
"Come and see us as soon as you can," shewed us how
the experienced hand can manufacture an effective exit.
He went to the door with the words "Come and see us as
soon." Then he nerved himself; opened the door; turned
dauntlessly; and with raised voice and sparkling eyes
hurled the significant words "as you can" in the teeth of
the gallery. Naturally we were all struck with admiration,
because it was just the thing that none of us would have
thought of or known how to do.

Mr Lewis Waller managed to get a moment of real
acting into the end of the first act, and then relapsed into
nonsensical solemnity for the rest of the evening. I do not
know what he was thinking of; but it can hardly have

been of the play. He delivered his lines with the automatic
gravity of a Brompton Cemetery clergyman repeating the
burial service for the thousandth time. He uttered endless
strings of syllables; but he did not divide them into words,
much less phrases. "IcannotIwillnotlistentothisIwonthear-
ofit," was the sort of thing he inflicted on us for three
mortal acts. As to Miss Florence West, if she persists in
using her privilege as the manager's wife to play melodramatic heroines, she will ruin the enterprise. Some years'
hard and continuous work might make her an accomplished performer in artificial comedy or in the Sardou-
Bernhardt line of sensational drama. At present she is
obviously a highly civilized modern London lady, whose
natural attitude towards melodramatic sentiment is one of
supercilious incredulity. There is about as much sense in
casting her for Kate Cregeen as there would be in casting
Mr Waller himself for Tony Lumpkin.

Told You So

MRS PONDERBURY'S PAST. A farcical comedy in three acts,
adapted by F. C. Burnand from Madame Mongodin. By
Ernest Blum and Raoul Toche.
A DANGEROUS RUFFIAN. Comedy in one act. By W. D.
Howells. Avenue Theatre.

[7 *December* 1895]

No truly magnanimous soul ever indulges in the mean
triumph of "I told you so." Exhibitions of magnanimity,
however, are not the business of a critic any more than
of a general in the field: for both alike the pursuit is as
important as the victory, though it may be a barbarous,
murderous, demoralizing cavalry business of cutting down
helpless fugitives. It was Lessing, the most eminent of
dramatic critics (so I am told by persons who have read
him), who was reproached by Heine for not only cutting
off his victims' heads but holding them up afterwards to
shew that there were no brains in them. The critical profession, in fact, is cruel in its nature, and demands for its
efficient discharge an inhuman person like myself. Therefore nobody need be surprised if I raise an exultant and
derisive laugh at the clouds of defeat, disappointment,
failure, perhaps ruin, which overhang the theatre at present. Where is your Manxman now, with his hired baby

and his real water? Has the desperate expedient of fitting
Her Advocate with a new act and a new hero saved it
from destruction? What of the adipose humors of Poor
Mr Potton?—do its authors still believe that the cheaper
the article the wider the consumption; or are they mourning with Mr Jerome K. Jerome and Mr Willard over the
ingratitude of an imaginary public of idiots to whose level
they have condescended in vain? I am not, I hope, an
exacting critic: I have been reproached from my own side
for approving of Miss Brown and disapproving of Mrs
Ebbsmith; and although I should have advised, and been
right in advising, Mr Lewis Waller to produce Ibsen's
hitherto unacted and impossible Emperor or Galilean
rather than The Manxman, since it would have secured
him at least a fortnight's business, not to mention a lifetime of artistic credit, yet something as enjoyable as The
Passport or The Prude's Progress would have quite satisfied me. I graciously tolerated these plays; and they
flourished: I frowned on the others; and they withered
from the stage. In this I acted as most sages do, making
an easy guess at what was going to happen, and taking
care to prophesy it. Dick Hallward, Her Advocate, and
The Manxman were nothing but lame attempts to compete
with the conventicle by exploiting the rooted love of the
public for moralizing and homiletics. Nobody, I hope, will
at this time of day raise a senseless braying against preaching in the theatre. The work of insisting that the church is
the house of God and the theatre the house of Satan may
be left to those poor North Sea islanders who have been
brought up to believe that it is wrong to enter a playhouse.
The theatre is really the week-day church; and a good play
is essentially identical with a church service as a combination of artistic ritual, profession of faith, and sermon.
Wherever the theatre is alive, there the church is alive
also: Italy, with its huge, magnificent, empty churches, and
slovenly, insincere services, has also its huge, magnificent,
empty theatres, with slovenly insincere plays. The countries which we call Scandinavian (to the exasperation of
all true Norwegians, somehow) produce saints and preach-
ers, dramatists and actors, who influence all Europe. The
fundamental unity of Church and Theatre—a necessary
corollary of the orthodox doctrine of omnipresence—is
actually celebrated on the stage in such dramas as Brand,
and in the Parsifal performance at Bayreuth, which is

nothing less than the Communion presented in theatrical
instead of ecclesiastical form. Indeed, the matter comes
out in a simpler way. Some time ago I had occasion to
deliver a public address on the Problems of Poverty in
Bristol. Following the custom of those who understand
such problems, I put up at the most expensive hotel in the
town, where I arrived the night before that appointed for
my own performance. After dinner I went into the hall of
the hotel to study the theatrical announcements exhibited
for the convenience of playgoing visitors. There, among
bills of pantomimes and melodramas, I found, in carved
wooden frames of "ecclesiastical" gothic design, and with
capital letters suggestive of the ten commandments, the
announcements of the churches, with the hours of service,
and details of the musical arrangements, as to which
"special attention" was guaranteed. Leaving all theological
and sectarian considerations out of account, I have no
doubt whatever that the Bristol churchgoer has a better
time of it in point of comfort, decency, cheapness, music,
interest, edification, rest and recreation than the Bristol
playgoer. I sometimes believe that our playgoers in London are simply stupid people who have not found out those
great "draws," the services in St Paul's and Westminster
Abbey. Certainly, when I recall some of the evening
services I have attended in cathedrals, and compare them
with the dull drudgery of sitting out The Manxman, even
in a complimentary stall (what must it be in the shilling
gallery?) I begin to understand why it is that only the
weaklings, the sentimentalists, the unbusinesslike people
go to the theatre, whilst the solid, acquisitive, industrious,
safely selfish Englishman who *will* have the best value for
his money, sticks to the church.

In the face of these facts it cannot be pretended that
either our late experiments in melodrama or any other
enterprises of the kind in England have ever failed through
preaching and sermonizing. The British public likes a
sermon, and resents an exhibition of human nature. If you
bring on the stage the Englishman who lives in a single-
room tenement, as many Englishmen do, and who beats
his wife, as all Englishmen do under such circumstances
except when their wives beat them, you will be denounced
as the author of "a problem play." If you substitute an
actor-preacher who declares that "the man who would
lift his hand to a woman save in the way of kindness,

etc.," it will be admitted on all hands that your feelings do you credit. Your popular Adelphi actor may lack every qualification save one—pious unction. And his most popular act is contrite confession, just as the most popular "evangelist" is the converted collier or prizefighter, who can delight his hearers with the atrocities he committed before his second birth, whilst sanctifying the wicked story with penitent tears and sighs of gratitude for his redemption. I have followed the revivalist preacher through many an incarnation; and now he cannot elude my recognition by merely taking refuge in a theatre. In vain does he mount the stage in a barrister's wig and gown and call his familiar emotional display acting. I am not to be deceived: in his struggles with his mock passion for the leading lady I recognize the old wrestle with the devil: in his muddy joy and relief at having won a verdict of acquittal for her I detect the rapture of the sinner saved. I see him at a glance in Dick Hallward, in Pete Quilliam, in Governor Christian. Mr Cartwright, well schooled at the Adelphi, has his trick to the life; Mr Willard spoils him by trying to act; Mr Lewis Waller utterly destroys him by treating him in the High Church manner; but, spoiled or unspoiled, there he is, all over the stage; and there, too, in the auditorium, is the hysterical groan and sniff which passes with simple souls as evidence of grace abounding. Why, then, has he been so unsuccessful of late? The answer is easy: he has failed to carry conviction. The congregation has said to itself, "This is not Spurgeon, it is Stiggins; and his lying lips are an abomination. The whole thing is put on to make money out of us. Does he take us for fools, with his babies and cradles, his policemen and criminal trials, his bottles of poison and slow music?" That attitude is fatal. Any gospel or anti-gospel will succeed as long as the author and the audience are making for the same end, whether by affirmation and praise, or by satire and negation. But when an author is openly insulting his patrons in the gallery by flattering their conscious hypocrisy, and complimenting them on what he conceives to be their weaknesses and superstitions, and what they themselves equally conceive to be their weaknesses and superstitions, he is predestined to damnation. To be publicly and obviously played down to is more than human nature can bear.

The New Boy and The Strange Adventures of Miss

Brown, on the other hand, are genuine appeals to our sense
of fun. The authors frankly do their best to tickle us; and
we are under no obligation to laugh if they fail, as we
are to say Amen to the hypocrisies of the melodramatist.
When they do not fail, they prove that they possess some
humorous faculty, however schoolboyish it may be; and
they seldom pretend to anything more. The danger of the
Miss Brown business is that it leads actor-managers—Mr
Kerr, for instance, if I may judge from a report of his
speech at the Playgoers' Club—into the wild error that
people want to be amused and pleased, and go to the
theatre with that object. As a matter of fact, they want
nothing of the sort. They want to be excited, and upset,
and made miserable, to have their flesh set creeping, to
gloat and quake over scenes of misfortune, injustice,
violence, and cruelty, with the discomfiture and punishment of somebody to make the ending "happy." The only
sort of horror they dislike is the horror that they cannot
fasten on some individual whom they can hate, dread, and
finally torture after revelling in his crimes. For instance,
if Ibsen were to rewrite Ghosts, and make Mrs Alving
murder her husband, flog Regina, burn down the orphanage purposely, and be killed with a hatchet by Engstrand
just a moment too late to save Oswald from filially taking
her guilt on himself and then, after drinking poison to
escape the scaffold, dying to slow music in the act of being
united to Regina by Pastor Manders, the play would have
an immense vogue, and be declared full of power and pity.
Ibsen, being apparently of opinion that there is quite
enough horror in the ordinary routine of respectable life
without piling Pelion on Ossa, sends away his audience
with their thirst for blood and revenge unsatisfied and
their self-complacency deeply wounded. Hence their mur-
murs against him. What is the secret of the overwhelming
reputation of Edmund Kean among the English actors of
this century? Hazlitt reveals it thus: "Mr Kean's imagination appears not to have the principles of joy or hope or
love in it. He seems chiefly sensible to pain or to the passions that spring from it, and to the terrible energies of
mind or body which are necessary to grapple with it." I
know that some of our theatrical experts believe that the
truly popular trait for a stage hero nowadays is the sort
of maudlin goodnature that is an essential part of the
worthlessness of the average Strand bar-loafer. But I

have never seen much evidence in favor of this idea; and my faith in it is not increased by the entire concurrence of the public in my view of Dick Hallward and the barrister in Her Advocate. What the public likes is a villain to torment and persecute the heroine, and a hero to thrash and baffle the villain. Not that it matters much, since what the public likes is entirely beside the question of what it can get. When the popular tribune demands "good words" from Coriolanus, he replies, "He that will give good words to thee will flatter beneath abhorring"; and no great play can ever be written by a man who will allow the public to dictate to him. Even if the public really knew what it likes and what it dislikes—a consummation of wisdom which it is as far from as any child—the true master-dramatist would still give it, not what it likes, but what is good for it.

This brings me to the announcement of the last nights of The Benefit of the Doubt. A run of two months, though not brilliant in comparison with that of Charley's Aunt, is not bad for an entirely serious work of art, especially when it is considered that some of the most important parts are so badly acted that I had to point out after the first night that they might possibly lead to the failure of the piece. The sympathetic part of the play is original and unconventional, so that the sympathy does not flow in the old ready-made channels. Now it is only by a poignant beauty of execution that new channels can be cut in the obdurate rock of the public's hardened heart; and the best stage execution that Mr Pinero could command was for the most part ugly and clumsy. We shall presently have him sharing the fate of Ibsen, and having his plays shirked with wise shakes of the head by actor-managers who have neither the talent to act them nor the brains to understand them. Why was I born into such a generation of duffers?

.   .   .   .

The Old Acting and the New

THE COMEDY OF ERRORS. Performance by the Elizabethan Stage Society in Gray's Inn Hall, 7 December 1895.

[14 *December* 1895]

For a delightful, as distinguished from a commercially promising first night, the palm must be given this season to the Elizabethan Stage Society's performance of The Comedy of Errors in Gray's Inn Hall this day week. Usually I enjoy a first night as a surgeon enjoys an operation: this time I enjoyed it as a playgoer enjoys a pleasant performance. I have never, I hope, underrated the importance of the amateur; but I am now beginning to cling to him as the savior of theatrical art. He alone among the younger generation seems to have any experience of acting. Nothing is more appalling to the dramatic author than the discovery that professional actors of ten years standing have acquired nothing but a habit of brazening out their own incompetence. What is an actor nowadays, or an actress? In nine cases out of ten, simply a person who has been "on tour" with half a dozen "London successes," playing parts that involve nothing but a little business thoughtlessly copied from the performances of their London "creators," with long intervals spent between each tour in the ranks of the unemployed. At the end of a lifetime so spent, the "actor" will no doubt be a genuine expert at railway travelling, at taking lodgings, and at cajoling and bullying landladies; but a decent amateur of two years standing, and of the true irrepressible sort, will beat him hopelessly at his art. What a fate is that of these unhappy young professionals, sick to desperation of a provincial routine compared to which that of a commercial traveller is a dream of romance, longing for a chance which they have not skill enough to turn to account even if some accident thrust it upon them, and becoming less interesting and attractive year by year at a profession in which the steady increase of personal fascination should have no limit but positive senility and decrepitude! I remember, years ago, when the Playgoers' Club was in its infancy, hearing Mr Pinero, in the course of an address to that body, break into an enthusiastic eulogium on the actor of the past, produced by the old stock-company system, versatile, a singer, a dancer, a fencer, an elocutionist, ready to play any part at a day's notice, and equally expert in comedy, drama, melodrama, Christmas pantomime, and the "legitimate." There is some German novel in which a crowd of mediaeval warriors, fired by the eloquence of Peter the Hermit, burns with a Christian longing to rush to the Holy Land and charge in serried ranks on the Paynim hosts—all except one man, who is obviously not impressed. Indignant at his coldness, they demand what he means by it. "I've been there," is his sufficient explanation. That is how I

felt when I was listening to Mr Pinero. Having been
brought up on the old stock-company actor, I knew that
he was the least versatile of beings—that he was nailed
helplessly to his own line of heavy or light, young or old,
and played all the parts that fell to him as the representa-
tive of that line in exactly the same way. I knew that his
power of hastily "swallowing" the words of a part and
disgorging them at short notice more or less inaccurately
and quite unimprovably (three months rehearsal would
have left him more at sea than three hours) was incom-
patible with his ever knowing his part in any serious sense
at all. I remembered his one absurd "combat" that passed
for fencing, the paltry stepdance between the verses of his
song in the pantomime that constituted him a dancer, the
obnoxiousness of utterance which he called elocution and
would impart to pupils for a consideration, the universal
readiness which only meant that in his incorrigible remote-
ness from nature and art it mattered nothing what he did.
Mr Pinero madly cited Sir Henry Irving as an example of
the product of the stock-company training; but the fact
is, when Sir Henry first attempted classical acting at the
Lyceum, he did not know the A B C of it, and only succeeded by his original and sympathetic notions of the
X Y Z. Nobody who is familiar with the best technical
work of the Irving of today, its finish, dignity, and grace,
and the exactitude of its expression of his thought and
feeling, can (unless he remembers) form any idea of what
our chief actor had to teach himself before he could
carry veteran playgoers with him in his breach with the
tradition of superhuman acting of which Barry Sullivan
was, as far as I know, the last English exponent (need I
say that the great Irish actor was born in Birmingham?).
Barry Sullivan was a splendidly monstrous performer in
his prime: there was hardly any part sufficiently heroic for
him to be natural in it. He had deficiencies in his nature,
or rather blanks, but no weaknesses, because he had what
people call no heart. Being a fine man, as proud as Lucifer,
and gifted with an intense energy which had enabled him
to cultivate himself physically to a superb degree, he was
the very incarnation of the old individualistic, tyrannical
conception of a great actor. By magnifying that conception
to sublimity, he reduced it to absurdity. There were just
two serious parts which he could play—Hamlet and Richelieu—the two loveless parts in the grand repertory. I

know that some people do not like to think of Hamlet
as loveless, and that the Irving Hamlet has his heart in
the right place, and almost breaks it in the scene with
Ophelia; but this I take to be the actor's rebuke to Shakespear rather than an attempt to fulfil his intentions. Sir
Henry Irving has never thought much of the immortal
William, and has given him more than one notable lesson
—for instance, in The Merchant of Venice, where he gave
us, not "the Jew that Shakespear drew," but the one he
ought to have drawn if he had been up to the Lyceum
mark. Barry Sullivan, with his gift of lovelessness, *was*
Hamlet, and consequently used to put his Ophelias out of
countenance more than it is easy to describe. In Hamlet,
as in Richelieu, it was right to create a figure whose utter
aloofness from his fellows gave him an almost supernatural
distinction, and cut him off from all such trifling intimacy
with them as love implies. And it was his success in producing this very curious and very imposing effect that
made for Barry Sullivan, in his best days (I am not now
speaking of the period after 1870 or thereabout), a unique
provincial and Australian reputation which carried him
over parts he could not play at all, such as Othello, through
which he walked as if the only line in the play that conveyed any idea to him was the description of Othello as
"perplexed in the extreme," or Macbeth, who was simply
Cibber's Richard (a favorite part of his) in mutton-chop
whiskers. No doubt his temperament, with its exceptional
combination of imaginative energy with coldness and
proud timidity of the sympathetic passions, accentuated
the superhuman pretension in the style of acting which he
practised; but his predecessor, Macready (if I may judge
from that extremely depressing document, his diary), must
have been much more like him than Sir Henry Irving.
At all events, both Macready and Sullivan had abominable
tempers, and relied for their stage climaxes on effects of
violence and impetuosity, and for their ordinary impressiveness on grandiose assumption of style. Once, when
my father mentioned to me that he had seen Macready
play Coriolanus, and I asked him what it was like, he
replied that it was like a mad bull. I do not offer this as
evidence that my critical faculty is an inherited one—
clearly there must have been some artistic method in the
bull's madness to have gained such a reputation—but I
feel quite sure that when Sir Henry Irving fulfils his prom-

ise to appear as Coriolanus, no father will describe him to
his son as my father described Macready to me. Barry
Sullivan, then, represented the grandiose and the violent
on its last legs, and could do nothing for the young
Irving but mislead him. Irving's mission was to re-establish
on the stage the touching, appealing nobility of sentiment
and affection—the dignity which only asserts itself when
it is wounded; and his early attempts to express these by
the traditional methods of the old domineering, self-assertive, ambitious, thundering, superb school led him for a
time into a grotesque confusion of style. In playing villains, too, his vein of callous, humorous impishness, with
its occasional glimpses of a latent bestial dangerousness,
utterly defied the methods of expression proper to the
heaven-defying, man-quelling tyrant, usurper, and murderer, who was the typical villain of the old school, and
whose flavorless quintessence will be found by the curious
distilled into that instructive Shakespearean forgery, Ireland's Vortigern. In short, Irving had to find the right expression for a perfectly new dignity and a perfectly new
indignity; and it was not until he had done this that he
really accomplished his destiny, broke the old tradition,
and left Barry Sullivan and Macready half a century behind. I will not say that he also left Shakespear behind:
there is too much of the "not for an age but for all time"
about our bard for that; but it is a pity that the new acting
was not applied to a new author. For though Sir Henry
Irving's acting is no longer a falsification of the old style,
his acting versions are falsifications of the old plays. His
Hamlet, his Shylock, his Lear, though interesting in their
own way, are spurious as representations of Shakespear.
His Othello I have never seen: his Macbeth I thought fine
and genuine, indicating that his business is with Shakespear's later plays and not with his earlier ones. But he
owes it to literature to connect his name with some greater
modern dramatist than the late Wills, or Tennyson, who
was not really a dramatist at all. There is a nice bishop's
part in Ibsen's—but I digress.

My point is that Sir Henry Irving's so-called training
under the old stock-company system not only did not give
him the individuality of his style—for to that it did not
pretend—but that it failed to give him even those generali-
ties of stage deportment which are common to all styles.
The stock actor, when the first travelling companies came

along, vanished before them, unwept, unhonored, and un-
sung, because the only sentiment he had inspired in the
public was an intense desire for some means of doing without him. He was such an unpresentable impostor that the
smart London person, well dressed and well spoken, figur-
ing in plays ingeniously contrived so as to dispense with
any greater powers of acting than every adroit man of the
world picks up, came as an inexpressible relief. Dare I
now confess that I am beginning to have moments of regret for him. The smart nullity of the London person is
becoming intolerably tedious; and the exhaustion of the
novelty of the plays constructed for him has stripped them
of their illusion and left their jingling, rickety mechanism
patent to a disgusted public. The latest generation of
"leading ladies" and their heroes simply terrify me: Mr
Bourchier, who had the good fortune to learn his business
as an amateur, towers above them as an actor. And the
latest crop of plays has been for the most part deliberately
selected for production because of the very abjectness and
venality which withered them, harvestless, almost as soon
as they were above ground.

And yet there is more talent now than ever—more skill
now than ever—more artistic culture—better taste, better
acting, better theatres, better dramatic literature. Mr Tree,
Mr Alexander, Mr Hare, have made honorable experiments; Mr Forbes-Robertson's enterprise at the Lyceum is
not a sordid one; Mr Henry Arthur Jones and Mr Pinero
are doing better work than ever before, and doing it without any craven concession to the follies of "the British
public." But it is still necessary, if you want to feel quite
reassured, to turn your back on the ordinary commercial
west end theatre, with its ignoble gambling for "a
catch-on," and its eagerly envious whisperings of how
much Mr Penley has made by Charley's Aunt, to watch
the forlorn hopes that are led from time to time by artists
and amateurs driven into action by the starvation of their
artistic instincts. The latest of these is the Elizabethan
Stage Society; and I am delighted to be able to taunt those
who missed the performance in Gray's Inn Hall with being
most pitiably out of the movement. The Lyceum itself
could not have drawn a more distinguished audience; and
the pleasant effect of the play, as performed on the floor
of the hall without proscenium or fittings of any kind, and
played straight through in less than an hour and a half

without any division into acts, cannot be as much as
imagined by any frequenter of our ordinary theatres. The
illusion, which generally lapses during performances in our
style whenever the principal performers are off the stage,
was maintained throughout: neither the torchbearers on
the stage nor the very effective oddity of the Dromio costumes interfering with it in the least. Only, the modern
dresses of the audience, the gasaliers, and the portrait of
Manisty next that of Bacon, were anachronisms which one
had to ignore. The stage management was good as regards
the exits, entrances, and groupings—not so good in the
business of the speeches, which might have been made
more helpful to the actors, especially to Adriana, whose
best speeches were underdone. On the whole the acting
was fair—much better than it would have been at an average professional performance. Egeon, one of the Dromios,
and the courtezan distinguished themselves most. The evening wound up with a Dolmetsch concert of lute and viol,
virginal and voice, a delectable entertainment which defies
all description by the pen.

New Year Dramas

A WOMAN'S REASON. By Charles H. E. Brookfield and F. C.
Philips. Shaftesbury Theatre, 27 December 1895.

THE LATE MR CASTELLO. A new and original farce in three
acts. By Sydney Grundy. Comedy Theatre, 28 December
1895.

[4 *January* 1896]

It was such pleasure to see Mr Lewis Waller and his
company divested of the trappings of Manxmanity and in
their right minds again, that we all received A Woman's
Reason with more gaiety and enthusiasm than can easily
be justified in cold blood. The play has been produced, as
far as I can guess, by the follc. ing process. One of the
authors, whom I take to be Mr Philips, wrote a commonplace Froufrou play, in a style so conscientiously and intolerably literary that the persons of the drama do not hesitate to remark familiarly to their nearest and dearest that
"Convention speaks one thing, whilst some sweeter voice
whispers another." The sweeter voice in the composing of
the play, I assume, was Mr Brookfield's. Mr Brookfield is
an assiduous collector of conversational *jeux d'esprit,* and

is witty enough to be able to contribute occasionally to the museum himself. Such a collection, from its very miscellaneousness, is better for ordinary theatrical purposes than a complete philosophy reduced to aphorisms; and by sticking its plums into Mr Philips's literary dough with reckless profusion, Mr Brookfield has produced a sufficiently toothsome pudding.

The worst of it is that the Brookfieldian plums digest and are forgotten, whilst the Philipian suet remains heavy on soul and stomach. I cannot now remember a single one of Mr Brookfield's sallies, not even the one in which I recognized a long-lost child of my own. On the other hand, I do recollect, with a growing sense of injury, the assumption that the relation between a British officer and a cultivated Jewish gentleman who makes a trifle of seventy thousand a year or so in the City is the relation between Ivanhoe and Isaac of York, with its offensiveness somewhat accentuated by modern snobbery. When Captain Crozier proceeded to explain haughtily to Mr Stephen D'Acosta that it was useless for two persons in their respective conditions to discuss a question of honor, as they could not possibly understand one another, I seemed to hear a voice from my boyhood—the voice of Howard Paul—singing:

> I'm Captain Jinks of the Horse Marines;
> And I feed my horse on kidney beans:
> Of course it far exceeds the means
> Of a captain in the army.

It is to this rustic conception of "a captain in the army" that we owe Crozier. And yet—would you believe it?—the performance at the Shaftesbury leaves one with a stronger sense of the reality of Captain Crozier than of any other person in the drama. This is largely due, no doubt, to Mr Coghlan, who, having given himself a complete rest from acting during his assumption of the part of Mercutio at the Lyceum, now resumes it at the Shaftesbury with all the vigor of a man who has had a thorough holiday. I do not say that Mr Coghlan's effects are made with the utmost economy of time and weight; but then it is perfectly in the character of the part and in the interest of the drama that Captain Crozier should be a comparatively slow, heavy person, in contrast to the keen, alert Jew. The presentation of a British officer as an over-eating, under-thinking person, professionally the merest routiner, one who by dint of sincere aspiration and conscientious plodding has learnt to play cards and billiards, to shoot, to bet, to do the correct thing in social emergencies, and in an irreproachably gentlemanly way to make women aware of his readiness to accept any degree of intimacy they may care to admit him to, is fair criticism of life; for wherever the social soil is manured by "independent incomes," it still produces large crops of such men (very pleasant fellows, many of them), though certainly the army has of late years become a much less eligible career for them than it was in the days of Captain Rawdon Crawley. The difficulty of giving the authors of A Woman's Reason credit for a clever study of an officer of this type lies in the fact that, as I have already hinted, his speeches to D'Acosta shew a quite romantic ignorance of the healthy promiscuity by which English society protects itself against all permanent Faubourg-St Germain formations. Thanks to the truly blessed institution of primogeniture constantly thrusting down the great bulk of our aristocratic stock into the ranks of the commoners, we are the most republican country in the world; and the ideas expressed by Captain Crozier at the Shaftesbury, though they might pass as part of the established currency on the Continent, and even in America, are here only the affectations of dukes' housekeepers and Hampton Court pensioners. Nor can we, when the Captain foolishly hides in the lady's bedroom from her husband, believe much more in him than in the domestic architecture which cuts that sacred apartment off from all ingress and egress save through the drawing room. In fact, the bedroom incident elicited one of those jeers from the audience which will soon force even the most conservative west end manager to abjure through terror of the gallery that insane faith in worn-out stage tricks which seem proof against the printed persuasion of the stalls. There is much else in Captain Crozier's part which is differentiated from the conventional seducer and villain business of melodrama rather by Mr Coghlan's acting than by the words put into his mouth; but the final touch, where he "does the right thing" by telling the usual divorce-court lie as to the lady's spotlessness, and offering to marry her when he perceives that he runs no risk of being accepted in view of her imminent reconciliation with her husband, is a genuine stroke of comedy and character.

Mr Coghlan created the part, like a true actor, by the

simple but very unusual method of playing it from its own point of view. The tradition of the stage is a tradition of villains and heroes. Shakespear was a devout believer in the existence of the true villain—the man whose terrible secret is that his fundamental moral impulses are by some freak of nature inverted, so that not only are love, pity, and honor loathsome to him, and the affectation of them which society imposes on him a constant source of disgust, but cruelty, destruction, and perfidy are his most luxurious passions. This is a totally different phenomenon from the survivals of the ape and the tiger in a normal man. The average normal man is covetous, lazy, selfish; but he is not malevolent, nor capable of saying to himself, "Evil: be thou my good." He only does wrong as a means to an end, which he always represents to himself as a right end. The case is exactly reversed with a villain; and it is my melancholy duty to add that we sometimes find it hard to avoid a cynical suspicion that the balance of social advantage is on the side of gifted villainy, since we see the able villain, Mephistopheles-like, doing a huge amount of good in order to win the power to do a little darling evil, out of which he is as likely as not to be cheated in the end; whilst your normal respectable man will countenance, connive at, and grovel his way through all sorts of meanness, baseness, servility, and cruel indifference to suffering in order to enjoy a miserable twopenn'orth of social position, piety, comfort, and domestic affection, of which he, too, is often ironically defrauded by Fate. I could point to a philanthropist or two—even to their statues—whom Posterity, should it ever turn from admiring the way they spent their money to considering the way they got it, will probably compare very unfavorably with Guy Fawkes.

However, these reflections are beside the present purpose, which is only to shew how our actors have been placed at cross-purposes with our authors by the traditional stage villain being a monster, or perversion of nature, like Iago; whilst the gentleman who serves as a foil to the hero in a modern west end play is not a villain at all, but at worst a comparatively selfish, worthless fellow. As far as he is taken from life at all, he is suspiciously like the average man of the world as portrayed by Thackeray. Indeed, in the best modern plays, and even in the best modern melodramas (for example, Held by the Enemy), there is no wicked person at all. Ever since Milton struck

the popular fancy by changing the devil into a romantic
gentleman who was nobody's enemy but his own, and
thereby practically abolished the real devil, or god of villains, as a necessary figure in the world drama, playgoers
have been learning to know themselves well enough to
recognize that quite mischief enough for the plot of any
ordinary play can be made by average ladies and gentlemen like themselves. Captain Crozier is not the least bit
of a villain. He shews abject weakness in allowing Mrs
D'Acosta to ruin him and make him ridiculous by drag-
ging him out of a seventy-thousand-a-year mansion in
which he is most comfortably installed as tame cat, with
the certainty that she will throw him over without scruple
as a moral outcast the moment she is tired of him; but one
feels that, after all, it does not greatly matter, since the
elopement is only a stage convention—one of those events
which you let pass in the theatre because they lead to interesting scenes, on the understanding that nobody is to be
held morally responsible for them. (Otherwise, it may be
remarked, Mrs D'Acosta's treatment of Captain Crozier
must be condemned as severely as her treatment of her
husband.) Crozier, in all the points at which he can reasonably be regarded as exercising free will, behaves like
a gentleman according to his lights; and when I say that
Mr Coghlan's success was due to his taking the character
from its own point of view, I mean that he so played it as
to make clear, when Crozier finally walked out, that he
was filled with the most complete sense of having done
everything that the most exacting social critic could have
expected of him, and done it handsomely and adroitly.
And the effect left upon us was that of having made the
acquaintance of Captain Crozier, instead of merely seeing
Mr Coghlan with a new suit of clothes on.

The part of Stephen D'Acosta fitted Mr Lewis Waller so
closely that it was not necessary for him to make any great
impersonative effort; and the same may be said of Miss
Florence West, who happily obliterated all memory of her
struggles with the Manxwoman. The pleasant personal
qualities with which we are familiar carried Mr Waller
through sympathetically; and though there was one speech
in which the authors evidently intended him to play much
more forcibly—that in which Stephen D'Acosta gives his
father-in-law a piece of his mind—I cannot blame him for
refusing to exert himself violently for its sake, since it was

hardly equal to, say, the exhortation which Molière puts
into the mouth of Don Juan's father on the subject of the
true gentleman. Still, the underplaying was a little hard on
Mr Brookfield, whose elaborate exit, as of a man utterly
crumpled up, would have been more effective had Mr
Waller done the crumpling with due energy. Mrs Beerbohm Tree, to whom some malignant fairy godmother must
have denied the gifts of emptyheaded sentimentality
and hysterical incontinence which are essential to success
in our drama, substituting for them the fatal disqualifica-
tions of brains, individuality, and positiveness of character,
gave an amazingly ingenious imitation of the conventional
Froufrou. Only once, through the genius of another member of the company, was she carried into a sincere bit of
acting. This talented colleague was a Mr Stewart Dawson,
an actor not yet in his teens, but with a pleasant voice, a
blarneying smile, a simplicity of manner all irresistible. The
house took to him as if he were its own son; and so apparently did Mrs Tree. I can only say that if Mr Dawson's
fascination increases with his years, it is a grave question
whether he ought to be allowed to grow up. Mrs Tree,
by the way, was announced as appearing "by arrangement," as if all the rest had dropped in by accident. What
has had to be arranged is evidently either Mrs Tree's
objection to appear "by kind permission of Mr Tree," or
Mr Tree's objection to give the kind permission. This observation is, of course, not serious; but I make it for the
sake of calling attention to the absurdity, and indeed the
indelicacy, of the "kind permission" formula by which
managers insist on publicly asserting proprietary rights in
artists who are under engagement to them. Imagine one of
the Reviews announcing an article on the theatre by Mr
Clement Scott as "by kind permission of the Editor of the
Daily Telegraph"! Why should the manager of a theatre
have worse manners than an editor?

Of the other characters, Lord Bletchley, half convention,
half burlesque, is cleverly played by Mr Brookfield. He
should be warned, however, that his tricky diction occasionally prevents his sentences from being quite clearly
caught. The Rev. Cosmo Pretious, all burlesque, and unenlightened burlesque at that, is very well played by Mr
Henry Kemble, whose sense of character and artistic feeling have been too much wasted on plays with no characters in them. Agatha Pretious, also a burlesque figure, is a

part quite unworthy of Miss Maude Millett. She has evidently been cast for it merely to drag another popular name into the bill.

I have forgotten to mention, by the way, that A Woman's Reason is a play with a purpose—the same purpose as that of Daniel Deronda. All the Jews in it are heroes and heroines, and all the Christians the meanest and feeblest wretches conceivable. Serve them right!

And now for The Late Mr Castello, which has replaced The Benefit of the Doubt at the Comedy. In this work Mr Sydney Grundy has—but on second thoughts I think I will confine myself to offering Mr Grundy and Mr Comyns Carr and Miss Winifred Emery and Miss Rose Leclercq and everyone else concerned, my devoted compliments. We shall meet again soon—very soon.

Michael and His Lost Angel

MICHAEL AND HIS LOST ANGEL. A new and original play of modern English life. In five acts. By Henry Arthur Jones. Lyceum Theatre, 15 January 1896.

[18 *January* 1896]

One of the great comforts of criticizing the work of Mr Henry Arthur Jones is that the critic can go straight to the subject matter without troubling about the dramatic construction. In the born writer the style is the man; and with the born dramatist the play is the subject. Mr Jones's plays grow: they are not cut out of bits of paper and stuck together. Mr Grundy or Sardou, at their respective worsts, perform such feats of carpentry in constructing show-cases for some trumpery little situation, that the critics exhaust all their space in raptures over the mechanical skill displayed. But Mr Jones's technical skill is taken as a matter of course. Nobody ever dreams of complimenting him about it: we proceed direct to abusing his ideas without delay. This is quite right and natural. If you invent a mechanical rabbit, wind it up, and set it running round the room for me, I shall be hugely entertained, no matter how monstrously unsuccessful it may be as a representation of nature; but if you produce a real rabbit which begins running about without being wound up at all, I simply say "why shouldnt it?" and take down my gun. Similarly, on Mr Jones producing a live play, which starts into perfectly

natural action on the rising of the curtain without being
wound up during an act or two of exposition, I say "Why
shouldnt it?" and, as aforesaid, take down my gun.

When I respond to the appeal of Mr Jones's art by throwing myself sympathetically into his characteristic attitude
of mind, I am conscious of no shortcoming in Michael and
his Lost Angel. It then seems to me to be a genuinely
sincere and moving play, feelingly imagined, written with
knowledge as to the man and insight as to the woman by
an author equipped not only with the experience of an
adept playwright, and a kindly and humorous observer's
sense of contemporary manners, but with that knowledge
of spiritual history in which Mr Jones's nearest competitors seem so stupendously deficient. Its art is in vital contact with the most passionate religious movement of its
century, as fully quickened art always has been. On comparing it in this relation with the ordinary personal sentiment of Mr Grundy, and with those grotesque flounderings
after some sort of respectably pious foothold which have
led Mr Pinero to his rescue of the burning Bible from Mrs
Ebbsmith's stove, and his redemption of Mrs Fraser by the
social patronage of the Bishop's wife, I unhesitatingly class
Mr Jones as first, and eminently first, among the surviving
fittest of his own generation of playwrights.

But when, instead of throwing myself sympathetically
into Mr Jones's attitude, I remain obstinately in my own, I
find myself altogether unable to offer to Michael that final
degree of complete sympathy and approval which is implied in the conviction that I would have written the play
myself if I could. As to the first two acts, I ask nothing
better; but at the beginning of the third comes the parting
of our ways; and I can point out the exact place where the
roads fork. In the first act Michael, a clergyman, compels
a girl who has committed what he believes to be a deadly
sin to confess it publicly in church. In the second act he
commits that sin himself. At the beginning of the third he
meets the lady who has been his accomplice; and the following words pass between them:

AUDRIE. Youre sorry?
MICHAEL. No. And you?
AUDRIE. No.

Now, after this, what does the clergyman do? Without
giving another thought to that all-significant fact that he

is not sorry—that at the very point where, if his code and creed were valid, his conscience would be aching with remorse, he is not only impenitent, but positively glad, he proceeds to act as if he really were penitent, and not only puts on a hair shirt, but actually makes a confession to his congregation in the false character of a contrite sinner, and goes out from among them with bowed head to exile and disgrace, only waiting in the neighborhood until the church is empty to steal back and privily contradict his pious imposture by picking up and hiding a flower which the woman has thrown on the steps of the altar. This is perfectly true to nature: men do every day, with a frightful fatalism, abjectly accept for themselves as well as others all the consequences of theories as to what they ought to feel and ought to believe, although they not only do not so feel or believe, but often feel and believe the very reverse, and find themselves forced to act on their real feeling and belief in supreme moments which they are willing with a tragically ridiculous self-abnegation to expiate afterwards even with their lives.

Here you have the disqualification of Michael and his Lost Angel for full tragic honors. It is a play without a hero. Let me rewrite the last three acts, and you shall have your Reverend Michael embracing the answer of his own soul, thundering it from the steps of his altar, and marching out through his shocked and shamed parishioners, with colors flying and head erect and unashamed, to the freedom of faith in his own real conscience. Whether he is right or wrong is nothing to me as a dramatist: he must follow his star, right or wrong, if he is to be a hero. In Hamlet one cannot approve unreservedly of the views of Fortinbras; but, generations of foolish actor-managers to the contrary notwithstanding, what true Shakespearean ever thinks of Hamlet without seeing Fortinbras, in his winged helmet, swoop down at the end, and take, by the divine right of a born "captain of his soul," the crown that slips through the dead fingers of the philosopher who went, at the bidding of his father's ghost, in search of a revenge which he did not feel and a throne which he did not want? Fortinbras can, of course, never be anything more than an Adelphi hero, because his bellicose instincts and imperial ambitions are comfortably vulgar; but both the Adelphi hero and the tragic hero have fundamentally the same heroic qualification—fearless pursuit of their own ends and championship of their own faiths *contra mundum*.

Michael fails to satisfy this condition in an emergency where a heroic self-realization alone could save him from destruction; and if this failure were the subject of Mr Jones's last three acts, then the play without a hero might be as tragic as Rosmersholm. But Mr Jones does not set Michael's situation in that light: he shares his fatalism, accepting his remorse, confession, and disgrace as inevitable, with a monastery for the man and death for the woman as the only possible stage ending—surely not so much an ending as a slopping up of the remains of the two poor creatures. The last act is only saved from being a sorry business by the man's plucking a sort of courage out of abandonment, and by a humorous piteousness in the dying woman, who, whilst submitting, out of sheer feebleness of character, to Michael's attitude, is apologetically conscious of having no sincere conviction of sin. When the priest offers his services, she replies, "No, thanks, Ive been dreadfully wicked—doesnt much matter, eh? Cant help it now. Havnt strength to feel sorry. So sorry I cant feel sorry." This gives a pleasant quaintness of the hackneyed pathos of a stage death; but it does not obliterate the fact that Audrie is dying of nothing but the need for making the audience cry, and that she is a deplorable disappointment considering her promise of force and originality in the first two acts. A play without a hero may still be heroic if it has a heroine; and had Mr Jones so laid out his play as to pose the question, "What will this woman do when she discovers that the saint of Cleveheddon is nothing but a hysterical coward, whose religion is a morbid perversion of his sympathetic instincts instead of the noblest development of them?" the answer of a capable woman to such a question might have given the last three acts the attraction of strength and hope, instead of their present appeal *ad misericordiam* of sentimental despair and irrelevant bodily disease. But Audrie, though she has a certain salt of wit in her, is as incapable of taking her fate into her own hands as Michael; and the two, hypnotized by public opinion, let themselves be driven abjectly, she to the shambles and he to the dustbin, without a redeeming struggle.

It is clear, I think, that if the public were of my way of thinking, the play, good as it is of its kind, would fail;

for the public is not sympathetic enough to throw itself
into Mr Jones's attitude, and enjoy the play from his point
of view, unless it can do so without going out of its own
way. And I cannot help thinking that the public dislike a
man of Michael's stamp. After all, stupid as we are, we are
not Asiatics. The most pigheaded Englishman has a much
stronger objection to be crushed or killed by institutions
and conventions, however sacred or even respectable, than
a Russian peasant or a Chinaman. If he commits a sin, he
either tells a lie and sticks to it, or else demands "a
broadening of thought" which will bring his sin within
the limits of the allowable. To expiation, if it can possibly
be avoided, he has a wholesome and energetic objection.
He is an individualist, not a fatalist: with all his apparent
conventionality there is no getting over the fact that institutions—moral, political, artistic, and ecclesiastical—
which in more Eastern lands have paralysed whole races,
making each century a mere stereotype of the one before,
are mere footballs for the centuries in England. It is an
instinct with me personally to attack every idea which has
been full grown for ten years, especially if it claims to be
the foundation of all human society. I am prepared to
back human society against any idea, positive or negative,
that can be brought into the field against it. In this—except
as to my definite intellectual consciousness of it—I am, I
believe, a much more typical and popular person in England than the conventional man; and I believe that when
we begin to produce a genuine national drama, this apparently anarchic force, the mother of higher law and hu-
maner order, will underlie it, and that the public will lose
all patience with the conventional collapses which serve for
last acts to the serious dramas of today. Depend upon it,
the miserable doctrine that life is a mess, and that there is
no way out of it, will never nerve any man to write a truly
heroic play west of the Caucasus. I do not for a moment
suspect Mr Jones of really holding that doctrine himself.
He has written Michael as a realist on the unheroic plane,
simply taking his contemporaries as he finds them on that
plane.

Perhaps it is unfair to Mr Jones to substitute to this extent a discussion of the philosophy of his play for a criticism of its merits on its own ground. But the performance
at the Lyceum has taken all the heart out of my hopes
of gaining general assent to my high estimate of Michael

and his Lost Angel. The public sees the play as it is acted, not as it ought to be acted. The sooner Mr Jones publishes it the better for its reputation. There never was a play more skilfully designed to fit the chief actors than this was for Mr Forbes Robertson and Mrs Patrick Campbell. But though Mr Jones was able to write for Mrs Campbell such a part as she is not likely to get the refusal of soon again, he had to depend on Mrs Campbell's own artistic judgment to enable her to perceive the value of the chance. The judgment was apparently not forthcoming: at all events, Mrs Patrick Campbell vanished from the bills as the day of battle drew nigh. In such an emergency your London manager has only one idea—send for Miss Marion Terry. Miss Marion Terry was accordingly sent for—sent for to play the bad angel; to be perverse, subtly malign, infernally beautiful; to sell her soul and her lover's to the Devil, and bite her arm through as a seal to the bargain; to do everything that is neither in her nature, nor within the scope of her utmost skill in dissimulation. The result was a touching little sham, very charming in the first act, where her entry rescued the play just as it was staggering under the weight of some very bad acting in the opening scene; and very affecting at the end, where she died considerately and prettily, as only an inveterately amiable woman could. But not for the most infinitesimal fraction of a second was she Audrie Lesden; and five acts of Michael and his Lost Angel without Audrie Lesden were not what the author intended. As to Mr Forbes Robertson, Mr Jones had undertaken to make the actor's outside effective if he in return would look after the inside of the Reverend Michael. Mr Jones kept to his bargain: Mr Forbes Robertson was unable to fulfil his. He made the mistake—common in an irreligious age—of conceiving a religious man as a lugubrious one. All the sympathy in the first act depended on his making it clear that the force that swept Rose Gibbard to the altar to confess was the priest's rapturous faith in the gladness of an open and contrite heart, natural to a man made over-sanguine by spiritual joy. Mr Forbes Robertson threw away all this sympathy, and set the audience against him and against the play from the outset by adopting the solemn, joyless, professional manner and the preachy utterance of the Low-Church apostle of mortification and wrath. It is quite impossible to exaggerate the disastrous effect of this initial mistake on

the performance. The more saintly Mr Robertson looked,
the slower, gloomier, more depressingly monotonous he
became, until at last, in spite of Miss Terry's spoonfuls of
sweet syrup, I half expected to see the infuriated author
rush on the stage and treat us to a realistic tableau of the
stoning of St Stephen. What is the use of the dramatist
harmonizing the old Scarlet-Letter theme in the new Pu-
seyite mode if the actor is to transpose it back again into
the old Calvinistic minor key?

As to the rest, their woodenness is not to be described,
though woodenness is hardly the right word for Mr
Mackintosh, in whose performance, however, I could discover neither grace nor verisimilitude. Miss Brooke need
not be included in this wholesale condemnation; but her
part was too small to make any difference to the general
effect. The melancholy truth of the matter is that the English stage got a good play, and was completely and ignominiously beaten by it. Mr Jones has got beyond the penny
novelette conventions which are actable in our theatre. I
fear there is no future for him except as a dramatic critic.

The play is well mounted, though the church scene is an
appalling example of the worst sort of German "restora-
tion." And it has the inevitable defect of all stage
churches: the voices will not echo nor the footsteps ring
through its canvas naves and aisles. Mr Forbes Robertson
has been specially generous in the matter of the band. Mr
Armbruster was able to give between the acts a genuine
orchestral performance of the slow movement from Raff's
Im Walde Symphony, and as much of the andante of Mendelssohn's Italian Symphony as there was time for.

Dear Harp of My Country!

THE COLLEEN BAWN; OR, THE BRIDES OF GARRYOWEN. Dion
Boucicault's Great Drama (sic), in three acts. Princess's
Theatre, 25 January 1896.

[1 February 1896]

I have lived to see The Colleen Bawn with real water in
it; and perhaps I shall live to see it some day with real
Irishmen in it, though I doubt if that will heighten its
popularity much. The real water lacks the translucent
cleanliness of the original article, and destroys the illusion
of Eily's drowning and Myles na Coppaleen's header to a

quite amazing degree; but the spectacle of the two performers taking a call before the curtain, sopping wet, and
bowing with a miserable enjoyment of the applause, is one
which I shall remember with a chuckle whilst life remains.

When I imply, as above, that the Irishmen in The Colleen Bawn are not real Irishmen, I do not mean for a
moment to challenge the authenticity of Mr Richard
Purdon, who succeeds Dion Boucicault as Myles. Nor do
I even accuse him of demonstrating the undeniable fact
that the worst stage Irishmen are often real Irishmen.
What I mean is that Dion Boucicault, when he invented
Myles, was not holding the mirror up to nature, but blarneying the British public precisely as the Irish car-driver,
when he is "cute" enough, blarneys the English tourist.
To an Irishman who has any sort of social conscience, the
conception of Ireland as a romantic picture, in which the
background is formed by the Lakes of Killarney by moonlight, and a round tower or so, whilst every male figure is
"a broth of a bhoy," and every female one a colleen in a
crimson Connemara cloak, is as exasperating as the conception of Italy as a huge garden and art museum, in-
habited by picturesque artists' models, is to a sensible
Italian. The Kerry peasant is no more a Myles na Coppaleen (his real name is Smith, or, at most, Ryan) than the
real Wiltshire peasant is a Mark Tapley; and as for Eily,
Dolly Varden as a typical English tradesman's daughter is
a masterpiece of realism in comparison. The occupation
of the Irish peasant is mainly agricultural; and I advise the
reader to make it a fixed rule never to allow himself to
believe in the alleged Arcadian virtues of the half-starved
drudges who are sacrificed to the degrading, brutalizing,
and, as far as I can ascertain, entirely unnecessary pursuit
of unscientific farming. The virtues of the Irish peasant are
the intense melancholy, the surliness of manner, the incapacity for happiness and self-respect that are the tokens
of his natural unfitness for a life of wretchedness. His
vices are the arts by which he accommodates himself to
his slavery—the flattery on his lips which hides the curse
in his heart; his pleasant readiness to settle disputes by
"leaving it all to your honor," in order to make something
out of your generosity in addition to exacting the utmost
of his legal due from you; his instinctive perception that by
pleasing you he can make you serve him; his mendacity
and mendicity; his love of a stolen advantage; the super-

stitious fear of his priest and his Church which does not
prevent him from trying to cheat both in the temporal
transactions between them; and the parasitism which
makes him, in domestic service, that occasionally convenient but on the whole demoralizing human barnacle,
the irremovable old retainer of the family. Of all the tricks
which the Irish nation have played on the slow-witted
Saxon, the most outrageous is the palming off on him of
the imaginary Irishman of romance. The worst of it is, that
when a spurious type gets into literature, it strikes the
imagination of boys and girls. They form themselves by
playing up to it; and thus the unsubstantial fancies of the
novelists and music-hall song-writers of one generation are
apt to become the unpleasant and mischievous realities of
the next. The obsoletely patriotic Englishman of today is
a most pestilent invention of this sort; and ever since the
formation of the German Empire, the German has been
dramatized with such success that even the Emperor
spends most of his time in working up the character.
Ireland, always foremost in the drama, may claim the
credit of having invented the Irishman out of nothing—
invented him without the stimulus of empire, national independence, knowledge of her own history, united population, common religion, or two-pennorth of prestige of any
sort, her very rebellions having only attained eminence by
giving the national genius for treachery an opportunity of
surpassing all recorded achievements in that important department of revolutionary politics. Fortunately the same
talent that enabled Ireland to lead the way in inventing
and dramatizing national types now keeps her to the front
in the more salutary work of picking them to pieces, a
process which appeals to her barbarous humor on the one
hand, and on the other to her keen common sense and
intelligent appreciation of reality. Of course it sacrifices
the advantages which the imposture secured, as I have
good reason to feel; for nobody can be better aware than
I am of the convenience to an Irishman in England of
being able, by an occasional cunning flourish of his na-
tionality, to secure all the privileges of a harmless lunatic
without forfeiting the position of a responsible member of
society. But there is a point at which shams become so
deadly tiresome that they produce ungovernable nausea,
and are rejected at all risks. There are signs that Ireland,
never very tolerant of the stage Irishman within her own

coasts, is disaffected to him even in the literature by which her scribes habitually impose on England and America. Quite lately a London publisher, Mr Arnold, sent me a novel with the suggestive title of Misther O'Ryan, who turned out to be the traditional blend of Myles na Coppaleen, Robert Emmett, Daniel O'Connell, Thomas Moore, Fin McCoul, and Brian Boru, as compounded and impersonated by a vulgar rascal—an Irish Silas Wegg—whose blackguardism and irremediable worthlessness the writer, evidently that very rare literary bird, an Irish author living in Ireland, had sketched with a vengeful zest that was highly refreshing and, I should say, very wholesome just at present. Take any of the pictures Balzac or Maupassant have painted for us of the spiritual squalor of the routine of poor middle-class life, in which the education, the income, the culture of the family are three-quarters abject pretence; and you will not find it more depressing and even appalling than those which break through the usually imaginative atmosphere of Mr T. P. O'Connor's reviews when the book in hand happens to touch Irish life. I shewed my own appreciation of my native land in the usual Irish way by getting out of it as soon as I possibly could; and I cannot say that I have the smallest intention of settling there again as long as the superior attractions of St Helena (not to mention London) are equally available; but since I cannot disguise from myself the helpless dependence of the British Empire on us for vital elements of talent and character (without us the English race would simply die of respectability within two generations), I am quite ready to help the saving work of reducing the sham Ireland of romance to a heap of unsightly ruins. When this is done, my countrymen can consider the relative merits of building something real in the old country, or taking a hint from that other clever people, the Jews, and abandoning their Palestine to put on all the rest of the world as a shepherd putteth on his garment, beginning with English journalism and American politics as a convenient intermediary stage to soften the transition from their present habits.

These considerations, though they bear more or less on the performance at the Princess's, are not absolutely indispensable to a reasonable enjoyment of it. I have always had a special respect for Mr Richard Purdon because his father was Lord Mayor of Dublin when I was an impres-

sionable boy; and I am, therefore, probably apt to overrate
his talent as a comedian. Still, I can see that his Myles is
not the inimitable Myles of Dion Boucicault. It is a case
of the words of Mercury being harsh after the songs of
Apollo. Boucicault had a charming brogue: not even the
speech of the eminent journalist and M.P. named in a
former paragraph of this article is more musical in sound
or irresistible in insinuation—"sloothering" would be the
right word, were it current here—than his. But Mr Purdon
unhappily did not learn to speak in Galway or Kerry. He
bewrays the respectable Dublin citizen, whose knowledge
of the brogue is derived from domestic servants drawn
chiefly from the neighboring counties, and corrupted by
the tongue of Dublin itself, which, like all crowded capitals, somehow evolves a peculiar villainous accent of its
own. With such opportunities Mr Purdon, having a strong
sense of fun, and being a born mimic, has no difficulty in
producing a brogue; but it is not a pretty one. Further, his
voice, a little coarsened, perhaps, by many years' vigorous
exploitation in the interests of the aforesaid sense of fun,
which seems unchastened by any very vigilant sense of
beauty, is rougher than that of the late author. He has to
omit the song in which Boucicault effortlessly persuaded us
to accept the statement that "old Ireland was his country,
and his name it was Molloy," as a complete and satisfying
apologia pro sua vita. And the attempt to humbug Father
Tom is an obvious and blundering evasion instead of what
it used to be—an artless outpouring of the innocence of a
poor lad who had not the wit to understand what the priest
was asking, much less tell a lie to his reverence. Boucicault
was a coaxing, blandandhering sort of liar, to whom you
could listen without impatience long enough to allow the
carpenters time to set the most elaborate water-scene behind the front cloth. Mr Purdon is just half a trifle too
grating and boisterous, though of course the generation
which does not recollect Boucicault hardly feels this. On
the other hand, Miss Beaumont Collins is a much better
Eily than Mrs Boucicault, who now plays Mrs Cregan,
used to be. Mrs Boucicault was always hopelessly ladylike,
and usually made Hardress Cregan's complaints of her
rusticity ridiculous by being more refined than he. Miss
Collins speaks the part, which is really an engaging and
almost poetic one, very prettily, and is always right about
the feeling of it. Mr Cockburn does nothing with Father

Tom; but as the character happens to suit his personality, his performance passes, and is even highly praised. Mr Tom Terriss does capitally for Hardress, besides being in earnest about his work, and so sustaining the reputation of his name. Miss Agnes Hewitt does all that can be done with the part of Anne Chute, an Irish edition of Lady Gay Spanker, and therefore one of the dreariest of Boucicault's pet vulgarities. Miss Clifton as Shelah, and Messrs Kenney and Rochelle as Corrigan and Danny Mann, were fully equal to the occasion, though Danny did not shew any of Charles II's sense of the tediousness of a prolonged death agony. Mrs Boucicault's competence in the stagey work to which Mrs Cregan is condemned goes without saying. The play, as a whole, in spite of an obsolete passage or two, and of the stupid mutilations imposed by the censorship of its day, is so far superior to the average modern melo-drama, that I shall not be surprised if it repays the man-agement handsomely for reviving it.

I regret to say that the patrons of the gallery at the Princess's, being admitted at half the usual west end price, devote the saving to the purchase of sausages to throw at the critics. I appeal to the gentleman or lady who success-fully aimed one at me to throw a cabbage next time, as I am a vegetarian, and sausages are wasted on me.

.   .   .   .

The Return of Mrs Pat

FOR THE CROWN. A romantic play in four acts, done into English by John Davidson, from François Coppée's Pour la Couronne. Lyceum Theatre, 27 February 1896.

[7 *March* 1896]

Have you observed, reader, how almost every critic who praises For the Crown thinks it necessary to apologize for the fifteenth century? Fancy sane men trying to extenuate a guarantee of beauty! However, since that appears to be the proper thing to do, let me be in the fashion. Yes, there is no denying it: Mr Forbes Robertson wears a caftan instead of a frock-coat, and an exquisite martial cap of metal and ivory instead of a masterpiece by Lincoln & Bennett. Mrs Patrick Campbell's dresses are not made by Worth: no controversy can possibly arise over her sleeves: worst of all, she does not once appear in a hat. It is true, on my credit—four acts, and not one hat. Playgoer: be generous. Overlook this: they mean well, these people at the Lyceum. But what can you expect from an actor who is a painter, and an actress who is a musician?

For the Balkan Mountains and Bulgaria no apology is necessary. Honor to whom honor is due! I—I who pen these lines—first rooted the Balkan mountains on the English stage in Arms and the Man—I first saw the immense dramatic possibilities of Bulgaria. And—let me confess it—I cannot help feeling a little sore that the work of adapting La Couronne was not entrusted to me on this account. I feel that I could have given that heroic tale a turn which Mr Davidson, with all his inspiration, has missed.

Somehow, I find I cannot bring myself to pass over this ridiculous apologizing for the fifteenth century with a mere ironic laugh. What does it mean? It is not the puerile chaff which the modern revival of artistic and religious feeling provoked earlier in the century, when our journalists and comic-opera parodists were too ignorant and callous to be ashamed to jeer like street boys at the pre-Raphaelite and Wagnerian movements, until even George Eliot, though on the materialist side herself, protested indignantly against "debasing the moral currency." All that ribaldry is obsolete: nobody now dreams of sneering at Mr Forbes-Robertson as "æsthetic," or conceives that to compare him to a mediaeval hero-saint, in "stained glass attitudes" or otherwise, would be anything but a high compliment to him. And yet there is the unmistakeable vein of apology and deprecation, if not about the costumes and scenery, at least about the play. And here we have the secret of it. The apologetic critics are thinking, not of the golden age of the arts and crafts, but of the later horrors of historical drama in five acts and in blank verse, which no more belong to the sensuously artistic fifteenth century than to the religiously artistic fourteenth century, or the sanely, humorously artistic thirteenth, since they are in fact a characteristic product of the rhetorical, intellectual, idealistic, inquisitive, logical, scientific, commercial, essentially anti-artistic period which we count as beginning with the sixteenth century, and in which we trace, not the beautiful growth and flowering of the arts, but their consummation and devastation in the giant hands of Michael Angelo and Shakespear. Those who desire to rejoice in Shakespear must confine themselves (as they generally do) to reading his own plays. Read those which have been written since he overwhelmed English dramatic poetry with his impossible example, and you will wish that he had never been born.

In order to write a true dramatic poem, one must possess very deep human feeling. In order to write historical drama in rhetorical blank verse, one only need possess imagination—a quite different and much cheaper article. Shakespear had both in an extraordinary degree: consequently his rhetoric, monstrous as much of it is, is so quickened by flashes and turns of feeling that it is impossible to be bored by it; whilst his feeling expresses itself so spontaneously in rhetorical forms that at the climaxes of his plays rhetoric and poetry become one. And so, since his time, every poor wretch with an excitable imagination, a command of literary bombast, and metric faculty enough to march in step, has found himself able to turn any sort of thematic material, however woodenly prosaic, into rhetorical blank verse; whereupon, foolishly conceiving himself to be another Shakespear, he has so oppressed the stage with yards upon yards and hours upon hours of barren imagery, that at last the announcement of a new historical play in verse at a London theatre produces an involuntary start of terror among the critics, followed by reassuring explanations that although it *is* a fifteenth-century business (more or less), it is really not so bad after all.

François Coppée, as a Frenchman, has not caught the rhetorical itch in its full Shakespearean virulence; but unfortunately the milder form in which it afflicts him is duller than the English variety by just as much as Racine and Corneille are weaker than our immortal William. Therefore Mr Davidson, as a countryman of Shakespear's—or, at any rate, of Macbeth's—has felt bound to prepare La Couronne for the English stage by intensifying the sublimity of its balderdash to an extent which no audience unaccustomed to Shakespear would stand without amazement and laughter. Accordingly Miss Winifred Emery, having to convey to us that she is somewhat bored, is condemned to do so by shrieking for the Balkan Mountains to move, and the Day of Judgment to dawn, with nothing to sustain her in this vortex of academic nonsense except the silly popular delusion that there is something fine in it all—a delusion which I will not insult her intelligence by assuming her to share. I need say no more about this aspect of the play beyond mentioning that wherever Mr Davidson has attempted to outdo M. Coppée in rhetorical folly, he has easily succeeded. I admit that the heightened effect proves, on the whole, that when you set out to be nonsensical, the more nonsensical you are the better. But fifty million lines of such stuff will not extract from me an admission that the writer is a dramatist, much less a poet. The utmost I will concede is that since poets so great as Shakespear and Shelley did not escape the infection, we must forgive Mr Davidson for it, though only, I hope, on the distinct understanding that it is not to occur again.

Unfortunately for the liveliness of the play, M. Coppée's power of imagining ready-made heroic situations and characters is not fortified by any power of developing them. Bazilide and Michael Brancomir never get beyond the point at which they are first dumped on the stage: they keep saying the same things about themselves and one another over and over again until at last the spectator feels that the play would be greatly improved if most of it were presented by accomplished pantomimists in dumb show. The second act—the Lady Macbeth act—is especially wearisome in this way. A Turkish spy forces the hand of Bazilide by the masterly argument that if Michael Brancomir does not betray his country somebody else will— probably the scullion. Bazilide passes on the argument to Michael, improving the scullion into a horseboy. But poor Michael is quite unable to get any forwarder with his conventional compunction, whilst Bazilide is equally at a loss for any idea except the horseboy, on whom she falls back again and again, the whole conversation being strung up to concert pitch of absurdity by the monstrously tall talk in which it is carried on. The pair prance as if they were bounding over the Alps; but they do not advance an inch. One has only to think for a moment of Lady Macbeth tempting Macbeth, or Iago tempting Othello, to realize how comparatively stupid the poet is, and how, of all methods of marking time, the most futile is to mark it in blank verse. Even in the striking scene of the parricide, there is hardly a human note struck, except in the preliminary chat between the sentinel and the shepherd, which is a welcome relief after Bazilide's fustian. When the catastrophe approaches, father and son do not rise for a mo-

ment into any human relation with one another. The more
terribly the emergency presses, the more literary do they
become, taking it by turns to deliver tearing apostrophes
to heaven, hell, honor, history, hope, memory, Christianity,
the fatherland, the past and the future; each waiting with
great politeness until the other has finished, the audience
meanwhile watching patiently for the fight and the finish.
In short, except as a display of rhetoric for the sake of
rhetoric—a form of entertainment which is chiefly interesting as the only known means by which an author or
speaker can make the public respect him for unmercifully
boring it—the play has no value apart from the force of
the main situation and the charm of the pretty love scenes
between Militza and Constantine.

The acting, though full of matter for the critic, is mostly
but poor sport for the lay spectator. Miss Winifred Emery
was not well advised to accept the part of Bazilide. The
original Bazilide of Coppée is a passably credible Bernhardtian wicked woman of the stage, corseted into alexandrines, but not bombasted and hyperbolicized out of all
humanity, like the pen-and-ink monster Mr Davidson has
produced in the ferment of his imagination. Nothing but a
specific artistic talent, and a most tactful virtuosity in the
artificial declamation and heroic bearing of the rhetorical
school, could enable an actress to get through such a part
with credit. Now Miss Emery's talent is a specifically
prosaic one: we have repeatedly seen that the more closely
her parts touch the actual life and society of our day in the
classes which she has under her own daily observation, the
better she acts. In The Benefit of the Doubt she almost persuaded us that she was the best actress on our stage. Re-
move the venue even so small a distance towards the
imaginative region as the plays of the late W. G. Wills, and
she is comparatively colorless. Shift it completely to the
Sahara of rhetorical blank verse or the heights of genuine
dramatic poetry, and she holds her own merely as a pretty
woman and a clever professional. For Bazilide she has not
even the right sort of prettiness: she is no "docile rhythmic
serpent of the East." Her habit of speech is positively sub-
versive of the poetry of tone and measure. When she says
"Nothing must tarnish the greater glory of Michael's love
for me," the words "greater glory" came out with a fashionable smartness at which it is hardly possible not to
smile. All that can be said for her Bazilide is that by dint

of going at her business with great spirit, and with a cleverness that only stops short of perceiving that she had better
not have gone at it at all, she gets safely through, thanks
to her great popularity, her good looks, and a resolute
application of her vigorous stage talent to a bold experiment in ranting, on the pretty safe chance of the public
rising at it as Partridge rose at the King in Hamlet. Which
the public obediently does, like the silly lamb it is in its
moments of pretension to fine connoisseurship.

And Mrs Patrick Campbell, what of her? Ah, the change
from that mournful first night of the slain Michael and the
Lost Angel, when we were all singing, both on the stage
and off:

> But what are vernal joys to me?
> Where thou art not, no Spring can be.

What a ballad could have been written then with the title
Come back from Dorchester; and what terrible heart twist-
ings we suffered when we knew that she would not come
unless we gave her Henry Arthur Jones's head on a
charger! Well, we gave it to her; and on the first night of
For the Crown we agreed, before she had been three sec-
onds on the stage, that her return was cheap at the price:
nay, we would have given her Shakespear's head as a
makeweight if she had given the faintest pout of dissatis-
faction. You will tell me, no doubt, that Mrs Patrick
Campbell cannot act. Who said she could?—who wants her
to act?—who cares twopence whether she possesses that
or any other second-rate accomplishment? On the highest
plane one does not act, one *is*. Go and see her move, stand,
speak, look, kneel—go and breathe the magic atmosphere
that is created by the grace of all these deeds; and then
talk to me about acting, forsooth! No, Mrs Campbell's
Militza is an embodied poem; and if it is much more a
lyric poem than a dramatic one, why, so much the worse
for dramatic poetry! This time, too, the poetry was not
without a little tenderness as well as much beauty of
movement and tone. The old vituperative note was not
heard; and there was an access of artistic earnestness and
power. Possibly the vituperative mood had exhausted itself
on the devoted author of Michael.

Mr Forbes Robertson was torn by a struggle between
the riotous high spirits he was evidently enjoying in his
own person, and the remorse and horror which racked

him as Constantine Brancomir. However, art is never the
worse for a happy inspiration; and though in filling the
part of Constantine he was really filling a brainless void,
he filled it like an artist. Miss Sarah Brooke played a
small part well; and Mr Dalton, as the elder Brancomir,
outfaced the nothingness of his part with sufficient assurance to impress the Partridges almost as successfully as
Miss Emery did. It was all that he could do under the circumstances.

The play is worth seeing for its mounting alone by
those who, like myself, care very little for the spouting of
Marlovian mighty lines. Everything, from the captured
standards of the Turks to Signor Lucchesi's equestrian
statue in the style of Verrocchio, shows the choice of the
artist, not the fulfilment of an order by a tradesman. The
first scene, Mr Walter Hann's Citadel in the Balkans, with
its most unrhetorical, delicately beautiful mountains
stretching to the horizon in a sea of snowy peaks, is so
good that one asks with some indignation whether some
means cannot be invented of doing away with the ridiculous "sky borders" which deface the firmament. The stage
management in this first act, by the way, is excellent. Later
on it is perhaps a trifle unimaginative; and Mr Forbes
Robertson has not yet mastered the art of arranging the
Lyceum stage so as to disguise its excessive spaciousness
when interiors are to be represented. For instance, in the
second act, since there is neither a Court procession to
enter nor a ballet to be danced, the room, in view of the
biting climate and Bazilide's light draperies, might be made
a trifle snugger with advantage to the illusion.

In short, then, everything—except perhaps the play—
is worth seeing. The spoilt children of the public have
certainly strained their privilege hard by their treatment of
Michael and his Lost Angel; but still, since Michael was
succeeding in spite of its having completely beaten the
company, whereas all the forces concerned have their
share in the success of For the Crown—since, above all,
we can now see Mrs Patrick Campbell every evening if
we will, the change in the Lyceum bill will be forgiven.
No doubt Mr Jones has lost a thousand or two; but in
every other respect he has gained; and, after all, what is
the loss of a thousand pounds to a successful dramatic
author? Merely a stimulant to increased production, the
first fruits of which we shall presently receive at the hands

of Mr Willard. And so let us be jocund, and book our
places at the Lyceum without delay.

Boiled Heroine

TRUE BLUE. A new and original drama of the Royal Navy.
In five acts. By Leonard Outram and Stuart Gordon, Lieut.
R.N. Olympic Theatre, 19 March 1896.

[28 *March* 1896]

I am often told by people who never go to the theatre
that they like melodramas, because they are so funny.
Those who do go know better than that. A melodrama
must either succeed as a melodrama or else fail with the
uttermost ignominies of tedium. But I am fain to admit
that True Blue is an exception to this rule. It is funnier
by a good deal than H.M.S. Pinafore in the absurd parts,
and not bad, as melodramas go, in the presentable parts.
The authorship has evidently been divided among many
hands. In some of the epithets which Mrs Raleigh, as the
lady matador, hurls at the villain, it is impossible not to
recognize the vivid style of Mr Raleigh. One of the un-
named authors—I do not know which—is clearly an
idiot; for it is not conceivable that the unspeakable fatui-
ties of the plot can have proceeded from the same brain
as the part of Strachan, or the dialogue, a good deal of
which is animated and businesslike. Probably the idiot was
the original begetter of the drama. As I conjecture, he
submitted his play to Mr Leonard Outram, who, as an
experienced actor, at once fell under the spell which unredeemed literary and dramatic idiocy never fails to throw
over his profession. He called in Lieutenant Stuart Gordon
to look after the naval realism, and supply technically
correct equivalents for the Avast Heavings, and Abaft the
Binnacles, and Splicing the Main Braces which we may
presume the original manuscript to have contained. The
Lieutenant, not being an experienced actor, no doubt suggested that if his naval realism could be supplemented by a
gleam or two of common sense, it would be all the better;
and I can imagine Sir Augustus Harris, on being approached on the subject of finance, not only supporting
the naval officer's view with some vehemence, but taking
the dialogue in hand to a certain extent himself, with his
popular collaborator, Mr Raleigh, to lend a hand when

time ran short. If this hypothesis be correct, we get four authors besides the nameless idiot; and it is in no small degree remarkable that the play has succeeded because the collaborators, in a sort of inspired desperation, played up to the idiot instead of trying to reclaim him. Take for example the main situation of the piece. A British cruiser is anchored at Gibraltar. Its deck is used as a sort of dramatic exchange where villains and villainesses, heroes and heroines, stroll in, like bolts out of the blue, to hatch plots and make love. First there is the lady matador who loves the captain and hates the heroine whom the captain loves. Then there is the heroine, who also loves the captain. And there is the heroine's maid, who loves the comic sailor, who loves the bottle. Suddenly the cruiser is ordered to up anchor and sweep England's enemies from the seas. The women resolve not to desert the men they love in the hour of danger. The matadoress, a comparatively experienced and sensible woman, slips quietly into the pantry adjoining the captain's cabin. The maid gets into one of those settee music boxes which are, it appears, common objects on the decks of cruisers, and is presently carried into the captain's cabin. The heroine, taught by love to divine a surer hiding-place, gets into one of the ship's boilers. Here the hand of the idiot is apparent, striking out a situation which would never have occurred to Shakespear. Once fairly at sea, the matadoress gives way to an inveterate habit of smoking, and is smelt out by the captain. She throws her arms boldly about him, and declares that he is hers for ever. Enter, inopportunely, the navigating officer. He is scandalized, but retires. When he thinks it safe to return, it is only to find the maid emerging from the settee to dispute possession of the captain, on behalf of the heroine, with the matadoress. Hereupon he describes the ship as the captain's harem, and is placed under arrest. Then comes the great dramatic opportunity of the matadoress. Becoming acquainted, Heaven knows how, with the hiding-place of the heroine, she takes the stage alone, and draws a thrilling picture of her rival's impending doom. She describes her in the clammy darkness and dank cold of that boiler, listening to the wild beats of her own heart. Then the sensation of wet feet, the water rising to her ankles, her knees, her waist, her neck, until only by standing on tiptoe, with frantic upturned face, can she breathe. One mercy alone seems

vouchsafed to her: the water has lost its deadly chill. Nay,
it is getting distinctly warm, even hot—hotter—*scalding!*
Immortal Powers, it is BOILING; and what a moment ago
was a beautiful English girl, in the first exquisite budding
of her beautiful womanhood, is now but a boilerful of
soup, and in another moment will be a condenserful of
low-pressure steam. I must congratulate Mrs Raleigh on
the courage with which she hurled this terrible word-
picture at a house half white with its purgation by pity
and terror, and half red with a voiceless, apoplectic laughter. Need I describe the following scene in the stokehold
("stokehole," it appears, is a solecism)—how the order
comes to fill the boiler; how the comic sailor, in shutting
the manhole thereof, catches sight of the white finger of
the captain's young lady; how the matadoress in disguise
comes in, and has all but turned on the boiling water when
the comic sailor disables the tap by a mighty blow from a
sledge-hammer; how he rushes away to tell the captain of
his discovery; how in his absence the fires are lighted and
the cold water turned on; and how at the last moment the
captain dashes in, shouting "Draw the fires from No. 7"
(the heroine is in No. 7), rushes up the ladder to the manhole, and drags out the heroine safe and sound, without
a smudge on her face or a crumple in her pretty white
frock, amid the delirious cheers of an audience which
contemplates the descending curtain as men who have
eaten of the insane root that takes the reason prisoner.
Many more terrors does that melodrama contain, including
the public drowning of the matadoress like a rat in a trap,
but nothing quite so novel as the boiling scene. The last
act degenerates into mere ordinary blood and thunder,
only relieved by the touching acting of Mr Rignold on
becoming suddenly penetrated, for no mortal reason that
anybody can discover, with a sense of his own unworthi-
ness and the nobility of his donkey of a captain, who,
though a sufficiently handsome and pleasant fellow, displays just ability enough to justify a steamboat company in
trusting him, under the guidance of an intelligent boy, with
the sale of tickets for a Thames steamer. Mr Rignold,
however, is not the man to allow himself to be bereaved
of a bit of acting by the absence of any motive for it. He
has the only real part in the play: and he makes the most
of it to the end.

Nearly thirty actors and actresses, most of them capable

and vigorous people with more or less distinct stage talents,
are provided with salaries by this melodrama. They have
for the most part about as much to do as the hundreds of
painted spectators in the first scene (which I forgot to
mention, as it is only a bullfight). Mr Bucklaw, as the
gallant, but brainless, captain, shewed that he only needs
to smarten himself a little—mostly in the way of enunci-
ating his consonants—to become popular in such parts.
Miss Laura Graves was irresistible as the parboiled heroine, being powerfully aided by the fact that the authors
of the dialogue have thoroughly mastered the great Shakespearean secret of always making the woman woo the
man. In actual life there is no point upon which individuals
vary more widely than in the effect of publicity on the
demonstrativeness of their affections. Some people would
rather die than offer or receive the slightest endearment
with anyone looking on. Others are stimulated to exceptional ardor by the presence of an audience; and it is a
tragic fact that these diverse temperaments are rather apt
to attract one another. The shy, conscious man whose
impulsive and warmhearted wife *will* caress him before a
roomful of people, and the fastidious reticent woman
whose husband's attitude is openly and blubberingly
amorous, are familiar figures in our civilization. But I
cannot recall on the stage any *ingénue* quite so reckless
under the sway of the tenderer emotions as the one played
by Miss Laura Graves. On all public occasions she positively showers kisses on the objects of her attachment. One
wonders what a French audience would think of her. It is
only when she is alone with the captain in his cabin that
she subsides into something like the customary reserve of
the bright and beautiful English girls of whom she is
offered as an authentic type. The maid is hardly behind her
mistress in respect of her indifference to publicity; but she
does not take the initiative—is, in fact, more kissed against
than kissing—the effect being so much worse that nobody
less clever than Miss Kate Phillips could make the part
popular. As it is, I congratulate the part on Miss Phillips,
without in any way congratulating Miss Phillips on the
part.

One of the humors of the piece is that the three stow-
away ladies never enter twice in the same costume. They
change as freely as if Worth had a branch establishment
on board. The fact that this gross impossibility does not

interfere in the least with the illusion (such as it is) of the
drama is an illustration of the fact that melodramatic stage
illusion is not an illusion of real life, but an illusion of the
embodiment of our romantic imaginings. If melodramatists
would only grasp this fact, they would save themselves a
good deal of trouble and their audiences a good deal of
boredom. Half the explanations and contrivances with
which they burden their pieces are superfluous attempts to
persuade the audience to accept, as reasonably brought
about, situations which it is perfectly ready to accept without any bringing about whatever. The second-rate dramatist always begins at the beginning of his play; the first-
rate one begins in the middle; and the genius—Ibsen, for ✕
instance—begins at the end. Nothing is odder about True
Blue than the way in which the same authors who heroically disregard the commonest physical possibilities in the
matter of boilers and millinery, timidly and superstitiously
waste half the first and second acts in useless explanations
of the villain's designs. The thousands of fiery Spaniards
waiting for the bull to appear in the ring are repeatedly
supposed to sit in respectful silence for five minutes at a
stretch whilst the first and second villains stroll into the
arena to discuss at great length the political situation which
has led to the presence of a British cruiser at Gibraltar
(as if that were the most improbable place for it in the
world), and which renders it desirable, from their own
point of view, that the cruiser should be sunk. Even if
these explanations were intelligible or plausible, they would
only waste time: as it is, they are stupid.

In looking over one or two criticisms of True Blue I
have been astonished to find the writers complaining that
there is too much realism and too little melodrama in it.
When a man who has just been regaled on boiled heroine
asks for more, it is only good manners to congratulate him
on his appetite; but it is also well to point out that he has
not the public on his side. The really entertaining part of
True Blue is Lieutenant Stuart Gordon's part. The cook-
ing of Alice Marjoribanks is only funny as a bogus mon-
strosity at a fair is funny; but the weighing of the anchor
is both interesting and exciting. It is true that the interest
is not strictly dramatic: it is the sort of interest that makes
people visit a man-of-war at Portsmouth; but then this is
the very sort of interest to which True Blue is addressed.
The fact that I did not catch half the expository dialogue

in the first act did not disappoint me in the least—quite the contrary; but I deeply resented the gruff unintelligibility of the orders by which the anchor-weighing process was directed, as I really wanted to know about that. What True Blue wants is more of the fresh naval routine, and less of the stale melodramatic routine. Why not allow the captain to descry the Venezuelan fleet on the horizon, and give us the process of preparing for action? Why not display in the third act a more interesting section of the ship shewing us both above and between decks? Why allow the catastrophe to be brought about by an impossible valet lamely rubbing out the pencil-marks on the captain's chart with a piece of india-rubber, instead of by a torpedo, or a hundred-ton projectile from the enemy, or—if the maximum of probability is preferable—a collision with some other British cruiser? I am convinced, with all respect to the contrary opinion of some of my colleagues, that in this play Lieutenant Gordon worked on the right lines, and his melodramatist collaborators on the wrong ones. The play is emphatically not the thing at the Olympic; and that is precisely why True Blue is better worth seeing than most exhibitions of its class.

Henry IV

Henry IV. Part I. Haymarket Theatre, 8 May 1896.

[16 *May* 1896]

This is a miserably incompetent world. The average doctor is a walking compound of natural ignorance and acquired witchcraft, who kills your favorite child, wrecks your wife's health, and orders you into habits of nervous dram-drinking before you have the courage to send him about his business, and take your chance like a gentleman. The average lawyer is a nincompoop, who contradicts your perfectly sound impressions on notorious points of law, involves you in litigation when your case is hopeless, compromises when your success is certain, and cannot even make your will without securing the utter defeat of your intentions if anyone takes the trouble to dispute them. And so on, down to the bootmaker whose boots you have to make your tortured feet fit, and the tailor who clothes you as if you were a cast-iron hot-water apparatus. You imagine that these people have professions; and you find that what they have is only, in the correct old word, their "mystery"—a humbug, like all mysteries. And yet, how we help to keep up the humbug! I know men of quite exceptional intelligence—men so sceptical that they have freed their minds from all philosophic and religious dogma, who nevertheless read the Lancet and the British Medical Journal from end to end every week as devoutly as any superstitious washerwoman ever read Zadkiel or Old Moore, and not only believe it all, but long tremblingly for the next symptom that will give them an excuse for calling in the medicine man to mistake typhoid fever for influenza or paint their tonsils with caustic when their kidneys are out of order. Every week they have some joyful tidings for me. Another disease has been traced to its germ; an infallible destroyer of that germ has been discovered; the disease has been annihilated. What wonderful triumphs has not science enjoyed in my time! Smallpox has been made totally impossible; hydrophobia has vanished; epilepsy has yielded to the simplest of operations; the pangs of angina pectoris have been relieved as if by magic; consumption is a dream of the past; and now there is to be no more diphtheria. Instead of vainly seeking, as of old, for a universal remedy, we are the proud discoverers of a dozen, and can change with the fashion from one to another. Mercury, salicylic acid, iodide and bromide of potassium, hashed thyroid, antipyrine, with lymphs innumerable: there they are, making us all safe and happy until we are unfortunate enough to fall down in a fit, or get bitten by a mad dog, or fall sick with an ugly rash and a bad pain in our backs, when we promptly place ourselves in the hands of the very gentleman who wrote to The Times to pledge his honor and reputation, founded on a pyramid of vivisected rabbits, that such things could never happen again. Depend upon it, if Macbeth had killed Macduff, he would have gone back to the Witches next day to ask their advice as to the best way of dealing with Malcolm.

It is the same with all the professions. I have other friends who are law-mad—who believe that lawyers are wise, judges high-minded and impartial, juries infallible, and codes on the brink of perfection. The military-mad and the clergy-mad stalk at large throughout the kingdom. Men believe in the professions as they believe in ghosts, because they want to believe in them. Fact-blindness—the

most common sort of blindness—and the resolute lying of
respectable men, keep up the illusion. No mortal, however
hard-headed, can feel very safe in his attempts to sift the
gold of fact and efficiency out of the huge rubbish heap
of professionalism.

My own weakness is neither medicine, nor law, nor tai-
loring, nor any of the respectable departments of bogus-
dom. It is the theatre. The mystery-man who takes me in
is not the doctor nor the lawyer, but the actor. In this
column I have prated again and again of the mission of
the theatre, the art of the actor, of his labor, his skill, his
knowledge, his importance as a civilizing agent, his function as a spiritual doctor. Surely I have been in this the
most ridiculous of all dupes. But before you lay me down
in derision, never to read my articles again, hear my excuse. There is one sort of human accomplishment that
cannot be dismissed as a figment of the spectator's imagination. The skill with which a man does that which he has
done every day for twenty years is no illusion. When the
operative at his mule in the cotton-mill pieces the broken
yarn, when Paderewski at his Erard grand plays a sonata,
he is not hypnotizing you, or inviting you to make-believe.
He is actually doing things that would be miracles if done
by an untrained man. Or take him who, with no eye to
cotton cloth or the interpretation of Beethoven, does difficult things for the sake of their difficulty, simply as mar-
vels: for instance, the acrobat. You cannot deny the reality
of his feats. His complete physical self-possession, his
ambidextrous grace, his power of making several deliberate
movements in the space of a pang of terror—as when, for
example, he will coolly alter the disposition of his body
at a given moment, whilst he is falling headlong through
the air: all these accomplishments of his really exist, and
are by no means the product of the imagination of an
innocent clergyman, sitting in the auditorium with his nose
buried in a volume of Shakespear, and ready to take the
word of the newspapers next day for what is happening
on the stage. Now, am I to be greatly blamed for having
supposed that the actor was a genuinely skilled artist like
the acrobat, only adding to the skilled mastery of his
powers of movement a mastery of his powers of speech,
with an ear for verse, a sense of character, a cultivated
faculty of observation and mimicry, and such higher qualities as Nature might throw into the bargain? There were

great examples to mislead me: Kean was a harlequin as
well as a Hamlet; Duse's Camille is positively enthralling
as an exhibition of the gymnastics of perfect suppleness
and grace; and I have seen Salvini come out before the
curtain to accept a trophy from an admirer in a stage box
with more art and more fascination—the whole thing
being carried out in strict accordance with certain rules
of his art—than an ordinary skirt dancer could get into
the clumsy imposture she calls dancing after two years'
hard practice. Further, it has been a matter of common
observation in my generation that the burlesque of the
Byron-Farnie-Reece-Burnand period did not, as it turned
out, prove a bad training for the people who played in it.
Nobody will contend, I imagine, that the training was intellectual: the secret lay in the music, the dancing, the
marching, the fantastic walks round, the boundless scope
for physical agility, the premium which the very barren-
ness and vulgarity of the entertainment placed on personal
feats and on mimicry. Even that terrible stage calamity the
stock actor of the old régime learnt something more from
the Christmas pantomime than he would have known
without it.

I plead, then, that acting is potentially an artistic profession, and that by training and practice a person can
qualify himself or herself to come to a manager or author
and say, "Within the limits imposed by my age and sex,
I can do all the ordinary work of the stage with perfect
certainty. I know my vowels and consonants as a phonetic
expert, and can speak so as to arrest the attention of the
audience whenever I open my mouth, forcibly, delicately,
roughly, smoothly, prettily, harshly, authoritatively, sub-
missively, but always artistically, just as you want it. I
can sit, stand, fall, get up, walk, dance, and otherwise use
my body with the complete command of it that marks the
physical artist." An actor might know all this, and yet, for
want of the power to interpret an author's text and invent
the appropriate physical expression for it, never, without
coaching, get beyond Rosencrantz or Seyton. It is, therefore, only the minimum qualification of a skilled stage
hand; and if an actor is not that, then he is merely a stage-
struck unskilled laborer or handy man, and his "conceptions" of Ibsen or Shakespear are mere impertinences. I
naturally concluded that the minimum was in force, and
acting a real profession. Alas! that only proves that my

desire and hope got the better of my observation—my imagination of my experience.

However, I am cured now. It is all a delusion: there is no profession, no art, no skill about the business at all. We have no actors: we have only authors, and not many of them. When Mendelssohn composed Son and Stranger for an amateur performance, he found that the bass could only sing one note. So he wrote the bass part all on that one note; and when it came to the fateful night, the bass failed even at that. Our authors do as Mendelssohn did. They find that the actors have only one note, or perhaps, if they are very clever, half a dozen. So their parts are confined to these notes, often with the same result as in Mendelssohn's case. If you doubt me, go and see Henry IV at the Haymarket. It is as good work as our stage can do; but the man who says that it is skilled work has neither eyes nor ears; the man who mistakes it for intelligent work has no brains; the man who finds it even good fun may be capable of Christy Minstrelsy but not of Shakespear. Everything that charm of style, rich humor, and vivid natural characterization can do for a play are badly wanted by Henry IV, which has neither the romantic beauty of Shakespear's earlier plays nor the tragic greatness of the later ones. One can hardly forgive Shakespear quite for the worldly phase in which he tried to thrust such a Jingo hero as his Harry V down our throats. The combination of conventional propriety and brute masterfulness in his public capacity with a low-lived blackguardism in his private tastes is not a pleasant one. No doubt he is true to nature as a picture of what is by no means uncommon in English society, an able young Philistine inheriting high position and authority, which he holds on to and goes through with by keeping a tight grip on his conventional and legal advantages, but who would have been quite in his place if he had been born a gamekeeper or a farmer. We do not in the first part of Henry IV see Harry sending Mrs Quickly and Doll Tearsheet to the whipping-post, or handing over Falstaff to the Lord Chief Justice with a sanctimonious lecture; but he repeatedly makes it clear that he will turn on them later on, and that his self-indulgent good-fellowship with them is consciously and deliberately treacherous. His popularity, therefore, is like that of a prizefighter: nobody feels for him as for Romeo or Hamlet. Hotspur, too, though he is stimulating

as ginger cordial is stimulating, is hardly better than his
horse; and King Bolingbroke, preoccupied with his crown
exactly as a miser is preoccupied with his money, is equally
useless as a refuge for our affections, which are thus
thrown back undivided on Falstaff, the most human person in the play, but none the less a besotted and disgusting
old wretch. And there is neither any subtlety nor (for
Shakespear) much poetry in the presentation of all these
characters. They are labelled and described and insisted
upon with the roughest directness; and their reality and
their humor can alone save them from the unpopularity of
their unlovableness and the tedium of their obviousness.
Fortunately, they offer capital opportunities for interesting
acting. Bolingbroke's long discourse to his son on the
means by which he struck the imagination and enlisted the
snobbery of the English people gives the actor a chance
comparable to the crafty early scenes in Richelieu. Prince
Hal's humor is seasoned with sportsmanlike cruelty and
the insolence of conscious mastery and contempt to the
point of occasionally making one shudder. Hotspur is full
of energy; and Falstaff is, of course, an unrivalled part
for the right sort of comedian. Well acted, then, the play
is a good one in spite of there not being a single tear in
it. Ill acted—O heavens!

Of the four leading parts, the easiest—Hotspur—becomes pre-eminent at the Haymarket, not so much by Mr
Lewis Waller's superiority to the rest as by their inferiority
to him. Some of the things he did were astonishing in an
actor of his rank. At the end of each of his first vehement
speeches, he strode right down the stage and across to the
prompt side of the proscenium on the frankest barnstorm-
ing principles, repeating this absurd "cross"—a well-known
convention of the booth for catching applause—three
times, step for step, without a pretence of any dramatic
motive. In the camp scene before the battle of Shrewsbury,
he did just what I blamed Miss Violet Vanbrugh for trying to do in Monsieur de Paris: that is, to carry through a
long crescendo of excitement by main force after beginning fortissimo. Would it be too far-fetched to recommend
Mr Waller to study how Mozart, in rushing an operatic
movement to a spirited conclusion, knew how to make it,
when apparently already at its utmost, seem to bound
forward by a sudden pianissimo and lightsome change of
step, the speed and force of the execution being actually

reduced instead of intensified by the change? Such skilled, resourceful husbandry is the secret of all effects of this kind; and it is in the entire absence of such husbandry that Mr Waller shewed how our miserable theatre has left him still a novice for the purposes of a part which he is fully equipped by nature to play with most brilliant success, and which he did play very strikingly considering he was not in the least sure how to set about it, and hardly dared to stop blazing away at full pitch for an instant lest the part should drop flat on the boards. Mr Mollison presented us with an assortment of effects, and tones, and poses which had no reference, as far as I could discover, to the part of Bolingbroke at any single point. I did not catch a glimpse of the character from one end of his performance to the other, and so must conclude that Shakespear has failed to convey his intention to him. Mr Gillmore's way of playing Hal was as bad as the traditional way of playing Sheridan. He rattled and swaggered and roystered, and followed every sentence with a forced explosion of mirthless laughter, evidently believing that, as Prince Hal was reputed to be a humorous character, it was his business to laugh at him. Like most of his colleagues, he became more tolerable in the plain sailing of the battle scene, where the parts lose their individuality in the general warlike excitement, and an energetic display of the commonest sort of emotion suffices. Mr Tree only wants one thing to make him an excellent Falstaff, and that is to get born over again as unlike himself as possible. No doubt, in the course of a month or two, when he begins to pick up a few of the lines of the part, he will improve on his first effort; but he will never be even a moderately good Falstaff. The basket-work figure, as expressionless as that of a Jack in the Green; the face, with the pathetic wandering eye of Captain Swift belying such suggestion of character as the lifeless mask of paint and hair can give; the voice, coarsened, vulgarized, and falsified without being enriched or colored; the hopeless efforts of the romantic imaginative actor, touching only in unhappy parts, to play the comedian by dint of mechanical horseplay: all that is hopeless, irremediable. Mr Tree might as well try to play Juliet; and if he were wise he would hand over his part and his breadbasket to Mr Lionel Brough, whose Bardolph has the true comic force which Mr Tree never attains for a moment.

Two ideas have been borrowed from the last London revival of Henry V by Mr Coleman at the Queen's Theatre in Long Acre. One is the motionless battle tableau, which is only Mr Coleman's Agincourt over again, and which might just as well be cut out of cardboard. The other is the casting of Miss Kate Phillips for Mrs Quickly. As Mrs Quickly is plainly a slovenly, greasy, Gampish old creature, and Miss Phillips is unalterably trim, smart, and bright, a worse choice could not have been made. One would like to have seen Miss Mansfield in the part. Mrs Tree, as Lady Percy, did what I have never seen her do before: that is, played her part stupidly. The laws of nature seem to be suspended when Shakespear is in question. A Lady Percy who is sentimentally affectionate, who recites her remonstrance with Percy in the vein of Clarence's dream in Richard III, and who comes on the stage to share the applause elicited by the combats in the battle of Shrewsbury, only makes me rub my eyes and wonder whether I am dreaming.

Besides Mr Lionel Brough and Mr Lewis Waller, there were three performers who came off with credit. Mr Holman Clark played Glendower like a reasonable man who could read a Shakespearean play and understand it —a most exceptional achievement in his profession, as it appears. Mr D. J. Williams, who played William in As You Like It the other day at the Métropole, and played him well, was a Smike-like and effective Francis; and Miss Marion Evans was a most musical Lady Mortimer, both in her Welsh song and Welsh speech.

The chief merit of the production is that the play has been accepted from Shakespear mainly as he wrote it. There are cuts, of course, the worst of them being the sacrifice of the nocturnal innyard scene, a mutilation which takes the reality and country midnight freshness from the Gadshill robbery, and reduces it to a vapid interlude of horseplay. But the object of these cuts is to save time: there is no alteration or hotch-potch, and consequently no suspicion of any attempt to demonstrate the superiority of the manager's taste and judgment to Shakespear's, in the Daly fashion. This ought to pass as a matter of course; but as things are at present it must be acknowledged as highly honorable to Mr Tree. However, it is not my cue just now to pay Mr Tree compliments. His *tours de force* in the art of make-up do not impose on me: any man can

get into a wicker barrel and pretend to be Falstaff, or put
on a false nose and call himself Svengali. Such tricks
may very well be left to the music-halls: they are altogether unworthy of an artist of Mr Tree's pretensions.
When he returns to the serious pursuit of his art by playing a part into which he can sincerely enter without disguise or mechanical denaturalization, may I be there to
see! Until then let him guard the Haymarket doors against
me; for I like him best when he is most himself.

Magda

MAGDA. A play in four acts. Translated by Louis N. Parker
from Hermann Sudermann's Home. Lyceum Theatre, 3 June
1896. [*From* "The New Magda and the New Cyprienne."]

.   .   .   .   .

[6 *June* 1896]
In all the arts there is a distinction between the mere
physical artistic faculty, consisting of a very fine sense of
color, form, tone, rhythmic movement, and so on, and
that supreme sense of humanity which alone can raise the
art work created by the physical artistic faculties into a
convincing presentment of life. Take the art of acting, for
instance. The physically gifted actor can fill in a conventional artistic outline with great charm. He—or she (I
really mean she, as will appear presently)—can move
exquisitely within the prescribed orbit of a dance, can
ring out the measure of a line of blank verse to a hair's-
breadth, can devise a dress well and wear it beautifully,
can, in short, carry out with infinite fascination the design
of any dramatic work that aims at sensuous and romantic
beauty alone. But present this same fascinating actress
with a work to the execution of which the sense of humanity is the only clue, in which there is no verse to guide
the voice and no dance to guide the body, in which every
line must appear ponderously dull and insignificant unless
its truth as the utterance of a deeply moved human soul
can be made apparent, in which the epicurean admiration
of her as an exquisite apparition, heightened, of course, by
sex attraction, can be but a trifling element in the deep
sympathy with her as a fellow-creature which is produced
by a great dramatist's revelation of ourselves to our own
consciousness through her part, and then you may very

possibly see your bewitching artist making a quite childish
failure on the very boards where a little while before she
was disputing the crown of her profession with the greatest
actresses in the world.

If you doubt me, then do you, if you have had the good
fortune to see Mrs Patrick Campbell play Militza in For
the Crown like an embodied picture or poem of the decorative romantic type, now go and see her play Magda.
And go soon; for the play will not run long: human nature
will not endure such a spectacle for many weeks. That is
not the fault of the play, which does not fail until she kills
it. At the end of the first act, before Magda appears, the
applause has a rising flood in it which shews that the
house is caught by the promise of the drama. Ten minutes
after Mrs Campbell's entry it is all over: thenceforward
the applause, though complimentary and copious, is from
the lips outward. The first-night audience had for the most
part seen Bernhardt and Duse in the part, and knew what
could be done with it. Nobody, I presume, was so foolishly
unreasonable as to expect anything approaching the wonderful impersonation by Duse at Drury Lane, when she
first played the part here last year. Mrs Campbell has not
lived long enough to get as much work crammed into her
entire repertory as Duse gets into every ten minutes of her
Magda. Nor has she had sufficient stage experience to
polish off the part with the businesslike competence of
the golden Sarah, coming down with her infallible stroke
on every good stage point in the dialogue, and never letting the play drag for an instant. But even if the audience
had never seen either Bernhardt or Duse, it could not have
mistaken Mrs Campbell for a competent Magda, although
it might very possibly have mistaken the play for a dull
and prosy one. The fact is, if Mrs Campbell's irresistible
physical gifts and her cunning eye for surface effects had
only allowed her to look as silly as she really was in the
part (and in one or two passages she very nearly achieved
this), her failure would have been as obvious to the green-
est novice in the house as it was to me. Take such a
dramatic moment, for instance, as that in which Magda
receives, first the card, and then the visit of Von Keller,
the runaway father of her child. Let us leave Duse's incomparable acting of that scene out of the question, even
if it is impossible to forget it. But with Mrs Campbell it
was not merely a falling short of Duse that one had to

complain of. She literally did nothing. From the point at which Miss Caldwell, as the servant, brought in the card, to the point at which Magda, her emotion mastered, good-humoredly shakes hands with the fellow (how capitally vulgarly Sarah did that!), Mrs Campbell did not display as much feeling as an ordinary woman of fifty does at the arrival of the postman. Whether her nonentity at this point was the paralysis of a novice who does not know how to express what she feels, or whether it was the vacuity of a woman who does not feel at all, I cannot determine. The result was that the audience did not realize that anything particular was supposed to be happening; and those who had seen the play before wondered why it should be so much less intelligible in English than in a foreign language.

Let me give one other instance. Quite the easiest line in the piece is the prima donna's remark, when she hears about Marie's lieutenant lover, "A lieutenant! with us it's always a tenor." Mrs Campbell actually succeeded in delivering that speech without making anyone smile. At the other end of the compass of the piece we have the terrible line which strikes the Colonel dead at the end—"How do you know that he was the only one?" (meaning "How do you know that this man Von Keller, whom you want me to marry to make an honest woman of me, is the only man who has been my lover?"). Mrs Campbell made an obvious attempt to do something with this line at the last moment. But there is nothing to be done with it except prepare its effect by acting beforehand so as to make the situation live, and then let it do its own work. Between these two failures I can recall no success; indeed, I can hardly recall any effort that went far enough to expose Mrs Campbell to the risk of active failure. Although she was apparently doing her best with the part, her best let its best slip by her, and only retained its commonplaces.

The part of Magda is no doubt one in which a young actress may very well be excused for failing. But from the broad point of view of our national interest in art, it is necessary, when work of the class of Sudermann's is in question, to insist on the claim of the public to have the best dramas of the day presented in English by the fittest talent. Mrs Campbell was entitled to her turn; but now that it is clear that the part does not suit her, are we to have it locked up lest any other actress should demonstrate

that it can be done better? Are we to have no chance of
seeing how it would come out in the hands of the actresses
who have shewn a special aptitude for this class of work?
Miss Elizabeth Robins would certainly not play Militza
half as effectively as Mrs Campbell; but can it be doubted
by anyone who has seen her play Hilda Wangel that she
would play Magda, especially in the self-assertive scenes,
twenty times better than Mrs Campbell? Miss Robins can
assert herself more youthfully, and pity herself more pathetically, than any actress on our stage. Doubtless she
might fail to convince us in the sympathetic, grandly maternal phases of the character; but what about Miss Janet
Achurch for that side of it? Miss Achurch, with no copyright monopoly of A Doll's House, has never been approached as Nora Helmer: Mrs Campbell's attempt at
Magda is the merest baby-play in comparison with that
performance. These able and energetic women who pio-
neered the new movement have had, so far, little to repay
them except unlimited opportunities of looking on at
fashionable dramas, in which placidly pretty and pleasant
actresses enjoy a heyday of popular success by exhibiting
themselves in expensive frocks, and going amiably through
half a dozen tricks which they probably amuse themselves
by teaching to their poodles when they are at a loss for
something better to do. The managers are quite right to
keep actresses of the calibre of Miss Achurch and Miss
Robins out of such business: they would be more likely
to knock an ordinary fashionable play to pieces than to
become popular pets in it—after all, one does not want a
Great Western locomotive to carry one's afternoon tea
upstairs. But if the managers are going in for Sudermann
and Ibsen, and serious work generally, then in the name of
common sense let them shew us something more of the
people who have proved themselvs able to handle such
work, and keep their pretty dolls for dolls' work. However, if Mrs Patrick Campbell has just shewn that she is
not yet a great actress, she is at any rate an artist; and
nobody can complain of her having tried Magda, if only
there is no attempt to prevent others from trying also. The
circumstances were not altogether favorable to her. It is
true that she was supported by the best Pastor Hefferdingh
we have seen—Mr Forbes Robertson was admirable in
the character; but the all-important Colonel Schwartze
was disastrous: Mr Fernandez exhibited every quality of

the old actor except the quality of being able to understand his part. Miss Alice Mansfield, as the agitated aunt, forgot that she was playing first-class drama in the Lyceum Theatre, and treated us to the grimaces and burlesque prolongations of her words with which she is accustomed to raise a laugh in farcical comedies. And Mr Gillmore, as Lieutenant Max, had not a touch of the smart German subaltern about him. Otherwise there was nothing to complain of. Mr Scott Buist, whose success as Tesman in Hedda Gabler has taught him the value of thoroughly modern parts, did not, especially in the earlier scenes, adapt himself sufficiently to the large size of the theatre, nor could he surpass the inimitable Von Keller of Sarah Bernhardt's company; but, for all that, he understood the part and played it excellently. Miss Brooke's Marie was spoiled by Mrs Campbell's Magda. She conveyed the impression of being a respectable young woman, with a rather loose and good-for-nothing kind of sister, instead of being clearly weaker in her conventionality than Magda in her independence.

·   ·   ·   ·   ·   ·   ·

"The Spacious Times"

DOCTOR FAUSTUS. By Christopher Marlowe. Acted by members of the Shakespear Reading Society at St George's Hall, on a stage after the model of the Fortune Playhouse, 2 July 1896.

·   ·   ·   ·   ·

[11 *July* 1896]

Mr William Poel, in drawing up an announcement of the last exploit of the Elizabethan Stage Society, had no difficulty in citing a number of eminent authorities as to the superlative merits of Christopher Marlowe. The dotage of Charles Lamb on the subject of the Elizabethan dramatists has found many imitators, notably Mr Swinburne, who expresses in verse what he finds in books as passionately as a poet expresses what he finds in life. Among them, it appears, is a Mr G. B. Shaw, in quoting whom Mr Poel was supposed by many persons to be quoting me. But though I share the gentleman's initials, I do not share his views. He can admire a fool: I cannot, even when his folly not only expresses itself in blank verse, but actually

invents that art form for the purpose. I admit that Marlowe's blank verse has charm of color and movement; and
I know only too well how its romantic march caught the
literary imagination and founded that barren and horrible
worship of blank verse for its own sake which has since
desolated and laid waste the dramatic poetry of England.
But the fellow was a fool for all that. He often reminds me,
in his abysmally inferior way, of Rossini. Rossini had
just the same trick of beginning with a magnificently impressive exordium, apparently pregnant with the most
tragic developments, and presently lapsing into arrant triviality. But Rossini lapses amusingly; writes "Excusez du
peu" at the double bar which separates the sublime from
the ridiculous; and is gay, tuneful and clever in his frivolity. Marlowe, the moment the exhaustion of the imaginative fit deprives him of the power of raving, becomes
childish in thought, vulgar and wooden in humor, and
stupid in his attempts at invention. He is the true Elizabethan blank-verse beast, itching to frighten other people
with the superstitious terrors and cruelties in which he does
not himself believe, and wallowing in blood, violence, mus-
cularity of expression and strenuous animal passion as
only literary men do when they become thoroughly de-
praved by solitary work, sedentary cowardice, and starvation of the sympathetic centres. It is not surprising to learn
that Marlowe was stabbed in a tavern brawl: what would
be utterly unbelievable would be his having succeeded in
stabbing anyone else. On paper the whole obscene crew
of these blank-verse rhetoricians could outdare Lucifer
himself: Nature can produce no murderer cruel enough
for Webster, nor any hero bully enough for Chapman,
devout disciples, both of them, of Kit Marlowe. But you
do not believe in their martial ardor as you believe in the
valor of Sidney or Cervantes. One calls the Elizabethan
dramatists imaginative, as one might say the same of a
man in delirium tremens; but even that flatters them; for
whereas the drinker can imagine rats and snakes and
beetles which have some sort of resemblance to real ones,
your typical Elizabethan heroes of the mighty line, having
neither the eyes to see anything real nor the brains to
observe it, could no more conceive a natural or convincing
stage figure than a blind man can conceive a rainbow or
a deaf one the sound of an orchestra. Such success as they
have had is the success which any fluent braggart and liar

may secure in a pothouse. Their swagger and fustian, and their scraps of Cicero and Aristotle, passed for poetry and learning in their own day because their public was Philistine and ignorant. Today, without having by any means lost this advantage, they enjoy in addition the quaintness of their obsolescence, and, above all, the splendor of the light reflected on them from the reputation of Shakespear. Without that light they would now be as invisible as they are insufferable. In condemning them indiscriminately, I am only doing what Time would have done if Shakespear had not rescued them. I am quite aware that they did not get their reputations for nothing; that there were degrees of badness among them; that Greene was really amusing, Marston spirited and silly-clever, Cyril Tourneur able to string together lines of which any couple picked out and quoted separately might pass as a fragment of a real organic poem, and so on. Even the brutish pedant Jonson was not heartless, and could turn out prettily affectionate verses and foolishly affectionate criticisms; whilst the plausible firm of Beaumont and Fletcher, humbugs as they were, could produce plays which were, all things considered, not worse than The Lady of Lyons. But these distinctions are not worth making now. There is much variety in a dust-heap, even when the rag-picker is done with it; but we throw it indiscriminately into the "destructor" for all that. There is only one use left for the Elizabethan dramatists, and that is the purification of Shakespear's reputation from its spurious elements. Just as you can cure people of talking patronizingly about "Mozartian melody" by shewing them that the tunes they imagine to be his distinctive characteristic were the commonplaces of his time, so it is possible, perhaps, to cure people of admiring, as distinctively characteristic of Shakespear, the false, forced rhetoric, the callous sensation-mongering in murder and lust, the ghosts and combats, and the venal expenditure of all the treasures of his genius on the bedizenment of plays which are, as wholes, stupid toys. When Sir Henry Irving presently revives Cymbeline at the Lyceum, the numerous descendants of the learned Shakespearean enthusiast who went down on his knees and kissed the Ireland forgeries will see no difference between the great dramatist who changed Imogen from a mere name in a story to a living woman, and the manager-showman who exhibited her with the gory trunk of a newly beheaded man in her arms. But why should we, the heirs of so many greater ages, with the dramatic poems of Goethe and Ibsen in our hands, and the music of a great dynasty of musicians, from Bach to Wagner, in our ears—why should we waste our time on the rank and file of the Elizabethans, or encourage foolish modern persons to imitate them, or talk about Shakespear as if his moral platitudes, his jingo claptraps, his tavern pleasantries, his bombast and drivel, and his incapacity for following up the scraps of philosophy he stole so aptly, were as admirable as the mastery of poetic speech, the feeling for nature, and the knack of character-drawing, fun, and heart wisdom which he was ready, like a true son of the theatre, to prostitute to any subject, any occasion, and any theatrical employment? The fact is, we are growing out of Shakespear. Byron declined to put up with his reputation at the beginning of the nineteenth century; and now, at the beginning of the twentieth, he is nothing but a household pet. His characters still live; his word pictures of woodland and wayside still give us a Bank-holiday breath of country air; his verse still charms us; his sublimities still stir us; the commonplaces and trumperies of the wisdom which age and experience bring to all of us are still expressed by him better than by anybody else; but we have nothing to hope from him and nothing to learn from him —not even how to write plays, though he does that so much better than most modern dramatists. And if this is true of Shakespear, what is to be said of Kit Marlowe?

Kit Marlowe, however, did not bore me at St George's Hall as he has always bored me when I have tried to read him without skipping. The more I see of these performances by the Elizabethan Stage Society, the more I am convinced that their method of presenting an Elizabethan play is not only the right method for that particular sort of play but that any play performed on a platform amidst the audience gets closer home to its hearers than when it is presented as a picture framed by a proscenium. Also, that we are less conscious of the artificiality of the stage when a few well-understood conventions, adroitly handled, are substituted for attempts at an impossible scenic verisimilitude. All the old-fashioned tale-of-adventure plays, with their frequent changes of scene, and all the new problem plays, with their intense intimacies, should be done in this way.

The E.S.S. made very free with Doctor Faustus. Their

devils, Baliol and Belcher to wit, were not theatrical devils with huge pasteboard heads, but pictorial Temptation-of-St-Anthony devils such as Martin Schongauer drew. The angels were Florentine fifteenth-century angels, with their draperies sewn into Botticellian folds and tucks. The Emperor's bodyguard had Maximilianesque uniforms copied from Holbein. Mephistophilis made his first appearance as Mr Joseph Pennell's favorite devil from the roof of Notre Dame, and, when commanded to appear as a Franciscan friar, still proclaimed his modernity by wearing an electric bulb in his cowl. The Seven Deadly Sins were *tout ce qu'il y a de plus fin de siècle,* the five worst of them being so attractive that they got rounds of applause on the strength of their appearance alone. In short, Mr William Poel gave us an artistic rather than a literal presentation of Elizabethan conditions, the result being, as always happens in such cases, that the picture of the past was really a picture of the future. For which result he is, in my judgment, to be highly praised. The performance was a wonder of artistic discipline in this lawless age. It is true, since the performers were only three or four instead of fifty times as skilful as ordinary professional actors, that Mr Poel has had to give up all impetuosity and spontaneity of execution, and to have the work done very slowly and carefully. But it is to be noted that even Marlowe, treated in this thorough way, is not tedious; whereas Shakespear, rattled and rushed and spouted and clattered through in the ordinary professional manner, all but kills the audience with tedium. For instance, Mephistophilis was as joyless and leaden as a devil need be—it was clear that no stage-manager had ever exhorted him, like a lagging horse, to get the long speeches over as fast as possible, old chap—and yet he never for a moment bored us as Prince Hal and Poins bore us at the Haymarket. The actor who hurries reminds the spectators of the flight of time, which it is his business to make them forget. Twenty years ago the symphonies of Beethoven used to be rushed through in London with the sole object of shortening the agony of the audience. They were then highly unpopular. When Richter arrived he took the opposite point of view, playing them so as to prolong the delight of the audience; and Mottl dwells more lovingly on Wagner than Richter does on Beethoven. The result is that Beethoven and Wagner are now popular. Mr Poel has proved that the same result will be attained as soon as blank-verse plays are produced under the control of managers who like them, instead of openly and shamelessly treating them as inflictions to be curtailed to the utmost. The representation at St George's Hall went without a hitch from beginning to end, a miracle of diligent preparedness. Mr Mannering, as Faustus, had the longest and the hardest task; and he performed it conscientiously, punctually, and well. The others did no less with what they had to do. The relief of seeing actors come on the stage with the simplicity and abnegation of children, instead of bounding on to an enthusiastic reception with the "Here I am again" expression of the popular favorites of the ordinary stage, is hardly to be described. Our professional actors are now looked at by the public from behind the scenes; and they accept that situation and glory in it for the sake of the "personal popularity" it involves. What a gigantic reform Mr Poel will make if his Elizabethan Stage should lead to such a novelty as a theatre to which people go to see the play instead of to see the cast!

.   .   .   .   .   .

Daly Undaunted

THE COUNTESS GUCKI. An entirely new comedy in three acts, adapted from the original of Franz von Schonthan by Augustin Daly. Comedy Theatre, 11 July 1896.

.   .   .   .   .

[18 *July* 1896]

O Mr Daly! Unfortunate Mr Daly! What a play! And we are actually assured that The Countess Gucki was received with delight in America! Well, perhaps it is true. After all, it may very well be that a nation plunged by its political circumstances into the study of tracts on bimetallism may have found this "entirely new comedy" quite a page of romance after so many pages of the ratio between gold and silver. But in London, at the end of a season of undistracted gaiety, it is about as interesting as a second-hand ball dress of the last season but ten. When the curtain goes up, we are in Carlsbad in 1819, talking glibly about Goethe and Beethoven for the sake of local and temporal color. Two young lovers, who provide what one may call the melancholy relief to Miss Rehan, enter upon a mad-

deningly tedious exposition of the relationship and movements of a number of persons with long German titles. As
none of these people have anything to do with the play as
subsequently developed, the audience is perhaps expected
to discover, when the curtain falls, that the exposition was
a practical joke at their expense, and to go home laughing
good-humoredly at their own discomfiture. But I was far
too broken-spirited for any such merriment. These
wretched lovers are supposed to be a dull, timid couple,
too shy to come to the point; and as the luckless artists
who impersonate them have no comic power, they present
the pair with such conscientious seriousness that reality
itself could produce nothing more insufferably tiresome.
At last Miss Rehan appears, her entry being worked up
with music—O Mr Daly, Mr Daly, when will you learn
the time of day in London?—in a hideous Madame de
Staël costume which emphasizes the fact that Miss Rehan,
a woman in the prime of life with a splendid physique, is
so careless of her bodily training that she looks as old as I
do. She, too, talks about Goethe and Beethoven, and,
having the merest chambermaid's part, proceeds heart-
lessly to exhibit a selection of strokes and touches broken
off from the old parts in which she has so often enchanted
us. This rifling of the cherished trophies of her art to make
a miserable bag of tricks for a part and a play which the
meekest leading lady in London would rebel against, was
to me downright sacrilege: I leave Miss Rehan to defend
it if she can. The play, such as it is, begins with the entry
of a gigantic coxcomb who lays siege to the ladies of the
household in a manner meant by the dramatist to be
engaging and interesting. In real life a barmaid would
rebuke his intolerable gallantries: on the stage Miss Rehan
is supposed to be fascinated by them. Later on comes the
one feeble morsel of stale sentiment which saves the play
from the summary damnation it deserves. An old General,
the coxcomb's uncle, loved the Countess Gucki when she
was sixteen. They meet again: the General still cherishes
his old romance: the lady is touched by his devotion. The
dramatist thrusts this ready-made piece of pathos in your
face as artlessly as a village boy thrusts a turnip-headed
bogie; but, like the bogie, it has its effect on simple folk;
and Miss Rehan, with callous cleverness, turns on one of
her best Twelfth Night effects, and arrests the sentimental
moment with a power which, wasted on such trivial stuff,

is positively cynical and shocking. But this oasis is soon left behind. The old General, not having a line that is worth speaking, looks solemn and kisses Miss Rehan's hand five or six times every minute; the coxcomb suddenly takes the part of circus clown, and, in pretended transports of jealousy, thrusts a map between the pair, and shifts it up and down whilst they dodge him by trying to see one another over or under it. But, well as we by this time know Mr Daly's idea of high comedy, I doubt if I shall be believed if I describe the play too closely. The whole affair, as a comedy presented at a West End house to a London audience by a manager "starring" a first-rate actress, ought to be incredible—ought to indicate that the manager is in his second childhood. But I suppose it only indicates that audiences are in their first childhood. If it pays, I have no more to say.

Mr Lewis and Mrs Gilbert, like Miss Rehan, are still faithful to Mr Daly, in spite of his wasting their talent on trash utterly unworthy of them. Remonstrance, I suppose, is useless. At best it could only drive Mr Daly into another of his fricassees of Shakespear.

   ·   ·   ·   ·   ·   ·   ·

Blaming the Bard

CYMBELINE. By Shakespear. Lyceum Theatre, 22 September 1896.

[26 *September* 1896]

I confess to a difficulty in feeling civilized just at present. Flying from the country, where the gentlemen of England are in an ecstasy of chicken-butchering, I return to town to find the higher wits assembled at a play three hundred years old, in which the sensation scene exhibits a woman waking up to find her husband reposing gorily in her arms with his head cut off.

Pray understand, therefore, that I do not defend Cymbeline. It is for the most part stagey trash of the lowest melodramatic order, in parts abominably written, throughout intellectually vulgar, and, judged in point of thought by modern intellectual standards, vulgar, foolish, offensive, indecent, and exasperating beyond all tolerance. There are moments when one asks despairingly why our stage should ever have been cursed with this "immortal" pilferer of

other men's stories and ideas, with his monstrous rhetorical
fustian, his unbearable platitudes, his pretentious reduction
of the subtlest problems of life to commonplaces against
which a Polytechnic debating club would revolt, his incredible unsuggestiveness, his sententious combination of
ready reflection with complete intellectual sterility, and his
consequent incapacity for getting out of the depth of even
the most ignorant audience, except when he solemnly says
something so transcendently platitudinous that his more
humble-minded hearers cannot bring themselves to believe
that so great a man really meant to talk like their grand-
mothers. With the single exception of Homer, there is no
eminent writer, not even Sir Walter Scott, whom I can
despise so entirely as I despise Shakespear when I measure
my mind against his. The intensity of my impatience with
him occasionally reaches such a pitch, that it would positively be a relief to me to dig him up and throw stones
at him, knowing as I do how incapable he and his worshippers are of understanding any less obvious form of
indignity. To read Cymbeline and to think of Goethe, of
Wagner, of Ibsen, is, for me, to imperil the habit of studied
moderation of statement which years of public responsibility as a journalist have made almost second nature in me.

But I am bound to add that I pity the man who cannot
enjoy Shakespear. He has outlasted thousands of abler
thinkers, and will outlast a thousand more. His gift of
telling a story (provided some one else told it to him first);
his enormous power over language, as conspicuous in his
senseless and silly abuse of it as in his miracles of expression; his humor; his sense of idiosyncratic character; and
his prodigious fund of that vital energy which is, it seems,
the true differentiating property behind the faculties, good,
bad, or indifferent, of the man of genius, enable him to
entertain us so effectively that the imaginary scenes and
people he has created become more real to us than our
actual life—at least, until our knowledge and grip of actual
life begins to deepen and glow beyond the common. When
I was twenty I knew everybody in Shakespear, from Hamlet to Abhorson, much more intimately than I knew my
living contemporaries; and to this day, if the name of Pistol
or Polonius catches my eye in a newspaper, I turn to the
passage with more curiosity than if the name were that
of—but perhaps I had better not mention any one in
particular.

How many new acquaintances, then, do you make in
reading Cymbeline, provided you have the patience to
break your way into it through all the fustian, and are old
enough to be free from the modern idea that Cymbeline
must be the name of a cosmetic and Imogen of the latest
scientific discovery in the nature of a hitherto unknown
gas? Cymbeline is nothing; his queen nothing, though some
attempt is made to justify her description as "a woman
that bears all down with her brain"; Posthumus, nothing
—most fortunately, as otherwise he would be an endur-
ably contemptible hound; Belarius, nothing—at least, not
after Kent in King Lear (just as the Queen is nothing after
Lady Macbeth); Iachimo, not much—only a *diabolus ex
machina* made plausible; and Pisanio, less than Iachimo.
On the other hand, we have Cloten, the prince of numb-
sculls, whose part, indecencies and all, is a literary masterpiece from the first line to the last; the two princes—fine
presentments of that impressive and generous myth, the
noble savage; Caius Lucius, the Roman general, urbane
among the barbarians; and, above all, Imogen. But do,
please, remember that there are two Imogens. One is a
solemn and elaborate example of what, in Shakespear's
opinion, a real lady ought to be. With this unspeakable
person virtuous indignation is chronic. Her object in life
is to vindicate her own propriety and to suspect everybody else's, especially her husband's. Like Lothaw in the
jeweller's shop in Bret Harte's burlesque novel, she cannot be left alone with unconsidered trifles of portable silver
without officiously assuring the proprietors that she has
stolen naught, nor would not, though she had found gold
strewed i' the floor. Her fertility and spontaneity in nasty
ideas is not to be described: there is hardly a speech in her
part that you can read without wincing. But this Imogen
has another one tied to her with ropes of blank verse
(which can fortunately be cut)—the Imogen of Shakespear's genius, an enchanting person of the most delicate
sensitiveness, full of sudden transitions from ecstasies of
tenderness to transports of childish rage, and reckless of
consequences in both, instantly hurt and instantly ap-
peased, and of the highest breeding and courage. But for
this Imogen, Cymbeline would stand about as much chance
of being revived now as Titus Andronicus.

The instinctive Imogen, like the real live part of the
rest of the play, has to be disentangled from a mass of

stuff which, though it might be recited with effect and ap-
propriateness by young amateurs at a performance by the
Elizabethan Stage Society, is absolutely unactable and un-
utterable in the modern theatre, where a direct illusion of
reality is aimed at, and where the repugnance of the best
actors to play false passages is practically insuperable. For
the purposes of the Lyceum, therefore, Cymbeline had to
be cut, and cut liberally. Not that there was any reason
to apprehend that the manager would flinch from the
operation: quite the contrary. In a true republic of art Sir
Henry Irving would ere this have expiated his acting versions on the scaffold. He does not merely cut plays: he
disembowels them. In Cymbeline he has quite surpassed
himself by extirpating the antiphonal third verse of the
famous dirge. A man who would do that would do anything—cut the coda out of the first movement of Beethoven's Ninth Symphony, or shorten one of Velasquez's
Philips into a kitcat to make it fit over his drawing room
mantelpiece. The grotesque character tracery of Cloten's
lines, which is surely not beyond the appreciation of an
age educated by Stevenson, is defaced with Cromwellian
ruthlessness; and the patriotic scene, with the Queen's
great speech about the natural bravery of our isle, magnificent in its Walkürenritt swing, is shorn away, though
it might easily have been introduced in the Garden scene.
And yet, long screeds of rubbish about "slander, whose
edge is sharper than the sword," and so on, are preserved
with superstitious veneration.

This curious want of connoisseurship in literature would
disable Sir Henry Irving seriously if he were an interpre-
tative actor. But it is, happily, the fault of a great quality
—the creative quality. A prodigious deal of nonsense has
been written about Sir Henry Irving's conception of this,
that, and the other Shakespearean character. The truth is
that he has never in his life conceived or interpreted the
characters of any author except himself. He is really as
incapable of acting another man's play as Wagner was of
setting another man's libretto; and he should, like Wagner,
have written his plays for himself. But as he did not find
himself out until it was too late for him to learn that
supplementary trade, he was compelled to use other men's
plays as the framework for his own creations. His first
great success in this sort of adaptation was with the
Merchant of Venice. There was no question then of a bad

Shylock or a good Shylock: he was simply not Shylock at all; and when his own creation came into conflict with Shakespear's, as it did quite openly in the Trial scene, he simply played in flat contradiction of the lines, and positively acted Shakespear off the stage. This was an original policy, and an intensely interesting one from the critical point of view; but it was obvious that its difficulty must increase with the vividness and force of the dramatist's creation. Shakespear at his highest pitch cannot be set aside by any mortal actor, however gifted; and when Sir Henry Irving tried to interpolate a most singular and fantastic notion of an old man between the lines of a fearfully mutilated acting version of King Lear, he was smashed. On the other hand, in plays by persons of no importance, where the dramatist's part of the business is the merest trash, his creative activity is unhampered and uncontradicted; and the author's futility is the opportunity for the actor's masterpiece. Now I have already described Shakespear's Iachimo as little better than any of the lay figures in Cymbeline—a mere *diabolus ex machina*. But Irving's Iachimo is a very different affair. It is a new and independent creation. I knew Shakespear's play inside and out before last Tuesday; but this Iachimo was quite fresh and novel to me. I witnessed it with unqualified delight: it was no vulgar bagful of "points," but a true impersonation, unbroken in its life-current from end to end, varied on the surface with the finest comedy, and without a single lapse in the sustained beauty of its execution. It is only after such work that an artist can with perfect naturalness and dignity address himself to his audience as "their faithful and loving servant"; and I wish I could add that the audience had an equal right to offer him their applause as a worthy acknowledgment of his merit. But when a house distributes its officious first-night plaudits impartially between the fine artist and the blunderer who roars a few lines violently and rushes off the stage after compressing the entire art of How Not to Act into five intolerable minutes, it had better be told to reserve its impertinent and obstreperous demonstrations until it has learnt to bestow them with some sort of discrimination. Our first-night people mean well, and will, no doubt, accept my assurance that they are donkeys with all possible good humor; but they should remember that to applaud for the sake of applauding, as schoolboys will cheer for the sake of cheering, is to destroy our own power of complimenting those who, as the greatest among us, are the servants of all the rest.

Over the performances of the other gentlemen in the cast let me skate as lightly as possible. Mr Norman Forbes's Cloten, though a fatuous idiot rather than the brawny "beef-witted" fool whom Shakespear took from his own Ajax in Troilus and Cressida, is effective and amusing, so that one feels acutely the mangling of his part, especially the cutting of that immortal musical criticism of his upon the serenade. Mr Gordon Craig and Mr Webster are desperate failures as the two noble savages. They are as spirited and picturesque as possible; but every pose, every flirt of their elfin locks, proclaims the wild freedom of Bedford Park. They recite the poor maimed dirge admirably, Mr Craig being the more musical of the twain; and Mr Webster's sword-and-cudgel fight with Cloten is very lively; but their utter deficiency in the grave, rather somber, uncivilized primeval strength and Mohican dignity so finely suggested by Shakespear, takes all the ballast out of the fourth act, and combines with the inappropriate prettiness and sunniness of the landscape scenery to handicap Miss Ellen Terry most cruelly in the trying scene of her awakening by the side of the flower-decked corpse: a scene which, without every accessory to heighten its mystery, terror, and pathos, is utterly and heart-breakingly impossible for any actress, even if she were Duse, Ristori, Mrs Siddons, and Miss Terry rolled into one. When I saw this gross and palpable oversight, and heard people talking about the Lyceum stage management as superb, I with difficulty restrained myself from tearing out my hair in handfuls and scattering it with imprecations to the four winds. That cave of the three mountaineers wants nothing but a trellised porch, a bamboo bicycle, and a nice little bed of standard roses, to complete its absurdity.

With Mr Frederic Robinson as Belarius, and Mr Tyars as Pisanio, there is no reasonable fault to find, except that they might, perhaps, be a little brighter with advantage; and of the rest of their male colleagues I think I shall ask to be allowed to say nothing at all, even at the cost of omitting a tribute to Mr Fuller Mellish's discreet impersonation of the harmless necessary Philario. There remains Miss Geneviève Ward, whose part, with the Neptune's park speech lopped off, was not worth her playing, and Miss Ellen Terry, who invariably fascinates me so much that I have not the smallest confidence in my own judgment respecting her. There was no Bedford Park about the effect she made as she stepped into the King's garden; still less any of the atmosphere of ancient Britain. At the first glance, we were in the Italian fifteenth century; and the house, unversed in the cinquecento, but dazzled all the same, proceeded to roar until it stopped from exhaustion. There is one scene in Cymbeline, the one in which Imogen receives the summons to "that same blessed Milford," which might have been written for Miss Terry, so perfectly does its innocent rapture and frank gladness fit into her hand. Her repulse of Iachimo brought down the house as a matter of course, though I am convinced that the older Shakespeareans present had a vague impression that it could not be properly done except by a stout, turnip-headed matron, with her black hair folded smoothly over her ears and secured in a classic bun. Miss Terry had evidently cut her own part; at all events the odious Mrs Grundyish Imogen had been dissected out of it so skilfully that it went without a single jar. The circumstances under which she was asked to play the fourth act were, as I have explained, impossible. To wake up in the gloom amid the wolf and robber-haunted mountain gorges which formed the Welsh mountains of Shakespear's imagination in the days before the Great Western existed is one thing: to wake up at about three on a nice Bank-holiday afternoon in a charming spot near the valley of the Wye is quite another. With all her force, Miss Terry gave us faithfully the whole process which Shakespear has presented with such dramatic cunning—Imogen's bewilderment, between dreaming and waking, as to where she is; the vague discerning of some strange bedfellow there; the wondering examination of the flowers with which he is so oddly covered; the frightful discovery of blood on the flowers, with the hideous climax that the man is headless and that his clothes are her husband's; and it was all ruined by that blazing, idiotic, prosaic sunlight in which everything leapt to the eye at once, rendering the mystery and the slowly growing clearness of perception incredible and unintelligible, and spoiling a scene which, properly stage-managed, would have been a triumph of histrionic intelligence. Cannot somebody be hanged for this?—men per-

ish every week for lesser crimes. What consolation is it to
me that Miss Terry, playing with infinite charm and
delicacy of appeal, made up her lost ground in other
directions, and had more than as much success as the
roaring gallery could feel the want of?

A musical accompaniment to the drama has been specially composed; and its numbers are set forth in the bill
of the play, with the words "LOST PROPERTY" in conspicuous red capitals in the margin. Perhaps I can be of some
use in restoring at least some of the articles to their rightful owner. The prelude to the fourth act belongs to
Beethoven—first movement of the Seventh Symphony.
The theme played by "the ingenious instrument" in the
cave is Handel's, and is familiar to lovers of Judas Macca-
beus as O never bow we down to the rude stock or sculp-
tured stone. J. F. R. will, I feel sure, be happy to carry
the work of identification further if necessary.

Sir Henry Irving's next appearance will be on Bosworth
Field. He was obviously astonished by the startling shout
of approbation with which the announcement was received.
We all have an old weakness for Richard. After that, Madame Sans-Gêne, with Sardou's Napoleon.

Ibsen Ahead!

DONNA DIANA. A poetical comedy in four acts. Adapted, and
to a great extent rewritten, from the German version of
Moreto's El Desden con el Desden, by Westland Marston.
Special revival. Prince of Wales Theatre, 4 November 1896.

[7 *November* 1896]

Few performances have struck such terror into me as
that of Westland Marston's Donna Diana on Wednesday
afternoon. Hitherto I have looked tranquilly on at such
reversions to the classically romantic phase which held
the English stage from the time of Otway to that of
Sheridan Knowles and Westland Marston, because the
trick of its execution had been so completely lost that the
performances were usually as senselessly ridiculous as an
attempt to give one of Hasse's operas at Bayreuth with
Sucher and Vogl in the principal parts would be. But such
occasions have always provoked the disquieting reflection
that since it is quite certain Mrs Siddons produced extraordinary effects in such plays in times when they were, except in point of ceremonious manners, just as remote from

real life as they are at present, there must clearly be some
way of attacking them so as to get hold of an audience
and escape all suggestion of derision. And on that came the
threatening thought—suppose this way should be redis-
covered, could any mortal power prevent the plays coming back to their kingdom and resuming their rightful
supremacy? I say rightful; for they have irresistible credentials in their staginess. The theatrical imagination, the
love of the boards, produced this art and nursed it. When
it was at its height the touches of nature in Shakespear
were not endured: the passages were altered and the events
reshaped until they were of a piece with the pure-bred
drama engendered solely by the passion of the stage-
struck, uncrossed by nature, character, poetry, philosophy,
social criticism, or any other alien stock. Stage kings and
queens, stage lovers, stage tyrants, stage parents, stage
villains, and stage heroes were alone to be found in it;
and, naturally, they alone were fit for the stage or in their
proper place there. Generations of shallow critics, mostly
amateurs, have laughed at Partridge for admiring the King
in Hamlet more than Hamlet himself (with Garrick in
the part), because "anyone could see that the King was an
actor." But surely Partridge was right. He went to the
theatre to see, not a real limited monarch, but a stage
king, speaking as Partridges like to hear a king speaking,
and able to have people's heads cut off, or to browbeat
treason from behind an invisible hedge of majestically
asserted divinity. Fielding misunderstood the matter because in a world of Fieldings there would be neither kings
nor Partridges. It is all very well for Hamlet to declare
that the business of the theatre is to hold the mirror up to
nature. He is allowed to do it out of respect for the bard,
just as he is allowed to say to a minor actor, "Do not saw
the air thus," though he has himself been sawing the air
all the evening, and the unfortunate minor actor has hardly
had the chance of cutting a chip off with a penknife. But
everybody knows perfectly well that the function of the
theatre is to realize for the spectators certain pictures
which their imagination craves for, the said pictures being
fantastic as the dreams of Alnaschar. Nature is only
brought in as an accomplice in the illusion: for example,
the actress puts rouge on her cheek instead of burnt cork
because it looks more natural; but the moment the illusion
is sacrificed to nature, the house is up in arms and the

play is chivied from the stage. I began my own dramatic
career by writing plays in which I faithfully held the
mirror up to nature. They are much admired in private
reading by social reformers, industrial investigators, and
revolted daughters; but on one of them being rashly exhibited behind the footlights, it was received with a paroxysm of execration, whilst the mere perusal of the others
induces loathing in every person, including myself, in
whom the theatrical instinct flourishes in its integrity.
Shakespear made exactly one attempt, in Troilus and
Cressida, to hold the mirror up to nature; and he probably
nearly ruined himself by it. At all events, he never did it
again; and practical experience of what was really popular
in the rest of his plays led to Venice Preserved and Donna
Diana. It was the stagey element that held the stage, not
the natural element. In this way, too, the style of execution proper to these plays, an excessively stagey style, was
evolved and perfected, the "palmy days" being the days
when nature, except as a means of illusion, had totally
vanished from both plays and acting. I need not tell over
again the story of the late eclipse of the stagey drama
during the quarter-century beginning with the success of
Robertson, who, by changing the costume and the form of
dialogue, and taking the Du Maurieresque, or garden
party, plane, introduced a style of execution which effectually broke the tradition of stagey acting, and has left
us at the present moment with a rising generation of actors
who do not know their business. But ever since the gar-
den-party play suddenly weakened and gave way to The
Sign of the Cross and The Red Robe—ever since Mr
Lewis Waller as Hotspur, Mr Alexander as King Rassen-
dyl, and Mr Waring as Gil de Berault have suddenly
soared from a position of general esteem as well-tailored
sticks into enthusiastic repute as vigorous and imaginative
actors—it has become only too probable that the genuine
old stagey drama only needs for its revival artists who,
either by instinct or under the guidance of the Nestors of
the profession, shall hit on the right method of execution.

Judge, then, of my consternation when Miss Violet
Vanbrugh, with Nestor Hermann Vezin looking on from
a box, and officially announced as the artistic counsellor
of the management, attacked the part of Donna Diana in
Westland Marston's obsolete play with the superbly
charged bearing, the picturesque plastique, and the im-

passioned declamation which one associates with the Siddons school! More terrifying still, the play began to live
and move under this treatment. Cold drops stood on my
brow as, turning to Mr Archer, whose gloomy and bodeful
eye seemed to look through and through Donna Diana to
immeasurable disaster beyond, I said, "If this succeeds, we
shall have the whole Siddons repertory back again." And,
in a way, it did succeed. If Westland Marston had been a
trifle less tamely sensible and sedately literary, and if the
rest of the company had been able to play up to Miss
Vanbrugh's pitch, it might have succeeded with frightful
completeness. Fortunately none of the others quite attained the palmy plane. Mr Vibart's defiant convexity of
attitude had not the true classic balance—in fact, there
were moments when his keeping any balance at all seemed
to disprove gravitation. Mr Bourchier, if one must be
quite frank, is spreading himself at the waist so rapidly
that he is losing his smartness and vocal resonance, and
will, at his present rate of expansion, be fit for no part
except Falstaff in a few years more. The actor who drinks
is in a bad way; but the actor who eats is lost. Why, with
such excellent domestic influences around him, is Mr
Bourchier not restrained from the pleasures of the table?
He has also a trick of dashing at the end of a speech so
impetuously that he is carried fully three words into the
next before he can stop himself. If he has to say "How
do you do? Glad to see you. Is your mother quite well?" it
comes out thus: "How do you do glad to. See you is your
mother. Quite well." All of which, though alleviated by
tunics, tights, and blank verse, is the harder to bear because
Mr Bourchier would be one of our best comedians if only
he would exact that much, and nothing less, from himself.
Mr Elliot, cheered to find the old style looking up again,
played Perin with excellent discretion—was, indeed, the
only male member of the cast who materially helped the
play; and Mr Kinghorne, though seemingly more bewil-
dered than encouraged by the setting back of the clock,
took his turn as "the sovereign duke of Barcelona" like a
man to whom such crazy adventures had once been quite
familiar. Miss Irene Vanbrugh, as the malapert waiting
wench who, ever since the spacious times of great Elizabeth, has been the genteel blankversemonger's notion of
comic relief, fulfilled her doom with a not too ghastly
sprightliness; but the other ladies were out of the question:

they had not a touch of the requisite carriage and style, and presented themselves as two shapeless anachronisms, like a couple of English housemaids at the Court of Spain. Let us by all means congratulate ourselves to the full on the fact that our young actresses are at least not stagey; but let us also be careful not to confuse the actress who knows too much to be stagey with the actress who does not know enough.

For the rest, all I can say is that I was glad to look again on the front scenes of my youth, and to see Miss Vanbrugh, after announcing her skill as a lute player, appear with an imitation lyre, wrenched from the pedals of an old-fashioned grand piano, and gracefully pluck with her jewelled fingers at four brass bars about an eighth of an inch thick. If Miss Vanbrugh will apply to Mr Arnold Dolmetsch, he will, I have no doubt, be glad to shew her a real lute. She can return the service by shewing him how very effective a pretty woman looks when she is playing it the right way. Though, indeed, that can be learnt from so many fifteenth-century painters that the wonder is that Miss Vanbrugh should not know all about it.

What, then, is to be the end of all this revival of staginess? Is the mirror never again to be held up to nature in the theatre? Do not be alarmed, pious playgoer: people get tired of everything, and of nothing sooner than of what they most like. They will soon begin to loathe these romantic dreams of theirs, and crave to be tormented, vivisected, lectured, sermonized, appalled by the truths which they passionately denounce as monstrosities. Already, on the very top of the wave of stage illusion, rises Ibsen, with his mercilessly set mouth and seer's forehead, menacing us with a new play. Whereupon we realize how we have shirked the last one—how we have put off the torture of Little Eyolf as one puts off a visit to the dentist. But the torture tempts us in spite of ourselves; we feel that it must be gone through with; and now, accordingly, comes Miss Hedda Hilda Gabler Wangel Robins, christened Elizabeth, and bids us not only prepare to be tortured, but subscribe to enable her to buy the rack. A monstrous proposition, but one that has been instantly embraced. No sooner was it made than Mrs Patrick Campbell volunteered for the Rat-wife, the smallest part in Little Eyolf, consisting of a couple of dozen speeches in the first act only. (Clever Mrs Pat! it is, between our-

selves, the most fascinating page of the play.) Miss Janet
Achurch, the original and only Nora Helmer, jumped at
the appalling part of Rita, whom nobody else on the
stage dare tackle, for all her "gold and green forests." The
subscriptions poured in so fast that the rack is now ready,
and the executioners are practising so that no pang may
miss a moan of its utmost excruciation. Miss Robins herself will play Asta, the sympathetic sister without whom,
I verily believe, human nature could not bear this most
horrible play. The performances are announced to take
place on successive afternoons from the 23rd to the 27th
inclusive, at the Avenue Theatre; and there is a sort of
hideous humor in the addition that if three people wish
to get racked together, they can secure that privilege in
the stalls at eight shillings apiece, provided they apply
before the subscription closes on the 16th.

It will be remarked as a significant fact that though
the women's parts in Little Eyolf have attracted a volun-
teer cast which no expenditure could better—enormously
the strongest that has ever been brought to bear in England
on an Ibsen play—we do not hear of eminent actors vol-
unteering for the part of Allmers (to be played, I understand, by Mr Courtenay Thorpe, whose Oswald, in Ghosts,
made an impression in America). The reason is that the
actor who plays the man's part in Ibsen has to go under
the harrow equally with the audience, suffering the shameful extremity of a weak soul stripped naked before an
audience looking to him for heroism. Women do not
mind ill usage so much, because the strongest position for
a woman is that of a victim: besides, Ibsen is evidently
highly susceptible to women, on which account they will
forgive him anything, even such remorseless brutalities as
Rita's reproach to her husband for his indifference to his
conjugal privileges: "There stood your champagne; but
you tasted it not," which would be an outrage if it were
not a masterstroke. Apart from the sensational scene of
the drowning of Little Eyolf at the end of the first act, the
theatre and its characteristic imaginings are ruthlessly set
aside for the relentless holding up of the mirror to nature
as seen under Ibsen rays that pierce our most secret cup-
boards and reveal the grin of the skeleton there. The remorseless exposure and analysis of the marriage founded
on passion and beauty and gold and green forests, the
identity of its love with the cruellest hate, and of this same

hate with the affection excited by the child (the Kreutzer
Sonata theme), goes on, without the smallest concession to
the claims of staginess, until the pair are finally dismissed,
somewhat tritely, to cure themselves as best they can by
sea air and work in an orphanage. Yes, we shall have rare
afternoons at the Avenue Theatre. If we do not get our
eight shillings' worth of anguish it will not be Ibsen's
fault.

Oddly enough, Miss Robins announces that the profits
of the torture chamber will go towards a fund, under
distinguished auditorship, for the performance of other
plays, the first being the ultra-romantic, ultra-stagey Mariana of Echegaray. When, on the publication of that play
by Mr Fisher Unwin, I urged its suitability for production,
nobody would believe me, because events had not then
proved the sagacity of my repeated assertions that the
public were tired of tailormade plays, and were ripe for a
revival of color and costume; and now, alas! my prophecies
are forgotten in the excitement created by their fulfilment.
That is the tragedy of my career. I shall die as I have
lived, poor and unlucky, because I am like a clock that
goes fast: I always strike twelve an hour before noon.

Little Eyolf

LITTLE EYOLF. A play in three acts, by Henrik Ibsen. Avenue
Theatre, 23 November 1896.

[28 *November* 1896]

The happiest and truest epithet that has yet been applied
to the Ibsen drama in this country came from Mr Clement
Scott when he said that Ibsen was "suburban." That is the
whole secret of it. If Mr Scott had only embraced his
discovery instead of quarrelling with it, what a splendid
Ibsen critic he would have made! Suburbanity at present
means modern civilization. The active, germinating, life
in the households of today cannot be typified by an aristocratic hero, an ingenuous heroine, a gentleman-forger
abetted by an Artful Dodger, and a parlormaid who takes
half-sovereigns and kisses from the male visitors. Such
interiors exist on the stage, and nowhere else: therefore
the only people who are accustomed to them and at home
in them are the dramatic critics. But if you ask me where
you can find the Helmer household, the Allmers house-

hold, the Solness household, the Rosmer household, and all the other Ibsen households, I reply, "Jump out of a train anywhere between Wimbledon and Haslemere; walk into the first villa you come to; and there you are." Indeed you need not go so far: Hampstead, Maida Vale, or West Kensington will serve your turn; but it is as well to remind people that the true suburbs are now the forty-mile radius, and that Camberwell and Brixton are no longer the suburbs, but the overflow of Gower Street—the genteel slums, in short. And this suburban life, except in so far as it is totally vegetable and undramatic, is the life depicted by Ibsen. Doubtless some of our critics are quite sincere in thinking it a vulgar life, in considering the conversations which men hold with their wives in it improper, in finding its psychology puzzling and unfamiliar, and in forgetting that its bookshelves and its music cabinets are laden with works which did not exist for them, and which are the daily bread of young women educated very differently from the sisters and wives of their day. No wonder they are not at ease in an atmosphere of ideas and assumptions and attitudes which seem to them bewildering, morbid, affected, extravagant, and altogether incredible as the common currency of suburban life. But Ibsen knows better. His suburban drama is the inevitable outcome of a suburban civilization (meaning a civilization that appreciates fresh air); and the true explanation of Hedda Gabler's vogue is that given by Mr Grant Allen—"I take her in to dinner twice a week."

Another change that the critics have failed to reckon with is the change in fiction. Byron remarked that

> Romances paint at full length people's wooings,
> But only give a bust of marriages.

That was true enough in the days of Sir Walter Scott, when a betrothed heroine with the slightest knowledge of what marriage meant would have shocked the public as much as the same ignorance today would strike it as tragic if real, and indecent if simulated. The result was that the romancer, when he came to a love scene, had frankly to ask his "gentle reader" to allow him to omit the conversation as being necessarily too idiotic to interest anyone. We have fortunately long passed out of that stage in novels. By the time we had reached Vanity Fair and Middlemarch—both pretty old and prim stories now—mar-

riage had become the starting point of our romances. Love
is as much the romancer's theme as ever; but married love
and the courtships of young people who are appalled by
the problems of life and motherhood have left the gover-
nesses and curates, the Amandas and Tom Joneses of other
days, far out of sight. Ten years ago the stage was as far
behind Sir Walter Scott as he is behind Madame Sarah
Grand. But when Ibsen took it by the scruff of the neck
just as Wagner took the Opera, then, willy nilly, it had to
come along. And now what are the critics going to do? The
Ibsen drama is pre-eminently the drama of marriage. If
dramatic criticism receives it in the spirit of the nurse's
husband in Romeo and Juliet, if it grins and makes remarks about "the secrets of the alcove," if it pours forth
columns which are half pornographic pleasantry and the
other half sham propriety, then the end will be, not in the
least that Ibsen will be banned, but that dramatic criticism
will cease to be read. And what a frightful blow that would
be to English culture!

Little Eyolf is an extraordinarily powerful play, although none of the characters are as fascinatingly individualized as Solness or Rosmer, Hedda or Nora. The
theme is a marriage—an ideal marriage from the suburban
point of view. A young gentleman, a student and an ideal-
ist, is compelled to drudge at teaching to support himself.
He meets a beautiful young woman. They fall in love with
one another; and by the greatest piece of luck in the world
(suburbanly considered) she has plenty of money. Thus
he is set free by his marriage to live his own life in his
own way. That is just where an ordinary play leaves off,
and just where an Ibsen play begins. The husband begins
to make those discoveries which everybody makes, except,
apparently, the dramatic critics. First, that love, instead of
being a perfectly homogeneous, unchanging, unending passion, is of all things the most mutable. It will pass through
several well-marked stages in a single evening, and, whilst
seeming to slip back to the old starting point the next evening, will yet not slip quite back; so that in the course
of years it will appear that the moods of an evening were
the anticipation of the evolution of a lifetime. But the
evolution does not occur in different people at the same
time or in the same order. Consequently the hero of Little
Eyolf, being an imaginative, nervous, thoughtful person,
finds that he has had enough of caresses, and wants to

dream alone among the mountain peaks and solitudes, whilst his wife, a warm-blooded creature, has only found her love intensified to a fiercely jealous covetousness of him. His main refuge from this devouring passion is in his peacefully affectionate relations with his sister, and in certain suburban dreams very common among literary amateurs living on their wives' incomes: to wit, forming the mind and character of his child, and writing a great book (on Human Responsibility if you please). Of course the wife, in her jealousy, hates the sister, hates the child, hates the book, hates her husband for making her jealous of them, and hates herself for her hatreds with the frightful logic of greedy, insatiable love. Enter then our old friend, Ibsen's divine messenger. The Ratwife, alias the Strange Passenger, alias the Button Moulder, alias Ulrik Brendel, comes in to ask whether there are any little gnawing things there of which she can rid the house. They do not understand—the divine messenger in Ibsen is never understood, especially by the critics. So the little gnawing thing in the house—the child—follows the Ratwife and is drowned, leaving the pair awakened by the blow to a frightful consciousness of themselves, the woman as a mere animal, the man as a moonstruck nincompoop, keeping up appearances as a suburban lady and gentleman with nothing to do but enjoy themselves. Even the sister has discovered now that she is not really a sister—also a not unprecedented suburban possibility—and sees that the passionate stage is ahead of her too; so, though she loves the husband, she has to get out of his way by the pre-eminently suburban expedient of marrying a man whom she does not love, and who, like Rita, is warm-blooded and bent on the undivided, unshared possession of the object of his passion. At last the love of the woman passes out of the passionate stage; and immediately, with the practical sense of her sex, she proposes, not to go up into the mountains or to write amateur treatises, but to occupy herself with her duties as landed proprietress, instead of merely spending the revenues of her property in keeping a monogamic harem. The gentleman asks to be allowed to lend a hand; and immediately the storm subsides, easily enough, leaving the couple on solid ground. This is the play, as actual and near to us as the Brighton and South Coast Railway—this is the mercilessly heart-searching sermon, touching all of us somewhere, and some of us everywhere, which we, the

critics, have summed up as "secrets of the alcove." Our
cheeks, whose whiteness Mr Arthur Roberts has assailed
in vain, have mantled at "the coarseness and vulgarity
which are noted characteristics of the author" (I am quoting, with awe, my fastidiously high-toned colleague of the
Standard). And yet the divine messenger only meant to
make us ashamed of ourselves. That is the way divine mes-
sengers always do muddle their business.

The performance was of course a very remarkable one.
When, in a cast of five, you have the three best yet discovered actresses of their generation, you naturally look
for something extraordinary. Miss Achurch was the only
one who ran any risk of failure. The Ratwife and Asta are
excellent parts; but they are not arduous ones. Rita, on the
other hand, is one of the heaviest ever written: any single
act of it would exhaust an actress of no more than ordinary resources. But Miss Achurch was more than equal to
the occasion. Her power seemed to grow with its own expenditure. The terrible outburst at the end of the first act
did not leave a scrape on her voice (which appears to have
the compass of a military band) and threw her into victorious action in that tearing second act instead of wreck-
ing her. She played with all her old originality and success,
and with more than her old authority over her audience.
She had to speak some dangerous lines—lines of a kind
that usually find out the vulgar spots in an audience and
give an excuse for a laugh—but nobody laughed or wanted
to laugh at Miss Achurch. "There stood your champagne;
but you tasted it not," neither shirked nor slurred, but
driven home to the last syllable, did not elicit an audible
breath from a completely dominated audience. Later on I
confess I lost sight of Rita a little in studying the surprising capacity Miss Achurch shewed as a dramatic instrument.
For the first time one clearly saw the superfluity of power
and the vehemence of intelligence which make her often
so reckless as to the beauty of her methods of expression.
As Rita she produced almost every sound that a big human
voice can, from a creak like the opening of a rusty canal
lock to a melodious tenor note that the most robust Sieg-
fried might have envied. She looked at one moment like a
young, well-dressed, very pretty woman: at another she
was like a desperate creature just fished dripping out of the
river by the Thames Police. Yet another moment, and she
was the incarnation of impetuous, ungovernable strength.

Her face was sometimes winsome, sometimes listlessly wretched, sometimes like the head of a statue of Victory, sometimes suffused, horrible, threatening, like Bellona or Medusa. She would cross from left to right like a queen, and from right to left with, so to speak, her toes turned in, her hair coming down, and her slippers coming off. A more utter recklessness, not only of fashion, but of beauty, could hardly be imagined: beauty to Miss Achurch is only one effect among others to be produced, not a condition of all effects. But then she can do what our beautiful actresses cannot do: attain the force and terror of Sarah Bernhardt's most vehement explosions without Sarah's violence and abandonment, and with every appearance of having reserves of power still held in restraint. With all her cleverness as a realistic actress she must be classed technically as a heroic actress; and I very much doubt whether we shall see her often until she comes into the field with a repertory as highly specialized as that of Sir Henry Irving or Duse. For it is so clear that she would act an average London success to pieces and play an average actor-manager off the stage, that we need not expect to see much of her as that useful and pretty auxiliary, a leading lady.

Being myself a devotee of the beautiful school, I like being enchanted by Mrs Patrick Campbell better than being frightened, harrowed, astonished, conscience-stricken, devastated, and dreadfully delighted in general by Miss Achurch's untamed genius. I have seen Mrs Campbell play the Ratwife twice, once quite enchantingly, and once most disappointingly. On the first occasion Mrs Campbell divined that she was no village harridan, but the messenger of heaven. She played supernaturally, beautifully: the first notes of her voice came as from the spheres into all that suburban prose: she played to the child with a witchery that might have drawn him not only into the sea, but into her very bosom. Nothing jarred except her obedience to Ibsen's stage direction in saying "Down where all the rats are" harshly, instead of getting the effect, in harmony with her own inspired reading, by the most magical tenderness. The next time, to my unspeakable fury, she amused herself by playing like any melodramatic old woman, a profanation for which, whilst my critical life lasts, never will I forgive her. Of Miss Robins's Asta it is difficult to say much, since the part, played as she plays it, does not exhibit anything like the full extent of her powers. Asta is

a study of a temperament—the quiet, affectionate, endur-
ing, reassuring, faithful, domestic temperament. That is
not in the least Miss Robins's temperament: she is nervous,
restless, intensely self-conscious, eagerly energetic. In parts
which do not enable her to let herself loose in this, her
natural way, she falls back on pathos, on mute misery, on
a certain delicate plaintive note in her voice and grace in
her bearing which appeal to our sympathy and pity without realizing any individuality for us. She gave us, with
instinctive tact and refinement, the "niceness," the consid-
erateness, the ladylikeness, which differentiate Asta from
the wilful, passionate, somewhat brutal Rita. Perhaps only
an American playing against an Englishwoman could have
done it so discriminately; but beyond this and the pathos
there was nothing: Asta was only a picture, and, like a
picture, did not develop. The picture, being sympathetic
and pretty, has been much admired; but those who have
not seen Miss Robins play Hilda Wangel have no idea of
what she is like when she really acts her part instead of
merely giving an urbanely pictorial recommendation of it.
As to Allmers, how could he recommend himself to spectators who saw in him everything that they are ashamed
of in themselves? Mr Courtenay Thorpe played very intelli-
gently, which, for such a part, and in such a play, is saying
a good deal; but he was hampered a little by the change
from the small and intimate auditorium in which he has
been accustomed to play Ibsen, to the Avenue, which
ingeniously combines the acoustic difficulties of a large
theatre with the pecuniary capacity of a small one. Master
Stewart Dawson, as Eyolf, was one of the best actors in
the company. Mr Lowne, as Borgheim, was as much out of
tone as a Leader sunset in a Rembrandt picture—no fault
of his, of course (the audience evidently liked him), but
still a blemish on the play.

And this brings me to a final criticism. The moment I
put myself into my old attitude as musical critic, I at once
perceive that the performance, as a whole, was an unsatis-
factory one. You may remonstrate, and ask me how I can
say so after admitting that the performers shewed such
extraordinary talent—even genius. It is very simple, nevertheless. Suppose you take Isaye, Sarasate, Joachim, and
Hollmann, and tumble them all together to give a scratch
performance of one of Beethoven's posthumous quartets
at some benefit concert. Suppose you also take the two De

Reszkes, Calvé, and Miss Eames, and set them to sing a glee under the same circumstances. They will all shew prodigious individual talent; but the resultant performances of the quartet and glee will be inferior, as wholes, to that of an ordinary glee club or group of musicians who have practised for years together. The Avenue performance was a parallel case. There was nothing like the atmosphere which Lugné-Poë got in Rosmersholm. Miss Achurch managed to play the second act as if she had played it every week for twenty years; but otherwise the performance, interesting as it was, was none the less a scratch one. If only the company could keep together for a while! But perhaps that is too much to hope for at present, though it is encouraging to see that the performances are to be continued next week, the five matinees—all crowded, by the way—having by no means exhausted the demand for places.

Several performances during the past fortnight remain to be chronicled; but Ibsen will have his due; and he has not left me room enough to do justice to any one else this week.

Ibsen without Tears

[12 *December* 1896]

Little Eyolf, which began at the Avenue Theatre only the other day as an artistic forlorn hope led by Miss Elizabeth Robins, has been promoted into a full-blown fashionable theatrical speculation, with a Morocco Bound syndicate in the background, unlimited starring and billposting, and everything complete. The syndicate promptly set to work to shew us how Ibsen should really be done. They found the whole thing wrong from the root up. The silly Ibsen people had put Miss Achurch, an Ibsenite actress, into the leading part, and Mrs Patrick Campbell, a fashionable actress, into a minor one. This was soon set right. Miss Achurch was got rid of altogether, and her part transferred to Mrs. Campbell. Miss Robins, though tainted with Ibsenism, was retained, but only, I presume, because, having command of the stage-right in the play, she could not be replaced—say by Miss Maude Millet—without her own consent. The rest of the arrangements are economical rather than fashionable, the syndicate, to all appearance, being, like most syndicates, an association for the purpose of getting money rather than supplying it.

Mrs Patrick Campbell has entered thoroughly into the spirit of the alterations. She has seen how unladylike, how disturbing, how full of horror even, the part of Rita All-mers is, acted as Miss Achurch acted it. And she has remedied this with a completeness that leaves nothing to be desired—or perhaps only one thing. Was there not a Mr Arcedeckne who, when Thackeray took to lecturing, said, "Have a piano, Thack"? Well, Rita Allmers wants a piano. Mrs Tanqueray had one, and played it so beauti-fully that I have been her infatuated slave ever since. There need be no difficulty about the matter: the breezy Borgheim has only to say, "Now that Alfred is back, Mrs Allmers, wont you give us that study for the left hand we are all so fond of?" and there you are. However, even without the piano, Mrs Campbell succeeded wonderfully in eliminating all unpleasantness from the play. She looked charming; and her dresses were beyond reproach: she carried a mortgage on the "gold and green forests" on her back. Her performance was infinitely reassuring and pretty: its note was, "You silly people: what are you mak-ing all this fuss about? The secret of life is charm and self-possession, and not tantrums about drowned children." The famous line "There stood your champagne; but you tasted it not," was no longer a "secret of the alcove," but a good-humored, mock petulant remonstrance with a man whom there was no pleasing in the matter of wine. There was not a taste of nasty jealousy: this Rita tolerated her dear old stupid's preoccupation with Asta and Eyolf and his books as any sensible (or insensible) woman would. Goodness gracious, I thought, what things that evil-minded Miss Achurch did read into this harmless play! And how nicely Mrs Campbell took the drowning of the child! Just a pretty waving of the fingers, a moderate scream as if she had very nearly walked on a tin tack, and it was all over, without tears, without pain, without more fuss than if she had broken the glass of her watch.

At this rate, it was not long before Rita thoroughly gained the sympathy of the audience. We felt that if she could only get rid of that ridiculous, sentimental Asta (Miss Robins, blind to the object lesson before her, per-sisted in acting Ibsenitically), and induce her fussing, self-conscious, probably underbred husband not to cry for spilt milk, she would be as happy as any lady in the land. Unfortunately, the behaviour of Mr Allmers became more and more intolerable as the second act progressed, though he could not exhaust Rita's patient, slily humorous tolerance. As usual, he wanted to know whether she would like to go and drown herself; and the sweet, cool way in which she answered, "Oh, I dont know, Alfred. No: I think I should have to stay here with *you*—a *litt*-le while" was a lesson to all wives. What a contrast to Miss Achurch, who so unnecessarily filled the stage with the terror of death in this passage! This is what comes of exaggeration, of over-acting, of forgetting that people go to the theatre to be amused, and not to be upset! When Allmers shook his fist at his beautiful wife—O unworthy the name of Briton!—and shouted "*You* are the guilty one in this," her silent dignity overwhelmed him. Nothing could have been in better taste than her description of the pretty way in which her child had lain in the water when he was drowned—his mother's son all over. All the pain was taken out of it by the way it was approached. "I got Borgheim to go down to the pier with me [so nice of Borgheim, dear fellow!]." "And what," interrupts the stupid Allmers, "did you want there?" Rita gave a little laugh at his obtuseness, a laugh which meant "Why, you dear silly," before she replied, "To question the boys as to how it happened." After all, it is these Ibsenite people that create the objections to Ibsen. If Mrs Campbell had played Rita from the first, not a word would have been said against the play; and the whole business would have been quietly over and the theatre closed by this time. But nothing would serve them but their Miss Achurch; and so, instead of a pretty arrangement of the "Eyolf" theme for boudoir pianette, we had it flung to the "Götterdämmerung" orchestra, and blared right into our shrinking souls.

In the third act, the smoothness of the proceedings was somewhat marred by the fact that Mrs Campbell, not knowing her words, had to stop acting and frankly bring the book on the stage and read from it. Now Mrs Campbell reads very clearly and nicely; and the result of course was that the Ibsenite atmosphere began to assert itself, just as it would if the play were read aloud in a private room. However, that has been remedied, no doubt, by this time; and the public may rely on an uninterruptedly quiet evening.

The main drawback is that it is impossible not to feel that Mrs Campbell's Rita, with all her charm, is terribly hampered by the unsuitability of the words Ibsen and Mr Archer have put into her mouth. They were all very well for Miss Achurch, who perhaps, if the truth were known, arranged her acting to suit them; but they are forced, strained, out of tune in all sorts of ways in the mouth of Mrs Campbell's latest creation. Why cannot the dialogue be adapted to her requirements and harmonized with her playing, say by Mr William Black? Ibsen is of no use when anything really ladylike is wanted: you might as well put Beethoven to compose Chaminades. It is true that no man can look at the new Rita without wishing that Heaven had sent him just such a wife, whereas the boldest man would hardly have envied Allmers the other Rita if Miss Achurch had allowed him a moment's leisure for such impertinent speculations; but all the same, the evenings at the Avenue Theatre are likely to be a little languid. I had rather look at a beautiful picture than be flogged, as a general thing; but if I were offered my choice between looking at the most beautiful picture in the world continuously for a fortnight and submitting to, say, a dozen, I think I should choose the flogging. For just the same reason, if I had to choose between seeing Miss Achurch's Rita again, with all its turns of beauty and flashes of grandeur obliterated, and nothing left but its insane jealousy, its agonizing horror, its lacerating remorse, and its maddening unrest, the alternative being another two hours' contemplation of uneventful feminine fascination as personified by Mrs Patrick Campbell, I should go like a lamb to the slaughter. I prefer Mrs Campbell's Rita to her photograph, because it moves and talks; but otherwise there is not so much difference as I expected. Mrs Campbell, as Magda, could do nothing with a public spoiled by Duse. I greatly fear she will do even less, as Rita, with a public spoiled by Miss Achurch.

The representation generally is considerably affected in its scale and effect by the change of Ritas. Mr Courtenay Thorpe, who, though playing *con tutta la forza,* could hardly avoid seeming to underact with Miss Achurch, has now considerable difficulty in avoiding overacting, since he cannot be even in earnest and anxious without producing an effect of being good-humoredly laughed at by Mrs Campbell. Miss Robins, as Asta, has improved greatly on the genteel misery of the first night. She has got complete

hold of the part; and although her old fault of resorting to
the lachrymose for all sorts of pathetic expression produces something of its old monotony, and the voice clings
to one delicate register until the effect verges on affectation, yet Asta comes out as a distinct person about whose
history the audience has learnt something, and not as an
actress delivering a string of lines and making a number of
points more or less effectively. The difficulty is that in this
cheap edition of Little Eyolf Asta, instead of being the
tranquillizing element, becomes the centre of disturbance;
so that the conduct of Allmers in turning for the sake of
peace and quietness from his pretty, coaxing, soothing
wife to his agitated high-strung sister becomes nonsensical.
I pointed out after the first performance that Miss Robins
had not really succeeded in making Asta a peacemaker;
but beside Miss Achurch she easily seemed gentle, whereas
beside Mrs Campbell she seems a volcano. It is only necessary to recall her playing of the frightful ending to the first
act of Alan's Wife, and compare it with Mrs Campbell's
finish to the first act of Little Eyolf, to realize the pre-
posterousness of their relative positions in the cast. Mrs
Campbell's old part of the Ratwife is now played by Miss
Florence Farr. Miss Farr deserves more public sympathy
than any of the other Ibsenite actresses; for they have only
damaged themselves professionally by appearing in Ibsen's
plays, whereas Miss Farr has complicated her difficulties
by appearing in mine as well. Further, instead of either devoting herself to the most personally exacting of all the arts
or else letting it alone, Miss Farr has written clever novels
and erudite works on Babylonish lore; has managed a
theatre capably for a season; and has only occasionally
acted. For an occasional actress she has been rather successful once or twice in producing singular effects in singular parts—her Rebecca in Rosmersholm was remarkable
and promising—but she has not pursued her art with sufficient constancy to attain any authoritative power of carrying out her conceptions, which are, besides, only skin deep.
Her Ratwife is a favorable example of her power of producing a certain strangeness of effect; but it is somewhat
discounted by want of sustained grip in the execution. Miss
Farr will perhaps remedy this if she can find time enough
to spare from her other interests to attend to it. The rest
of the cast is as before. One has no longer any real belief
in the drowning of Master Stewart Dawson, thanks to the

gentle method of Mrs Campbell. Mr Lowne's sensible, healthy superiority to all this morbid Ibsen stuff is greatly reinforced now that Rita takes things nicely and easily.

I cannot help thinking it a great pity that the Avenue enterprise, just as it seemed to be capturing that afternoon classical concert public to which I have always looked for the regeneration of the classical drama, should have paid the penalty of its success by the usual evolution into what is evidently half a timid speculation in a "catch-on," and half an attempt to slacken the rate at which the Avenue Theatre is eating its head off in rent. That evolution of course at once found out the utter incoherence of the enterprise. The original production, undertaken largely at Miss Robins's individual risk, was for the benefit of a vaguely announced Fund, as to the constitution and purpose of which no information was forthcoming, except that it proposed to produce Echegaray's Mariana, with Miss Robins in the title-part. But neither Miss Robins's nor anyone else's interests in this fund seem to have been secured in any way. The considerable profit of the first week of Little Eyolf may, for all that is guaranteed to the contrary, be devoted to the production of an opera, a shadow play from Paris, or a drama in which neither Miss Robins nor any of those who have worked with her may be offered any part or share whatever. There is already just such a fund in existence in the treasury of the Independent Theatre, which strove hard to obtain Little Eyolf for production, and which actually guaranteed part of the booking at the Avenue. But here the same difficulty arose. Miss Achurch would no doubt have trusted the Independent, for the excellent reason that her husband is one of the directors; but no other artist playing for it would have had the smallest security that, had its fortunes been established through their efforts, they would ever have been cast for a part in its future productions. On the other hand, Miss Achurch had no hold on the new fund, which had specially declared its intention of supporting Miss Robins. This has not prevented the production of Little Eyolf, though it has greatly delayed it; for everybody finally threw security to the winds, and played by friendly arrangement on such terms as were possible. As it happened, there was a substantial profit, and it all went to the Fund. Naturally, however, when the enterprise entered upon a purely commercial phase, the artists at once refused to work for the profit of a syndicate on the enthusiastic terms (or no terms) on which they had worked for Ibsen and for one another. The syndicate, on the other hand, had no idea of wasting so expensive a star as Mrs Patrick Campbell on a small part that could be filled for a few pounds, when they could transfer her to the leading part and save Miss Achurch's salary. If they could have substituted an inferior artist for Miss Robins, they could have effected a still further saving, relying on Mrs Pat to draw full houses; but that was made impossible by Miss Robins's power over the stage-right. Consequently, the only sufferer was Miss Achurch; but it is impossible for Miss Robins and Mrs Campbell not to feel that the same thing might have happened to them if there had been no stage-right, and if the syndicate had realized that, when it comes to Ibsen, Miss Achurch is a surer card to play than Mrs Campbell.

Under these circumstances, what likelihood is there of the experiment being resumed or repeated on its old basis? Miss Robins will probably think twice before she creates Mariana without some security that, if she succeeds, the part will not immediately be handed over to Miss Winifred Emery or Miss Julia Neilson. Miss Achurch, triumphantly as she has come out of the comparison with her successor, is not likely to forget her lesson. Mrs Campbell's willingness to enlist in forlorn hopes in the humblest capacity may not improbably be received in future as Laocoon received the offer of the wooden horse. I do not presume to meddle in the affairs of all these actors and authors, patrons and enthusiasts, subscribers and guarantors, though this is quite as much my business as theirs; but after some years' intimate experience of the results of unorganized Ibsenism, I venture to suggest that it would be well to have some equitable form of theatrical organization ready to deal with Ibsen's new play, on the translation of which Mr Archer is already at work.

Richard Himself Again

RICHARD III. Lyceum Theatre, 19 December 1896.

[26 *December* 1896]

The world being yet little better than a mischievous schoolboy, I am afraid it cannot be denied that Punch and Judy holds the field still as the most popular of dra-

matic entertainments. And of all its versions, except those
which are quite above the head of the man in the street,
Shakespear's Richard III is the best. It has abundant
devilry, humor, and character, presented with luxuriant
energy of diction in the simplest form of blank verse.
Shakespear revels in it with just the sort of artistic uncon-
scionableness that fits the theme. Richard is the prince of
Punches: he delights Man by provoking God, and dies
unrepentant and game to the last. His incongruous conventional appendages, such as the Punch hump, the conscience, the fear of ghosts, all impart a spice of outra-
geousness which leaves nothing lacking to the fun of the
entertainment, except the solemnity of those spectators
who feel bound to take the affair as a profound and subtle
historic study.

Punch, whether as Jingle, Macaire, Mephistopheles, or
Richard, has always been a favorite part with Sir Henry
Irving. The craftily mischievous, the sardonically impudent, tickle him immensely, besides providing him with a
welcome relief from the gravity of his serious impersonations. As Richard he drops Punch after the coronation
scene, which, in deference to stage tradition, he makes a
turning-point at which the virtuoso in mischief, having
achieved his ambition, becomes a savage at bay. I do not
see why this should be. In the tent scene, Richard says:

> There is no creature loves me;
> And if I die no soul will pity me.

Macbeth repeats this patch of pathos, and immediately
proceeds to pity himself unstintedly over it; but Richard
no sooner catches the sentimental cadence of his own voice
than the mocker in him is awakened at once, and he adds,
quite in Punch's vein,

> Nay, wherefore should they? since that I myself
> Find in myself no pity for myself.

Sir Henry Irving omits these lines, because he plays, as he
always does, for a pathetically sublime ending. But we
have seen the sublime ending before pretty often; and this
time it robs us of such strokes as Richard's aristocratically
cynical private encouragement to his entourage of peers:

> Our strong arms be our conscience, swords our law.
> March on; join bravely; let us to't pell-mell,
> If not to Heaven, then hand in hand to hell;

followed by his amusingly blackguardly public address to
the rank and file, quite in the vein of the famous and more
successful appeal to the British troops in the Peninsula.
"Will you that are Englishmen fed on beef let yourselves
be licked by a lot of —— Spaniards fed on oranges?"
Despair, one feels, could bring to Punch-Richard nothing
but the exultation of one who loved destruction better than
even victory; and the exclamation

> A thousand hearts are great within my bosom

is not the expression of a hero's courage, but the evil
ecstasy of the destroyer as he finds himself, after a weak,
piping time of peace, back at last in his native element.

Sir Henry Irving's acting edition of the play is so enormously superior to Cibber's, that a playgoer brought up,
as I was, on the old version must needs find an overwhelming satisfaction in it. Not that I object to the particular lines which are now always flung in poor Cibber's face.
"Off with his head: so much for Buckingham!" is just as
worthy of Shakespear as "I'll hear no more. Die, prophet,
in thy speech," and distinctly better than "Off with his son
George's head."

> Hark! the shrill trumpet sounds. To horse! Away!
> My soul's in arms, and eager for the fray,

is ridiculed because Cibber wrote it; but I cannot for the
life of me see that it is inferior to

> Go muster men. My counsel is my shield.
> We must be brief when traitors brave the field.

"Richard's himself again" is capital of its kind. If you
object to the kind, the objection is stronger against Shakespear, who set Cibber the example, and was proclaimed
immortal for it, than against an unfortunate actor who
would never have dreamt of inventing the art of rhetorical
balderdash for himself. The plain reason why the public
for so many generations could see no difference in merit
between the famous Cibber points and

> A horse! A horse! My kingdom for a horse!

was that there was no difference to see. When it came to
fustian, Jack was as good as his master.

The real objection to Cibber's version is that it is what

we call a "one man show." Shakespear, having no room in
a play so full of action for more than one real part, sur-
rounded it with figures whose historical titles and splendid
dresses, helped by a line or two at the right moment, impose on our imagination sufficiently to make us see the
whole Court of Edward IV. If Hastings, Stanley, the
"jockey of Norfolk," the "deep revolving witty Buckingham," and the rest, only bear themselves with sufficient
address not to contradict absolutely the dramatist's suggestion of them, the audience will receive enough impression of their reality, and even of their importance, to give
Richard an air of moving in a Court as the King's brother.
But Cibber could not bear that anyone on the stage should
have an air of importance except himself: if the subordinate members of the company could not act so well as he,
it seemed to him, not that it was his business as the pre-
senter of a play to conceal their deficiencies, but that the
first principles of justice and fair dealing demanded before
all things that his superiority should be made evident to
the public. (And there are not half a dozen leading actors
on the stage today who would not take precisely that view
of the situation.) Consequently he handled Richard III so
as to make every other actor in it obviously ridiculous and
insignificant, except only that Henry VI, in the first act,
was allowed to win the pity of the audience in order that
the effect might be the greater when Richard stabbed him.
No actor could have produced more completely, exactly,
and forcibly the effect aimed at by Cibber than Barry Sullivan, the one actor who kept Cibber's Richard on the stage
during the present half-century. But it was an exhibition,
not a play. Barry Sullivan was full of force, and very
clever: if his power had been less exclusively of the infernal order, or if he had devoted himself to the drama
instead of devoting the drama to himself as a mere means
of self-assertion, one might have said more for him. He
managed to make the audience believe in Richard; but as
he could not make it believe in the others, and probably
did not want to, they destroyed the illusion almost as fast
as he created it. This is why Cibber's Richard, though it
is so simple that the character plays itself as unmistakeably
as the blank verse speaks itself, can only be made endurable by an actor of exceptional personal force. The second
and third acts at the Lyceum, with their atmosphere of

Court faction and their presentation before the audience of
Edward and Clarence, make all the difference between the
two versions.

But the Lyceum has by no means emancipated itself
from superstition—even gross superstition. Italian opera
itself could go no further in folly than the exhibition of a
pretty and popular young actress in tights as Prince
Edward. No doubt we were glad to see Miss Lena Ashwell—for the matter of that we should have been glad to
see Mrs John Wood as the other prince—but from the
moment she came on the stage all serious historical illusion necessarily vanished, and was replaced by the most
extreme form of theatrical convention. Probably Sir Henry
Irving cast Miss Ashwell for the part because he has not
followed her career since she played Elaine in King
Arthur. She was then weak, timid, subordinate, with an
insignificant presence and voice which, contrasted as it
was with Miss Terry's, could only be described—if one
had the heart to do it—as a squawl. Since then she has
developed precipitously. If any sort of success had been
possible for the plays in which she has appeared this year
at the Duke of York's and Shaftesbury Theatres, she
would have received a large share of the credit of it. Even
in Carmen, when, perhaps for the sake of auld lang syne,
she squawled and stood on the tips of her heels for the last
time (let us hope), her scene with the dragoon in the first
act was the one memorable moment in the whole of that
disastrous business. She now returns to the Lyceum stage
as an actress of mark, strong in womanly charm, and not
in the least the sort of person whose sex is so little empha-
sized that it can be hidden by a doublet and hose. You
might as well put forward Miss Ada Rehan as a boy.
Nothing can be more absurd than the spectacle of Sir
Henry Irving elaborately playing the uncle to his little
nephew when he is obviously addressing a fine young
woman in rational dress who is very thoroughly her own
mistress, and treads the boards with no little authority and
assurance as one of the younger generation knocking vigorously at the door. Miss Ashwell makes short work of
the sleepiness of the Lyceum; and though I take urgent
exception to her latest technical theory, which is, that the
bridge of the nose is the seat of facial expression, I admit
that she does all that can be done to reconcile us to the

burlesque of her appearance in a part that should have
been played by a boy.

Another mistake in the casting of the play was Mr
Gordon Craig's Edward IV. As Henry VI, Mr Craig, who
wasted his delicacy on the wrong part, would have been
perfect. Henry not being available, he might have played
Richmond with a considerable air of being a young Henry
VII. But as Edward he was incredible: one felt that
Richard would have had him out of the way years ago if
Margaret had not saved him the trouble by vanquishing
him at Tewkesbury. Shakespear took plenty of pains with
the strong ruffian of the York family: his part in Henry
VI makes it quite clear why he held his own both in and
out of doors. The remedy for the misfit lay ready to the
manager's hand. Mr Cooper, his too burly Richmond,
shewed what a capital Edward he would have made when
he turned at the entrance to his tent, and said, with the
set air of a man not accustomed to be trifled with,

> O Thou, whose captain I account myself,
> Look on my forces with a gracious eye,
> Or you will have me to reckon with afterwards.

The last line was not actually spoken by Mr Cooper; but
he looked it, exactly as Edward IV might have done.

As to Sir Henry Irving's own performance, I am not
prepared to judge it, in point of execution, by what he did
on the first night. He was best in the Court scenes. In the
heavy single-handed scenes which Cibber loved, he was
not, as it seemed to me, answering his helm satisfactorily;
and he was occasionally a little out of temper with his
own nervous condition. He made some odd slips in the
text, notably by repeatedly substituting "you" for "I"—
for instance, "Shine out, fair sun, till you have bought a
glass." Once he inadvertently electrified the house by very
unexpectedly asking Miss Milton to get further up the
stage in the blank verse and penetrating tones of Richard.
Finally, the worry of playing against the vein tired him.
In the tent and battle scenes his exhaustion was too genuine to be quite acceptable as part of the play. The fight
was, perhaps, a relief to his feelings; but to me the spectacle of Mr Cooper pretending to pass his sword three
times through Richard's body, as if a man could be run
through as easily as a cuttle-fish, was neither credible nor

impressive. The attempt to make a stage combat look as imposing as Hazlitt's description of the death of Edmund Kean's Richard reads, is hopeless. If Kean were to return to life and do the combat for us, we should very likely find it as absurd as his habit of lying down on a sofa when he was too tired or too drunk to keep his feet during the final scenes.

Further, it seems to me that Sir Henry Irving should either cast the play to suit his acting or else modify his acting to suit the cast. His playing in the scene with Lady Anne—which, though a Punch scene, is Punch on the Don Giovanni plane—was a flat contradiction, not only of the letter of the lines, but of their spirit and feeling as conveyed unmistakeably by their cadence. This, however, we are used to: Sir Henry Irving never did and never will make use of a play otherwise than as a vehicle for some fantastic creation of his own. But if we are not to have the tears, the passion, the tenderness, the transport of dissimulation which alone can make the upshot credible—if the woman is to be openly teased and insulted, mocked, and disgusted, all through the scene as well as in the first "keen encounter of their wits," why not have Lady Anne presented as a weak, childish-witted, mesmerized creature, instead of as that most awful embodiment of virtue and decorum, the intellectual American lady? Poor Miss Julia Arthur honestly did her best to act the part as she found it in Shakespear; and if Richard had done the same she would have come off with credit. But how could she play to a Richard who would not utter a single tone to which any woman's heart could respond? She could not very well box the actor-manager's ears, and walk off; but really she deserves some credit for refraining from that extreme remedy. She partly had her revenge when she left the stage; for Richard, after playing the scene with her as if he were a Houndsditch salesman cheating a factory girl over a pair of second-hand stockings, naturally could not reach the raptures of the tremendous outburst of elation beginning

> Was ever woman in this humor wooed?
> Was ever woman in this humor won?

One felt inclined to answer, "Never, I assure you," and make an end of the scene there and then. I am prepared to admit that the creations of Sir Henry Irving's imagination

are sometimes—in the case of his Iachimo, for example—
better than those of the dramatists whom he is supposed
to interpret. But what he did in this scene, as well as in the
opening soliloquy, was child's play compared to what
Shakespear meant him to do.

The rest of the performance was—well, it was Lyceum
Shakespear. Miss Geneviève Ward was, of course, a very
capable Margaret; but she missed the one touchstone passage in a very easy part—the tenderness of the appeal to
Buckingham. Mr Macklin, equally of course, had no trouble with Buckingham; but he did not give us that moment
which makes Richard say:

> None are for me
> That look into me with considerate eyes.

Messrs Norman Forbes and W. Farren (junior) played the
murderers in the true Shakespearean manner: that is, as
if they had come straight out of the pantomime of The
Babes in the Wood; and Clarence recited his dream as if
he were an elocutionary coroner summing up. The rest
were respectably dull, except Mr Gordon Craig, Miss Lena
Ashwell, and, in a page's part, Miss Edith Craig, the only
member of the company before whom the manager visibly
quails.

Olivia

OLIVIA. A play in four acts. By the late W. G. Wills. Founded
on an episode in The Vicar of Wakefield. Revival. Lyceum
Theatre, 30 January 1897.

THE FREE PARDON. An original domestic drama in four acts.
By F. C. Philips and Leonard Meyrick. Olympic Theatre, 28
January 1897.

THE PRODIGAL FATHER. An extravagant farce in three acts.
By Glen Macdonough. Strand Theatre, 1 February 1897.

[6 *February* 1897]

The world changes so rapidly nowadays that I hardly
dare speak to my juniors of the things that won my affections when I was a sceptical, imperturbable, hard-headed
young man of twenty-three or thereabouts. Now that I am
an impressionable, excitable, sentimental—if I were a
woman everybody would say hysterical—party on the
wrong side of forty, I am conscious of being in danger

of making myself ridiculous unless I confine my public
expressions of enthusiasm to great works which are still
before their time. That is why, when Olivia was revived
at the Lyceum last Saturday, I blessed the modern custom
of darkening the auditorium during the performance, since
it enabled me to cry secretly. I wonder what our playgoing
freshmen think of Olivia. I do not, of course, mean what
they think of its opening by the descent of two persons to
the footlights to carry on an expository conversation beginning, "It is now twenty-five years since, etc.," nor the
antediluvian asides of the "I do but dissemble" order in
Thornhill's part, at which the gallery burst out laughing.
These things are the mere fashions of the play, not the
life of it. And it is concerning the life of it that I ask how
the young people who see it today for the first time as I
saw it nearly twenty years ago at the old Court Theatre
feel about it.

I must reply that I have not the least idea. For what has
this generation in common with me, or with Olivia, or
with Goldsmith? The first book I ever possessed was a
Bible bound in black leather with gilt metal rims and a
clasp, slightly larger than my sisters' Bibles because I was
a boy, and was therefore fitted with a bigger Bible, precisely as I was fitted with bigger boots. In spite of the
trouble taken to impress me with the duty of reading it
(with the natural result of filling me with a conviction that
such an occupation must be almost as disagreeable as
going to church), I acquired a considerable familiarity
with it, and indeed once read the Old Testament and the
four Gospels straight through, from a vainglorious desire
to do what nobody else had done. A sense of the sanctity
of clergymen, and the holiness of Sunday, Easter, and
Christmas—sanctity and holiness meaning to me a sort of
reasonlessly inhibitory condition in which it was wrong to
do what I liked and especially meritorious to make myself
miserable—was imbibed by me, not from what is called a
strict bringing-up (which, as may be guessed by my readers, I happily escaped), but straight from the social atmosphere. And as that atmosphere was much like the atmosphere of Olivia, I breathe it as one to the manner born.

The question is, then, has that atmosphere changed so
much that the play is only half comprehensible to the
younger spectators? That there is a considerable change I
cannot doubt; for I find that if I mention Adam and Eve,

or Cain and Abel, to people of adequate modern equipment under thirty, they do not know what I am talking
about. The Scriptural literary style which fascinated Wills
as it fascinated Scott is to them quaint and artificial.
Think of the difference between the present Bishop of
London's History of the Popes and anything that the Vicar
of Wakefield could have conceived or written! Think of
the eldest daughters of our two-horse-carriage vicars going
out, as female dons with Newnham degrees, to teach the
granddaughters of ladies shamefacedly conscious of having been educated much as Mrs Primrose was; and ponder
well whether such domestic incidents can give any clue to
poor Olivia going off by coach to be "companion" to
"some old tabby" in Yorkshire, and—most monstrous of
all—previously presenting her brothers with her Prayer-
book and her Pilgrim's Progress, and making them promise to pray for her every night at their mother's knee. Read
The Woman Who Did, bearing in mind its large circulation and the total failure of the attempt to work up the
slightest public feeling against it; and then consider how
obsolescent must be that part of the interest of Olivia
which depends on her sense of a frightful gulf between
her moral position as a legally married woman and that in
which she feels herself when she is told that the legal part
of the ceremony was not valid. Take, too, that old notion
of the home as a sort of prison in which the parents kept
their children locked up under their authority, and from
which, therefore, a daughter who wished to marry without
their leave had to escape through the window as from the
Bastille! Must not this conception, which alone can give
any reality to the elopement of Olivia, be very historical
and abstract to the class of people to whom a leading
London theatre might be expected to appeal? It is easy for
me, taught my letters as I was by a governess who might
have been Mrs Primrose herself, to understand the Wakefield vicarage; but what I want to know is, can it carry any
conviction to people who are a generation ahead of me in
years, and a century in nursery civilization?

If I, drowning the Lyceum carpet with tears, may be
taken as one extreme of the playgoing body, and a modern
lady who, when I mentioned the play the other day, dismissed it with entire conviction as "beneath contempt," as
the other, I am curious to see whether the majority of
those between us are sufficiently near my end to produce

a renewal of the old success. If not, the fault must lie with
the rate of social progress; for Olivia is by a very great deal
the best nineteenth-century play in the Lyceum repertory;
and it has never been better acted. The Ellen Terry of
1897 is beyond all comparison a better Olivia than the
Ellen Terry of 1885. The enchanting delicacy and charm
with which she first stooped to folly at the old Court
Theatre was obscured at the Lyceum, partly, perhaps, by a
certain wrathful energy of developed physical power,
pride, strength, and success in the actress, but certainly, as
I shall presently shew, by the Lyceum conditions. Today
the conditions are altered; the vanities have passed away
with the water under the bridges; and the delicacy and
charm have returned. We have the original Olivia again,
in appearance not discoverably a week older, and much
idealized and softened by the disuse of the mere brute
force of tears and grief, which Miss Terry formerly employed so unscrupulously in the scene of the presents and
of the elopement that she made the audience positively
howl with anguish. She now plays these scenes with infinite
mercy and art, the effect, though less hysterical, being
deeper, whilst the balance of the second act is for the first
time properly adjusted. The third act should be seen by
all those who know Ellen Terry only by her efforts to
extract a precarious sustenance for her reputation from
Shakespear: it will teach them what an artist we have
thrown to our national theatrical Minotaur. When I think
of the originality and modernity of the talent she revealed
twenty years ago, and of its remorseless waste ever since
in "supporting" an actor who prefers The Iron Chest to
Ibsen, my regard for Sir Henry Irving cannot blind me to
the fact that it would have been better for us twenty-five
years ago to have tied him up in a sack with every existing
copy of the works of Shakespear, and dropped him into
the crater of the nearest volcano. It really serves him right
that his Vicar is far surpassed by Mr Hermann Vezin's.
I do not forget that there never was a more beautiful, a
more dignified, a more polished, a more cultivated, a more
perfectly mannered Vicar than Sir Henry Irving's. He
annihilated Thornhill, and scored off everybody else, by
sheer force of behavior. When, on receiving that letter that
looked like a notice of distraint for rent, he said, with
memorable charm of diction, "The law never enters the
poor man's house save as an oppressor," it was difficult to

refrain from jumping on the stage and saying, "Heaven
bless you, sir, why dont you go to London and start a
proprietary chapel? You would be an enormous success
there." There is nothing of this about the Vezin Vicar. To
Farmer Flamborough he may be a fine gentleman; but to
Thornhill he is a very simple one. To the innkeeper he is
a prodigy of learning; but out in the world, looking for his
daughter, his strength lies only in the pathos of his anxious
perseverance. He scores off nobody except in his quaint
theological disputation with the Presbyterian; but he makes
Thornhill ashamed by not scoring off him. It is the appeal
of his humanity and not the beauty of his style that carries
him through; and his idolatry of his daughter is unselfish
and fatherly, just as her affection for him is at last touched
with a motherly instinct which his unworldly helplessness
rouses in her. Handling the part skilfully and sincerely
from this point of view, Mr Hermann Vezin brings the
play back to life on the boards where Sir Henry Irving,
by making it the occasion of an exhibition of extraordinary
refinement of execution and personality, very nearly killed
it as a drama. In the third act, by appealing to our admiration and artistic appreciation instead of to our belief and
human sympathy, Sir Henry Irving made Olivia an orphan.
In the famous passage where the Vicar tries to reprove his
daughter, and is choked by the surge of his affection for
her, he reproved Olivia like a saint and then embraced her
like a lover. With Mr Vezin the reproof is a pitiful stam-
mering failure: its break-down is neither an "effect" nor
a surprise: it is foreseen as inevitable from the first, and
comes as Nature's ordained relief when the sympathy is
strained to bursting point. Mr Vezin's entry in this scene is
very pathetic. His face is the face of a man who has been
disappointed to the very heart every day for months; and
his hungry look round, half longing, half anticipating another disappointment, gives just the right cue for his attitude towards Thornhill, to whom he says, "I forget you,"
not in conscious dignity and judgment, but as if he meant,
"Have I, who forget *myself,* any heart to remember *you*
whilst my daughter is missing?" When a good scene is
taken in this way, the very accessories become eloquent,
like the decent poverty of Mr Vezin's brown overcoat. Sir
Henry Irving, not satisfied to be so plain a person as the
Vicar of Wakefield, gave us something much finer and
more distinguished, the beauty of which had to stand as a

substitute for the pathos of those parts of the play which it destroyed. Mr Vezin takes his part for better for worse, and fits himself faithfully into it. The result can only be appreciated by those whose memory is good enough to compare the effect of the third act in 1885 and today. Also, to weigh Olivia with the Vicar right against Olivia with the Vicar wrong. I purposely force the comparison between the two treatments because it is a typical one. The history of the Lyceum, with its twenty years' steady cultivation of the actor as a personal force, and its utter neglect of the drama, is the history of the English stage during that period. Those twenty years have raised the social status of the theatrical profession, and culminated in the official recognition of our chief actor as the peer of the President of the Royal Academy, and the figure-heads of the other arts. And now I, being a dramatist and not an actor, want to know when the drama is to have its turn. I do not suggest that G.B.S. should condescend to become K.C.B.; but I do confidently affirm that if the actors think they can do without the drama, they are most prodigiously mistaken. The huge relief with which I found myself turning from Olivia as an effective exhibition of the extraordinary accomplishments of Sir Henry Irving to Olivia as a naturally acted story has opened my eyes to the extent to which I have been sinking the true dramatic critic in the connoisseur in virtuosity, and forgetting what they were doing at the Lyceum in the contemplation of how they were doing it. Henceforth I shall harden my heart as Wagner hardened his heart against Italian singing, and hold diction, deportment, sentiment, personality, and character as dust in the balance against the play and the credibility of its representation.

The rest of the company, not supporting, but supported *by* Mr Vezin and Miss Terry—thereby reverting to the true artistic relation between the principal parts and the minor ones—appear to great advantage. Only, one misses Mr Terriss as Thornhill, since Mr Cooper cannot remake himself so completely as to give much point to Olivia's line, once so effective, "As you stand there flicking your boot, you look the very picture of vain indifference." Mr Norman Forbes does not resume his old part of Moses, which is now played by Mr Martin Harvey. Mr Macklin as Burchell and Mr Sam Johnson as Farmer Flamborough, Master Stewart Dawson and Miss Valli Valli as Dick and

Bill, and Miss Julia Arthur as Sophia, all fall admirably into their places. Miss Maud Milton is a notably good Mrs Primrose: her share in the scene of the pistols, which attains a most moving effect, could not have been better. Miss Edith Craig makes a resplendent Bohemian Girl of the gipsy, the effect being very nearly operatic. Miss Craig may have studied her part from the life; but if so, I should be glad to know where, so that I may instantly ride off to have my fortune told by the original.

.   .   .   .

Shakespear in Manchester

ANTONY AND CLEOPATRA. Shakespearean revival by Mr Louis Calvert at the Queen's Theatre, Manchester.

[20 *March* 1897]

Shakespear is so much the word-musician that mere practical intelligence, no matter how well prompted by dramatic instinct, cannot enable anybody to understand his works or arrive at a right execution of them without the guidance of a fine ear. At the great emotional climaxes we find passages which are Rossinian in their reliance on symmetry of melody and impressiveness of march to redeem poverty of meaning. In fact, we have got so far beyond Shakespear as a man of ideas that there is by this time hardly a famous passage in his works that is considered fine on any other ground than that it sounds beautifully, and awakens in us the emotion that originally expressed itself by its beauty. Strip it of that beauty of sound by prosaic paraphrase, and you have nothing left but a platitude that even an American professor of ethics would blush to offer to his disciples. Wreck that beauty by a harsh, jarring utterance, and you will make your audience wince as if you were singing Mozart out of tune. Ignore it by "avoiding sing-song"—that is, ingeniously breaking the verse up so as to make it sound like prose, as the professional elocutionist prides himself on doing—and you are landed in a stilted, monstrous jargon that has not even the prosaic merit of being intelligible. Let me give one example: Cleopatra's outburst at the death of Antony:

> Oh withered is the garland of the war,
> The soldier's pole is fallen: young boys and girls
> Are level now with men: the odds is gone,

> And there is nothing left remarkable
> Beneath the visiting moon.

This is not good sense—not even good grammar. If you
ask what does it all mean, the reply must be that it means
just what its utterer feels. The chaos of its thought is a
reflection of her mind, in which one can vaguely discern
a wild illusion that all human distinction perishes with the
gigantic distinction between Antony and the rest of the
world. Now it is only in music, verbal or other, that the
feeling which plunges thought into confusion can be artistically expressed. Any attempt to deliver such music pro-
saically would be as absurd as an attempt to speak an
oratorio of Handel's, repetitions and all. The right way to
declaim Shakespear is the sing-song way. Mere metric
accuracy is nothing. There must be beauty of tone, expressive inflection, and infinite variety of *nuance* to sustain the
fascination of the infinite monotony of the chanting.

Miss Janet Achurch, now playing Cleopatra in Manchester, has a magnificent voice, and is as full of ideas as
to vocal effects as to everything else on the stage. The
march of the verse and the strenuousness of the rhetoric
stimulate her great artistic susceptibility powerfully: she is
determined that Cleopatra shall have rings on her fingers
and bells on her toes, and that she shall have music wherever she goes. Of the hardihood of ear with which she
carries out her original and often audacious conceptions of
Shakespearean music I am too utterly unnerved to give
any adequate description. The lacerating discord of her
wailings is in my tormented ears as I write, reconciling me
to the grave. It is as if she had been excited by the Hallelu-
jah Chorus to dance on the keyboard of a great organ with
all the stops pulled out. I cannot—dare not—dwell on it.
I admit that when she is using the rich middle of her voice
in a quite normal and unstudied way, intent only on the
feeling of the passage, the effect leaves nothing to be desired; but the moment she raises the pitch to carry out
some deeply planned vocal masterstroke, or is driven by
Shakespear himself to attempt a purely musical execution
of a passage for which no other sort of execution is possible, then—well then, hold on tightly to the elbows of your
stall, and bear it like a man. And when the feat is accom-
panied, as it sometimes is, by bold experiments in facial
expression which all the passions of Cleopatra, complicated by seventy-times-sevenfold demoniacal possession,

could but faintly account for, the eye has to share the anguish of the ear instead of consoling it with Miss Achurch's beauty. I have only seen the performance once; and I would not unsee it again if I could; but none the less I am a broken man after it. I may retain always an impression that I have actually looked on Cleopatra enthroned dead in her regal robes, with her hand on Antony's, and her awful eyes inhibiting the victorious Cæsar. I grant that this "resolution" of the discord is grand and memorable; but oh! how infernal the discord was whilst it was still unresolved! That is the word that sums up the objection to Miss Achurch's Cleopatra in point of sound: it is discordant.

I need not say that at some striking points Miss Achurch's performance shews the same exceptional inventiveness and judgment in acting as her Ibsen achievements did, and that her energy is quite on the grand scale of the play. But even if we waive the whole musical question— and that means waiving the better half of Shakespear— she would still not be Cleopatra. Cleopatra says that the man who has seen her "hath seen some majesty, and should know." One conceives her as a trained professional queen, able to put on at will the deliberate artificial dignity which belongs to the technique of court life. She may keep it for state occasions, like the unaffected Catherine of Russia, or always retain it, like Louis XIV, in whom affectation was nature; but that she should have no command of it—that she should rely in modern republican fashion on her personal force, with a frank contempt for ceremony and artificiality, as Miss Achurch does, is to spurn her own part. And then, her beauty is not the beauty of Cleopatra. I do not mean merely that she is not "with Phœbus' amorous pinches black," or brown, bean-eyed, and pickaxe-faced. She is not even the English (or Anglo-Jewish) Cleopatra, the serpent of old Thames. She is of the broad-browed, column-necked, Germanic type—the Wagner heroine type—which in England, where it must be considered as the true racial heroic type, has given us two of our most remarkable histrionic geniuses in Miss Achurch herself and our dramatic singer, Miss Marie Brema, both distinguished by great voices, busy brains, commanding physical energy, and untameable impetuosity and originality. Now this type has its limitations, one of them being that it has not the genius of worthlessness, and so cannot present it

on the stage otherwise than as comic depravity or master-
ful wickedness. Adversity makes it superhuman, not sub-
human, as it makes Cleopatra. When Miss Achurch comes
on one of the weak, treacherous, affected streaks in Cleopatra, she suddenly drops from an Egyptian warrior queen
into a naughty English *petite bourgeoise,* who carries off a
little greediness and a little voluptuousness by a very unheroic sort of prettiness. That is, she treats it as a stroke of
comedy; and as she is not a comedian, the stroke of
comedy becomes in her hands a bit of fun. When the
bourgeoise turns into a wild cat, and literally snarls and
growls menacingly at the bearer of the news of Antony's
marriage with Octavia, she is at least more Cleopatra; but
when she masters herself, as Miss Achurch does, not in
gipsy fashion, but by a heroic-grandiose act of self-
mastery, quite foreign to the nature of the "tripled turned
wanton" (as Mr Calvert bowdlerizes it) of Shakespear, she
is presently perplexed by fresh strokes of comedy—

> He's very knowing.
> I do perceive 't: theres nothing in her yet:
> The fellow has good judgment.

At which what can she do but relapse farcically into the
bourgeoise again, since it is not on the heroic side of her to
feel elegantly self-satisfied whilst she is saying mean and
silly things, as the true Cleopatra does? Miss Achurch's
finest feat in this scene was the terrible look she gave the
messenger when he said, in dispraise of Octavia, "And I
do think she's thirty"—Cleopatra being of course much
more. Only, as Miss Achurch had taken good care not to
look more, the point was a little lost on Manchester. Later
on she is again quite in her heroic element (and out of
Cleopatra's) in making Antony fight by sea. Her "I have
sixty sails, Cæsar none better," and her overbearing of the
counsels of Enobarbus and Canidius to fight by land are
effective, but effective in the way of a Boadicea, worth ten
guzzling Antonys. There is no suggestion of the petulant
folly of the spoiled beauty who has not imagination enough
to know that she will be frightened when the fighting begins. Consequently when the audience, already puzzled as
to how to take Cleopatra, learns that she has run away
from the battle, and afterwards that she has sold Antony
to Cæsar, it does not know what to think. The fact is,
Miss Achurch steals Antony's thunder and Shakespear's

thunder and Ibsen's thunder and her own thunder so that
she may ride the whirlwind for the evening; and though
this *Walkürenritt* is intense and imposing, in spite of the
discords, the lapses into farce, and the failure in comedy
and characterization—though once or twice a really memorable effect is reached—yet there is not a stroke of Cleopatra in it; and I submit that to bring an ardent Shakespearean like myself all the way to Manchester to see
Antony and Cleopatra with Cleopatra left out, even with
Brynhild-cum-Nora Helmer substituted, is very different
from bringing down soft-hearted persons like Mr Clement
Scott and Mr William Archer, who have allowed Miss
Achurch to make Ibsen-and-Wagner pie of our poor Bard's
historical masterpiece without a word of protest.

And yet all that I have said about Miss Achurch's Cleopatra cannot convey half the truth to those who have not
seen Mr Louis Calvert's Antony. It is on record that
Antony's cooks put a fresh boar on the spit every hour,
so that he should never have to wait long for his dinner.
Mr Calvert looks as if he not only had the boars put on
the spit, but ate them. He is inexcusably fat: Mr Bourchier
is a sylph by comparison. You will conclude, perhaps, that
his fulness of habit makes him ridiculous as a lover. But
not at all. It is only your rhetorical tragedian whose effec-
tiveness depends on the oblatitude of his waistcoat. Mr
Calvert is a comedian—brimming over with genuine humane comedy. His one really fine tragic effect is the burst
of laughter at the irony of fate with which, as he lies dying,
he learns that the news of Cleopatra's death, on the receipt
of which he mortally wounded himself, is only one of her
theatrical, sympathy-catching lies. As a lover, he leaves
his Cleopatra far behind. His features are so pleasant, his
manner so easy, his humor so genial and tolerant, and
his portliness so frank and unashamed, that no goodnatured woman could resist him; and so the topsiturvitude
of the performance culminates in the plainest evidence
that Antony is the seducer of Cleopatra instead of Cleopatra of Antony. Only at one moment was Antony's girth
awkward. When Eros, who was a slim and rather bony
young man, fell on his sword, the audience applauded
sympathetically. But when Antony in turn set about the
Happy Despatch, the consequences suggested to the imagination were so awful that shrieks of horror arose in the
pit; and it was a relief when Antony was borne off by four

stalwart soldiers, whose sinews cracked audibly as they heaved him up from the floor.

Here, then, we have Cleopatra tragic in her comedy, and Antony comedic in his tragedy. We have Cleopatra heroically incapable of flattery or flirtation, and Antony with a wealth of blarney in every twinkle of his eye and every fold of his chin. We have, to boot, certain irrelevant but striking projections of Miss Achurch's genius, and a couple of very remarkable stage pictures invented by the late Charles Calvert. But in so far as we have Antony and Cleopatra, we have it partly through the genius of the author, who imposes his conception on us through the dialogue in spite of everything that can be done to contradict him, and partly through the efforts of the secondary performers.

Of these Mr George F. Black, who plays Octavius Cæsar, speaks blank verse rightly, if a little roughly, and can find his way to the feeling of the line by its cadence. Mr Mollison—who played Henry IV here to Mr Tree's Falstaff—is Enobarbus, and spouts the description of the barge with all the honors. The minor parts are handled with the spirit and intelligence that can always be had by a manager who really wants them. A few of the actors are certainly very bad; but they suffer rather from an insane excess of inspiration than from apathy. Charmian and Iras (Miss Ada Mellon and Miss Maria Fauvet) produce an effect out of all proportion to their scanty lines by the conviction and loyalty with which they support Miss Achurch; and I do not see why Cleopatra should ungratefully take Iras's miraculous death as a matter of course by omitting the lines beginning "Have I the aspic in my lips," nor why Charmian should be robbed of her fine reply to the Roman's "Charmian, is this well done?" "It is well done, and fitted for a princess descended of so many royal kings." No doubt the Cleopatras of the palmy days objected to anyone but themselves dying effectively, and so such cuts became customary; but the objection does not apply to the scene as arranged in Manchester. Modern managers should never forget that if they take care of the minor actors the leading ones will take care of themselves.

May I venture to suggest to Dr Henry Watson that his incidental music, otherwise irreproachable, is in a few places much too heavily scored to be effectively spoken

through? Even in the *entr'actes* the brass might be spared
in view of the brevity of the intervals and the almost continuous strain for three hours on the ears of the audience.
If the music be revived later as a concert suite, the wind
can easily be restored.

Considering that the performance requires an efficient
orchestra and chorus, plenty of supernumeraries, ten or
eleven distinct scenes, and a cast of twenty-four persons,
including two leading parts of the first magnitude; that
the highest price charged for admission is three shillings;
and that the run is limited to eight weeks, the production
must be counted a triumph of management. There is not
the slightest reason to suppose that any London manager
could have made a revival of Antony and Cleopatra more
interesting. Certainly none of them would have planned
that unforgettable statue death for Cleopatra, for which,
I suppose, all Miss Achurch's sins against Shakespear will
be forgiven her. I begin to have hopes of a great metropolitan vogue for that lady now, since she has at last done
something that is thoroughly wrong from beginning to end.

Mr Pinero on Turning Forty

THE PHYSICIAN. A new play of modern life in four acts. By
Henry Arthur Jones. Criterion Theatre, 25 March 1897.

THE PRINCESS AND THE BUTTERFLY, OR THE FANATICS. An
original comedy in five acts. By Arthur W. Pinero. St James's
Theatre, 29 March 1897.

[3 *April* 1897]

When I was a fastidious youth, my elders, ever eager to
confer bad advice on me and to word it with disgusting
homeliness, used to tell me never to throw away dirty
water until I got in clean. To which I would reply that as
I had only one bucket, the thing was impossible. So until
I grew middle-aged and sordid, I acted on the philosophy
of Bunyan's couplet:

A man there was, tho' some did count him mad,
The more he cast away, the more he had.

Indeed, in the matter of ideals, faiths, convictions and the
like, I was of opinion that Nature abhorred a vacuum,
and that you might empty your bucket boldly with the
fullest assurance that you would find it fuller than ever

before you had time to set it down again. But herein I
youthfully deceived myself. I grew up to find the genteel
world full of persons with empty buckets. Now The Physician is a man with an empty bucket. "By God!" he says
(he doesnt believe in God), "I dont believe theres in any
London slum, or jail, or workhouse, a poor wretch with
such a horrible despair in his heart as I have today. I tell
you Ive caught the disease of our time, of our society, of
our civilization—middle age, disillusionment. My youth's
gone. My beliefs are gone. I enjoy nothing. I believe in
nothing. Belief! Thats the placebo I want. That would
cure me. My work means nothing to me. Success means
nothing to me. I cure people with a grin and a sneer. I
keep on asking myself, 'To what end? To what end?' "

O dear! Have we not had enough of this hypochondriasis
from our immortal bard in verse which—we have it on his
own authority—"not marble, nor the gilded monuments
of princes, shall outlive"? It is curable by Mr Meredith's
prescription—the tonic of comedy; and when I see a
comedian of Mr Wyndham's skill and a dramatist of Mr
Jones's mother-wit entering into a physicianly conspiracy
to trade in the disease it is their business to treat, I abandon all remorse, flatly refuse to see any "sympathetic"
drama in a mere shaking of the head at life, and vow that
at least one of Dr Carey's audience shall tell him that
there is nothing in the world more pitiably absurd than
the man who goes about telling his friends that life is not
worth living, when they know perfectly well that if he
meant it he could stop living much more easily than go on
eating. Even the incorrigible Hamlet admitted this, and
made his excuse for not resorting to the bare bodkin; but
Dr Carey, who says "I never saw a man's soul," has not
Hamlet's excuse. His superstitions are much cruder: they
do not rise above those of an African witch-finder or
Sioux medicine-man. He pretends to "cure" diseases—
Mother Carey is much like Mother Seigel in this respect
—and holds up a test-tube, whispering, "I fancy I'm on the
track of the cancer microbe: I'm not sure I havent got
my gentleman here." At which abject depth of nineteenth-
century magicianism he makes us esteem Dr Diafoirus
and the Apothecary in Romeo and Juliet as, in comparison,
dazzling lights of science.

And now, as if it were not bad enough to have Mr Jones
in this state of mind, we have Mr Pinero, who was born,

as I learn from a recent biographic work of reference, in 1855, quite unable to get away from the same tragic preoccupation with the horrors of middle age. He has launched at us a play in five acts—two and a half of them hideously superfluous—all about being over forty. The heroine is forty, and can talk about nothing else. The hero is over forty, and is blind to every other fact in the universe. Having this topic of conversation in common, they get engaged in order that they may save one another from being seduced by the attraction of youth into foolish marriages. They then fall in love, she with a fiery youth of twenty-eight, he with a meteoric girl of eighteen. Up to the last moment I confess I had sufficient confidence in Mr Pinero's saving sense of humor to believe that he would give the verdict against himself, and admit that the meteoric girl was too young for the hero (twenty-seven years' discrepancy) and the heroine too old for the fiery youth (thirteen years' discrepancy). But no: he gravely decided that the heart that loves never ages; and now perhaps he will write us another drama, limited strictly to three acts, with, as heroine, the meteoric girl at forty with her husband at sixty-seven, and, as hero, the fiery youth at forty-nine with his wife at sixty-two.

Mr Henry Arthur Jones is reconciled to his own fate, though he cannot bear to see it overtake a woman. Hear Lady Val in his play! "I smell autumn; I scent it from afar. I ask myself how many years shall I have a man for my devoted slave. . . . Oh, my God, Lewin [she is an Atheist], it never can be worth while for a woman to live one moment after she has ceased to be loved." This, I admit, is as bad as Mr Pinero: the speech is actually paraphrased by Mrs St Roche in the St James's play. But mark the next sentence: "And you men have the laugh of us. Age doesnt wither you or stale your insolent, victorious, self-satisfied, smirking, commonplace durability! Oh, you brutes, I hate you all, because youre warranted to wash and wear for fifty years." Observe, *fifty* years, not forty. I turn again to my book of reference, and find, as I expected, that Mr Jones was born in 1851. I discover also that I myself was born in 1856. And this is '97. Well, my own opinion is that sixty is the prime of life for a man. Cheer up, Mr Pinero: courage, Henry Arthur! "What though the grey do something mingle with our younger brown" (excuse my quoting Shakespear), the world is as young as ever. Go look at the people in Oxford Street: they are always the same age.

As regards any conscious philosophy of life, I am bound to say that there is not so much (if any) difference between Mr Jones and Mr Pinero as the very wide differences between them in other respects would lead us to suppose. The moment their dramatic inventiveness flags, and they reach the sentimentally reflective interval between genuine creation and the breaking off work until next day, they fall back on the two great Shakespearean grievances—namely, that we cannot live for ever and that life is not worth living. And then they strike up the old tunes—"Out, out, brief candle!" "Vanitas vanitatum," "To what end?" and so on. But in their fertile, live moments they are as unlike as two men can be in the same profession. At such time Mr Pinero has no views at all. Our novelists, especially those of the Thackeray-Trollope period, have created a fictitious world for him; and it is about this world that he makes up stage stories for us. If he observes life, he does so as a gentleman observes the picturesqueness of a gipsy. He presents his figures coolly, clearly, and just as the originals like to conceive themselves—for instance, his ladies and gentlemen are not real ladies and gentlemen, but ladies and gentlemen as they themselves (mostly modelling themselves on fiction) aim at being; and so Bayswater and Kensington have a sense of being understood by Mr Pinero. Mr Jones, on the other hand, works passionately from the real. By throwing himself sympathetically into his figures he gives them the stir of life; but he also often raises their energy to the intensity of his own, and confuses their feelings with the revolt of his own against them. Above all, by forcing to the utmost their aspect as they really are as against their pose, he makes their originals protest violently that he cannot draw them—a protest formerly made, on exactly the same grounds, against Dickens. For example, Lady Val in The Physician is a study of a sort of clever fashionable woman now current; but it is safe to say that no clever fashionable woman, nor any admirer of clever fashionable women, will ever admit the truth or good taste of the likeness. And yet she is very carefully studied from life, and only departs from it flatteringly in respect of a certain energy of vision and intensity of conscience that belong to Mr Jones and not in the least to herself.

Compare with Lady Val the Princess Pannonia in Mr Pinero's play. You will be struck instantly with the comparative gentlemanliness of Mr Pinero. He seems to say, "Dear lady, do not be alarmed: I will shew just enough of your weaknesses to make you interesting; but otherwise I shall take you at your own valuation and make the most of you. I shall not forget that you are a Princess from the land of novels. My friend Jones, who would have made an excellent Dissenting clergyman, has a vulgar habit of bringing persons indiscriminately to the bar of his convictions as to what is needful for the life and welfare of the real world. You need apprehend no such liberties from me. I have no convictions, no views, no general ideas of any kind: I am simply a dramatic artist, only too glad to accept a point of view from which you are delightful. At the same time, I am not insensible to the great and tragic issues that meet us wherever we turn. For instance, it is hardly possible to reach the age of forty without etc. etc. etc." And accordingly you have a cool, tasteful, polished fancy picture which reflects the self-consciousness of Princesses and the illusions of their imitators much more accurately than if Mr Jones had painted it.

The two plays present an extraordinary contrast in point of dramatic craft. It is no exaggeration to say that within two minutes from the rising of the curtain Mr Jones has got tighter hold of his audience and further on with his play than Mr Pinero within two hours. During those two hours, The Princess marks time complacently on the interest, the pathos, the suggestiveness, the awful significance of turning forty. The Princess has done it; Sir George Lamorant has done it; Mrs St Roche has done it; so has her husband. Lady Chichele, Lady Ringstead, and Mrs Sabiston have all done it. And they have all to meditate on it like Hamlet meditating on suicide; only, since soliloquies are out of fashion, nearly twenty persons have to be introduced to listen to them. The resultant exhibition of High Life Above Stairs is no doubt delightful to the people who had rather read the fashionable intelligence than my articles. To me not even the delight of playing Peeping Tom whilst Princess Pannonia was getting out of bed and flattering me with a vain hope that the next item would be her bath could reconcile me to two hours of it. If the women had worn some tolerable cap-and-apron uniform I could have borne it better; but those

dreadful dresses, mostly out of character and out of complexion—I counted nine failures to four successes—upset
my temper, which was not restored by a witless caricature
of Mr Max Beerbohm (would he had written it himself!),
or by the spectacle of gilded youth playing with toys whilst
Sir George Lamorant put on a fool's cap and warned
them that they would all be forty-five presently, or even by
the final tableau, unspeakably sad to the British mind, of
the host and hostess retiring for the night to separate apart-
ments instead of tucking themselves respectably and do-
mestically into the same feather bed. Yet who shall say
that there is no comedy in the spectacle of Mr Pinero
moralizing, and the public taking his reflections seriously?
He is much more depressing when he makes a gentleman
throw a glass of water at another gentleman in a drawing
room, thereby binding the other gentleman in honor to
attack his assailant in the street with a walking stick,
whereupon the twain go to France to fight a duel for all
the world as if they were at the Surrey Theatre. However,
when this is over the worst is over. Mr Pinero gets to
business at about ten o'clock, and the play begins in the
middle of the third act—a good, old-fashioned, well-sea-
soned bit of sentimental drawing room fiction, daintily put
together, and brightening at the end into a really light-
hearted and amusing act of artificial comedy. So, though
it is true that the man who goes to the St James's Theatre
now at 7.45 will wish he had never been born, none the
less will the man who goes at 9.30 spend a very pleasant
evening.

The two authors have not been equally fortunate in respect of casting. Half Mr Jones's play—the women's half
—is obliterated in performance. His Edana is a sterling,
convinced girl-enthusiast. "Her face," says the Doctor,
"glowed like a live coal." This sort of characterization
cannot be effected on the stage by dialogue. Enthusiasts
are magnetic, not by what they say, or even what they do,
but by how they say and do it. Mr Jones could write "yes"
and "no"; but it rested with the actress whether the affirmation and denial should be that of an enthusiast or not.
Edana at the Criterion is played by Miss Mary Moore.
Now Miss Moore is a dainty light comedian; and her
intelligence, and a certain power of expressing grief rather
touchingly and prettily, enable her to take painful parts
on occasion without making herself ridiculous. But they

do not enable her to play an enthusiast. Consequently her Edana is a simple substitution of what she can do for what she is required to do. The play is not only weakened by this—all plays get weakened somewhere when they are performed—it is dangerously confused, because Edana, instead of being a stronger character than Lady Val, and therefore conceivably able to draw the physician away from her, is just the sort of person who would stand no chance against her with such a man. To make matters worse, Lady Val is played by Miss Marion Terry, who is in every particular, from her heels to her hairpins, exactly what Lady Val could not be, her qualities being even more fatal to the part than her faults. A more hopeless pair of misfits has never befallen an author. On the other hand, Mr Jones has been exceptionally fortunate in his men. Mr Alfred Bishop's parson and Mr J. G. Taylor's Stephen Gurdon are perfect. Mr Thalberg does what is wanted to set the piece going on the rising of the curtain with marked ability. The easy parts—which include some racy village studies—are well played. Mr Leslie Kenyon, as Brooker, has the tact that is all the part requires; and the Physician is played with the greatest ease by Mr Wyndham himself, who will no doubt draw all Harley Street to learn what a consulting room manner can be in the hands of an artist. The performance as a whole is exceptionally fine, the size of the theatre admitting of a delicacy of handling without which Mr Jones's work loses half its sincerity.

In The Princess matters are better balanced. There is a fearful waste of power: out of twenty-nine performers, of whom half are accustomed to play important parts in London, hardly six have anything to do that could not be sufficiently well done by nobodies. Mr Pinero seems to affirm his supremacy by being extravagant in his demands for the sake of extravagance; and Mr Alexander plays up to him with an equally high hand by being no less extravagant in his compliances. So the piece is at all events not underplayed; and it has crowned the reputation of Miss Fay Davis, whose success, the most sensational achieved at the St James's Theatre since that of Mrs Patrick Campbell as Paula Tanqueray, is a success of cultivated skill and self-mastery on the artist's part, and not one of the mere accidents of the stage. Miss Neilson, ever fair and fortunate, puts a pleasant face on a long and uninteresting part,

all about the horrors of having reached forty without losing "the aroma of a stale girlhood." The Princess is ladylike and highly literary. When, in the familiar dilemma of
the woman of forty with an inexperienced lover, she is
forced to prevent his retiring in abashed despair by explaining to him that her terrifying fluster over his more
personal advances only means that she likes them and
wants some more, she choicely words it, "I would not have
it otherwise." And his ardor is volcanic enough to survive
even that. The lover's part falls to Mr H. B. Irving, who
is gaining steadily in distinction of style and strength of
feeling. Mr Alexander has little to do beyond what he has
done often before—make himself interesting enough to
conceal the emptiness of his part. He laments his forty-five
years as mercifully as such a thing may be done; and he
secures toleration for the silly episodes of the fool's cap
and the quarrel with Maxime. Mr Esmond makes the
most of a comic scrap of character; and Miss Rose Leclercq is duly exploited in the conventional manner as
Lady Ringstead. Miss Patty Bell's Lady Chichele is not
bad: the rest I must pass over from sheer exhaustion.

Mainly about Shakespear

ANTONY AND CLEOPATRA. Olympic Theatre, 24 May 1897.

.   .   .   .   .

[29 *May* 1897]

If only I were a moralist, like Shakespear, how I could
improve the occasion of the fall of the once Independent
Theatre! A fortnight ago that body, whose glory was its
freedom from actor-managership and its repertory of plays
which no commercial theatre would produce, was hanging
the wreath on the tip-top of the Independent tower over
its performance of the Wild Duck. This week it has offered
us, as choice Independent fare, the thirty-year-old "acting
version" of Shakespear's Antony and Cleopatra, with
which Miss Janet Achurch made a sensation the other
day in Manchester. I ask the directors of the Independent
Theatre what they mean by this? I ask it as a shareholder
who put down his hard-earned money for the express purpose of providing a refuge from such exhibitions. I ask it
as a member of the body politic, whose only hope of
dramatic nutrition is in the strict specialization of these

newly and painfully evolved little organs, the Independent and New Century Theatres. I ask it as a critic who has pledged himself for the integrity of the Independent Theatre as recklessly as Falstaff did for Pistol's honesty. Even Pistol was able to retort on Falstaff, "Didst thou not share? Hadst thou not fifteen pence?" But I have not had fifteen pence: I have only had an afternoon of lacerating anguish, spent partly in contemplating Miss Achurch's overpowering experiments in rhetoric, and partly in wishing I had never been born.

If I speak intemperately on this matter, please to remember what I have endured throughout a quarter of a century of playgoing. Years ago—how many does not matter —I went to the theatre one evening to see a play called The Two Roses, and was much struck therein by the acting of one Henry Irving, who created a modern realistic character named Digby Grand in a manner which, if applied to an Ibsen play now, would astonish us as much as Miss Achurch's Nora astonished us. When next I saw that remarkable actor, he had gone into a much older established branch of his business, and was trying his hand at Richelieu. He was new to the work; and I suffered horribly; the audience suffered horribly; and I hope (though I am a humane man, considering my profession) that the actor suffered horribly. For I knew what rhetoric ought to be, having tasted it in literature, music, and painting; and as to the stage, I had seen great Italians do it in the days when Duse, like Ibsen, had not arrived. After a long period of convalescence, I ventured again to the Lyceum, and saw Hamlet. There was a change, Richelieu had been incessantly excruciating: Hamlet had only moments of violent ineptitude separated by lengths of dulness; and though I yawned, I felt none the worse next morning. When some unaccountable impulse led me to the Lyceum again (I suspect it was to see Miss Ellen Terry), The Lady of Lyons was in the bill. Before Claude Melnotte had moved his wrist and chin twice, I saw that he had mastered the rhetorical style at last. His virtuosity of execution soon became extraordinary. His Charles I, for instance, became a miracle of the most elaborate class of this sort of acting. It was a hard-earned and well-deserved triumph; and by it his destiny was accomplished; the anti-Irvingites were confuted; the caricaturists were disconcerted; and the foreign actor could no longer gasp at us when we talked

of Irving as a master of his art. But suppose he had fore-
gone this victory! Suppose he had said, "I can produce
studies of modern life and character like Digby Grand. I
can create weird supernatural figures like Vanderdecken
(Vanderdecken, now forgotten, was a masterpiece), and
all sorts of grotesques. But if I try this rhetorical art of
making old-fashioned heroics impressive and even beautiful, I shall not only make a fool of myself as a beginner
where I have hitherto shone as an adept, but—what is of
deeper import to me and the world—I shall give up a
fundamentally serious social function for a fundamentally
nonsensical theatrical accomplishment." What would have
been the result of such a renunciation? We should have
escaped Lyceum Shakespear; and we should have had the
ablest manager of the day driven by life-or-death necessity
to extract from contemporary literature the proper food
for the modern side of his talent, and thus to create a
new drama instead of galvanizing an old one and cutting
himself off from all contact with the dramatic vitality of
his time. And what an excellent thing that would have been
both for us and for him!

Now what Sir Henry Irving has done, for good or evil,
Miss Janet Achurch can do too. If she is tired of being
"an Ibsenite actress" and wants to be a modern Ristori, it
is clear that the public will submit to her apprenticeship
as humbly as they submitted to Sir Henry Irving's. Mr
Grossmith may caricature her at his recitals; flippant critics
may pass jests through the stalls or pittites with an ungovernable sense of the ludicrous burst into guffaws; the
orchestra may writhe like a heap of trodden worms at
each uplifting of her favorite tragic wail; but now, as at
the Lyceum of old, the public as a whole is clearly at her
mercy; for in art the strength of a chain is its strongest
link; and once the power to strike a masterstroke is clearly
felt, the public will wait for it patiently through all ex-
tremities of experimental blundering. But the result will
repeat itself as surely as the process. Let Miss Achurch
once learn to make the rhetorical drama plausible, and
thenceforth she will never do anything else. Her interest
in life and character will be supplanted by an interest in
plastique and execution; and she will come to regard emotion simply as the best of lubricants and stimulants, caring
nothing for its specific character so long as it is of a sufficiently obvious and facile sort to ensure a copious flow

without the fatigue of thought. She will take to the one-part plays of Shakespear, Schiller, Giacometti, and Sardou, and be regarded as a classic person by the Corporation of Stratford-on-Avon. In short, she will become an English Sarah Bernhardt. The process is already far advanced. On Monday last she was sweeping about, clothed with red Rossettian hair and beauty to match; revelling in the power of her voice and the steam pressure of her energy; curving her wrists elegantly above Antony's head as if she were going to extract a globe of gold fish and two rabbits from behind his ear; and generally celebrating her choice between the rare and costly art of being beautifully natural in lifelike human acting, like Duse, and the comparatively common and cheap one of being theatrically beautiful in heroic stage exhibition. Alas for our lost leaders! Shakespear and success capture them all.

. . . .

Robertson Redivivus

CASTE. By T. W. Robertson. Revival. Court Theatre, 10 June 1897.

. . . . .

[19 *June* 1897]

The revival of Caste at the Court Theatre is the revival of an epoch-making play after thirty years. A very little epoch and a very little play, certainly, but none the less interesting on that account to mortal critics whose own epochs, after full deductions for nonage and dotage, do not outlast more than two such plays. The Robertsonian movement caught me as a boy; the Ibsen movement caught me as a man; and the next one will catch me as a fossil.

It happens that I did not see Mr Hare's revival of Caste at the Garrick, nor was I at his leave-taking at the Lyceum before his trip to America; so that until last week I had not seen Caste since the old times when the Hare-Kendal management was still in futurity, and the Bancrofts had not left Tottenham Court Road. During that interval a great many things have happened, some of which have changed our minds and morals more than many of the famous Revolutions and Reformations of the historians. For instance, there was supernatural religion then; and eminent physicists, biologists, and their disciples were "infidels." There was a population question then; and what men and women knew about one another was either a family secret or the recollection of a harvest of wild oats. There was no social question—only a "social evil"; and the educated classes knew the working classes through novels written by men who had gathered their notions of the subject either from a squalid familiarity with general servants in Pentonville kitchens, or from no familiarity at all with the agricultural laborer and the retinues of the country house and west end mansion. Today the "infidels" are bishops and church-wardens, without change of view on their part. There is no population question; and the young lions and lionesses of Chronicle and Star, Keynote and Pseudonym, without suspicion of debauchery, seem to know as much of erotic psychology as the most liberally educated Periclean Athenians. The real working classes loom hugely in middle-class consciousness, and have pressed into their service the whole public energy of the time; so that now even a Conservative Government has nothing for the classes but "doles," extracted with difficulty from its preoccupation with instalments of Utopian Socialism. The extreme reluctance of Englishmen to mention these changes is the measure of their dread of a reaction to the older order which they still instinctively connect with strict applications of religion and respectability.

Since Caste has managed to survive all this, it need not be altogether despised by the young champions who are staring contemptuously at it, and asking what heed they can be expected to give to the opinions of critics who think such stuff worth five minutes' serious consideration. For my part, though I enjoy it more than I enjoyed The Notorious Mrs Ebbsmith, I do not defend it. I see now clearly enough that the eagerness with which it was swallowed long ago was the eagerness with which an ocean castaway, sucking his bootlaces in an agony of thirst in a sublime desert of salt water, would pounce on a spoonful of flat salutaris and think it nectar. After years of sham heroics and superhuman balderdash, Caste delighted everyone by its freshness, its nature, its humanity. You will shriek and snort, O scornful young men, at this monstrous assertion. "Nature! Freshness!" you will exclaim. "In Heaven's name [if you are not too modern to have heard of Heaven], where is there a touch of nature in Caste?" I reply, "In the windows, in the doors, in the walls, in the carpet, in the ceiling, in the kettle, in the fireplace, in the ham, in the tea, in the bread and butter, in the bassinet, in the hats and sticks and clothes, in the familiar phrases, the quiet, unpumped, everyday utterance: in short, the commonplaces that are now spurned because they are commonplaces, and were then inexpressibly welcome because they were the most unexpected of novelties."

And yet I dare not submit even this excuse to a detailed examination. Charles Mathews was in the field long before Robertson and Mr Bancroft with the art of behaving like an ordinary gentleman in what looked like a real drawing room. The characters are very old stagers, very thinly "humanized." Captain Hawtrey may look natural now in the hands of Mr Fred Kerr; but he began by being a very near relation of the old stage "swell," who pulled his moustache, held a single eyeglass between his brow and cheekbone, said "Haw, haw" and "By Jove," and appeared in every harlequinade in a pair of white trousers which were blacked by the clown instead of his boots. Mr Henry Arthur Jones, defending his idealized early impressions as Berlioz defended the forgotten Dalayrac, pleads for Eccles as "a great and vital tragi-comic figure." But the fond plea cannot be allowed. Eccles is caricatured in the vein and by the methods which Dickens had made obvious; and the implied moral view of his case is the common Pharisaic one of his day. Eccles and Gerridge together epitomize mid-century Victorian shabby-genteel ignorance of the working classes. Polly is comic relief pure and simple; George and Esther have nothing but a milkcan to differentiate them from the heroes and heroines of a thousand sentimental dramas; and though Robertson happens to be quite right—contrary to the prevailing opinion among critics whose conception of the aristocracy is a theoretic one—in representing the "Marquizzy" as insisting openly and jealously on her rank, and, in fact, having an impenitent and resolute flunkeyism as her class characteristic, yet it is quite evident that she is not an original study from life, but simply a ladyfication of the conventional haughty mother whom we lately saw revived in all her original vulgarity and absurdity at the Adelphi in Maddison Morton's All that Glitters is not Gold, and who was generally associated on the stage with the swell from whom Captain Hawtrey is evolved. Only, let it not be forgotten that in both there really is a humanization, as humanization was understood in the 'sixties: that is, a discovery of saving sympathetic qualities in personages thitherto deemed beyond redemption. Even theology had to be humanized then by the rejection of the old doctrine of eternal punishment. Hawtrey is a good fellow, which the earlier "swell" never was; the Marquise is dignified and affectionate at heart, and is neither made ridiculous by a grotesque headdress nor embraced by the drunken Eccles; and neither of them is attended by a supercilious footman in plush whose head is finally punched powderless by Sam Gerridge. And if from these hints you cannot gather the real nature and limits of the tiny theatrical revolution of which Robertson was the hero, I must leave you in your perplexity for want of time and space for further exposition.

Of the performance I need say nothing. Caste is a task for amateurs: if its difficulties were doubled, the Court company could without effort play it twice as well as it need be played. Mr Hare's Eccles is the *tour de force* of a refined actor playing a coarse part; but it is all the more enjoyable for that. Of the staging I have one small criticism to offer. If George D'Alroy's drawing room is to be dated by a cluster of electric lights, Sam Gerridge must not come to tea in corduroy trousers, dirty shirt-sleeves, and a huge rule sticking out of his pocket. No "mechanic" nowadays would dream of doing such a thing. A stockbroker in moleskins would not be a grosser solecism.

.   .   .   .

Lorenzaccio

LORENZACCIO. A drama in five acts. By Alfred de Musset. Adapted for the stage by M. Armand d'Artois. Adelphi Theatre, 17 June 1897.

.   .   .   .   .

[26 *June* 1897]

What was the Romantic movement? I dont know, though I was under its spell in my youth. All I can say is that it was a freak of the human imagination, which created an imaginary past, an imaginary heroism, an imaginary poetry out of what appears to those of us who are no longer in the vein for it as the show in a theatrical costumier's shop window. Everybody tells you that it began

with somebody and ended with somebody else; but all its
beginners were anticipated; and it is going on still. Byron's
Laras and Corsairs look like the beginning of it to an
elderly reader until he recollects The Castle of Otranto;
yet The Castle of Otranto is not so romantic as Otway's
Venice Preserved, which, again, is no more romantic than
the tales of the knights errant beloved of Don Quixote.
Romance is always, I think, a product of *ennui,* an attempt to escape from a condition in which real life appears
empty, prosaic, and boresome—therefore essentially a
gentlemanly product. The man who has grappled with real
life, flesh to flesh and spirit to spirit, has little patience
with fools' paradises. When Carlyle said to the emigrants,
"Here and now is your America," he spoke as a realist to
romanticists; and Ibsen was of the same mind when he
finally decided that there is more tragedy in the next suburban villa than in a whole imaginary Italy of unauthentic
Borgias. Indeed, in our present phase, romance has become
the literary trade of imaginative weaklings who have
neither the energy to gain experience of life nor the genius
to divine it: wherefore I would have the State establish a
public Department of Literature, which should affix to
every romance a brief *dossier* of the author. For example:
"The writer of this story has no ascertainable qualifications
for dealing with the great personages and events of history.
His mind is stored with fiction, and his imagination in-
flamed with alcohol. His books, full of splendid sins, in
no respect reflect his life, as he is too timid not to be con-
ventionally respectable, and has never fought a man or
tempted a woman. He cannot box, fence, or ride, and is
afraid to master the bicycle. He appears to be kept alive
mainly by the care of his wife, a plain woman, much worn
by looking after him and the children. He is unconscious
that he has any duties as a citizen; and the Secretary of
State for Literature has failed to extract from him any
intelligible answer to a question as to the difference between an Urban Sanitary Authority and the Holy Roman
Empire. The public are therefore warned to attach no
practical importance to the feats of swordsmanship, the
breakneck rides, the intrigues with Semiramis, Cleopatra,
and Catherine of Russia, and the cabinet councils of
Julius Cæsar, Charlemagne, Richelieu, and Napoleon, as
described in his works; and he is hereby declared liable
to quadruple assessment for School Board rates in con-

sideration of his being the chief beneficiary, so far, by the
efforts made in the name of popular education to make
reading and writing coextensive with popular ignorance."

For all that, the land of dreams is a wonderful place;
and the great Romancers who found the key of its gates
were no Alnaschars. These artists, inspired neither by
faith and beatitude, nor by strife and realization, were
neither saints nor crusaders, but pure enchanters, who
conjured up a region where existence touches you delicately to the very heart, and where mysteriously thrilling
people, secretly known to you in dreams of your childhood, enact a life in which terrors are as fascinating as
delights; so that ghosts and death, agony and sin, become,
like love and victory, phases of an unaccountable ecstasy.
Goethe bathed by moonlight in the Rhine to learn this
white magic, and saturated even the criticism and didac-
ticism of Faust with the strangest charm by means of it.
Mozart was a most wonderful enchanter of this kind: he
drove very clever men—Oublicheff, for example—clean
out of their wits by his airs from heaven and blasts from
hell in Le Nozze di Figaro and Don Giovanni. From the
middle of the eighteenth to the middle of the nineteenth
century Art went crazy in its search for spells and dreams;
and many artists who, being neither Mozarts nor Goethes,
had their minds burnt up instead of cleansed by "the
sacred fire," yet could make that fire cast shadows that
gave unreal figures a strange majesty, and phantom land-
scapes a "light that never was on sea or land." These
phrases which I quote were then the commonplaces of
critics' rhapsodies.

Today, alas!—I mean thank goodness!—all this rhap-
sodizing makes people stare at me as at Rip Van Winkle.
The lithographs of Delacroix, the ghostly tam-tam march
in Robert the Devil, the tinkle of the goat's bell in Dinorah,
the illustrations of Gustave Doré, mean nothing to the
elect of this stern generation but an unintelligible refuse of
bad drawing, barren, ugly orchestral tinkering, senseless,
and debased ambition. We have been led forth from the
desert in which these mirages were always on the horizon
to a land overflowing with reality and earnestness. But if
I were to be stoned for it this afternoon by fervent Wag-
nerites and Ibsenites, I must declare that the mirages were
once dear and beautiful, and that the whole Wagnerian
criticism of them, however salutary (I have been myself

one of its most ruthless practitioners), has all along been
a pious dialectical fraud, because it applies the tests of
realism and revelation to the arts of illusion and trans-
figuration. From the point of view of the Building Act the
palaces built by Mr Brock, the pyrotechnist, may be most
pestilent frauds; but that only shews that Mr Brock's point
of view is not that of the Building Act, though it might
be very necessary to deliberately force that criticism on
his works if real architecture shewed signs of being seduced by the charms of his colored fires. It was just such
an emergency that compelled Wagner to resort to the pious
dialectical fraud against his old romanticist loves. Their
enchantments were such that their phantasms, which
genius alone could sublimate from real life, became the
models after which the journeyman artist worked and was
taught to work, blinding him to nature and reality, from
which alone his talent could gain nourishment and originality, and setting him to waste his life in outlining the
shadows of shadows, with the result that Romanticism
became, at second hand, the blight and dry rot of Art.
Then all the earnest spirits, from Ruskin and the pre-
Raphaelites to Wagner and Ibsen, rose up and made war
on it. Salvator Rosa, the romantic painter, went down
before the preaching of Ruskin as Delacroix has gone
down before the practice of John Maris, Von Uhde, and
the "impressionists" and realists whose work led up to
them. Meyerbeer was brutally squelched, and Berlioz put
out of countenance, by the preaching and practice of
Wagner. And after Ibsen—nay, even after the cup-and-
saucer realists—we no longer care for Schiller; Victor
Hugo, on his spurious, violently romantic side, only incom-
modes us; and the spirit of such a wayward masterpiece of
Romanticism as Alfred de Musset's Lorenzaccio would
miss fire with us altogether if we could bring ourselves to
wade through the morass of pseudo-mediaeval Florentine
chatter with which it begins.

De Musset, though a drunkard, with his mind always
derelict in the sea of his imagination, yet had the sacred
fire. Lorenzaccio is a reckless play, broken up into scores
of scenes in the Shakespearean manner, but without Shakespear's workmanlike eye to stage business and to cumula-
tive dramatic effect; for half these scenes lead nowhere;
and the most gaily trivial of them—that in which the two
children fight—is placed in the fifth act, *after* the catas-

trophe, which takes place in the fourth. According to all
the rules, the painter Tebaldeo must have been introduced
to stab somebody later on, instead of merely to make
Lorenzaccio feel like a cur; Filippo Strozzi is a Virginius-
Lear wasted; the Marquise was plainly intended for something very fine in the seventeenth act, if the play ever got
so far; and Lorenzaccio's swoon at the sight of a sword in
the first act remains a mystery to the end of the play. False
starts, dropped motives, no-thoroughfares, bewilder the
expert in "construction" all through; but none the less
the enchanter sustains his illusion: you are always in the
Renaissant Italian city of the Romanticist imagination, a
murderous but fascinating place; and the characters, spectral as they are, are yet as distinct and individual as Shakespear's, some of them—Salviati, for instance—coming out
with the rudest force in a mere mouthful of lines. Only,
the force never becomes realism: the romantic atmosphere
veils and transfigures everything: Lorenzaccio himself,
though his speeches bite with the suddenest vivacity, never
emerges from the mystic twilight of which he seems to be
only a fantastic cloud, and no one questions the consistency of the feet stealing through nameless infamy and
the head raised to the stars. In the Romantic school horror
was naturally akin to sublimity.

In the Romantic school, too, there was nothing incongruous in the man's part being played by a woman, since
the whole business was so subtly pervaded by sex instincts
that a woman never came amiss to a romanticist. To him
she was not a human being or a fellow-creature, but simply
the incarnated divinity of sex. And I regret to add that
women rather liked being worshipped on false pretences
at first. In America they still do. So they play men's parts
fitly enough in the Romantic school; and the contralto in
trunk hose is almost a natural organic part of romantic
opera. Consequently, the announcement that Sarah Bernhardt was to play Lorenzaccio was by no means incongruous and scandalous, as, for instance, a proposal on her part
to play the Master Builder would have been. Twenty years
ago, under the direction of a stage manager who really
understood the work, she would probably have given us a
memorable sensation with it. As it is—well, as it is, perhaps you had better go and judge for yourself. A stall will
only cost you a guinea.

Perhaps I am a prejudiced critic of French acting, as it

seems to me to be simply English acting fifty years out of
date, always excepting the geniuses like Coquelin and
Réjane, and the bold pioneers like Lugné-Poë and his company. The average Parisian actor was quaint and interesting to me at first; and his peculiar mechanical cadence,
which he learns as brainlessly as a costermonger learns his
street cry, did not drive me mad as it does now. I have
even wished that English actors were taught their alphabet
as he is taught his. But I have worn off his novelty by this
time; and I now perceive that he is quite the worst actor
in the world. Every year Madame Bernhardt comes to us
with a new play, in which she kills somebody with any
weapon from a hairpin to a hatchet; intones a great deal
of dialogue as a sample of what is called "the golden
voice," to the great delight of our curates, who all produce
more or less golden voices by exactly the same trick; goes
through her well-known feat of tearing a passion to tatters
at the end of the second or fourth act, according to the
length of the piece; serves out a certain ration of the celebrated smile; and between whiles gets through any ordinary acting that may be necessary in a thoroughly businesslike and competent fashion. This routine constitutes
a permanent exhibition, which is refurnished every year
with fresh scenery, fresh dialogue, and a fresh author,
whilst remaining itself invariable. Still, there are real parts
in Madame Bernhardt's repertory which date from the
days before the travelling show was opened; and she is
far too clever a woman, and too well endowed with stage
instinct, not to rise, in an offhanded, experimental sort of
way, to the more obvious points in such an irresistible new
part as Magda. So I had hopes, when I went to see Lorenzaccio, that the fascination which, as Dona Sol, she once
gave to Hernani, might be revived by De Musset's romanticism. Those hopes did not last a minute after her first
entry. When the retort *"Une insulte de prêtre doit se faire
en latin"* was intoned on one note with Melissindian sweet-
ness, like a sentimental motto out of a cracker, I concluded that we were to have no Lorenzaccio, and that poor
De Musset's play was only a new pretext for the old exhibition. But that conclusion, though sound in the main,
proved a little too sweeping. Certainly the Lorenzaccio of
De Musset, the filthy wretch who is a demon and an angel,
with his fierce, serpent-tongued repartees, his subtle blas-
phemies, his cynical levity playing over a passion of horror

at the wickedness and cowardice of the world that tolerates him, is a conception which Madame Bernhardt has failed to gather from the text—if she has troubled herself to gather any original imaginative conception from it, which I cannot help doubting. But the scene of the stealing of the coat of mail, with its incorporated fragment of the earlier scene with the painter, was excellently played; and the murder scene was not a bad piece of acting of a heavy conventional kind, such as a good Shakespearean actor of the old school would turn on before killing Duncan or Desdemona, or in declaiming "Oh that this too too solid flesh would melt!" I seriously suggest to Madame Bernhardt that she might do worse than attempt a round of Shakespearean heroes. Only, I beg her not to get M. Armand d'Artois to arrange Shakespear's plays for the stage as he has so kindly arranged Lorenzaccio.

The company supporting Madame Bernhardt is, as far as I can judge, up to standard requirements. They delivered De Musset's phrases in the usual French manner, so that the words "Alexandre de Médicis" rang through my head all night like "extra special" or "Tuppence a barskit." Only one actor succeeded in pronouncing "Strozzi" properly; and even he drew the line at Venturi, which became frankly French. And yet when Mr Terriss, with British straightforwardness, makes the first syllable in Valclos rhyme to "hall," and pronounces "Contesse" like contest with the final *t* omitted, the British playgoer whispers that you would never hear a French actor doing such a thing. The truth is that if Mr Terriss were to speak as we have often heard M. Mounet Sully speak, he would be removed to an asylum until he shewed signs of returning humanity. As a rule, when an Englishman can act, he knows better than to waste that invaluable talent on the stage; so that in England an actor is mostly a man who cannot act well enough to be allowed to perform anywhere except in a theatre. In France, an actor is a man who has not common sense enough to behave naturally. And that, I imagine, is just what the English actor was half a century ago.

·　　·　　·　　·　　·　　·　　·

Mr Grundy's Improvements on Dumas

THE SILVER KEY. A comedy in four acts, adapted from
Alexandre Dumas' Mlle de Belleisle by Sydney Grundy. Her
Majesty's Theatre, 10 July 1897.

[17 *July* 1897]

I must say I take the new Dumas adaptation in anything
but good part. Why on earth cannot Mr Grundy let well
alone? Dumas *père* was what Gounod called Mozart, a
summit of art. Nobody ever could, or did, or will improve
on Mozart's operas; and nobody ever could, or did, or will
improve on Dumas' romances and plays. After Dumas you
may have Dumas-and-water, or you may have, in Balzac,
a quite new and different beginning; but you get nothing
above Dumas on his own mountain: he is the summit, and
if you attempt to pass him you come down on the other
side instead of getting higher. Mr Grundy's version of the
Marriage sous Louis Quinze did not suggest that he was in
the absurd position of being the only expert in the world
who did not know this; but the chorus of acclamation with
which we greeted that modest and workmanlike achievement seems to have dazzled him; for in his version of
Mademoiselle de Belleisle he treats us to several improvements of his own, some of them pruderies which spare us
nothing of the original except its wit; others, like the
dreams and the questioning of the servant in her mistress's
presence by the jealous lover, wanton adulterations; and
all, as it seems to me, blunders in stagecraft. They remind
me of the "additional accompaniments" our musicians
used to condescend to supply when an opera by some
benighted foreigner of genius was produced here. If Mr
Grundy were a painter and composer as well as a dramatist, I dare say he could rescore Don Giovanni and repaint
Velasquez' Philip to the entire satisfaction of people who
know no better; but if he were an artist, he would not
want to do so, and would feel extremely indignant with
anyone who did. I hope I am no fanatic as to the reverence
with which the handiwork of a great man should be
treated. If Dumas had failed to make any point in his
story clear, then I should no more think of blaming Mr
Grundy for putting in a speech, or even a little episode, to
elucidate it, than I blame Wagner for helping out Beethoven in the Ninth Symphony in places where the most

prominent melody in the written score was, as a matter of physical fact, inaudible when performed, or where there were distortions caused by deficiencies in instruments since provided with a complete scale. But Mademoiselle de Belleisle is expounded by its author with a dramatic perspicacity far beyond our most laborious efforts at play construction; and the net result of Mr Grundy's meddling is that the audience does not fully understand until the end of the third act (the original fourth) the mistake on which the whole interest of the scene in the second (third) between Richelieu and the two lovers depends. It is almost as if Mr Grundy were to adapt Cymbeline, which is the same play with a slight difference of treatment, and to send the audience home with the gravest doubts as to what really took place between Iachimo and Imogen. The resource of "construction" cannot reasonably be denied to authors who have not the natural gift of telling a story; but when the whole difficulty might have been avoided by dealing faithfully with the work of one of the best storytellers, narrative or dramatic, that ever lived, I feel driven to express myself shrewishly. As to the ending of the play with a crudely dragged in title-tag (The Silver King, or something like it), it is—well, I do not wish to be impolite; so I will simply ask Mr Grundy whether he really thinks highly of it himself.

The acting at Her Majesty's is not precisely what one calls exquisite; and for perfect interpretation of Dumas acting should be nothing less. Such delicacy of execution as there is on our stage never comes within a mile of virtuosity. As virtuosity in manners was the characteristic mode of eighteenth-century smart society, it follows that we get nothing of the eighteenth century at Her Majesty's, except that from time to time the persons of the drama alarm us by suddenly developing symptoms of strychnine poisoning, which are presently seen to be intended for elaborate bows and curtseys. This troubles the audience very little. The manners of Mr Tree and Mr Waller are better than eighteenth-century manners; and I, for one, am usually glad to exchange old lamps for new ones in this particular. But it takes no very subtle critic to see that the exchange makes the play partly incredible. Mr Waller suffers more in this respect than Mr Tree, because his late-nineteenth-century personality is hopelessly incompat-

ible with the eighteenth-century cut-and-dried ideals of
womanhood and chivalry of the hero he represents. Mr
Tree is in no such dilemma. The lapse of a century has left
Richelieu (described by Macaulay as "an old fop who had
passed his life from sixteen to sixty in seducing women
for whom he cared not one straw") still alive and familiar.
What people call vice is eternal: what they call virtue is
mere fashion. Consequently, though Mr Waller's is the
most forcible acting in the piece—though he alone selects
and emphasizes the dramatically significant points which
lead the spectator clearly through the story, yet his performance stands out flagrantly as a *tour de force* of acting
and not as life; whilst Mr Tree, who makes no particular
display of his powers as an actor except for a moment in
the duel with dice, produces a quite sufficient illusion.

There is one quality which is never absent in Dumas,
and never present in English performances of him; and
that is a voluntary naïveté of humorous clearsightedness.
Dumas' invariable homage to the delicacy of his heroines
and the honor of his heroes has something in it of that
maxima reverentia which the disillusionment of mature age
pays to the innocence of youth. He handles his lovers as if
they were pretty children, giving them the charm of childhood when he can, and unconsciously betraying a wide
distinction in his own mind between the ideal virtues which
he gives them as a romantic sinner might give golden
candlesticks to a saint's altar, and the real ones which he is
prepared to practise as well as preach—high personal
loyalty, for instance. Hence it is that his stories are always
light-hearted and free from that pressure of moral responsibility without which an Englishman would burst like a
fish dragged up from the floor of the Atlantic deeps. At
Her Majesty's the two performers with the strongest sense
of comedy—Mrs Tree and Mr Lionel Brough—do contrive to bear the burden of public morality easily; but the
rest carefully clear themselves of all suspicion of Continental levity: even Richelieu contrives to convey that whatever may happen in the Marquise's bedroom, he will be
found at the strait gate in the narrow way punctually at
eleven next Sunday morning. As to Miss Millard, she impersonated Mademoiselle de Belleisle with the most chas-
tising propriety. She evidently knew all about Richelieu's
ways from the beginning, and was simply lying in wait for

effective opportunities of pretending to be amazed and horrified at them. I have seen nothing more ladylike on the stage. It was magnificent; but it was not Dumas.

Miss Gigia Filippi—sister, I presume, to that clever actress Miss Rosina Filippi—played the waiting-maid Mariette according to a conception of her art upon which I shall preach a little sermon, because I believe it to be a misleading conception, and because nevertheless it is one which no less an exponent of stage art than Miss Ellen Terry has carried out with undeniable success. It came about, as I guess, in this way. Miss Terry, as we all know, went on the stage in her childhood, and not only "picked up" her profession, but was systematically taught it by Mrs Charles Kean, with the result that to this day her business is always thoroughly well done, and her part gets over the footlights to the ends of the house without the loss of a syllable or the waste of a stroke. But if Mrs Charles Kean qualified her to be the heroine of a play, Nature presently qualified her to be the heroine of a picture by making her grow up quite unlike anybody that had ever been seen on earth before. I trust Nature has not broken the mould: if she has, Miss Terry's portraits will go down to posterity as those of the only real New Woman, who was never repeated afterwards. The great painters promptly pounced on her as they did on Mrs Morris and Mrs Stillman. She added what she learnt in the studio to what she had already learnt on the stage so successfully that when I first saw her in Hamlet it was exactly as if the powers of a beautiful picture of Ophelia had been extended to speaking and singing. It was no doubt her delight in this pictorial art that made her so easily satisfied with old-fashioned rhetorical characters which have no dramatic interest for any intelligent woman nowadays, much less for an ultramodern talent like Miss Terry's. When she came to the "touches of nature" in such characters (imagine a school of drama in which nature is represented only by "touches"!) she seized on them with an enjoyment and a tender solicitude for them that shewed the born actress; but after each of them she dropped back into the pictorial as unquestioningly as Patti, after two bars of really dramatic music in an old-fashioned aria, will drop back into purely decorative roulade. And here you have the whole secret of the Lyceum: a drama worn by age into great holes, and the holes filled up with the art of the picture gallery. Sir Henry Irving as King Arthur, going solemnly through a Crummles broadsword combat with great beauty of deportment in a costume designed by Burne-Jones, is the *reductio ad absurdum* of it. Miss Ellen Terry as a beautiful living picture in the vision in the prologue is its open reduction to the art to which it really belongs. And Miss Ellen Terry as Madame Sans-Gêne is the first serious struggle of dramatic art to oust its supplanter and reclaim the undivided service of its wayward daughter.

The most advanced audiences today, taught by Wagner and Ibsen (not to mention Ford Madox Brown), cannot stand the drop back into decoration after the moment of earnest life. They want realistic drama of complete brainy, passional texture all through, and will not have any pictorial stuff or roulade at all—will not even have the old compromise by which drama was disguised and denaturalized in adaptations of the decorative forms. The decorative play, with its versified rhetoric, its timid little moments of feeling and blusterous big moments of raving nonsense, must now step down to the second-class audience, which is certainly more numerous and lucrative than the first-class, but is being slowly dragged after it, in spite of the reinforcement of its resistance by the third-class audience hanging on to its coat tails. It screams and kicks most piteously during the process; but it will have to submit; for the public must finally take, willy-nilly, what its greatest artists choose to give it, or else do without art. And so even the second-class public, though it still likes plenty of pictorial beauty and distinction (meaning mostly expensiveness and gentility) in the setting, and plenty of comfortable optimistic endearment and cheap fun in the substance, nevertheless needs far more continuous drama to bind the whole together and compel sustained attention and interest than it did twenty years ago. Consequently the woman who now comes on the stage with carefully cultivated qualifications as an artist's model, and none as an actress, no longer finds herself fitting exactly into leading parts even in the fashionable drama of the day, and automatically driving the real actresses off the stage. Miss Ellen Terry innocently created a whole school of such pictorial leading ladies. They went to the Lyceum, where, not being skilled critics, they recognized the heroine's pictorial triumphs as art, whilst taking such occasional sallies of acting

as the Shakespearean "touches of nature" admitted of as
the spontaneous operation of Miss Terry's own charming
individuality. I am not sure that I have not detected that
simple-minded Terry theory in more critical quarters. The
art, of course, lay on the side where it was least suspected.
The nervous athleticism and trained expertness which
have enabled Miss Terry, without the least appearance of
violence to hold her audiences with an unfailing grip in a
house which is no bandbox, and where really weak acting,
as we have often seen, drifts away under the stage door
and leaves the audience coughing, are only known by their
dissimulative effect: that is, they are not known at all for
what they really are; whereas the pictorial business, five-
sixths of which is done by trusting to nature, proceeds, as
to the other sixth, by perfectly obvious methods. In this
way, an unenlightened observation of Miss Ellen Terry
produced the "æsthetic" actress, or living picture. Such a
conception of stage art came very easily to a generation of
young ladies whose notions of art were centred by the
Slade School and the Grosvenor Gallery.

Now Miss Gigia Filippi is original enough not to directly
imitate Miss Terry or any other individual artist. But I
have never seen the pictorial conception carried out with
greater industry and integrity. Miss Filippi was on the
stage when the curtain went up; and before it was out of
sight I wanted a kodak. Every movement ended in a
picture, not a Burne-Jones or Rossetti, but a dark-eyed,
red-cheeked, full-lipped, pearly-toothed, coquettish Fildes
or Van Haanen. The success of the exhibition almost justified the labor it must have cost. But that is not acting. It
is a string that a finished actress may add to her bow if she
has the faculty for it, like Miss Terry; but as a changeling
for acting it will not do, especially in a play by Dumas.
When Miss Filippi speaks, she takes pains to make her
voice soft and musical; but as she has never had a competent person sitting in the gallery to throw things at her
head the moment she became unintelligible, the consonants
often slip away unheard, and nothing remains but a musical murmur of vowels, soothing to the ear, but baffling and
exasperating to people whose chief need at the moment is
to find out what the play is about. On the other side of the
Haymarket Miss Dairolles has a precisely similar part.
Miss Dairolles seeks first to live as the clever lady's-maid
of the play in the imagination of the audience; and all the

other things are added unto her without much preoccupation on her part. Miss Filippi prefers to stand composing
pretty pictures, and exhibiting each of them for nearly half
a minute, instead of for the tenth part of a second, as a
skilled actress would. Now an effect prolonged for even
an instant after artist and audience have become conscious
of it is recognized as an end with the artist instead of a   .
means, and so ceases to be an effect at all. It is only applauded by Partridge, with his "anybody can see that the
king is an actor," or, in Miss Filippi's case, by dramatically
obtuse painters and Slade School students on the watch for
pictures everywhere. I earnestly advise Miss Filippi to
disregard their praises and set about finding a substitute
for Mrs Charles Kean at once.

Hamlet

[2 *October* 1897]
The Forbes-Robertson Hamlet at the Lyceum is, very
unexpectedly at that address, really not at all unlike Shakespear's play of the same name. I am quite certain I saw
Reynaldo in it for a moment; and possibly I may have
seen Voltimand and Cornelius; but just as the time for
their scene arrived, my eye fell on the word "Fortinbras"
in the program, which so amazed me that I hardly know
what I saw for the next ten minutes. Ophelia, instead of
being a strenuously earnest and self-possessed young lady
giving a concert and recitation for all she was worth, was
mad—actually mad. The story of the play was perfectly
intelligible, and quite took the attention of the audience off
the principal actor at moments. What is the Lyceum coming to? Is it for this that Sir Henry Irving has invented a
whole series of original romantic dramas, and given the
credit of them without a murmur to the immortal bard
whose profundity (as exemplified in the remark that good
and evil are mingled in our natures) he has just been
pointing out to the inhabitants of Cardiff, and whose works
have been no more to him than the word-quarry from
which he has hewn and blasted the lines and titles of masterpieces which are really all his own? And now, when he
has created by these means a reputation for Shakespear,
he no sooner turns his back for a moment on London than
Mr Forbes-Robertson competes with him on the boards
of his own theatre by actually playing off against him the

authentic Swan of Avon. Now if the result had been the
utter exposure and collapse of that impostor, poetic justice must have proclaimed that it served Mr Forbes-Robertson right. But alas! the wily William, by literary tricks
which our simple Sir Henry has never quite understood,
has played into Mr Forbes-Robertson's hands so artfully
that the scheme is a prodigious success. The effect of this
success, coming after that of Mr Alexander's experiment
with a Shakespearean version of As You Like It, makes it
almost probable that we shall presently find managers
vying with each other in offering the public as much of
the original Shakespearean stuff as possible, instead of, as
heretofore, doing their utmost to reassure us that everything that the most modern resources can do to relieve the
irreducible minimum of tedium inseparable from even the
most heavily cut acting version will be lavished on their
revivals. It is true that Mr Beerbohm Tree still holds to the
old scepticism, and calmly proposes to insult us by offering
us Garrick's puerile and horribly caddish knockabout farce
of Katharine and Petruchio for Shakespear's Taming of
the Shrew; but Mr Tree, like all romantic actors, is incorrigible on the subject of Shakespear.

Mr Forbes-Robertson is essentially a classical actor, the
only one, with the exception of Mr Alexander, now established in London management. What I mean by classical
is that he can present a dramatic hero as a man whose
passions are those which have produced the philosophy,
the poetry, the art, and the statecraft of the world, and not
merely those which have produced its weddings, coroners'
inquests, and executions. And that is just the sort of actor
that Hamlet requires. A Hamlet who only understands his
love for Ophelia, his grief for his father, his vindictive
hatred of his uncle, his fear of ghosts, his impulse to snub
Rosencrantz and Guildenstern, and the sportsman's excitement with which he lays the "mousetrap" for Claudius,
can, with sufficient force or virtuosity of execution, get a
great reputation in the part, even though the very intensity
of his obsession by these sentiments (which are common
not only to all men but to many animals) shews that the
characteristic side of Hamlet, the side that differentiates
him from Fortinbras, is absolutely outside the actor's consciousness. Such a reputation is the actor's, not Hamlet's.
Hamlet is not a man in whom "common humanity" is
raised by great vital energy to a heroic pitch, like Coriola-

nus or Othello. On the contrary, he is a man in whom the
common personal passions are so superseded by wider and
rarer interests, and so discouraged by a degree of critical
self-consciousness which makes the practical efficiency of
the instinctive man on the lower plane impossible to him,
that he finds the duties dictated by conventional revenge
and ambition as disagreeable a burden as commerce is to
a poet. Even his instinctive sexual impulses offend his intellect; so that when he meets the woman who excites them
he invites her to join him in a bitter and scornful criticism
of their joint absurdity, demanding "What should such
fellows as I do crawling between heaven and earth?" "Why
wouldst thou be a breeder of sinners?" and so forth, all of
which is so completely beyond the poor girl that she naturally thinks him mad. And, indeed, there is a sense in
which Hamlet is insane; for he trips over the mistake
which lies on the threshold of intellectual selfconscious-
ness: that of bringing life to utilitarian or Hedonistic tests,
thus treating it as a means instead of an end. Because
Polonius is "a foolish prating knave," because Rosencrantz
and Guildenstern are snobs, he kills them as remorselessly
as he might kill a flea, shewing that he has no real belief in
the superstitious reason which he gives for not killing himself, and in fact anticipating exactly the whole course of
the intellectual history of Western Europe until Schopenhauer found the clue that Shakespear missed. But to call
Hamlet mad because he did not anticipate Schopenhauer is
like calling Marcellus mad because he did not refer the
Ghost to the Psychical Society. It is in fact not possible
for any actor to represent Hamlet as mad. He may (and
generally does) combine some notion of his own of a man
who is the creature of affectionate sentiment with the
figure drawn by the lines of Shakespear; but the result is
not a madman, but simply one of those monsters produced
by the imaginary combination of two normal species, such
as sphinxes, mermaids, or centaurs. And this is the invariable resource of the instinctive, imaginative, romantic
actor. You will see him weeping bucketsful of tears over
Ophelia, and treating the players, the gravedigger, Horatio,
Rosencrantz, and Guildenstern as if they were mutes at his
own funeral. But go and watch Mr Forbes-Robertson's
Hamlet seizing delightedly on every opportunity for a bit
of philosophic discussion or artistic recreation to escape
from the "cursed spite" of revenge and love and other

common troubles; see how he brightens up when the
players come; how he tries to talk philosophy with Rosencrantz and Guildenstern the moment they come into the
room; how he stops on his country walk with Horatio to
lean over the churchyard wall and draw out the grave-
digger whom he sees singing at his trade; how even his fits
of excitement find expression in declaiming scraps of
poetry; how the shock of Ophelia's death relieves itself in
the fiercest intellectual contempt for Laertes's ranting,
whilst an hour afterwards, when Laertes stabs him, he
bears no malice for that at all, but embraces him gallantly
and comradely; and how he dies as we forgive everything
to Charles II for dying, and makes "the rest is silence" a
touchingly humorous apology for not being able to finish
his business. See all that; and you have seen a true classical
Hamlet. Nothing half so charming has been seen by this
generation. It will bear seeing again and again.

And please observe that this is not a cold Hamlet. He is
none of your logicians who reason their way through the
world because they cannot feel their way through it: his
intellect is the organ of his passion: his eternal self-
criticism is as alive and thrilling as it can possibly be. The
great soliloquy—no: I do NOT mean "To be or not to
be": I mean the dramatic one, "O what a rogue and
peasant slave am I!"—is as passionate in its scorn of brute
passion as the most bull-necked affirmation or sentimental
dilution of it could be. It comes out so without violence:
Mr Forbes-Robertson takes the part quite easily and spontaneously. There is none of that strange Lyceum intensity
which comes from the perpetual struggle between Sir
Henry Irving and Shakespear. The lines help Mr Forbes
Robertson instead of getting in his way at every turn,
because he wants to play Hamlet, and not to slip into his
inky cloak a changeling of quite another race. We may
miss the craft, the skill double-distilled by constant peril,
the subtlety, the dark rays of heat generated by intense
friction, the relentless parental tenacity and cunning with
which Sir Henry nurses his own pet creations on Shakespearean food like a fox rearing its litter in the den of a
lioness; but we get light, freedom, naturalness, credibility,
and Shakespear. It is wonderful how easily everything
comes right when you have the right man with the right
mind for it—how the story tells itself, how the characters
come to life, how even the failures in the cast cannot con-

fuse you, though they may disappoint you. And Mr Forbes-
Robertson has certainly not escaped such failures, even in
his own family. I strongly urge him to take a hint from
Claudius and make a real ghost of Mr Ian Robertson at
once; for there is no sort of use in going through that
scene night after night with a Ghost so solidly, comfortably, and dogmatically alive as his brother. The voice is
not a bad voice; but it is the voice of a man who does not
believe in ghosts. Moreover, it is a hungry voice, not that
of one who is past eating. There is an indescribable little
complacent drop at the end of every line which no sooner
calls up the image of purgatory by its words than by its
smug elocution it convinces us that this particular penitent
is cosily warming his shins and toasting his muffin at the
flames instead of expiating his bad acting in the midst of
them. His aspect and bearing are worse than his recita-
tions. He beckons Hamlet away like a beadle summoning
a timid candidate for the post of junior footman to the
presence of the Lord Mayor. If I were Mr Forbes-Robertson I would not stand that from any brother: I would
cleave the general ear with horrid speech at him first. It is
a pity; for the Ghost's part is one of the wonders of the
play. And yet, until Mr Courtenay Thorpe divined it the
other day, nobody seems to have had a glimpse of the
reason why Shakespear would not trust anyone else with
it, and played it himself. The weird music of that long
speech which should be the spectral wail of a soul's bitter
wrong crying from one world to another in the extremity
of its torment, is invariably handed over to the most
squaretoed member of the company, who makes it sound,
not like Rossetti's Sister Helen, or even, to suggest a possible heavy treatment, like Mozart's statue-ghost, but like
Chambers's Information for the People.

Still, I can understand Mr Ian Robertson, by sheer force
of a certain quality of sententiousness in him, overbearing
the management into casting him for the Ghost. What I
cannot understand is why Miss Granville was cast for the
Queen. It is like setting a fashionable modern mandolinist
to play Haydn's sonatas. She does her best under the circumstances; but she would have been more fortunate had
she been in a position to refuse the part.

On the other hand, several of the impersonations are
conspicuously successful. Mrs Patrick Campbell's Ophelia
is a surprise. The part is one which has hitherto seemed

incapable of progress. From generation to generation actresses have, in the mad scene, exhausted their musical skill, their ingenuity in devising fantasias in the language of flowers, and their intensest powers of portraying anxiously earnest sanity. Mrs Patrick Campbell, with that complacent audacity of hers which is so exasperating when she is doing the wrong thing, this time does the right thing by making Ophelia really mad. The resentment of the audience at this outrage is hardly to be described. They long for the strenuous mental grasp and attentive coherence of Miss Lily Hanbury's conception of maiden lunacy; and this wandering, silly, vague Ophelia, who no sooner catches an emotional impulse than it drifts away from her again, emptying her voice of its tone in a way that makes one shiver, makes them horribly uncomfortable. But the effect on the play is conclusive. The shrinking discomfort of the King and Queen, the rankling grief of Laertes, are created by it at once; and the scene, instead of being a pretty interlude coming in just when a little relief from the inky cloak is welcome, touches us with a chill of the blood that gives it its right tragic power and dramatic significance. Playgoers naturally murmur when something that has always been pretty becomes painful; but the pain is good for them, good for the theatre, and good for the play. I doubt whether Mrs Patrick Campbell fully appreciates the dramatic value of her quite simple and original sketch—it is only a sketch—of the part; but in spite of the occasional triviality of its execution and the petulance with which it has been received, it seems to me to settle finally in her favor the question of her right to the very important place which Mr Forbes-Robertson has assigned to her in his enterprises.

I did not see Mr Bernard Gould play Laertes: he was indisposed when I returned to town and hastened to the Lyceum; but he was replaced very creditably by Mr Frank Dyall. Mr Martin Harvey is the best Osric I have seen: he plays Osric from Osric's own point of view, which is, that Osric is a gallant and distinguished courtier, and not, as usual, from Hamlet's, which is that Osric is "a waterfly." Mr Harrison Hunter hits off the modest, honest Horatio capitally; and Mr Willes is so good a Gravedigger that I venture to suggest to him that he should carry his work a little further, and not virtually cease to concern himself with the play when he has spoken his last line and handed

Hamlet the skull. Mr Cooper Cliffe is not exactly a subtle
Claudius; but he looks as if he had stepped out of a picture
by Madox Brown, and plays straightforwardly on his very
successful appearance. Mr Barnes makes Polonius robust
and elderly instead of aged and garrulous. He is good in
the scenes where Polonius appears as a man of character
and experience; but the senile exhibitions of courtierly tact
do not match these, and so seem forced and farcical.

Mr Forbes-Robertson's own performance has a continuous charm, interest, and variety which are the result not
only of his well-known grace and accomplishment as an
actor, but of a genuine delight—the rarest thing on our
stage—in Shakespear's art, and a natural familiarity with
the plane of his imagination. He does not superstitiously
worship William: he enjoys him and understands his methods of expression. Instead of cutting every line that can
possibly be spared, he retains every gem, in his own part
or anyone else's, that he can make time for in a spiritedly
brisk performance lasting three hours and a half with very
short intervals. He does not utter half a line; then stop to
act; then go on with another half line; and then stop to
act again, with the clock running away with Shakespear's
chances all the time. He plays as Shakespear should be
played, on the line and to the line, with the utterance and
acting simultaneous, inseparable and in fact identical. Not
for a moment is he solemnly conscious of Shakespear's
reputation or of Hamlet's momentousness in literary history: on the contrary, he delivers us from all these boredoms instead of heaping them on us. We forgive him the
platitudes, so engagingly are they delivered. His novel and
astonishingly effective and touching treatment of the final
scene is an inspiration, from the fencing match onward.
If only Fortinbras could also be inspired with sufficient
force and brilliancy to rise to the warlike splendor of his
helmet, and make straight for that throne like a man who
intended to keep it against all comers, he would leave
nothing to be desired. How many generations of Hamlets,
all thirsting to outshine their competitors in effect and
originality, have regarded Fortinbras, and the clue he gives
to this kingly death for Hamlet, as a wildly unpresentable
blunder of the poor foolish old Swan, than whom they all
knew so much better! How sweetly they have died in that
faith to slow music, like Little Nell in The Old Curiosity
Shop! And now how completely Mr Forbes-Robertson has

bowled them all out by being clever enough to be simple.

By the way, talking of slow music, the sooner Mr Hamilton Clark's romantic Irving music is stopped, the better. Its effect in this Shakespearean version of the play is absurd. The four Offenbachian young women in tights should also be abolished, and the part of the player-queen given to a man. The courtiers should be taught how flatteringly courtiers listen when a king shews off his wisdom in wise speeches to his nephew. And that nice wooden beach on which the ghost walks would be the better for a seaweedy looking cloth on it, with a handful of shrimps and a pennorth of silver sand.

Chin Chon Chino

THE CAT AND THE CHERUB. By Chester Bailey Fernald. Lyric Theatre, 30 October 1897.

THE FIRST BORN. By Francis Powers. Globe Theatre, 1 November 1897.

A RETROSPECT OF THE STAGE FESTIVALS OF 1876. By Richard Wagner. Translated by W. Ashton Ellis. In Richard Wagner's Prose Works, Vol. VI, Part 2. London: Kegan Paul. 1897.

[6 *November* 1897]

The latest attempt to escape from hackneydom and cockneydom is the Chinatown play, imported, of course, from America. There is no reason, however, why it should not be manufactured in England. I beg respectfully to inform managers and syndicates that I am prepared to supply "Chinese plays," music and all, on reasonable terms, at the shortest notice. A form of art which makes a merit of crudity need never lack practitioners in this country. The Chinese music, which we are spared at the Lyric, is unmitigated humbug. At the Globe it is simply very bad American music, with marrowbones and cleaver, teatray and cat-call, *ad lib.* And the play is nothing but Wilkie Collins fiction disguised in pigtail and petticoats.

The result is worth analysing. The dramatic art of our day has come to such a pass of open artificiality and stale romantic convention that the sudden repudiation of all art produces for the moment almost as refreshing a sensation as its revival would. In The First Born the death of the little boy at the end of the first scene, and the murder of

the man whose corpse is propped up against the doorpost
by his murderer and made to counterfeit life whilst the
policeman passes, might be improvised in a schoolroom:
yet they induce a thrill which all the resources of the St
James's Theatre, strained during five long acts to their utmost, cannot attain to for the briefest instant. Truly the
secret of wisdom is to become as a little child again. But
our art-loving authors will not learn the lesson. They cannot understand that when a great genius lays hands on a
form of art and fascinates all who understand its language
with it, he makes it say all that it can say, and leaves it
exhausted. When Bach has got the last word out of the
fugue, Mozart out of the opera, Beethoven out of the
symphony, Wagner out of the symphonic drama, their
enraptured admirers exclaim: "Our masters have shewn
us the way: let us compose some more fugues, operas,
symphonies, and Bayreuth dramas." Through just the same
error the men who have turned dramatists on the frivolous
ground of their love for the theatre have plagued a weary
world with Shakespearean dramas in five acts and in blank
verse, with artificial comedies after Congreve and Sheridan,
and with the romantic goody-goody fiction which was
squeezed dry by a hundred strong hands in the first half
of this century. It is only when we are dissatisfied with
existing masterpieces that we create new ones: if we merely
worship them, we only try to repeat the exploit of their
creator by picking out the titbits and stringing them together, in some feeble fashion of our own, into a "new
and original" botching of what our master left a good and
finished job. We are encouraged in our folly by the need
of the multitude for intermediaries between its childishness
and the maturity of the mighty men of art, and also by the
fact that art fecundated by itself gains a certain lapdog
refinement, very acceptable to lovers of lapdogs. The Incas
of Peru cultivated their royal race in this way, each Inca
marrying his sister. The result was that an average Inca
was worth about as much as an average fashionable drama
bred carefully from the last pair of fashionable dramas,
themselves bred in the same way, with perhaps a cross of
novel. But vital art work comes always from a cross between art and life: art being of one sex only, and quite
sterile by itself. Such a cross is always possible; for though
the artist may not have the capacity to bring his art into
contact with the higher life of his time, fermenting in its

religion, its philosophy, its science, and its statesmanship
(perhaps, indeed, there may not be any statesmanship
going), he can at least bring it into contact with the obvious life and common passions of the streets. This is what
has happened in the case of the Chinatown play. The
dramatist, compelled by the nature of his enterprise to
turn his back on the fashionable models for "brilliantly"
cast plays, and to go in search of documents and facts in
order to put a slice of Californian life on the stage with
crude realism, instantly wakes the theatre up with a piece
which has some reality in it, though its mother is the
cheapest and most conventional of the daughters of art,
and its father the lowest and darkest stratum of Amer-
icanized yellow civilization. The phenomenon is a very old
one. When art becomes effete, it is realism that comes to
the rescue. In the same way, when ladies and gentlemen
become effete, prostitutes become prime ministers; mobs
make revolutions; and matters are readjusted by men who
do not know their own grandfathers.

This moral of the advent of the Chinatown play is
brought out strikingly by the contrast between the rival
versions at the Lyric and at the Globe. The Lyric version,
entitled The Cat and the Cherub, and claiming to be the
original (a claim which is apparently not contradicted),
is much the more academic of the two. It is a formal play,
with comparatively pretentious acting parts, and the local
color blended into the dramatic business in the most ap-
proved literary manner: the whole ending with a complicated death struggle, in which the victim is strangled with
his own pigtail, and performs an elaborate stage fall. In
the Globe version there is comparatively no art at all: we
see the affair as we see a street row, with all the incidents
of the Chinatown slum going on independently—vulgar,
busy, incongruous, irrelevant, indifferent, just as we see
them in a London slum whilst the policeman is adjusting
some tragedy at the corner. Placed between an academic
play and a vulgar play, the high-class London critic cannot hesitate. He waves the Globe aside with scorn and
takes the Lyric to his bosom. It seems to me that the
popular verdict must go the other way. It is of course
eminently possible that people may not care to pay West
End theatre prices for a very short entertainment which,
at best, would make an excellent side show at Earl's
Court. But if they choose either way, they will probably

like the crude, coarse, curious, vivid and once or twice even thrilling hotch-potch at the Globe, better than the more sedate and academic drama at the Lyric. A good deal will depend on which they see first. Nine-tenths of the charm of Chinatown lies in its novelty; and a comparison of the opinions of those who saw the two plays in the order of their production, and those who, like myself, saw the Globe play first, will prove, I think, that the first experience very heavily discounts the second.

I am not sure that there is not more initiative for art in commercial speculations like these sham Chinese plays than in academic-revolutionary bodies like the New Century Theatre, the Independent Theatre, or the Bayreuth Festival Playhouse. These enterprises, indifferent to public demand, can do no more than create a taste for the already achieved works of the artists who seem to them at the moment of their foundation to be the most advanced of their time. It is no doubt heroic of the Independent Theatre to send out a mission to accustom the demoralized and recalcitrant provincial playgoer to Ibsen's plays and mine. It is at least prudent, if not glorious, for the New Century Theatre to promote the spread of the New Drama by sitting tightly on its copyrights and neither performing its Echegaray and Ibsen plays itself nor allowing anyone else to do so. Bayreuth no doubt makes the most of its opportunities by steadily exploiting the reputation of its dead founder, and keeping Parsifal as a luxury for tourists. But what did the great founder of Bayreuth say to it himself? We can now learn that in his own words; for Mr Ashton Ellis's translation of Wagner's writings has now passed safely through the pregnant but labored essays of the master's middle age, and has arrived at the clear, humorous, wise journalism of his Bayreuth time, when he cast back to his early ways as a musical critic in Paris, and anticipated the most entertaining features of modern Saturday Reviewing. His style does not lose in the hands of Mr Ashton Ellis: nobody but Carlyle has ever before made English German so fascinating. The irony of Ein Rückblick auf die Bühnenfestspiele des Jahres 1876 is brought out with a vengeance. Wagner's description of his triumphant achievement of the building of the great Festspielhaus, and the first Bayreuth festival in 1876, is one of the most amusing and thrilling documents in the history of art. There he tells of his gallery of kings, every one of

whom complimented him on his indomitable pluck, and
confessed that they had never believed it possible for him
to pull it through, exactly as if he were Sir Augustus
Harris: not one of them having the faintest sense of what
he was really driving at. Then he goes on, with an intense
relish for the joke against himself, to tell how the thing
was really done—how the little congregations of worshippers who had been formed throughout Germany to provide
the festival with an audience of true worshippers, and
exclude all the fashionable heathen, were really speculators
who joined to get the seats and sell them again to the
aforesaid heathen, the result being as worldly and unpre-
pared an audience as one could desire at the private view
of the Royal Academy. The account of the collection of
the funds by an energetic lady, who was wonderfully
successful with people who did not know who Wagner was,
and actually levied her largest tributes on the Sultan and
the Khedive of Egypt, is the climax of the irony, though
perhaps the climax of the fun is the story of the ordering
of the dragon from a famous English firm, which, after
our commercial manner, delivered it in instalments at the
last moment, and finally sent the neck irrecoverably to
the wrong address. It would carry me too far to draw the
moral, but it certainly does not point to the founding of
societies and the building of theatres as being any better a
device in art than the founding of orders and the building
of cathedrals has proved in religion. Not that these things
are not worth doing, since they lead to so many incidental
improvements, especially in architecture. But it is certain
that they never do what the Master Builder meant them
to do.

.   .   .   .

Shakespear and Mr Barrie

THE TEMPEST. Performance by the Elizabethan Stage Society
at the Mansion House, 5 November 1897.

THE LITTLE MINISTER. A play in four acts. By J. M. Barrie,
founded on his novel of that name. Haymarket Theatre, 6
November 1897.

[13 *November* 1897]

It was a curious experience to see The Tempest one
night and The Little Minister the next. I should like to

have taken Shakespear to the Haymarket play. How well
he would have recognized it! For he also once had to take
a popular novel; make a shallow, unnatural, indulgent,
pleasant, popular drama of it; and hand it to the theatre
with no hint of his feelings except the significant title As
You Like It. And we have not even the wit to feel the
snub, but go on complacently talking of the manufacture
of Rosalinds and Orlandos (a sort of thing that ought
really to be done in a jam factory) as "delineation of
character" and the like. One feels Shakespear's position
most strongly in the plays written after he had outgrown
his interest in the art of acting and given up the idea of
educating the public. In Hamlet he is quite enthusiastic
about naturalness in the business of the stage, and makes
Hamlet hold forth about it quite Wagnerianly: in Cymbeline and The Tempest he troubles himself so little about
it that he actually writes down the exasperating clownish
interruptions he once denounced; brings on the god in the
car; and, having indulged the public in matters which he
no longer set any store by, took it out of them in poetry.
   The poetry of The Tempest is so magical that it would
make the scenery of a modern theatre ridiculous. The
methods of the Elizabethan Stage Society (I do not commit myself to their identity with those of the Elizabethan
stage) leave to the poet the work of conjuring up the
isle "full of noises, sounds and sweet airs." And I do not
see how this plan can be beaten. If Sir Henry Irving were
to put the play on at the Lyceum next season (why not,
by the way?), what could he do but multiply the expenditure enormously, and spoil the illusion? He would give
us the screaming violin instead of the harmonious viol;
"characteristic" music scored for wood-wind and percus-
sion by Mr German instead of Mr Dolmetsch's pipe and
tabor; an expensive and absurd stage ship; and some wind-
less, airless, changeless, soundless, electric-lit, wooden-
floored mockeries of the haunts of Ariel. They would cost
more; but would they be an improvement on the Mansion
House arrangement? Mr Poel says frankly, "See that singers' gallery up there! Well, lets pretend that it's the ship."
We agree; and the thing is done. But how could we agree
to such a pretence with a stage ship? Before it we should
say, "Take that thing away: if our imagination is to create
a ship, it must not be contradicted by something that apes
a ship so vilely as to fill us with denial and repudiation of

its imposture." The singing gallery makes no attempt to impose on us: it disarms criticism by unaffected submission to the facts of the case, and throws itself honestly on our fancy, with instant success. In the same way a rag doll is fondly nursed by a child who can only stare at a waxen simulacrum of infancy. A superstitious person left to himself will see a ghost in every ray of moonlight on the wall and every old coat hanging on a nail; but make up a really careful, elaborate, plausible, picturesque, blood-curdling ghost for him, and his cunning grin will proclaim that he sees through it at a glance. The reason is, not that a man can *always* imagine things more vividly than art can present them to him, but that it takes an altogether extraordinary degree of art to compete with the pictures which the imagination makes when it is stimulated by such potent forces as the maternal instinct, superstitious awe, or the poetry of Shakespear. The dialogue between Gonzalo and that "bawling, blasphemous, incharitable dog" the boatswain, would turn the House of Lords into a ship: in less than ten words—"What care these roarers for the name of king?"—you see the white horses and the billowing green mountains playing football with crown and purple. But the Elizabethan method would not do for a play like The White Heather, excellent as it is of its kind. If Mr Poel, on the strength of the Drury Lane dialogue, were to leave us to imagine the singers' gallery to be the bicycling ring in Battersea Park, or Boulter's Lock, we should flatly decline to imagine anything at all. It requires the nicest judgment to know exactly how much help the imagination wants. There is no general rule, not even for any particular author. You can do best without scenery in The Tempest and A Midsummer Night's Dream, because the best scenery you can get will only destroy the illusion created by the poetry; but it does not at all follow that scenery will not improve a representation of Othello. Maeterlinck's plays, requiring a mystical inscenation in the style of Fernand Knopf, would be nearly as much spoiled by Elizabethan treatment as by Drury Lane treatment. Modern melodrama is so dependent on the most realistic scenery that a representation would suffer far less by the omission of the scenery than of the dialogue. This is why the manager who stages every play in the same way is a bad manager, even when he is an adept at his one way. A great deal of the distinction of the Lyceum productions is due to the fact that Sir Henry Irving, when the work in hand is at all within the limits of his sympathies, knows exactly how far to go in the matter of scenery. When he makes mistakes, they are almost always mistakes in stage management, by which he sacrifices the effect of some unappreciated passage of dialogue of which the charm has escaped him.

Though I was sufficiently close to the stage at The Tempest to hear, or imagine I heard, every word of the dialogue, yet it was plain that the actors were not eminent after-dinner speakers, and had consequently never received in that room the customary warning to speak to the second pillar on the right of the door, on pain of not being heard. Though they all spoke creditably, and some of them remarkably well, they took matters rather too easily, with the result that the quieter passages were inaudible to a considerable number of the spectators. I mention the matter because the Elizabethan Stage Society is hardly yet alive to the acoustic difficulties raised by the lofty halls it performs in. They are mostly troublesome places for a speaker; for if he shouts, his vowels make such a roaring din that his consonants are indistinguishable; and if he does not, his voice does not travel far enough. They are too resonant for noisy speakers and too vast for gentle ones. A clean, athletic articulation, kept up without any sentimental or indolent relaxations, is indispensable as a primary physical accomplishment for the Elizabethan actor who "takes to the halls."

The performance went without a hitch. Mr Dolmetsch looked after the music; and the costumes were worthy of the reputation which the Society has made for itself in this particular. Ariel, armless and winged in his first incarnation, was not exactly a tricksy sprite; for as the wing arrangement acted as a strait waistcoat, he had to be content with the effect he made as a living picture. This disability on his part was characteristic of the whole performance, which had to be taken in a somewhat low key and slow tempo, with a minimum of movement. If any attempt had been made at the impetuosity and liveliness for which the English experts of the sixteenth century were famous throughout Europe, it would have not only failed, but prevented the performers from attaining what they did attain, very creditably, by a more modest ambition.

To our host the Lord Mayor I take off my hat. When I

think of the guzzling horrors I have seen in that room, and
the insufferable oratory that has passed through my head
from ear to ear on its way to the second pillar on the right
of the door (which has the advantage of being stone deaf),
I hail with sincere gratitude the first tenant of the Mansion
House who has bidden me to an entertainment worthy of
the first magistrate of a great city, instead of handing me
over to an army of waiters to be dealt with as one "whose
god is his belly."

The Little Minister is a much happier play than The
Tempest. Mr Barrie has no impulse to throw his adaptation of a popular novel at the public head with a sarcastic
title, because he has written the novel himself, and
thoroughly enjoys it. Mr Barrie is a born storyteller; and
he sees no further than his stories—conceives any discrepancy between them and the world as a shortcoming on
the world's part, and is only too happy to be able to
rearrange matters in a pleasanter way. The popular stage,
which was a prison to Shakespear's genius, is a playground
to Mr Barrie's. At all events he does the thing as if he
liked it, and does it very well. He has apparently no eye
for human character; but he has a keen sense of human
qualities, and he produces highly popular assortments of
them. He cheerfully assumes, as the public wish him to
assume, that one endearing quality implies all endearing
qualities, and one repulsive quality all repulsive qualities:
the exceptions being comic characters, who are permitted
to have "weaknesses," or stern and terrible souls who are
at once understood to be saving up some enormous sentimentality for the end of the last act but one. Now if there
is one lesson that real life teaches us more insistently than
another, it is that we must not infer one quality from
another, or even rely on the constancy of ascertained
qualities under all circumstances. It is not only that a brave
and good-humored man may be vain and fond of money;
a lovable woman greedy, sensual, and mendacious; a saint
vindictive; and a thief kindly; but these very terms are
made untrustworthy by the facts that the man who is
brave enough to venture on personal combat with a prizefighter or a tiger may be abjectly afraid of ghosts, mice,
women, a dentist's forceps, public opinion, cholera epi-
demics, and a dozen other things that many timorous
mortals face resignedly enough; the man who is stingy to
miserliness with coin, and is the despair of waiters and

cabmen, gives thousands (by cheque) to public institutions; the man who eats oysters by the hundred and legs of mutton by the dozen for wagers, is in many matters temperate, moderate, and even abstemious; and men and women alike, though they behave with the strictest conventional propriety when tempted by advances from people whom they do not happen to like, are by no means so austere with people whom they do like. In romance, all these "inconsistencies" are corrected by replacing human nature by conventional assortments of qualities. When Shakespear objected to this regulation, and wrote All's Well in defiance of it, his play was not acted. When he succumbed, and gave us the required assortment "as we like it," he was enormously successful. Mr Barrie has no scruples about complying. He is one with the public in the matter, and makes a pretty character as a milliner makes a pretty bonnet, by "matching" the materials. And why not, if everybody is pleased?

To that question I reply by indignantly refusing, as a contemporary of Master-Builder Solness, to be done out of my allowance of "salutary self-torture." People dont go to the theatre to be pleased: there are a hundred cheaper, less troublesome, more effective pleasures than an uncomfortable gallery can offer. We are led there by our appetite for drama, which is no more to be satisfied by sweetmeats than our appetite for dinner is to be satisfied with meringues and raspberry vinegar. One likes something solid; and that, I suppose, is why heroes and heroines with assorted qualities are only endurable when the author has sufficient tact and comic force to keep up an affectionate undercurrent of fun at their expense and his own. That was how Shakespear pulled his amiable fictions through; that is how Mr Carton does it; that is how Mr Barrie does it. Dickens, with his fundamental seriousness and social conscience always at war with his romantic instincts and idealism, and even with his unconquerable sense of humor, made desperate efforts to take his assorted heroines quite seriously by resolutely turning off the fun, with a result—Agnes Wickfield, Esther Summerson, and so forth —so utterly unbearable that they stand as a warning to all authors that it is dangerous to be serious unless you have something real to be serious about, even when you are a great genius. Happily, Mr Barrie is not serious about his little minister and his little minister's Babby. At most he is affectionate, which is quite a different thing. The twain are nine-tenths fun and the other tenth sentiment, which makes a very toothsome combination.

I should explain, however, that I took care not to read the novel before seeing the play; and I have not had time to read it since. But it is now clear to me that Mr Barrie has depended on the novel to make his hero and heroine known to the playgoer. Their parts consist of a string of amusing and sometimes touching trivialities; but it is easy to divine that the young minister's influence over his elders, and perhaps Babby's attraction for him, are more fully accounted for in the book. I should hope also that Rob Dow and the chief elder, who in the play are machine-made after a worn-out pattern, are more original and natural in the novel. Otherwise, I found the work self-sufficing.

As a success for the Haymarket Theatre the play has fulfilled and exceeded all expectation. It has every prospect of running into the next century. It is the first play produced under Mr Cyril Maude's own management that has given him a chance as an actor. It is quite characteristic of the idiotic topsyturviness of our stage that Mr Maude, who has a remarkable charm of quaintly naïve youthfulness, should have been immediately pitched upon—nay, have pitched on himself—as a born impersonator of old men. All he asked from the author was a snuff-box, a set of grease paints, and a part not younger than sixty-five to make him perfectly happy. There was Mr Grundy's Sowing the Wind, for instance: Mr Maude was never more pleased with himself than when, after spending the afternoon in pencilling impossible wrinkles all over his face, he was crustily taking snuff as the old man in that play. The spectacle used to exasperate me to such a degree that nothing restrained me from hurling the nearest opera-glass at those wrinkles but the fear that, as I am unfortunately an incorrigibly bad shot, I might lay Miss Emery low, or maim Mr Brandon Thomas for life. I do declare that of all the infuriating absurdities that human perversity has evolved, this painted-on "character-acting" is the only one that entirely justifies manslaughter. It was not that Mr Cyril Maude did it badly; on the contrary, he did it very cleverly indeed: it was that he ought to have been doing something else. The plague of the stage at present is the intolerable stereotyping of the lover: he is always the same sort of young man, with the same cast of features, the same crease down his new trousers, the same careful manners, the same air of behaving and dressing like a gentleman for the first time in his life and being overcome with the novelty and importance of it. Mr Maude was just the man to break this oppressive fashion; and instead of doing it, he amused himself with snuff, and crustiness, and wrinkles as aforesaid, perhaps for the sake of the novelty which gentility could not offer him. As the little minister he at last plays without disguise, and with complete success. He is naturally shy at shewing himself to the public for the first time; but the shyness becomes him in the part; and I dare say he will run Mr Forbes Robertson hard for the rest of the season as a much-admired man. Miss Winifred Emery, as Babby, has a rare time of it. She plays with the part like a child, and amuses herself and the audience unboundedly. Her sudden assumption of Red-Robe dignity for a few minutes in the fourth act constitutes what I think may be described safely as the worst bit of acting the world has yet seen from a performer of equal reputation, considering that it is supposed to represent the conduct of a girl just out of the schoolroom; but she soon relapses into an abandonment to fun compared to which Miss Rehan's most reckless attacks of that nature are sedate. Mr Kinghorne is, I think, the best of the elders; but Mr Brandon Thomas and Mrs Brooke are in great force. There was a good deal of curiosity among the women in the audience to see Mr Barrie, because of his evident belief that he was shewing a deep insight into feminine character by representing Babby as a woman whose deepest instinct was to find a man for her master. At the end, when her husband announced his intention of caning her if she deserved it, she flung her arms round his neck and exclaimed ecstatically that he was the man for her. The inference that, with such an experience of the sex, Mr Barrie's personality must be little short of godlike, led to a vociferous call for him when the curtain fell. In response, Mr Harrison appeared, and got as far as "Mr Barrie is far too modest a man—" when he was interrupted by a wild shriek of laughter. I do not doubt that many amiable ladies may from time to time be afflicted with the fancy that there is something voluptuous in getting thrashed by a man. In the classes where the majority of married women get that fancy gratified with

excessive liberality, it is not so persistent as Mr Barrie
might think. I seriously suggest to him that the samples of
his notion of "womanliness" given by Babby are nothing
but silly travesties of that desire to find an entirely trust-
worthy leader which is common to men and women.

Sir A. C. Mackenzie's overture was drowned by the
conversation, which was energetically led by the composer
and Sir George Lewis. But I caught some scraps of refreshingly workmanlike polyphony; and the *mélodrame*
at the beginning of the garden scene was charming.

Hamlet Revisited

[18 *December* 1897]

Public feeling has been much harrowed this week by
the accounts from America of the 144 hours' bicycle race;
but what are the horrors of such an exhibition compared
to those of the hundred-nights run of Hamlet! On Monday
last I went, in my private capacity, to witness the last lap
but five of the Lyceum trial of endurance. The performers
had passed through the stage of acute mania, and were
for the most part sleep-walking in a sort of dazed blank-
verse dream. Mr Barnes raved of some New England
maiden named Affection Poo; the subtle distinctions made
by Mrs Patrick Campbell between madness and sanity had
blurred off into a placid idiocy turned to favor and to
prettiness; Mr Forbes-Robertson, his lightness of heart all
gone, wandered into another play at the words "Sleep?
No more!" which he delivered as, "Sleep no more." Fortunately, before he could add "Macbeth does murder
sleep," he relapsed into Hamlet and saved the situation.
And yet some of the company seemed all the better for
their unnatural exercise. The King was in uproarious
spirits; and the Ghost, always comfortable, was now positively pampered, his indifference to the inconveniences of
purgatory having developed into a bean-fed enjoyment of
them. Fortinbras, as I judged, had sought consolation in
religion: he was anxious concerning Hamlet's eternal welfare; but his general health seemed excellent. As Mr Gould
did not play on the occasion of my first visit, I could not
compare him with his former self; but his condition was
sufficiently grave. His attitude was that of a castaway mariner who has no longer hope enough to scan the horizon

for a sail; yet even in this extremity his unconquerable generosity of temperament had not deserted him. When his cue came, he would jump up and lend a hand with all his old alacrity and resolution. Naturally the players of the shorter parts had suffered least: Rosencrantz and Guildenstern were only beginning to enjoy themselves; and Bernardo (or was it Marcellus?) was still eagerly working up his part to concert pitch. But there could be no mistake as to the general effect. Mr Forbes-Robertson's exhausting part had been growing longer and heavier on his hands; whilst the support of the others had been falling off; so that he was keeping up the charm of the representation almost single-handed just when the torturing fatigue and monotony of nightly repetition had made the task most difficult. To the public, no doubt, the justification of the effort is its success. There was no act which did not contain at least one scene finely and movingly played; indeed some of the troubled passages gained in verisimilitude by the tormented condition of the actor. But Hamlet is a very long play; and it only seems a short one when the high-mettled comedy with which it is interpenetrated from beginning to end leaps out with all the lightness and spring of its wonderful loftiness of temper. This was the secret of the delighted surprise with which the public, when the run began, found that Hamlet, far from being a funereally classical bore, was full of a celestial gaiety and fascination. It is this rare vein that gives out first when the exigencies of theatrical commerce force an actor to abuse it. A sentimental Hamlet can go on for two years, or ten for the matter of that, without much essential depreciation of the performance; but the actor who sounds Hamlet from the lowest note to the top of his compass very soon finds that compass contracting at the top. On Monday night the first act, the third act, and the fifth act from the entrance of Laertes onward, had lost little more than they had gained as far as Mr Forbes-Robertson was concerned; but the second act, and the colloquy with the grave-digger, which were the triumphs of the representation in its fresher stages, were pathetically dulled, with the result that it could no longer be said that the length of the play was forgotten.

The worst of the application of the long-run system to heroic plays is that, instead of killing the actor, it drives him to limit himself to such effects as he can repeat to infinity without committing suicide. The opposite system, in its extreme form of the old stock company playing two or three different pieces every night, led to the same evasion in a more offensive form. The recent correspondence in the Morning Post on The Stage as a Profession, to which I have myself luminously contributed, has produced the usual fallacious eulogies of the old stock company as a school of acting. You can no more prevent contributors to public correspondences falling into this twenty-times-exploded error than from declaring that duelling was a school of good manners, that the lash suppressed garotting, or any other of the gratuitous ignorances of the amateur sociologist. The truth is, it is just as impossible for a human being to study and perform a new part of any magnitude every day as to play Hamlet for a hundred consecutive nights. Nevertheless, if an actor is required to do these things, he will find some way out of the difficulty without refusing. The stock actor solved the problem by adopting a "line": for example, if his "line" was old age, he acquired a trick of doddering and speaking in a cracked voice: if juvenility, he swaggered and effervesced. With these accomplishments, eked out by a few rules of thumb as to wigs and face-painting, one deplorable step dance, and one still more deplorable "combat," he "swallowed" every part given to him in a couple of hours, and regurgitated it in the evening over the footlights, always in the same manner, however finely the dramatist might have individualized it. His infamous incompetence at last swept him from the reputable theatres into the barns and booths; and it was then that he became canonized, in the imagination of a posterity that had never suffered from him, as the incarnation of the one quality in which he was quite damnably deficient: to wit, versatility. His great contribution to dramatic art was the knack of earning a living for fifty years on the stage without ever really acting, or either knowing or caring for the difference between the Comedy of Errors and Box and Cox.

A moment's consideration will shew that the results of the long-run system at its worst are more bearable than the horrors of the past. Also, that even in point of giving the actor some chance of varying his work, the long-run system is superior, since the modern actor may at all events exhaust the possibilities of his part before it exhausts him, whereas the stock actor, having barely time to apply his bag of tricks to his daily task, never varies his treatment by a hair's breadth from one half century to another. The best system, of course, lies between these extremes. Take the case of the great Italian actors who have visited us, and whose acting is of an excellence apparently quite beyond the reach of our best English performers. We find them extremely chary of playing every night. They have a repertory containing plays which count as resting places for them. For example, Duse relieves Magda with Mirandolina just as our own Shakespearean star actors used to relieve Richard the Third and Othello with Charles Surface and Don Felix. But even with this mitigation no actor can possibly play leading parts of the first order six nights a week all the year round unless he underplays them, or routines them mechanically in the old stock manner, or faces a terrible risk of disablement by paralysis, or, finally, resorts to alcohol or morphia, with the usual penalties. What we want in order to get the best work is a repertory theatre with alternative casts. If, for instance, we could have Hamlet running at the Lyceum with Sir Henry Irving and Miss Ellen Terry on Thursdays and Saturdays, Mr Forbes-Robertson and Mrs Patrick Campbell on Wednesdays and Fridays, and the other two days devoted to comedies in which all four could occasionally appear, with such comedians as Mr Charles Wyndham, Mr Weedon Grossmith, Mr Bourchier, Mr Cyril Maude, and Mr Hawtrey, then we should have a theatre which we could invite serious people to attend without positively insulting them. I am aware that the precise combination which I have named is not altogether a probable one at present; but there is no reason why we should not at least turn our faces in that direction. The actor-manager system, which has hitherto meant the star system carried to its utmost possible extreme, has made the theatre so insufferable that, now that its monopoly has been broken up by the rise of the suburban theatres, there is a distinct weakening of the jealous and shameless individualism of the last twenty years, and a movement towards combination and cooperation.

By the way, is it quite prudent to start a public correspondence on the Stage as a Profession? Suppose someone were to tell the truth about it!

Tappertit on Cæsar

JULIUS CÆSAR. Her Majesty's Theatre, 22 January 1898.

[29 *January* 1898]

The truce with Shakespear is over. It was only possible whilst Hamlet was on the stage. Hamlet is the tragedy of private life—nay, of individual bachelor-poet life. It belongs to a detached residence, a select library, an exclusive circle, to no occupation, to fathomless boredom, to impenitent mugwumpism, to the illusion that the futility of these things is the futility of existence, and its contemplation philosophy: in short, to the dream-fed gentlemanism of the age which Shakespear inaugurated in English literature: the age, that is, of the rising middle class bringing into power the ideas taught it by its servants in the kitchen, and its fathers in the shop—ideas now happily passing away as the onslaught of modern democracy offers to the kitchen-taught and home-bred the alternative of achieving a real superiority or going ignominiously under in the class conflict.

It is when we turn to Julius Cæsar, the most splendidly written political melodrama we possess, that we realize the apparently immortal author of Hamlet as a man, not for all time, but for an age only, and that, too, in all solidly wise and heroic aspects, the most despicable of all the ages in our history. It is impossible for even the most judicially minded critic to look without a revulsion of indignant contempt at this travestying of a great man as a silly braggart, whilst the pitiful gang of mischief-makers who destroyed him are lauded as statesmen and patriots. There is not a single sentence uttered by Shakespear's Julius Cæsar that is, I will not say worthy of him, but even worthy of an average Tammany boss. Brutus is nothing but a familiar type of English suburban preacher: politically he would hardly impress the Thames Conservancy Board. Cassius is a vehemently assertive nonentity. It is only when we come to Antony, unctuous voluptuary and self-seeking sentimental demagogue, that we find Shakespear in his depth; and in his depth, of course, he is superlative. Regarded as a crafty stage job, the play is a triumph: rhetoric, claptrap, effective gushes of emotion, all the devices of the popular playwright, are employed with a profusion of power that almost breaks their backs. No doubt there are slips and slovenliness of the kind that careful revisers eliminate; but they count for so little in the mass of accomplishment that it is safe to say that the dramatist's art can be carried no further on that plane. If Goethe, who understood Cæsar and the significance of his death—"the most senseless of deeds" he called it—had treated the subject, his conception of it would have been as superior to Shakespear's as St John's Gospel is to the Police News; but his treatment could not have been more magnificently successful. As far as sonority, imagery, wit, humor, energy of imagination, power over language, and a whimsically keen eye for idiosyncrasies can make a dramatist, Shakespear was the king of dramatists. Unfortunately, a man may have them all, and yet conceive high affairs of state exactly as Simon Tappertit did. In one of the scenes in Julius Cæsar a conceited poet bursts into the tent of Brutus and Cassius, and exhorts them not to quarrel with one another. If Shakespear had been able to present his play to the ghost of the great Julius, he would probably have had much the same reception. He certainly would have deserved it.

When it was announced that Mr Tree had resolved to give special prominence to the character of Cæsar in his acting version, the critics winked, and concluded simply that the actor-manager was going to play Antony and not Brutus. Therefore I had better say that Mr Tree must stand acquitted of any belittlement of the parts which compete so strongly with his own. Before going to Her Majesty's I was curious enough to block out for myself a division of the play into three acts; and I found that Mr Tree's division corresponded exactly with mine. Mr Waller's opportunities as Brutus, and Mr McLeay's as Cassius, are limited only by their own ability to take advantage of them; and Mr Louis Calvert figures as boldly in the public eye as he did in his own production of Antony and Cleopatra last year at Manchester. Indeed, Mr Calvert is the only member of the company who achieves an unequivocal success. The preference expressed in the play by Cæsar for fat men may, perhaps, excuse Mr Calvert for having again permitted himself to expand after his triumphant reduction of his girth for his last appearance in London. However, he acted none the worse: in fact, nobody else acted so skilfully or originally. The others, more heavily burdened, did their best, quite in the spirit of the man who had never played the fiddle, but had no doubt he could if he tried. Without oratory, without style, without specialized vocal training, without any practice worth mentioning, they assaulted the play with cheerful self-sufficiency, and gained great glory by the extent to which, as a masterpiece of the playwright's trade, it played itself. Some small successes were not lacking. Cæsar's nose was good: Calpurnia's bust was worthy of her: in such parts Garrick and Siddons could have achieved no more. Miss Evelyn Millard's Roman matron in the style of Richardson—Cato's daughter as Clarissa—was an unlooked-for novelty; but it cost a good deal of valuable time to get in the eighteenth century between the lines of the first B.C. By operatic convention —the least appropriate of all conventions—the boy Lucius was played by Mrs Tree, who sang Sullivan's ultra-nineteenth-century Orpheus with his Lute, modulations and all, to a pizzicato accompaniment supposed to be played on a lyre with eight open and unstoppable strings, a feat complexly and absurdly impossible. Mr Waller, as Brutus, failed in the first half of the play. His intention clearly was to represent Brutus as a man superior to fate and circumstance; but the effect he produced was one of insensibility. Nothing could have been more unfortunate; for it is through the sensibility of Brutus that the audience have to learn what they cannot learn from the phlegmatic pluck of Casca or the narrow vindictiveness of Cassius: that is, the terrible momentousness, the harrowing anxiety and dread, of the impending catastrophe. Mr Waller left that function to the thunderstorm. From the death of Cæsar onward he was better; and his appearance throughout was effective; but at best his sketch was a water-color one. Mr Franklyn McLeay carried off the honors of the evening by his deliberate staginess and imposing assumptiveness: that is, by as much of the grand style as our playgoers now understand; but in the last act he was monotonously violent, and died the death of an incorrigible poseur, not of a noble Roman. Mr Tree's memory failed him as usual; and a good deal of the technical part of his work was botched and haphazard, like all Shakespearean work nowadays; nevertheless, like Mr Calvert, he made the audience believe in the reality of the character before them. But it is impossible to praise his performance in detail. I cannot recall any single passage in the scene after the murder that was well done: in fact, he only secured an effective curtain

by bringing Calpurnia on the stage to attitudinize over
Cæsar's body. To say that the demagogic oration in the
Forum produced its effect is nothing; for its effect is inevitable, and Mr Tree neither made the most of it nor
handled it with any pretence of mastery or certainty. But
he was not stupid, nor inane, nor Bard-of-Avon ridden;
and he contrived to interest the audience in Antony instead of trading on their ready-made interest in Mr Beerbohm Tree. And for that many sins may be forgiven him
nowadays, when the playgoer, on first nights at all events,
goes to see the cast rather than the play.

What is missing in the performance, for want of the
specific Shakespearean skill, is the Shakespearean music.
When we come to those unrivalled grandiose passages in
which Shakespear turns on the full organ, we want to hear
the sixteen-foot pipes booming, or, failing them (as we
often must, since so few actors are naturally equipped with
them), the ennobled tone, and the tempo suddenly steadied
with the majesty of deeper purpose. You have, too, those
moments when the verse, instead of opening up the depths
of sound, rises to its most brilliant clangor, and the lines
ring like a thousand trumpets. If we cannot have these
effects, or if we can only have genteel drawing room arrangements of them, we cannot have Shakespear; and that
is what is mainly the matter at Her Majesty's: there are
neither trumpets nor pedal pipes there. The conversation
is metrical and emphatic in an elocutionary sort of way;
but it makes no distinction between the arid prairies of
blank verse which remind one of Henry VI at its crudest,
and the places where the morass suddenly piles itself into
a mighty mountain. Cassius in the first act has a twaddling
forty-line speech, base in its matter and mean in its measure, followed immediately by the magnificent torrent of
rhetoric, the first burst of true Shakespearean music in
the play, beginning—

> Why, man, he doth bestride the narrow world
> Like a Colossus, and we petty men
> Walk under his huge legs and peep about
> To find ourselves dishonorable graves.

I failed to catch the slightest change of elevation or reinforcement of feeling when Mr McLeay passed from one to
the other. His tone throughout was dry; and it never
varied. By dint of energetic, incisive articulation, he drove

his utterances harder home than the others; but the best
lines seemed to him no more than the worst: there were
no heights and depths, no contrast of black thunder-cloud
and flaming lightning flash, no stirs and surprises. Yet he
was not inferior in oratory to the rest. Mr Waller certainly
cannot be reproached with dryness of tone; and his delivery of the speech in the Forum was perhaps the best
piece of formal elocution we got; but he also kept at much
the same level throughout, and did not at any moment attain to anything that could be called grandeur. Mr Tree,
except for a conscientiously desperate effort to cry havoc
and let slip the dogs of war in the robustious manner,
with no better result than to all but extinguish his voice,
very sensibly left oratory out of the question, and tried
conversational sincerity, which answered so well that his
delivery of "This was the noblest Roman of them all"
came off excellently.

The real hero of the revival is Mr Alma Tadema. The
scenery and stage coloring deserve everything that has been
said of them. But the illusion is wasted by want of discipline and want of thought behind the scenes. Every car-
penter seems to make it a point of honor to set the cloths
swinging in a way that makes Rome reel and the audience
positively seasick. In Brutus's house the door is on the
spectators' left: the knocks on it come from the right. The
Roman soldiers take the field each man with his two
javelins neatly packed up like a fishing-rod. After a battle,
in which they are supposed to have made the famous
Roman charge, hurling these javelins in and following them
up sword in hand, they come back carrying the javelins
still undisturbed in their rug-straps, in perfect trim for a
walk-out with the nursery-maids of Philippi.

The same want of vigilance appears in the acting version. For example, though the tribunes Flavius and Marul-
lus are replaced by two of the senators, the lines referring
to them by name are not altered. But the oddest oversight
is the retention in the tent scene of the obvious confusion
of the original version of the play, in which the death of
Portia was announced to Brutus by Messala, with the second version, into which the quarrel scene was written to
strengthen the fourth act. In this version Brutus, already
in possession of the news, reveals it to Cassius. The play
has come down to us with the two alternative scenes strung
together; so that Brutus's reception of Messala's news,

following his own revelation of it to Cassius, is turned into
a satire on Roman fortitude, the suggestion being that the
secret of the calm with which a noble Roman received the
most terrible tidings in public was that it had been carefully imparted to him in private beforehand. Mr Tree has
not noticed this; and the two scenes are gravely played
one after the other at Her Majesty's. This does not matter
much to our playgoers, who never venture to use their
common sense when Shakespear is in question; but it
wastes time. Mr Tree may without hesitation cut out Pin-
darus and Messala, and go straight on from the bowl of
wine to Brutus's question about Philippi.

The music, composed for the occasion by Mr Raymond
Roze, made me glad that I had already taken care to
acknowledge the value of Mr Roze's services to Mr Tree;
for this time he has missed the Roman vein rather badly.
To be a Frenchman was once no disqualification for the
antique, because French musicians used to be brought up
on Gluck as English ones were brought up on Handel.
But Mr Roze composes as if Gluck had been supplanted
wholly in his curriculum by Gounod and Bizet. If that
prelude to the third act were an attempt to emulate the
overtures to Alceste or Iphigenia I could have forgiven it.
But to give us the soldiers' chorus from Faust, crotchet for
crotchet and triplet for triplet, with nothing changed but
the notes, was really too bad.

I am sorry I must postpone until next week all consideration of Mr Pinero's Trelawney of the Wells. The
tragic circumstances under which I do are as follows. The
manager of the Court Theatre, Mr Arthur Chudleigh, did
not honor the Saturday Review with the customary invita-
tion to the first performance. When a journal is thus
slighted, it has no resource but to go to its telephone and
frantically offer any terms to the box-offices for a seat for
the first night. But on fashionable occasions the manager
is always master of the situation: there are never any seats
to be had except from himself. It was so on this occasion;
and the Saturday Review was finally brought to its knees
at the feet of the Sloane Square telephone. In response to
a humble appeal, the instrument scornfully replied that
"three lines of adverse criticism were of no use to it."
Naturally my curiosity was excited to an extraordinary degree by the fact that the Court Theatre telephone, which
knew all about Mr Pinero's comedy, should have such a

low opinion of it as to be absolutely certain that it would
deserve an unprecedentedly contemptuous treatment at
my hands. I instantly purchased a place for the fourth
performance, Charlotte Corday and Julius Cæsar occupy-
ing my time on the second and third nights; and I am now
in a position to assure that telephone that its misgivings
were strangely unwarranted, and that, if it will excuse my
saying so, it does not know a good comedietta when it sees
one. Reserving my reasons for next week, I offer Mr
Pinero my apologies for a delay which is not my own
fault. (Will the Mining Journal please copy, as Mr Pinero
reads no other paper during the current fortnight?)

I find this article has already run to such a length that I
must postpone consideration of Charlotte Corday also,
merely remarking for the present that I wish the play was
as attractive as the heroine.

Elizabethan Athletics at Oxford

ROMEO AND JULIET. Oxford University Dramatic Society,
New Theatre, Oxford, 16-22 February 1898.

.   .   .   .   .

[5 *March* 1898]

It is characteristic of the authorities at Oxford that they
should consider a month too little for the preparation of a
boat-race, and grudge three weeks to the rehearsals of one
of Shakespear's plays. The performance of Romeo and
Juliet by the Oxford University Dramatic Society naturally
did not, under these circumstances, approach the level of
skill attained on the Thames. The one advantage that
amateurs have over professionals—and it is such an overwhelming advantage when exhaustively used that the best
amateur performances are more instructive than the most
elaborate professional ones—is the possibility of unlimited
rehearsal. An amateur company prepared to rehearse Romeo and Juliet for six months would in some respects
easily beat an ordinary London company. But there is a
still better way within the reach of amateurs. Everyone
who has seen the annual performances of Latin plays at
Westminster School must have been struck by the absence
of that feebleness and futility of utterance which makes
the ordinary amateur so obnoxious. Yet the Westminster
plays get no such extraordinary measure of rehearsals.

Again, if we watch the amateur performances of Elizabethan drama with which Mr William Poel does such good work, we find that those performers who are members of the Shakespear Reading Society, or of the little private circles formed by inveterate Elizabethan readers, acquit themselves much better, in point of delivery, than average professional actors. This gives us the secret of the Westminster play. The schoolboy is well practised in the utterance of Latin, not colloquially as he utters English, but as a task in the nature of a performance to be submitted to the approval of his master, just as the Elizamaniac utters Shakespearean verse every week at least for the delectation of his circle. Here, surely, is the clue to the right course for the O.U.D.S. Let the members devote two nights a week all the year round to reading Elizabethan plays, and let it be a rule that no member shall be allotted a principal part without a very high average of attendances. A tradition of skill and practice in what is one of the finest of physical accomplishments will soon be established; and the O.U.D.S. will in course of time become popular as a club of artistic athletes instead of being ridiculed, as I fear it is to some extent at present, as a set of unrepresentative æsthetes. To play Shakespear without considerable technical skill and vocal power is, frankly, to make an ass of oneself; and the contempt of the average undergraduate for such exhibitions is by no means mere Philistinism. If the boat-race were rowed by men who never took an oar in their hands until the middle of February, and only did so then because they were vain enough to want to figure in some footling imitation of the Olympian games, the University would not care two straws about the boat-race. I am bound to say that it has had much the same reason for not concerning itself about the late performance of Romeo and Juliet. If the performers had been able to handle their vowels and consonants as bats and balls and sculls are handled at Oxford in the racket-courts and cricket-fields and on the river, then, whether they were able to act or not, the performance would have been full of technical interest; the gallery would have seethed with youthful hero-worship; and the performers, doing something that every undergraduate would like to do if he could, would now be holding their heads high even among the athletes. On no other lines is there the smallest chance of a dramatic club becoming a really vital organ of an English

University, or forcing the authorities, by sheer weight of
public opinion, to build a University theatre as an indispensable part of their educational equipment.

The amateur company which performed Romeo and
Juliet was under-trained and under-rehearsed to a degree
of which, I think, it had itself no suspicion. Consequently,
though its intentions were excellent, it had very little
power of carrying them out: ideas and taste were not
lacking; but executive power was at a huge premium.
Romeo had cultivated a pretty *mezza voce,* which carried
him in a sentimentally lyrical way through a performance
which certainly maintained a distinctly artistic character
and style all through, though it was deficient in variety
and power. Mercutio, when illustrating Tybalt's accomplishments as a fencer, fell and put his knee out. He rose,
with his knee-cap visibly in that excruciating condition,
and continued his performance with undiminished dash.
He did not faint; but I should certainly have done so if
the dislocation had not fortunately reduced itself in the
slow course of about two minutes. I protest against these
exhibitions of fortitude: the Spartans may have considered
them good manners; but a really considerate modern
should frankly yell when he is hurt, and thereby give the
sympathetic spectators an opportunity to relieve their
feelings with equal demonstrativeness. Except for his
hypocrisy in this matter, Mercutio deserved well of the
Club. The part is a puzzling one; and his notion of
handling it was by no means an unhappy one. Juliet was
a convincing illustration of the advantages of practice.
The balcony scene and the phial scene—that is to say, the
two scenes which she had probably often recited—were
quite presentable. The rest, got up merely for the occasion,
was uncertain and helpless. Friar Laurence got on tolerably well; and the effect of playing the last scene in its
entirety was decidedly good. But I desire to dwell on the
weak parts in the performance rather than on the passable
ones. It was not worth doing for its own immediate sake;
and as the candid friend of the O.U.D.S., I advise them
to drop Shakespear unless they are prepared to work continuously at the Elizabethan drama all the year round, in
the way I have suggested. They have not yet qualified
themselves to split the ears of the groundlings, which they
should all be able to do, in the style of the apprentice in
The Knight of the Burning Pestle, to begin with. Later on

they can keep within the modesty of nature; but it is the business of youth "to fetch up a couraging part" valiantly, and master all the technical difficulties and audacities of art, just as the pianist, at eighteen, dazzles us with transcendent execution, though he cannot play a Mozart sonata. The secret of art's humanity will come later, when the university has been exchanged for the real world.

.   .   .   .

The Drama in Hoxton

[9 *April* 1898]

Of late, I am happy to say, the theatres have been so uneventful that I should have fallen quite out of the habit of my profession but for a certain vigorously democratic clergyman, who seized me and bore me off to the last night of the pantomime at "the Brit." The Britannia Theatre is in Hoxton, not far from Shoreditch Church, a neighborhood in which the Saturday Review is comparatively little read. The manager, a lady, is the most famous of all London managers. Sir Henry Irving, compared to her, is a mushroom, just as his theatre, compared to hers, is a back drawing room. Over 4000 people pay nightly at her doors; and the spectacle of these thousands, serried in the vast pit and empyrean gallery, is so fascinating that the stranger who first beholds it can hardly turn away to look at the stage. Forty years ago Mrs Sara Lane built this theatre; and she has managed it ever since. It may be no such great matter to handle a single playhouse—your Irvings, Trees, Alexanders, Wyndhams, and other upstarts of yesterday can do that; but Mrs Lane is said to own the whole ward in which her theatre stands. Madame Sarah Bernhardt's diamonds fill a jewel-box: Mrs Lane's are reputed to fill sacks. When I had the honor of being presented to Mrs Lane, I thought of the occasion when the late Sir Augustus Harris, her only serious rival in managerial fame, had the honor of being presented to me. The inferiority of the man to the woman was manifest. Sir Augustus was, in comparison, an hysterical creature. Enterprise was with him a frenzy which killed him when it reached a climax of success. Mrs Lane thrives on enterprise and success, and is capable, self-contained, practical, vigilant, everything that a good general should be. A

West End star is to her a person to whom she once gave
so many pounds or shillings a week, and who is now, in
glittering and splendid anxiety, begging for engagements,
desperately wooing syndicates and potential backers, and
living on Alnaschar dreams and old press notices which
were unanimously favorable (if you excluded those which
were obviously malignant personal attacks). Mrs Lane,
well furnished with realities, has no use for dreams; and
she knows syndicates and capitalists only as suspicious
characters who want her money, not as courted deities with
powers of life and death in their hands. The fortune of her
productions means little to her: if the piece succeeds, so
much the better: if not, the pantomime pays for all.

The clergyman's box, which was about as large as an
average Metropolitan railway station, was approached from
the stage itself; so that I had opportunities of criticizing
both from before the curtain and behind it. I was struck
by the absence of the worthless, heartless, incompetent
people who seem to get employed with such facility—nay,
sometimes apparently by preference—in West End theatres.
The West End calculation for musical farce and pantomime appears to be that there is "a silver mine" to be made
by paying several pounds a week to people who are worth
nothing, provided you engage enough of them. This is not
Mrs Lane's plan. Mr Bigwood, the stage-manager, is a
real stage-manager, to whom one can talk on unembar-
rassed human terms as one capable man to another, and
not by any means an erratic art failure from Bedford
Park and the Slade School, or one of those beachcombers
of our metropolitan civilization who drift to the West End
stage because its fringe of short-lived ventures provide
congenital liars and impostors with unique opportunities
of drawing a few months' or weeks' salary before their
preoccupied and worried employers have leisure to realize
that they have made a bad bargain. I had not the pleasure
of making the prompter's acquaintance; but I should have
been surprised to find him the only person in the theatre
who could not read, though in the West I should have
expected to find that his principal qualification. I made
my way under the stage to look at the working of the star-
trap by which Mr Lupino was flung up through the boards
like a stone from a volcano; and there, though I found
eight men wasting their strength by overcoming a counter-
weight which, in an up-to-date French *théâtre de féerie,*

is raised by one man with the help of a pulley, the carpenter-machinist in command was at once recognizable as a well-selected man. On the stage the results of the same instinctive sort of judgment were equally apparent. The display of beauty was sufficiently voluptuous; but there were no good-for-nothings: it was a company of men and women, recognizable as fellow-creatures, and not as accidentally pretty cretinous freaks. Even the low comedians were not blackguards, though they were certainly not fastidious, Hoxton being somewhat Rabelaisian in its ideas of broad humor. One scene, in which the horrors of seasickness were exploited with great freedom, made the four thousand sons and daughters of Shoreditch scream with laughter. At the climax, when four voyagers were struggling violently for a single bucket, I looked stealthily round the box, in which the Church, the Peerage, and the Higher Criticism were represented. All three were in convulsions. Compare this with our West End musical farces, in which the performers strive to make some inane scene "go" by trying to suggest to the starving audience that there is something exquisitely loose and vicious beneath the dreary fatuity of the surface. Who would not rather look at and laugh at four men pretending to be sea-sick in a wildly comic way than see a row of young women singing a chorus about being "Gaiety Girls" with the deliberate intention of conveying to the audience that a Gaiety chorister's profession—their own profession—is only a mask for the sort of life which is represented in Piccadilly Circus and Leicester Square after midnight? I quite agree with my friend the clergyman that decent ladies and gentlemen who have given up West End musical farce in disgust will find themselves much happier at the Britannia pantomime.

I shall not venture on any searching artistic criticism of Will o' the Wisp, as the pantomime was called. If it were a West End piece, I should pitch into it without the slightest regard to the prestige and apparent opulence of the manager, not because I am incorruptible, but because I am not afraid of the mere shadow of success. I treat its substance, in the person of Mrs Lane, with careful respect. Shew me real capacity; and I bow lower to it than anybody. All I dare suggest to the Hoxtonians is that when they insist on an entertainment lasting from seven to close upon midnight, they have themselves to thank if the actors occasionally have to use all their ingenuity to spin out scenes of which a judicious playgoer would desire to have at least ten minutes less.

The enthusiasm of the pit on the last night, with no stalls to cut it off from the performers, was frantic. There was a great throwing of flowers and confectionery on the stage; and it would happen occasionally that an artist would overlook one of these tributes, and walk off, leaving it unnoticed on the boards. Then a shriek of tearing anxiety would arise, as if the performer were wandering blindfold into a furnace or over a precipice. Every factory girl in the house would lacerate the air with a mad scream of "Pick up, Topsy!" "Pick it up, Voylit!" followed by a gasp of relief, several thousand strong, when Miss Topsy Sinden or Miss Violet Durkin would return and annex the offering. I was agreeably astonished by Miss Topsy Sinden's dancing. Thitherto it had been my miserable fate to see her come on, late in the second act of some unspeakably dreary inanity at the West End, to interpolate a "skirt dance," and spin out the unendurable by the intolerable. On such occasions I have looked on her with cold hatred, wondering why the "varieties" of a musical farce should not include a few items from the conventional "assault-at-arms," culminating in some stalwart sergeant, after the usual slicing of lemons, leaden bars, and silk handkerchiefs, cutting a skirt-dancer in two at one stroke. At the Britannia Miss Sinden really danced, acted, and turned out quite a charming person. I was not surprised; for the atmosphere was altogether more bracing than at the other end of the town. These poor playgoers, to whom the expenditure of half a guinea for a front seat at a theatre is as outrageously and extravagantly impossible as the purchase of a deer forest in Mars is to a millionaire, have at least one excellent quality in the theatre. They are jealous *for* the dignity of the artist, not derisively covetous of his (or her) degradation. When a white statue which had stood for thirteen minutes in the middle of the stage turned out to be Mr Lupino, who forthwith put on a classic plasticity, and in a series of rapid poses claimed popular respect for "the antique," it was eagerly accorded; and his demon conflict with the powers of evil, involving a desperate broadsword combat, and the most prodigious plunges into the earth and projections therefrom by volcanic traps as aforesaid, was conducted with all the tragic dignity of Richard III and received in the true Aristotelean spirit by the audience. The fairy queen, a comedy prima donna who scorned all frivolity, was treated with entire respect and seriousness. Altogether, I seriously recommend those of my readers who find a pantomime once a year good for them, to go next year to the Britannia, and leave the West End to its boredoms and all the otherdoms that make it so expensively dreary.

·   ·   ·   ·   ·   ·   ·

Mr Charles Frohman's Mission

THE HEART OF MARYLAND. A drama in four acts. By David Belasco. Adelphi Theatre, 9 April 1898.

·   ·   ·   ·   ·

[16 *April* 1898]

After The Heart of Maryland, at the Adelphi, I begin to regard Mr Charles Frohman as a manager with a great moral mission. We have been suffering of late years in England from a wave of blackguardism. Our population is so large that even its little minorities of intellectual and moral dwarfs form a considerable body, and can make an imposing noise, so long as the sensible majority remain silent, with its clamor for war, for "empire," for savage sports, savage punishments, flogging, duelling, prizefighting, 144 hours' bicycle races, national war dances to celebrate the cautious pounding of a few thousand barbarians to death with machine projectiles, followed by the advance of a whole British brigade on the wretched survivors under "a withering fire" which kills twenty-three men, and national newspaper paragraphs in which British heroes of the rank and file, who will be flung starving on our streets in a year or two at the expiration of their short service, proudly describe the sport of village-burning, remarking, with a touch of humorous Cockney reflectiveness, on the amusing manner in which old Indian women get "fairly needled" at the spectacle of their houses and crops being burnt, and mentioning with honest pride how their officers were elated and satisfied with the day's work. My objection to this sort of folly is by no means purely humanitarian. I am quite prepared to waive the humanitarian point altogether, and to accept, for the sake of argument, the position that we must destroy or be destroyed. But I do not believe in the destructive force of a combination of de-

scriptive talent with delirium tremens. I do not feel safe
behind a rampart of music-hall enthusiasm: on the contrary, the mere thought of what these poor, howling, half-
drunk patriots would do if the roll of a hostile drum
reached their ears, brings out a cold sweat of pity and
terror on me. Imagine going to war, as the French did in
1870, with a stock of patriotic idealism and national enthusiasm instead of a stock of military efficiency. The
Dervishes have plenty of racial idealism and enthusiasm,
with religious fanaticism and personal hardihood to boot;
and much good it has done them! What would have happened to them if they had been confronted by the army of
the future is only conceivable because, after all, the limit
of possibility is annihilation, which is conceivable enough.
I picture that future army to myself dimly as consisting of
half-a-dozen highly paid elderly gentlemen provided with a
picnic basket and an assortment of implements of wholesale destruction. Depend upon it, its first meeting with our
hordes of Continental enslaved conscripts and thriftless
English "surplus population," disciplined into combining
all the self-helplessness of machinery with the animal dis-
advantages of requiring food and being subject to panic,
and commanded by the grown-up boyishness for which the
other professions have no use, will be the death of military
melodrama. It is quite clear, at all events, that the way out
of the present militaristic madness will be found by the
first nation that takes war seriously, or, as the melo-
dramatizers of war will say, cynically. It has always been
so. The fiery Rupert, charging for God and the King, got
on excellently until Cromwell, having some experience as
a brewer, made the trite experiment of raising the wages
of the Parliamentary soldier to the market value of respectable men, and immediately went over Rupert like a
steam-roller. Napoleon served out enthusiasm, carefully
mixed with prospects of loot, as cold-bloodedly as a pirate
captain serves out rum, and never used it as an efficient
substitute for facts and cannon. Wellington, with his characteristic Irish common sense, held a steadfast opinion of
the character of the average British private and the capacity of the average British officer which would wreck
the Adelphi theatre if uttered there; but he fed them carefully, and carried our point with them against the enemy.
At the present time, if I or anyone else were to propose
that enough money should be spent on the British soldier

to make him an efficient marksman, to attract respectable
and thrifty men to the service, to escape the necessity for
filling the ranks with undersized wasters and pretending
to believe the glaring lies as to their ages which the recruit-
ing sergeant has to suggest to them, and to abolish the
military prison with its cat-o'-nine-tails perpetually flour-
ishing before our guardsmen in Gibraltar "fortress orders"
and the like, there would be a howl of stingy terror from
the very taxpayers who are now weeping with national
enthusiasm over the heroism of the two Dargai pipers
who, five years hence, will probably be cursing, in their
poverty, the day they ever threw away their manhood on
the British War Office.

The question for the dramatic critic is, how is it possible
to knock all this blood-and-thunder folly out of the head
of the British playgoer? Satire would be useless: sense
still more out of the question. Mr Charles Frohman seems
to me to have solved the problem. You cannot make the
Britisher see that his own bunkum is contemptible. But
shew him the bunkum of any other nation, and he sees
through it promptly enough. And that is what Mr Frohman
is doing. The Heart of Maryland is an American melodrama of the Civil War. As usual, all the Southern
commanders are Northern spies, and all the Northern commanders Southern spies—at least that is the general impression produced. It may be historically correct; for obviously such an arrangement, when the troops once got used
to it, would not make the smallest difference; since a competition for defeat, if earnestly carried out on both sides,
would be just as sensible, just as exciting, just as difficult,
just as well calculated to call forth all the heroic qualities,
not to mention the Christian virtues, as a competition for
victory. Maryland Cawlvert (spelt Calvert) is "a Southern
woman to the last drop of her blood," and is, of course, in
love with a Northern officer, who has had the villain
drummed out of the Northern army for infamous conduct.
The villain joins the Southerns, who, in recognition no
doubt of his high character and remarkable record, at once
make him a colonel, especially as he is addicted to heavy
drinking. Naturally, he is politically impartial, and, as he
says to the hysterical Northerner (who is, of course, the
hero of the piece), fights for his own hand. "But the United
States!" pleads the hysterical one feebly. "Damn the
United States" replies the villain. Instantly the outraged

patriot assaults him furiously, shouting "Take back that.
Take it back." The villain prudently takes it back; and the
honor of America is vindicated. This is clearly the point
at which the audiences should burst into frantic applause.
No doubt American audiences do. Perhaps the Adelphi
audience would too if the line were altered to "Damn the
United Kingdom." But we are sensible enough about other
people's follies; and the incontinent schoolboyishness of the
hero is received with the coolest contempt. This, then, is
the moral mission of Mr Charles Frohman. He is snatching the fool's cap from the London playgoer and shewing
it to him on the head of an American. Meanwhile, our
foolish plays are going to America to return the compliment. In the end, perhaps, we shall get melodramas in
which the heroism is not despicable, puerile, and blackguardly, nor the villainy mere mechanical criminality.

For the rest, The Heart of Maryland is not a bad speci-
men of the American machine-made melodrama. The
actors know the gymnastics of their business, and work
harder and more smartly, and stick to it better than English actors. Mrs Leslie Carter is a melodramatic heroine
of no mean powers. Her dresses and graces and poses cast
a glamor of American high art on Mr Belasco's romance;
and her transports and tornadoes, in which she shews
plenty of professional temperament and susceptibility, give
intensity to the curtain situations, and secure her a flattering series of recalls. She disdains the silly and impossible
sensation scene with the bell, leaving it to a lively young-
lady athlete who shews with every muscle in her body that
she is swinging the bell instead of being swung by it. Mr
Morgan as the villain is received with special favor; and
Mr Malcolm Williams pretends to be a corpse in such a
life-like manner that he brings down the house, already well
disposed to him for his excellent acting before his decease.
Nobody else has much of a chance.

.   .   .   .

Van Amburgh Revived

THE CLUB BABY. A farce in three acts. By Edward G.
Knoblauch. Avenue Theatre, 28 April 1898.

THE MEDICINE MAN. A melodramatic comedy in five acts.
By H. D. Traill and Robert Hichens. Lyceum Theatre, 4
May 1898.

[7 *May* 1898]

The Club Baby at the Avenue ought to have been called
The Stage Baby's Revenge. The utter worthlessness of the
sentiment in which our actors and playgoers wallow is
shewn by their readiness to take an unfortunate little child
who ought to be in bed, and make fun of it on the stage
as callously as a clown at a country fair will make fun of
a sucking pig. But at the Avenue the baby turns the tables
on its exploiters. The play tumbled along on the first night
in an undeservingly funny way until the end of the second
act, when the baby was rashly brought on the stage. Then
it was all over. It was not so much that the audience
looked at the baby, for audiences, in their thoughtless moments, are stupid enough to look at anything without
blushing. But that baby looked at the audience; and its
gaze would have reclaimed a gang of convicts. The pained
wonder and unfathomable sadness with which it saw its
elders, from whom its childlike trust and reverence had
expected an almost godlike dignity, profanely making fools
of themselves with a string of ribald jests at its expense,
came upon us as the crowing of the cock came upon Peter.
We went out between the acts and drank heavily as the
best available substitute for weeping bitterly. If even one
man had the grace to hang himself I should still have some
hopes of the British public. As it is, I merely beg the Home
Secretary to ask the magistrate who is responsible for the
appearance of this child on the stage on what grounds he
went out of his way to permit it. We have been at the
trouble of passing an Act of Parliament to forbid the
commercial exploitation of children on the stage, except in
cases where the enforcement of the Act would banish from
the theatre some masterpiece of dramatic art written before
the passing of the Act. For instance, we did not wish to
make Richard III impossible by unconditionally abolishing
the little Duke of York, nor to suppress A Doll's House by
depriving Nora Helmer of her children. But The Club
Baby is a play newly written with the deliberate intention

of doing precisely what the Act was passed to prevent. It
is a play without merit enough of any sort to give it a
claim to the most trivial official indulgence, much less the
setting aside of an Act of Parliament in its interest. And
yet a magistrate licenses the employment in it, not of a
boy or girl, but actually of a child in arms who is handed
about the stage until eleven o'clock at night. It is useless
to appeal to playgoers, managers, authors, and people of
that kind in this matter. If the exhibition of a regiment
of new-born babies would raise an extra laugh or draw
half-a-guinea over its cost, that regiment of babies would
be ordered and a play written round it with the greatest
alacrity. But the Home Office is responsible for the pre-
vention of such outrages. Sir Matthew White Ridley is at
present receiving £5000 a year, partly at my expense, for
looking after the administration of the laws regulating the
employment of children. If a factory owner employed a
child under the specified age, or kept a "young person" at
work ten minutes after the specified hour, Sir Matthew
would be down on him like five thousand of brick. If the
factory owner were to plead that his factory was producing goods of vital utility and the rarest artistic value, the
plea would not be listened to for a moment. In the name
of common sense, why are speculators in Club Babies and
the like to enjoy illegal and anti-social privileges which are
denied to manufacturers?

I have been invited to the Strand Theatre to a play called
The J.P. In the bill the following appears: "Charles Vivian,
Junior. By a Baby Three Months old." What right has
Mr Edouin, the manager, to invite me to witness such an
outrage?

I suggest to the Home Office that a rigid rule should be
made against the licensing of children for any new entertainment whatsoever. With regard to old plays, a privileged
list might be made of works of the Richard III order; but
the licences given under this list should be limited to
specified parts: for example, the Richard III privilege
should apply solely to the part of the Duke of York, and
not be made an excuse for introducing a coronation scene
with a procession of five-year-old infants strewing flowers.
If it were once understood that applications for licences
outside this list would be refused as a matter of course,
the present abuses would disappear without further legis-
lation. I would remind my critical colleagues that about

six years ago a sort of epidemic of child exhibition broke out at the theatres devoted to comic opera. I was a critic of music at that time; and I remember an opera at the Lyric Theatre in which a ballet of tiny Punchinellos was danced between eleven o'clock and midnight by a troop of infants in a sort of delirium induced by the conflict between intense excitement and intense sleepiness. I vainly tried to persuade some of the most enlightened of my fellow-critics to launch the thunder of the press at this abomination. Unfortunately, having little children of their own, and having observed that a single night's private theatricals gave much innocent delight to their babes, they thought it was quite a charming thing that the poor little Punchinellos should have such fun every night for several months. Truly, as Talleyrand said, the father of a family is capable of anything. I was left to launch the little thunder I could wield myself; and the result, I am happy to say, was that the managers, including a well-known stage-manager since deceased, suffered so much anguish of mind from my criticisms, without any counterbalancing conviction that their pieces were drawing a farthing more with the children than they would have drawn without them, that they mended their ways. But of late the epidemic has shewn signs of breaking out again. I therefore think it only fair to say that I also am quite ready to break out again, and that I hope by this time my colleagues have realized that their "bless-its-little-heart" patrosentimentality is not publicism.

As to the performance of The Club Baby, all I need say is that a long string of popular comedians do their best with it, and that a Miss Clare Greet, whom I do not remember to have seen before, distinguishes herself very cleverly in the part of the country girl.

Now that Sir Henry Irving has taken to encouraging contemporary literature, it cannot be denied that he has set to work in a sufficiently original fashion. Mr H. D. Traill is an academic literary gentleman who, like Schopenhauer, conceives the world as Will and the intellectual representations by which Man strives to make himself conscious of his will; only Mr Traill conceives these things in a professional mode, the will being to him not a Will to Live, but a Will to Write Books, and the process of making us conscious of these books by intellectual representation being simply reviewing. Some time in the eighties London

rose up in revolt against this view. The New Journalism
was introduced. Lawless young men began to write and
print the living English language of their own day instead
of the prose style of one of Macaulay's characters named
Addison. They split their infinitives, and wrote such
phrases as "a man nobody ever heard of" instead of "a
man of whom nobody had ever heard," or, more classical
still, "a writer hitherto unknown." Musical critics, instead
of reading books about their business and elegantly re-
gurgitating their erudition, began to listen to music and
distinguish between sounds; critics of painting began to
look at pictures; critics of the drama began to look at
something else besides the stage; and descriptive writers
actually broke into the House of Commons, elbowing the
reporters into the background, and writing about political
leaders as if they were mere play-actors. The interview,
the illustration and the cross-heading, hitherto looked on
as American vulgarities impossible to English literary
gentlemen, invaded all our papers; and, finally, as the
climax and masterpiece of literary Jacobinism, the Saturday Review appeared with a signed article in it. Then Mr
Traill and all his generation covered their faces with their
togas and died at the base of Addison's statue, which all
the while ran ink. It is true that they got up and went home
when the curtain fell; but they made no truce with Jacobinism; and Mr Traill fled into the fortress of the Times,
and hurled therefrom, under the defiant title of Literature,
a destructive mass of reviews and publishers' advertise-
ments which caught me one morning in a railway carriage
and nearly killed me. One of the Jacobins was Mr Hichens.
He paid me the compliment of following up the assault on
Academicism on my old lines—those of musical criticism.
He was well received by a revolutionary and licentious
generation; but whatever circulation his novels and articles
might achieve, it was not to be expected that Mr Traill
would ever consent to be seen speaking to him in the
street. And yet Sir Henry Irving, in the calmest manner,
seems to have ordered a play from the twain jointly. What
is more, he has got it. I hardly know how to describe the
result. I trace the theme of the piece to a story, well known
to Mr Traill's generation, of the lion-tamer Van Amburgh,
who professed to quell the most ferocious animals, whether
human or not, by the power of his eye alone. Challenged
to prove this power on the person of a very rough-looking

laborer, he approached the man and fixed a soul-searching gaze on him. The laborer soon evinced the greatest disquietude, became very red and self-conscious, and finally knocked Van Amburgh down, accompanying the blow with a highly garnished demand as to who he was staring at. In The Medicine Man we have Van Amburgh with the period of quelling contemplation extended to five acts, and including not only the laborer, Bill Burge, but also a beauteous maiden named Sylvia. One can understand the humorous insanity of such a story fascinating Mr Hichens, and Mr Traill chuckling secretly at having planted it on the young Jacobin as a new idea. I find myself totally unable to take it seriously: it sends me into a paroxysm of laughter whenever I think of it. I wonder which of the two authors gave the muscular victim of Van Amburgh Tregenna the name of a very eminent contemporary pugilist, known affectionately to the fancy as the Coffee Cooler. If Mr Burge should take the suggested portrait at all amiss, and should seek personal redress at the hands of the authors or the manager, one shudders at the possible consequences to literature and the stage.

There was infinite comedy in the first night of the play at the Lyceum. It lasted from eight to past eleven, and contained just matter enough for a half-hour pantomimic sketch by Mr Martinetti. Sir Henry Irving, pleased by the lion-taming notion, was perfectly delighted with his part, and would evidently have willingly gone on impressing and mesmerizing his devoted company for three hours longer. Miss Ellen Terry, on the other hand, was quite aware of the appalling gratuitousness of his satisfaction. To save the situation she put forth all her enchantments, and so beglamored the play act by act that she forced the audience to accept Sylvia as a witching and pathetically lovely creation of high literary drama. The very anguish the effort caused her heightened the effect. When, after some transcendently idiotic speech that not even her art could give any sort of plausibility to, she looked desperately at us all with an expression that meant "Dont blame me: *I* didnt write it," we only recognized a touch of nature without interpreting it, and were ravished. Hand-in-hand with the innocently happy Sir Henry, she endured the curtain calls with a proud reticence which said to us plainly enough, "I will play this part for you unworthy people, since you have no better use to make of me; but I will not pretend to like it," which was really hardly fair; for we were, as I have said, in a state of enchantment, and thought it all adorable. Mr Mackintosh as Bill Burge is laboriously impossible. His Hogarthian make-up is not like anything now discoverable at the docks; his dialect has no touch of the East End in it; he is as incapable of walking out of a room naturally as a real dock laborer is of "doing an exit." However, it does not matter much; the whole business is such utter nonsense that a stagy dock laborer is quite in keeping with the freakish humors of Mr Hichens, to whom the life of the poor is a tragi-comic phantasmagoria with a good deal of poker and black eye in it. Only at a West End theatre could such a picture pass muster. Some of it—the humors of Mrs Burge, for instance—is an outrage on humanity. But Mr Hichens will retrieve The Medicine Man easily enough, for he has by no means mistaken his vocation in writing for the stage, though he had better avoid collaboration with the chartered dullness of academic history and the solemn frivolity of academic literature. It would take ten years' hard descriptive reporting for the Star or Daily Mail to teach Mr Traill to observe life and to write seriously. The first tinker he meets will tell him a better ghost story than the vague figment, despicable to his own common sense, which he has thought good enough to make a theme for the most exacting of all the forms of literary art. That is your literary man all over— any old theme for a great occasion, provided only nobody can suspect you of believing in it.

Valedictory

[21 *May* 1898]

As I lie here, helpless and disabled, or, at best, nailed by one foot to the floor like a doomed Strasburg goose, a sense of injury grows on me. For nearly four years—to be precise, since New Year 1895—I have been the slave of the theatre. It has tethered me to the mile radius of foul and sooty air which has its centre in the Strand, as a goat is tethered in the little circle of cropped and trampled grass that makes the meadow ashamed. Every week it clamors for its tale of written words; so that I am like a man fighting a windmill: I have hardly time to stagger to my feet from the knock-down blow of one sail, when the next strikes me down. Now I ask, is it reasonable to expect me to spend my life in this way? For just consider my position. Do I receive any spontaneous recognition for the prodigies of skill and industry I lavish on an unworthy institution and a stupid public? Not a bit of it: half my time is spent in telling people what a clever man I am. It is no use merely doing clever things in England. The English do not know what to think until they are coached, laboriously and insistently for years, in the proper and becoming opinion. For ten years past, with an unprecedented pertinacity and obstination, I have been dinning into the public head that I am an extraordinarily witty, brilliant, and clever man. That is now part of the public opinion of England; and no power in heaven or on earth will ever change it. I may dodder and dote; I may potboil and platitudinize; I may become the butt and chopping-block of all the bright, original spirits of the rising generation; but my reputation shall not suffer: it is built up fast and solid, like Shakespear's, on an impregnable basis of dogmatic reiteration.

Unfortunately, the building process has been a most painful one to me, because I am congenitally an extremely modest man. Shyness is the form my vanity and self-consciousness take by nature. It is humiliating, too, after making the most dazzling displays of professional ability, to have to tell people how capital it all is. Besides, they get so tired of it, that finally, without dreaming of disputing the alleged brilliancy, they begin to detest it. I sometimes get quite frantic letters from people who feel that they cannot stand me any longer.

Then there are the managers. Are *they* grateful? No: they are simply forbearing. Instead of looking up to me as their guide, philosopher, and friend, they regard me merely as the author of a series of weekly outrages on their profession and their privacy. Worse than the managers are the Shakespeareans. When I began to write, William was a divinity and a bore. Now he is a fellow-creature; and his plays have reached an unprecedented pitch of popularity. And yet his worshippers overwhelm my name with insult.

These circumstances will not bear thinking of. I have never had time to think of them before; but now I have nothing else to do. When a man of normal habits is ill, everyone hastens to assure him that he is going to recover. When a vegetarian is ill (which fortunately very seldom happens), everyone assures him that he is going to die, and that they told him so, and that it serves him right. They implore him to take at least a little gravy, so as to give himself a chance of lasting out the night. They tell him awful stories of cases just like his own which ended fatally after indescribable torments; and when he tremblingly inquires whether the victims were not hardened meat-eaters, they tell him he must not talk, as it is not good for him. Ten times a day I am compelled to reflect on my past life, and on the limited prospect of three weeks or so of lingering moribundity which is held up to me as my probable future, with the intensity of a drowning man. And I can never justify to myself the spending of four years on dramatic criticism. I have sworn an oath to endure no more of it. Never again will I cross the threshold of a theatre. The subject is exhausted; and so am I.

Still, the gaiety of nations must not be eclipsed. The long string of beautiful ladies who are at present in the square without, awaiting, under the supervision of two gallant policemen, their turn at my bedside, must be reassured when they protest, as they will, that the light of their life will go out if my dramatic articles cease. To each of them I will present the flower left by her predecessor, and assure her that there are as good fish in the sea as ever came out of it. The younger generation is knocking at the door; and as I open it there steps spritely in the incomparable Max.

For the rest, let Max speak for himself. I am off duty for ever, and am going to sleep.

Index

W1